JOURNAL FOR THE STUDY OF THE NEW TESTAMENT SUPPLEMENT SERIES
154

Executive Editor
Stanley E. Porter

STUDIES IN SCRIPTURE IN EARLY JUDAISM AND CHRISTIANITY
6

Series Editors
Craig A. Evans
James A. Sanders

Sheffield Academic Press

The Function of Scripture in Early Jewish and Christian Tradition

edited by
Craig A. Evans
and
James A. Sanders

Journal for the Study of the New Testament
Supplement Series 154

Studies in Scripture in Early Judaism and Christianity 6

Copyright © 1998 Sheffield Academic Press

Published by
Sheffield Academic Press Ltd
Mansion House
19 Kingfield Road
Sheffield S11 9AS
England

Typeset by Sheffield Academic Press
and
Printed on acid-free paper in Great Britain
by Bookcraft Ltd
Midsomer Norton, Bath

British Library Cataloguing in Publication Data

A catalogue record for this book is available
from the British Library

ISBN 1-85075-830-1

CONTENTS

Part III
INTERPRETATION IN THE RABBINIC AND PATRISTIC PERIOD

PREFACE

The present volume is the sixth in the series Studies in Scripture in Early Judaism and Christianity, a series that has grown out of the Society of Biblical Literature program unit Scripture in Early Judaism and Christianity, founded by the editors and currently chaired by Kenneth E. Pomykala. The series produces occasional volumes that are published as Supplements to the *Journal for the Study of the Old Testament*, *Journal for the Study of the New Testament*, and *Journal for the Study of the Pseudepigrapha*. The first two volumes appeared in 1993: *Paul and the Scriptures of Israel*, edited by C.A. Evans and J.A. Sanders (JSNTSup, 83; SSEJC, 1) and *The Pseudepigrapha and Early Biblical Interpretation*, edited by J.H. Charlesworth and C.A. Evans (JSPSup, 14; SSEJC, 2). A third volume appeared in 1994: *The Gospels and the Scriptures of Israel*, edited by C.A. Evans and W.R. Stegner (JSNTSup, 104; SSEJC, 3). The fourth and fifth volumes appeared in 1997: *The Things Accomplished among Us: Prophetic Tradition in the Structual Pattern of Luke–Acts*, by R.I. Denova (JSNTSup, 141; SSEJC, 4) and *Early Christian Interpretation of the Scriptures of Israel: Investigations and Proposals*, edited by C.A. Evans and J.A. Sanders (JSNTSup, 148; SSEJC, 5). As in the case of these previous volumes, *The Function of Scripture in Early Jewish and Christian Tradition* represents a collection of studies concerned with the function of Israel's Scriptures in later sacred writings. The studies in this volume, however, treat the interpretive tendencies that shaped Scripture and gave rise to its later adaptations and applications, both in the second temple period, as well as in the later rabbinic and patristic period.

Almost all of the papers were read at annual meetings of the Society of Biblical Literature and then subsequently were revised for inclusion in the present volume. The editors wish to express their thanks to the many scholars who with industry and enthusiasm took part in the sessions of the Scripture in Early Judaism and Christianity program unit and especially to those scholars whose papers were prepared for inclusion in this volume.

Craig A. Evans
James A. Sanders
January 1998

ABBREVIATIONS

AB	Anchor Bible
ABD	David Noel Freedman (ed.), *The Anchor Bible Dictionary* (New York: Doubleday, 1992)
ABRL	Anchor Bible Reference Library
ANET	James B. Pritchard (ed.), *Ancient Near Eastern Texts Relating to the Old Testament* (Princeton: Princeton University Press, 1950)
ANTJ	Arbeiten zum Neuen Testament und Judentum
ArBib	Aramaic Bible
BHT	Beiträge zur historischen Theologie
Bib	*Biblica*
BIS	Biblical Interpretation Series
BJRL	*Bulletin of the John Rylands University Library of Manchester*
BJS	Brown Judaic Studies
BTB	*Biblical Theology Bulletin*
BZ	*Biblische Zeitschrift*
BZAW	Beihefte zur *ZAW*
CBET	Contributions to Biblical Exegesis and Theology
CBQ	*Catholic Biblical Quarterly*
CBQMS	*Catholic Biblical Quarterly*, Monograph Series
CRINT	Compendia rerum iudaicarum ad Novum Testamentum
CSCO	Corpus scriptorum christianorum orientalium
CSS	Cistercian Studies Series
CTM	*Concordia Theological Monthly*
EHAT	Exegetisches Handbuch zum Alten Testament
EphMar	*Ephemerides maxiologicae*
ETL	*Ephemerides theologicae lovanienses*
ExpTim	*Expository Times*
FRLANT	Forschungen zur Religion und Literatur des Alten und Neuen Testaments
GKC	*Gesenius' Hebrew Grammar* (ed. E. Kautzsch, revised and trans. A.E. Cowley; Oxford: Clarendon Press, 1910)
HAT	Handbuch zum Alten Testament
HSM	Harvard Semitic Monographs
HSS	Harvard Semitic Studies
HTR	*Harvard Theological Review*
HUCA	*Hebrew Union College Annual*
ICC	International Critical Commentary

IDB	George Arthur Buttrick (ed.), *The Interpreter's Dictionary of the Bible* (4 vols.; Nashville: Abingdon Press, 1962)
Int	*Interpretation*
IDBSup	*IDB*, Supplementary Volume
JAC	*Jahrbuch für Antike und Christentum*
JAOS	*Journal of the American Oriental Society*
JBL	*Journal of Biblical Literature*
JETS	*Journal of the Evangelical Theological Society*
JJS	*Journal of Jewish Studies*
JSHRZ	Jüdische Schriften aus hellenistisch-römischer Zeit
JSJ	*Journal for the Study of Judaism in the Persian, Hellenistic and Roman Period*
JSNT	*Journal for the Study of the New Testament*
JSNTSup	*Journal for the Study of the New Testament*, Supplement Series
JSOR	*Journal of the Society of Oriental Research*
JSOT	*Journal for the Study of the Old Testament*
JSOTSup	*Journal for the Study of the Old Testament*, Supplement Series
JSP	*Journal for the Study of the Pseudepigrapha*
JSS	*Journal of Semitic Studies*
JTS	*Journal of Theological Studies*
LCL	Loeb Classical Library
LTQ	*Lexington Theological Quarterly*
MSU	Mitteilungen des Septuaginta-Unternehmens der Akademie der Wissenschaft in Göttingen
NICOT	New International Commentary on the Old Testament
NTS	*New Testament Studies*
NumBS	Numen Book Series
OBO	Orbis biblicus et orientalis
OTL	Old Testament Library
OTS	*Oudtestamentische Studiën*
PG	J.-P. Migne (ed.), *Patrologia cursus completa... Series graeca* (166 vols.; Paris: Petit-Montrouge, 1857–83)
P(ST)J	*Perkins (School of Theology) Journal*
RevQ	*Revue de Qumran*
RHPR	*Revue d'histoire et de philosophie religieuses*
RSR	*Recherches de science religieuse*
SBET	*Scottish Bulletin of Evangelical Theology*
SBLDS	SBL Dissertation Series
SBLSCS	SBL Septuagint and Cognate Studies
SBT	Studies in Biblical Theology
SC	Sources chrétiennes
SJ	Studia judaica
SJT	*Scottish Journal of Theology*
SNTSMS	Society for New Testament Studies Monograph Series
TOTC	Tyndale Old Testament Commentaries
VT	*Vetus Testamentun*
VTSup	*Vetus Testamentum*, Supplements

WTJ	*Westminster Theological Journal*
WUNT	Wissenschaftliche Untersuchungen zum Neuen Testament
YJS	Yale Judaica Series
ZAW	*Zeitschrift für die alttestamentliche Wissenschaft*
ZNW	*Zeitschrift für die neutestamentliche Wissenschaft*

LIST OF CONTRIBUTORS

Paul Borgman
Gordon College, Wenham, MA

George Wesley Buchanan
Wesley Theological Seminary, Washington, DC

Randall Buth
Jerusalem University College

Ruth Anne Clements
Harvard Divinity School

Joan E. Cook
St Bonaventure University

Steve Delamarter
Western Evangelical Seminary, Portland, OR

Peter Enns
Westminster Theological Seminary, Philadelphia, PA

Richard A. Freund
University of Nebraska

Larry L. Lyke
Yale University

Esther M. Menn
University of Virginia

Judith H. Newman
Harvard University

Elaine A. Phillips
Gordon College, Wenham, MA

Will Soll
St Louis University, Missouri

Stephen S. Taylor
University of Pennsylvania

INTRODUCTION

A tradent is one who brings the past into the present in contemporary terms.

That statement makes two important points about the work of those who wrote for and will read this volume, and about the ancient traditions studied in it. First, a tradent is essentially a traditionist, that is, one who attempts to understand an earlier text in the terms the tradent knows; a tradent is specifically not a traditionalist, that is, one who attempts to make the present look like the past. Second, a tradent of necessity is limited to the terms of the culture, no matter how 'advanced' or refined, in which the tradent and his community live.[1]

These observations apply to scholars as well as practitioners for contemporary communities. Scholars have their professional as well as confessional communities, and they too have their limits and contours, no matter how broad or sophisticated. Some scholars like to think that they have no confessional community, but what that means is simply that they have made their professional community their confessional community. What scholars do that is different from what confessional practitioners do is to attempt to understand the ancient traditioning process in refined Renaissance and Enlightenment terms derived and inherited from ancient Greco-Roman cultural thought patterns. That is, all the authors in this volume, and most of the readers of it, are and will be heirs of the European rebirth of Greco-Roman thought patterns by which we attempt to understand what was happening in history when biblical texts were read by folk in antiquity. This has caused some problems in modern times (from, say, the eighteenth to the twentieth centuries) at those points when 'scholarly' tradents felt they could, with the eyes and the tools of the Enlightenment, judge everything they surveyed. And if they somehow missed the mark in this or that effort, they could always think that if they

1. J.A. Sanders, 'Scripture as Canon for Post-Modern Times', *BTB* 25 (1995), pp. 56-63.

studied harder and got smarter they could nail down the truth about the Bible in modern terms.

A major difficulty with such a postmodern observation on what has been happening in biblical scholarship for these three or so centuries of 'modernism' is that it can be misunderstood by confessional practitioners to mean that they now can read the Bible responsibly without engaging in serious historical scholarship.[2] But all that does is to reinforce the hermeneutic circle taught in their confessional communities with no challenge whatever to reading into the Bible what a particular current community wants to see there.

What one hopes for now that postmodernism has helped us see our own scholarly and human limitations, and has helped induce human humility in scholarly pursuit, is that scholars will find just that mix, of the modernist ability to use the refined and refining tools of historical investigation to make responsible historical judgments, with the postmodern humility of openness to the semitic strangeness of the Bible— strange indeed to Greco-Roman-Enlightenment thought forms and categories of reason, and not always reducible to those thought forms.

This volume, the sixth in our series, brings to a conclusion the first phase of work of the 'Section on Scripture in Early Judaism and Christianity' of the Society of Biblical Literature. The editors, who have been co-chairs of the Section since its inception, feel that serious work of study of the *Nachleben* of Scripture in early Jewish and Christian communities is well launched but has much yet to do in exploring Scripture's function as canon in its early expressions in those communities. The hermeneutic triangle (the confluence of text, socio-political context, and the hermeneutics by which the text was/is re-read) will remain the sharpest challenge to reading Scripture only through hermeneutic circles learned in confessional communities— even professional communities that have in effect become confessional.[3] The hermeneutic triangle was conceived at the juncture of

2.   See B. Chilton, 'Biblical Authority, Canonical Criticism, and Generative Exegesis', in C.A. Evans and S. Talmon (eds.), *The Quest for Context and Meaning: Studies in Biblical Intertextuality in Honor of James A. Sanders* (BIS, 28; Leiden: E.J. Brill, 1997), pp. 343-55.

3.   J.A. Sanders, *From Sacred Story to Sacred Text* (Minneapolis: Fortress Press, 1987), pp. 76-105. See also F.A. Spina, 'The "Face of God": Esau in Canonical Context', in Evans and Talmon (eds.), *The Quest for Context and Meaning*, pp. 3-25.

modern and postmodern understandings of biblical study, drawing on both but critical of each.[4]

The papers that make up the present volume fall under three major headings. The first section treats sacred tradition in the First Temple period. Elaine Phillips, in the first of her papers, treats the post-biblical interpretation of Abraham's and Sarah's incredulity in response to God's promise of an heir. She finds that later interpretive traditions explain the founders' apparent lack of faith in a variety of ways. Judith Newman examines ancient interpretation of Genesis 18–19, which narrates Lot's life and adventures in Sodom. Of particular interest is her comparison of the Sodom tradition with Jesus' warning against the cities of his time that had rejected his disciples. Paul Borgman probes the story of Abraham and Sarah, treating the reader to a survey of ancient and contemporary interpretation. He finds complementarity in the differing applications of Abraham's faith on the part of Paul and James. In her second contribution Elaine Phillips probes the tension in the Pentateuch with respect to the prophetic status of Moses. She analyzes in what ways interpreters of late antiquity wrestle with the ambiguities of the text in its description of the rivalry of Moses, Aaron, and Miriam. The first section concludes with George Buchanan's programmatic study of Isaiah's usage of Exodus tradition. He believes that the prophet gives evidence of an early form of midrash, which was practiced by his disciples.

The papers that make up the second section focus on biblical interpretation in the Second Temple period. In her second paper Judith Newman examines the prayer found in Nehemiah 9. In it she finds the presence of scriptural elements, concluding that it is an early exemplar of a genre of prayer that will become commonplace in Judaism and Christianity. Richard Freund treats the use and interpretation of the Decalogue in early Judaism and Christianity. He concludes that this list of commandments proved to be a vehicle for continuing revelation of morality rather than a fixed formulation of a single event that took place at a particular time in Israel's history. Peter Enns offers a study of the retelling of the Song of the Sea (Exodus 15) in Wisdom 10. Readers will find his comparisons with interpretive traditions in

4.   See the discussion by Richard Weis and David Carr, in R.D. Weis and D.M. Carr (eds.), *A Gift of God in Due Season: Essays on Scripture and Community in Honor of James A. Sanders* (JSOTSup, 225; Sheffield: Sheffield Academic Press, 1996), pp. 13-64.

rabbinic literature and other sources illuminative of exegetical efforts
of late antiquity. In his study Will Soll shows that although Tobit
offers readers an imaginative and delightful story, it advances important perspectives of family. Of especial interest is the light the book of
Tobit sheds on Jewish practices of endogamy. Randall Buth, a semitics
specialist, probes the much debated meaning of בר־אנשא ('son of
man'). He recommends that the Hebrew language be taken into consideration, not simply Greek and Aramaic. He suspects that Jesus'
sayings, in which reference is made to 'the son of (the) man', may
have been in Hebrew, with the epithet בר־אנשא appearing in Aramaic.
Sayings made up of Aramaic and Hebrew mixtures are well attested
in early rabbinic literature. The section concludes with Steve Delamarter's interesting study of the vilification of Jehoiakim, whose association with the evil king Manasseh was promoted in early Judaism
and formed part of a moral assessment of Israel's colorful history.

The papers found in the third section treat the issues that surround
interpretation in the rabbinic and patristic period. Esther Menn investigates *Targum Neofiti*'s creative retelling of the story of Tamar in
Genesis 38, in which both Judah and his daughter-in-law are excul-
pated. Joan Cook traces the history of early interpretation of Hannah's
song (1 Sam. 2.1-10). She finds that the eschatological paraphrase of
the song attested in the Targum and in other Jewish sources of late
antiquity parallels in important ways Mary's song, the Magnificat.
Larry Lyke ponders the significance of the women mentioned in
Matthew's genealogical list. He thinks Midrash *Ruth Rabbah* could
throw light on this question. Ruth Clements investigates the possible
influence of Palestinian Jewish exegesis on Origen's interpretation of
Exod. 12.5. She finds elements of Jewish interpretive tradition that
reflects the Hebrew version of Scripture, as opposed to the Greek
version, and reflects rabbinic midrash at many points. Stephen Taylor
rounds out the volume with a study of Aphrahat's use of the Pauline
corpus. Of especial interest is this Syriac father's understanding of law
and grace in the apostle.

As in previous volumes of Studies in Scripture in Early Judaism and
Christianity, the present volume hopes to turn new ground and to
blaze new trails in the field of biblical intertextuality and the function
of sacred tradition and texts in later writings. These studies explore
that logical phase in the history of sacred tradition and Bible that
bridges the great moments of revelation, through word and event, to

forces and circumstances that would give us canonical Scripture. Accordingly, these papers exhibit exegeses of particular texts on the one hand and yet, on the other, reflect an awareness of the larger context of canon. We hope that they not only shed light on particular passages and topics, but also stimulate greater understanding and appreciation for the canonical dimension of Scripture and the way in which it functions authoritatively for communities of faith.

Craig A. Evans
James A. Sanders

Part I
FORMATION OF SACRED TRADITION IN THE FIRST TEMPLE PERIOD

INCREDULITY, FAITH, AND TEXTUAL PURPOSES: POST-BIBLICAL RESPONSES TO THE LAUGHTER OF ABRAHAM AND SARAH

Elaine A. Phillips

Introduction

At the explicit announcements that Abraham and Sarah would have a son, each of them laughed in the presence of the Lord. As they laughed, they both articulated to themselves the reason for their incredulity; it was unlikely that two old bodies would produce a child. They even both kept their skeptical responses quite to themselves. In these somewhat parallel vignettes (Gen. 17.15-21 and Gen. 18.9-15), we find affirmation regarding the child's name from the experience of each of the parents. Furthermore, when Isaac was indeed named, it was Sarah who expressed the significance of his name for *her* (Gen. 21.6). Nevertheless, as the apparent incredulity was first voiced, Abraham was not questioned as to why he laughed but Sarah was. The reader cannot help but wonder why this was so.

While these narratives have customarily been assigned to separate sources and addressed on that basis,[1] how the 'finished product' was treated in post-biblical renditions of the story is what interests me. Toward that end, I first review briefly the narratives of God's promise to Abraham, summarizing the pertinent biblical texts and the interpretive questions they have raised. Then, I survey their re-presentation by significant post-biblical textual communities, addressing the differences among the approaches of these communities.

The Biblical Narratives: An Overview

The first thing we learn about the matriarch is that she was barren (Gen. 11.30). This was acknowledged even before God issued the call

---

1. Specifically, Gen. 17 is assigned to P, 18 to J, and 21 to E. See E.A. Speiser, *Genesis* (AB, 1; New York: Doubleday, 1964), p. 125.

to leave Mesopotamia, an event which occurred when Abram was 75 (Gen. 12.4) and Sarai was 65. They had had sufficient years to experience their childless estate.[2]

God promised 'seed' to Abram in Gen. 12.7 and reiterated the promise in Gen. 15.4, 5. Only after the detour with Hagar and the birth of Ishmael (Gen. 16) did Abram learn that it was Sarai who was to have the promised child. Appearing to Abram when he was 99, the Lord reiterated the promises of the covenant, indicating that he would increase Abram very much (Gen. 17.2). Abram's response was to fall on his face (Gen. 17.3). The Lord spoke further to the effect that Abraham would have a new name, representing his status as father of many nations, and his descendants would inherit the land. There is a multiplicity of references to offspring in this section. In the meantime, he was to be circumcised (Gen. 17.4-14). Then God promised a son to Abraham through Sarah.

> Abraham fell on his face and laughed and said in his heart: Will he be born to one who is 100 years old and will Sarah who is 90 bear?
> Abraham said to God: May Ishmael live before you!
> God said: But Sarah your wife will bear to you a son and you will call his name Isaac and I will establish my covenant with him as an everlasting covenant for his offspring after him. Regarding Ishmael, I have heard you...but my covenant I will establish with Isaac whom Sarah will bear to you at this time in another year.
> When God finished speaking with him, God went up from Abraham (Gen. 17.15-22).

Both times Abraham fell on his face (וַיִּפֹּל אַבְרָם עַל־פָּנָיו) it was because God had promised the seemingly impossible. While the second declaration was more explicit, mentioning Sarah, the first indicated that he would have a multitude of offspring. In both cases, Abraham's physical response may be indicative of consternation which accompanied his incredulity.[3]

---

2. Danna Nolan Fewell suggested that it was Abram's awareness of the hopelessness of this state that prompted him to pass Sarai off as his sister in Egypt in order to get rid of her and be able to father children with a woman who would successfully bear them ('Divine Calls, Human Responses: Another Look at Abraham and Sarah', *P(ST)J* 41.4, 1989], pp. 13-16 [14, 15]).

3. Other uses of some form of לִנְפֹּל אֶל/עַל פָּנִים seem to indicate that this is the way biblical characters responded when they were in a state of fear or consternation or were feeling overwhelmed. See, for example, Lev. 9.24; Num. 14.5; 16.4, 24;

Following Abraham's laughter at the naming of Sarah, God first addressed what Abraham said to himself about their ages. Then he responded to the audible request about Ishmael, denied it, and finally reiterated the promise that the son, to be named Isaac, would come in a year.[4]

It is important to view this first vignette in the wider narrative setting which presents and develops the figure of Abraham as the paradigmatic person of faith and subsequent obedience. To be sure, his attempts to take matters into his own hands were, in retrospect, the wrong choices, but we might argue that each was well-intentioned given the information which he had at that point. Though he appeared to falter here, falling on his face, laughing and suggesting that Ishmael really should be the object of God's promise, he quickly responded to the command to circumcise himself and his entire household as a sign of the covenant.[5]

It doesn't appear that the Lord was gone long. After Abraham, at the age of 99, circumcised himself and all the male members of his house, three visitors appeared at his tent. Abraham bowed (וישתחו ארצה) before them, proposed some rest and refreshment, and hurried about preparing to serve them. Once the meal was ready, he stood to serve them as they ate.

> They said to him[6]: Where is Sarah your wife? He said: Right here, in the tent.
>
> Then he said: I will surely return to you at the time of reviving (כעת חיה)[7] and your wife will have a son.

17.10 (Hebr); 20.6; Josh. 5.14; 7.6; 1 Sam. 14.4, 22; 17.49; 1 Chron. 21.16; Ezek. 1.28; 3.23; 9.8; 11.13; 43.3; 44.4.

4.   J. Gerald Janzen, *Abraham and All the Families of the Earth: A Commentary on the Book of Genesis 12–50* (Grand Rapids: Eerdmans, 1993), p. 51, indicated that there were two objections raised by Abraham to what God had said. One was a social consideration; Ishmael was by rights the first-born. This would mean forgoing the customary primogeniture procedures. Second, the physical improbability had a high profile for both Abraham and Sarah. Perhaps the Lord designated the name to remind Abraham of the fragility of his faith.

5.   In fact, the laughter is really an essential ingredient to the story. It was frank acknowledgment of the physically unrealistic aspect of the promise and was then followed by his obedience in spite of that seeming impossibility.

6.   There are three dots over three letters of the Hebrew text. As we shall see, the rabbis addressed the possible implications of these markings.

7.   The translation is literal; one might think of spring. The only other place

Sarah was listening at the door of the tent and he/she was behind him/it
(והוא אחריו).[8] Now Abraham and Sarah were old and advanced in days
and Sarah had ceased to be in the way of women. So Sarah laughed in
herself saying: After I am worn shall I have this pleasure[9] and my master
being old?

But the Lord said to Abraham: Why did Sarah laugh and say: Shall I
even surely bear a child when I am old? Is anything too wonderful for the
Lord? At this season, I shall return to you (כעת חיה) and Sarah shall have
a son.

Then Sarah lied: I did not laugh, because she was afraid but he said:
Ah, but you did laugh (Gen. 18.9-15).

This incident raises numerous questions, some of which are addressed
in subsequent treatments of the narrative. We wonder why 'they' asked
after Sarah's whereabouts; after all, they/he knew. Was it to attract
her attention and make certain that she was listening?[10] Is it a stylistic
nicety to elicit the maternal response of laughter in order to confirm
the name of the child? In the developing narrative, God had already
pronounced the name to Abraham in 17.21 but both parents' laughter
is poetic symmetry, a balance that is a subtle undertone in Genesis 21.
Was all of this to set the stage for the theological statement 'Is

where the expression occurs is 2 Kgs 4.16, 17 -למועד הזה כעת חיה. The context is
similar: a couple who had not yet had children. In order to understand Gen.
18.10 as 'this time next year', the reader is dependent on what had been said in
Gen. 17.21 which uses the expression למועד הזה.

8.   The ambiguity of the pronouns in this clause makes it difficult to render with
precision. The Samaritan Pentateuch reads והיא instead of והוא and the LXX has the
same tradition, indicating that Sarah was behind (him/it), meaning the messenger or
the tent. The source of the confusion is that הוא serves in the Pentateuch for both the
masculine and feminine singular nominative pronouns. See E. Kautzsch and A.E.
Cowley, *Gesenius' Hebrew Grammar* (Oxford: Clarendon Press, 2nd edn, 1910),
p. 321.

9.   Sarah used very explicit language to describe her condition. See Gerhard von
Rad, *Genesis* (trans. John H. Marks; Philadelphia: Westminster Press, 1961),
p. 202, and Claus Westermann, *Genesis 12–36* (trans. John J. Scullion; Minneapolis: Augsburg, 1985; English; first published 1981 by Neukirchener Verlag),
p. 281. בלה is used of worn out clothing (Josh. 9.13) and bones that have dried up
(Ps. 32.3). עדנה, used only here, seems to refer to sexual pleasure. In repeating her
sentiment, the Lord softened the tone considerably.

10. Janzen, *Abraham and All the Families of the Earth* (pp. 54, 55) suggested
that, in that culture, it would have been improper for strangers to speak with a
woman/wife directly. Thus, the messengers addressed Sarah through Abraham.

anything too wonderful for the Lord?'[11]. Why did the Lord change Sarah's quiet response when he repeated it to Abraham, leaving out the reference to *his* age? Furthermore, several of the pronouns in Hebrew are ambiguous, suggesting multiple interpretations. How are they to be understood in the development of the story? Finally, what did Sarah's laughter represent that it warranted a question from the Lord?

It is worth recalling that these three visitors had not clearly identified themselves as some manifestation of the divine presence. Sarah had only been working in the background. Thus, her knowledge of her own physical condition in conjunction with her lack of expectation that these strangers could speak with authority on such an issue would naturally prompt incredulity.[12]

On the other hand, after his outburst of laughter, Abraham had set about acting on his belief with the circumcision procedure. It is probable that Sarah knew of it. If they were living in close proximity to one another, it would be difficult not to know of the circumcision of all the male members of the household.[13] She may have also known something of the communication from God which was part of that covenant restatement.[14] As with Abraham, the Lord addressed what she had expressed only inwardly. That accounts for her fear and the subsequent audible lie. In response, God had the last word: She did indeed laugh.

In the intervening year, Sarah experienced one more episode as Abraham's sister in the territory of Abimelekh and finally she bore Isaac.

11. This is echoed in Lk. 1.37, another statement to a woman. Both express the very heart of faith.

12. 'Contrary to some interpreters, this is not the laughter of ridicule or mockery; Sarah's half-suppressed laughter arises from the comic disproportion between what is announced and what is possible…she knew better than anyone else, the absurdity of the promise…'. Bernhard Anderson, 'Abraham, the Friend of God', *Interpretation* 42 (1988), pp. 353-66 (361).

13. Later it appears that Abraham no longer lived in the same geographical location (Gen. 22.19 and 23.2) but that separation is not evident up to this point.

14. In fact it has been suggested that, because she knew this, her laughter, unlike Abraham's, was from stubborn unbelief. See Derek Kidner, *Genesis: An Introduction and Commentary* (TOTC; Downers Grove, IL: InterVarsity Press, 1967), p. 132.

The Lord visited Sarah as He had said and He did to her as He had spoken. Sarah conceived and bore to Abraham a son in his old age at the time which God had told him. And Abraham called the name of his son who was born to him and whom Sarah had born to him, Isaac. Abraham circumcised Isaac his son when he was eight days old as God had commanded him. Abraham was 100 years old when Isaac his son was born to him.

Sarah said: God has made for me laughter. Let all who hear laugh for me (Gen. 21.1-6).

This brief narrative draws together the threads from each of the preceding separate incidents. The son was born at the time God had promised. The fact that both Abraham and Sarah were responsible for the birth of the son is emphasized. Abraham named him Isaac and circumcised him in accordance with the command in ch. 17 and Sarah testified to God's fulfillment of the 'absurd' promise in giving her joy where pleasure had seemed impossible (18.12). This is a text of triumph; in fact, the name is perfect, combining the joy at seeing the unbelievable occur and the recognition of the fragility of faith.[15]

Post-biblical Responses

In the various genres of literature which responded to the biblical text, the treatments of these incidents vary depending on the purposes and the socioreligious contexts of each text. Because Abraham was set to become the paradigmatic figure for the faithful and ostensibly faith and incredulity are impossible bedfellows, his laughter was generally toned down or pains were taken to explain it. On the other hand, there were not such high theological stakes with Sarah's response and laughter. Some treatments entirely bypass that incident; several are concerned to rephrase some of her words in a more delicate manner; still others address questions raised by the accompanying textual ambiguities.

Translations

The Septuagint consistently renders 'laugh' in both Genesis 17 and 18 as γελάω, indicating general amusement, scorn or derision.[16] The

15. The word צחק, outside of this narrative, is not frequently used. See Gen. 19.14; 26.8; 39.14, 17; Exod. 32.6; Judg. 16.25.

16. Henry G. Liddell and Robert Scott, *A Greek–English Lexicon* (rev. Henry S. Jones; Oxford: Clarendon Press, 1973 repr.), pp. 341-42.

translators appear not to have been troubled by laughter at this point in the patriarch's life. The Septuagint demonstrates the typical substitution of 'mind' (διανοια) for 'heart' in Gen. 17.17 as Abraham laughed within himself. As in the Hebrew text, Sarah laughed 'in herself' (εν εαυτη). Finally, the Greek translation considerably softens Sarah's description of herself in 18.12.[17]

A more interpretive approach is evident in the Targums.[18] The general tenor of the Targums is that Abraham fell on his face and rejoiced[19] or was astonished.[20] Outright laughter seems to have been viewed as disrespectful. While several of the Targums represent Sarah as 'wondering' rather than laughing, her laughter was not uniformly a problem for these translators.[21] In fact, her laughter is necessary as the narrative of the rebuke continues. Instead, these communities addressed the meaning of the word עדנה, interpreting it as the pleasure of returning to youth and enjoying pregnancy. A further issue in the Targums is the pronoun ambiguity regarding who or what was behind what in v. 10; Ishmael was a prime candidate for lurking behind the tent.[22] Viewed in the context of story-telling, this potentially heightens the tension for the listening audience. These translators also rephrased the Lord's question to ask if anything was *hidden* (היתכסא) from him rather than anything being too difficult for him. This may have been for them an indirect connection to his discerning what she had only said to herself.

We can imagine why such changes were made for the sake of a listening synagogue audience. Clarification of textual ambiguities, linkage of ideas, development of the personalities in the narrative, and sensitivity to matters of faith and propriety all figure into these renditions. In regard to the last suggestion, perhaps the example in the

17. 'It has certainly not yet happened to me until now' (ουπω μεν μοι γεγονεν εως του νυν).

18. Targum texts consulted: *Onqelos, Neofiti I, Pseudo-Jonathan*, and the *Fragmentary Targums*.

19. *Onqelos*—חדי.

20. תמה (*Neofiti I, Pseudo-Jonathan, Fragmentary Targums*).

21. *Targum Onqelos* and the *Fragmentary Targums* use the word וחייכת ('and she laughed') while *Neofiti I* and *Pseudo-Jonathan* have ותמה ('she was astonished or wondered').

22. *Onqelos* is the only one of the Targum texts which does not identify the person behind the tent as Ishmael.

biblical text itself of God's toning down Sarah's evaluation of Abraham's potential served as a pattern.

Re-presentations of the Biblical Text

In *Jubilees* and Josephus, the treatments are very abbreviated and the broader issues in each narrative receive considerably more attention than the instances of laughter. We find in *Jub.* 15.17 that Abraham fell on his face and *rejoiced* and pondered in his heart whether a son would be born to one who was 100 years old.[23] This is similar to the approach of the Targums and avoids the possible impropriety of laughter on the part of the patriarch at what God said. The rest of the text of *Jubilees* is fundamentally the same as the biblical text where the focus of attention is circumcision.

Jubilees 16.2-3 is also very abbreviated. It succinctly rehearses Sarah's laughter, the rebuke, her fear and denial. In addition, she was told the name as it was written on the heavenly tablets, a significant motif in *Jubilees*, which emphasizes that the events in the lives of God's people were preordained.

In regard to Genesis 17, Josephus (*Ant.* 1.10.5) simply recorded the promise of a son who was to be named Isaac, the promise about kings to come from Abraham's offspring, and the command to circumcise in order to maintain purity. While Abraham's request on behalf of Ishmael is noted, his laughter is not. Josephus was equally brief with regard to Genesis 18 (*Ant.* 1.11.2) but did not shy away from mentioning Sarah's laughter. Strangers asked about Sarah and stated she would be pregnant. She laughed and said it was impossible given their respective ages. Then the angels revealed their identity and the focus moves to the overthrow of Sodom.

Texts with a Philosophical/Theological Agenda

For Philo, the potential contradiction between Abraham's belief and his laughter seems to have posed a serious problem which he addressed at length. He, too, was careful to indicate that Abraham's laughter was a matter of joy; thus, Isaac's name. The laughter of Sarah, who is consistently identified in Philo's allegorical scheme as virtue, is considered in the same light.

23. O.S. Wintermute (trans.), 'Jubilees', in James Charlesworth (ed.), *The Old Testament Pseudepigrapha* (2 vols.; New York: Doubleday, 1985), p. 86.

> Abraham, therefore, appears here to be in a state of joy, and to be laugh-
> ing because he is about to become the father of happiness, that is to say,
> of Isaac; and virtue, that is to say, Sarrah, laughs also. And the same
> prophet [Moses] will bear further witness, speaking thus, 'And it had
> ceased to be with Sarrah after the manner of women, and she laughed in
> her mind and said, such happiness has never happened to me to this time
> and my lord [kurios], that is to say, the Divine Lord, is older than I;' in
> whose power, however, this thing must inevitably be, and in whose
> power it is becoming to place confidence. For the offspring is laughter
> and joy.[24]

In Philo's presentation of Sarah as virtue, her incredulous expression is turned entirely into a statement of joyous belief. Nothing is
said about the question and rebuke; they do not fit the scheme.

Philo also waxed long on the significance of Abraham's falling
down in conjunction with his laughter; it was indicative of his humility and piety in the presence of God's goodness.[25] Further, Abraham
did not voice his incredulity but only thought it to himself, therefore
not incurring the guilt of doubt.

> The expression, 'he said in his mind' [Gen. 17.17] is not added without
> an object or gratuitously, for words which are articulated in the tongue
> and the mouth incur guilt, and become liable to punishment, but those
> which are restrained within the mind are not liable to punishment...[26]

> Since then it was not consistent for one who had already believed to
> doubt, he [Moses] has represented the doubt as of no long continuance,
> extending only as far as the mouth of the tongue, and stopping there at the
> mind which is endowed with such celerity of motion; for, says the scrip-
> ture, 'he said in his mind', which nothing, and no person ever so cele-
> brated for swiftness of foot, could ever be able to outstrip, since it outruns
> even all the winged natures.[27]

24. *Leg. All.* 3.217-19 (trans. C.D. Yonge; *The Works of Philo* [Peabody, MA:
Hendrickson, 1993]). A curious feature of this passage is the way the reference to
Abraham ('my Lord') is turned around to refer to God, presumably to connect with
the following biblical declaration about the power of God. See also *Leg. All.* 3.85-87
and *Quaest. in Gen.* 3.55 to the effect that he was filled with great hope at the promise.
    25. '...and both these feelings, namely, to laugh and also to fall, do at the same
time occur to a wise man who inherits good things beyond his expectation; the one
being his fate, as a proof that he is not over-proud because of his thorough knowledge of his mortal nothingness; and the other, by way of a confirmation of his piety
on account of his looking upon God as the sole case of all graces and all good things'
(*Mut. Nom.* 155). See also *Quaest. in Gen.* 3.55.
    26. *Quaest. in Gen.* 3.56; *Mut. Nom.* 178.
    27. *Mut. Nom.* 178.

> When, therefore, the virtuous man [Abraham] knew that the promise was
> uttering things full of reverence and prudent caution, according to his own
> mind, he admitted both these feelings into his breast, namely faith in God,
> and incredulity as to the creature...[28]

Philo's extensive treatment of the patriarch and matriarch is in
keeping with his allegorical approach and with his apparent concern to
establish the harmony within all of existence. The incongruities of the
human experience, in this case, faith and incredulity, obedience and
disbelief, pride and humility, are lifted to the allegorical plane and
brought into an integrated whole.

By way of contrast, the picture from the New Testament is focused
almost exclusively on Abraham and his faith. The only possible allusion to Abraham's laughter appears in Jn 8.56 if Jesus' words to the
effect that Abraham saw His day and *rejoiced* are a product of the
traditional interpretation of the incident in the first century. The general tenor of the translations would suggest this possibility. Because
Paul's intent was to demonstrate that Abraham is the father of the
faithful, all references to him in Romans and Galatians bypass entirely
the laughter incident; it did not serve his purpose. While Peter referred to the person of Sarah to illustrate submission (1 Pet. 3.5, 6), her
mirth was not a focal point. In other words, the theological teaching
agenda mandated selectivity on the part of each text.

Rabbinic Commentary: Bereshith Rabbah (Ber. R.)
Because the rabbis' focus was the text of Torah, they discovered their
answers to a variety of textual issues within the Hebrew Bible as a
whole. Their method was rooted in a network of interlocking biblical
characters and texts. Relatively little was said in response to the laughter of Abraham, perhaps because it is not really a textual issue. The
authorship of *Bereshith Rabbah* was instead characteristically interested in why Abraham was circumcised at the age of 99, how the cut-
ting of flesh could fit with the command to be *tamim* (Gen. 17.1), and
the implications of Abraham's falling on his face twice (*Ber. R.* 46
and 47). Also meriting attention was the change of names, especially
that of Sarah, perhaps because the significance of the change of her
name is not evident in the biblical text (*Ber. R.* 47).

When it comes to the second episode, the Sages extensively addressed the ambiguities of the biblical text in Genesis 18. They proposed

28. *Mut. Nom.* 201.

interpretations of the נְקוּדוֹת of v. 9.[29] They addressed the grammar and vocabulary of vv. 10 and 12.[30] They suggested a reason why the Lord changed the words that Sarah said as he repeated them back to Abraham.[31] Finally, and the punchline for our investigation, they presented an explanation for the different response to Sarah's laughter. Because this last was clearly a 'stock' item, appearing frequently throughout the text traditions, only its introductory declaration was presented in *Ber. R.* It was presumed that the rest was known. In the more complete rendition found in *Abot deRabbi Nathan B* 37, it reads:

> Sarah laughed inside saying... This is one of the things they changed for Ptolemy the king [from בְּקִרְבָּהּ to בִּקְרוֹבֶהָ 'with her relatives']. The difference is that Abraham said it to himself and God was not angry. Because He got angry with Sarah she must have said it out loud.[32]

29. 'Why does אֵלָיו have dots over three of the letters? R. Shimon ben Eleazer said: When you find the number of undotted letters prevailing over the number of pointed letters, you interpret the undotted letters (and vice versa). Here the dotted letters prevail and you read אַיּוֹ—where is Abraham [they were being polite and inquiring about both]. R. Azariah said: Just as they said to Abraham: Where is Sarah? so they said to Sarah: Where is Abraham?' (*Ber. R.* 48.9).

30. '*...and he was behind it* [or *it was behind him*]. This refers to Ishmael. *...and it was behind him*; because of privacy. *...and she* [הִיא instead of הוּא] *was behind him/it...*; she perceived that the traveler had come' (*Ber. R.* 48.10). '*...After I am worn out, will I still have this pleasure?* She said: A woman, all the time she was a young girl, she had ornaments... How do you know ornaments? [Ezek. 16.11 utilizes a related word.] All the time she was a young girl, she had periods... And my master is old. Judah: He has intercourse but is impotent. R. Judah in the name of R. Simon: You think of yourselves as young and your fellows old. Am I too old to do miracles?' (*Ber. R.* 48.12). According to R. Simon's interpretation, it was God who uttered those last words, joining together the issues of the age of Abraham with His own power in a fashion reminiscent of Philo (*Leg. All.* 3.217-19).

31. '*The Lord said to Abraham: Why did Sarah laugh?* Bar Kapara—Great is peace that even the Scriptures spoke fiction to keep peace between Abraham and Sarah. *Why did Sarah laugh saying: Shall I even bear a child...?* It does not say "my master is old" but "I am old"' (*Ber. R.* 48.13).

32. *Abot deRabbi Nathan B* 37; *Ber. R.* 48.12; b. *Meg.* 9a. See also *Mekilta deRabbi Ishmael, Pisha* 14, y. *Meg.* 1.9. Many of the changes ostensibly made for Ptolemy had to do in some sense with the presentation of God. Notably, care was taken to avoid plural forms. This one is clearly not in that category. While the rabbis noted over a dozen changes made 'for Ptolemy', many of them are not reflected in the LXX now.

Conclusion

In each of these post-biblical treatments, the agenda of that text determined whether and how the incidents were addressed. The Targums, most likely intended for synagogue reading and popular consumption, were made more 'presentable' and the ambiguities in the story-line were redefined by interpretive additions. Josephus and *Jubilees* presented the big picture, with more focus on the issues of covenant, circumcision, and the judgment against Sodom and Gomorrah. It was Philo's intention to discover the philosophical harmony behind the ever-present paradoxes of the biblical text. The New Testament selectively represented Abraham because of the issue of faith. *Bereshith Rabbah*, the first real commentary, took up philological and grammatical issues in the process of addressing broader interpretive issues in the context of Torah as a whole.

LOT IN SODOM: THE POST-MORTEM OF A CITY AND THE AFTERLIFE OF A BIBLICAL TEXT

Judith H. Newman

In our current age, the destruction of Sodom and Gomorrah described in Genesis 18–19 is invoked most frequently as a morality tale warning against the dangers of untrammeled homosexual lust. The connotations of the word sodomy also suggest that this interpretation is the predominant one in our society. This intepretation is also found in commentaries on Genesis. For instance, Speiser states that: 'to J, it was the city's sexual depravity, the manifest "sodomy" of its inhabitants that provided the sole and self-evident reason for its frightful fate'.[1] It is thus interesting that the early history of interpretation of this episode reveals a very different perspective on Sodom's iniquity.[2] Already in the first century of the common era, Josephus provides a vice list of the Sodomites in *Antiquities of the Jews* that only hints at their sexual behavior, but includes mention of their abhorrence of strangers. In rabbinic interpretation, the Sodomites are portrayed as wicked evildoers whose behavior encompasses a wide variety of sins, but foremost among them was their lack of hospitality and antagonism toward strangers.

In this essay, my aim is to disentangle a few filaments in the web of early post-biblical interpretation about Sodom found in Josephus and *Pirqe deRabbi Eliezer*, and to show how their interpretive strategy sought to harmonize the various depictions of the Sodomites in the

1. E.A. Speiser, *Genesis* (AB, 1; Garden City, NY: Doubleday, 1964), p. 142.
2. J.A. Loader has written a monograph on the early history of Jewish and Christian interpretation of the Sodom traditions that provides some welcome revisionism of the typical modern view that the 'sin of Sodom' was simply homosexuality. He argues in part that Augustine was largely responsible for a shift in emphasis from the 'social aspect' to the 'sexual aspect' of the interpretive tradition; *A Tale of Two Cities: Sodom and Gomorrah in the Old Testament, Early Jewish and Early Christian Traditions* (CBET, 1; Kampen: Kok, 1990).

Bible.[3] At the end, I will also suggest that the rhetorical force of the allusion to the fate of Sodom and Gomorrah in Mt. 10.15 reflects this early Jewish understanding of the sin of Sodom as inhospitality.

Sodom in the Hebrew Bible and Pseudepigrapha

To understand Jewish interpretation of this episode, it is helpful first to review other references to Sodom in the Hebrew Bible and the pseudepigrapha. Outside the book of Genesis, there are 12 references to Sodom or the Sodomites, either paired with Gomorrah, or cited alone. Of these, seven function in the text in much the same way.[4] They portray Sodom as the paradigm for the disastrous consequences of wickedness and disobedience, but do not cite any specific sin as reason for Sodom's destruction.

The other references to Sodom all appear in the prophetic corpus. Three of these make indirect connections to the sins of the Sodomites. Jeremiah 23.14 condemns the behavior of the Jerusalemite prophets for adultery, lying, and strengthening the hands of evildoers, and then likens their fate to that of the Sodomites. Isaiah 1.10 condemns the Jerusalemites for their empty religious practices and lack of social justice, referring to them as 'rulers of Sodom and people of Gomorrah'. In Zeph. 2.9-10, Moab's fate is compared to Sodom's because of their arrogance and their scoffing at the Israelites: תחת גאונם כי חרפו ויגדלו.

The most interesting passage to consider, however, is Ezekiel 16, both because it contains an *explicit* list of the sins of the Sodomites, and also because Ezek. 16.49 figures prominently in early interpretation of Genesis 19.

The reference to the sin of Sodom in Ezekiel comes in the context of a long passage in which Jerusalem's idolatrous behavior is likened

---

3. The learned reader will note the position taken in this essay differs from Loader's work in at least two ways. I understand early Jewish interpretation of the Sodom episode *primarily* as an *exegetical harmonization* of all the biblical references to the Sodomites. Loader suggests that both the narrative in Gen. 18–19 and the references to Sodom and Gomorrah in the prophetic literature are 'the same tradition with the same motifs and the same basic function...there is no fundamental difference in the view taken of Sodom and Gomorrah, of what their inhabitants did, and of what happened to them' (*A Tale of Two Cities*, p. 73). My second major disagreement with Loader is over the relationship between Ezek. 16 and Gen. 18–19, which he considers 'the fountainhead' of the Sodom traditions. See n. 7 below.

4. Jer. 49.18, Jer. 50.40, and also in Isa. 13.19, Amos 4.11, and Lam. 4.6.

allegorically to an unfaithful wife who betrays her husband, YHWH. Here the sin of Jerusalem is apostasy, portrayed metaphorically as sexual misconduct. In this passage that highlights sexual misdeeds, if only figuratively, it is striking that Sodom's sins are listed, but no sexual sins are included among them. Sodom is described as Jerusalem's younger sister, whose sins pale by comparison with her older sister's. In Ezek. 16.49-50, Sodom's guilt is spelled out:

גאון שבעת־לחם ושלות השקט היה לה ולבנותיה ויד־עני ואביון לא החזיקה

She and her daughters had arrogance, surfeit of bread, and prosperous security, and did not help the poor and needy.

Ezekiel 16.52 states that by comparison with the sexual misdeeds of Jerusalem, both Sodom (and Samaria, her other 'sister') appear righteous.[5] Thus the Hebrew Bible outside of Genesis suggests a number of ideas about the exact nature of Sodom's sin: adultery, social injustice, arrogance, and oppression of the poor. In literature outside the Hebrew Bible, the sin of Sodom seems to pick up these motifs, construing the Sodomites' wickedness in one of two ways. Ben Sira and *3 Maccabees* pick up the motif of arrogance mentioned in Ezekiel and Zephaniah. The *Testaments of the Twelve Patriarchs* and the book of *Jubilees* refer to Sodom's sin in terms of sexual misdeeds.[6] But of all of these, the book of Ezekiel offers the most explicit list of Sodom's offenses, none of which seems to be suggested from the story in Genesis 19 itself.[7] This divergence caused Walther Eichrodt to suggest

5. Another significant verse in this chapter in Ezekiel suggests that already by the time it was written, Sodom had a long reputation as having been destroyed for its misdeeds: 16.57 'Was not Sodom your sister a 'byword' שמועה (literally, 'a report or rumor in the mouth') already in the days of [Jerusalem's] exultation?'

6. Ben Sira 16.8 condemns the 'neighbors of Lot' for their arrogance. *3 Macc.* 2.5 mentions both the Sodomites' arrogance and their reputation for wickedness. Both *Testaments of the Twelve Patriarchs* and *Jubilees* mention the sexual sins of the Sodomites. In *T. Benj.* 9.1, Benjamin predicts that his descendants will emulate 'the promiscuity of the Sodomites', seemingly by their associations with 'loose women'. Cf. also *T. Levi* 14.6-8. *Jub.* 16.8 also focuses on sexual conduct. The Sodomites were 'polluting themselves by fornicating in their flesh and causing pollution upon the earth'. It is worth noting that sexual misconduct is not limited to homosexual behavior, but encompasses heterosexual behavior as well. It should also be added that *Jub.* 22 contains a reference to the Sodomites' sin in which it is understood to be idolatry.

7. Here I would have to take strong issue with Loader's comment, 'The gluttony, complacency and social irresponsibility should not be ascribed to a variant

that the author of Ezekiel 16 relied on another tradition about Sodom than the one now found in Genesis.[8] Von Rad suggests the explanation that the tale in Genesis 19 involving a town's abuse of its guests was only secondarily connected to Sodom, which had long had a reputation in Israel as the seat of all sin.[9] Both of these explanations for the differing accounts of the Sodomites' sin offer decidedly modern historical-critical solutions that recognize the complex editing process that lies behind the biblical texts.

But ancient interpreters were of course operating under quite different assumptions about the text. Wellhausen's documentary hypothesis was not even a glimmer in Rabbi Eliezer's eye. For as we shall see in our exploration of Josephus and some midrash on Genesis 18 and 19, early exegetes sought to harmonize divergent references to Sodom in the Torah and latter prophets. The study of early interpretation shows that from an early date, at least by the time of Josephus in the first century CE, these variant motifs about what constituted the sin of Sodom were combined. What appeared to Eichrodt and von Rad as incompatible characterizations of Sodom in Genesis 19 and Ezekiel 16 were used by the rabbis as jumping-off points for a synthetic exposition on the text.

The Sin of Sodom in Early Jewish Sources

Before looking at midrash in *Pirqe deRabbi Eliezer*, I want first to focus on a passage in Josephus's *Antiquities of the Jews* because unlike the aggadic interpretations in the Targums and midrash, it can be firmly dated to the late first century CE. This puts Josephus at roughly

tradition as opposed to a "mainline" tradition about the sexual sins depicted in Genesis 19' (*A Tale of Two Cities*, p. 65). His attempt to argue that Ezekiel's depiction of Sodom relies on the same 'complex of motifs' as does Gen. 18–19 is unconvincing. Granted, both passages understand Sodom to have been destroyed by God because of its wickedness, but divine punishment for wickedness is a theological constant in most of the Hebrew Bible. That alone does not function as a 'motif'. Specificity in details—in this case, the exact conception of Sodom's sins—marks one 'motif' as distinct from another. Thus I cannot accept Loader's claim that 'Ezekiel's social motif is essentially the same as that of the Sodom cycle'.

8.   Walther Eichrodt, *Ezekiel* (OTL; Philadelphia: Westminster Press, 1970), p. 168.

9.   Gerhard von Rad, *Genesis* (OTL; Philadelphia: Westminster Press, 1972), p. 221.

the same time as the Gospel of Matthew, and so presumably reflects one snapshot of the state of early Jewish interpretation at the time. Josephus describes the fall of Sodom in *Ant.* 1.11. The chapter begins with this 'editorial comment' of sorts before the story of Abraham's encounter with the three messengers (in other words, before what would be Genesis 18 in the MT):

> About this time the Sodomites grew arrogant on account of their riches and great wealth: they became unjust toward men, and impious toward God, in that they did not remember the advantages they received from him: they hated strangers, and abused themselves with Sodomite practices.

Josephus's account of the destruction of Sodom is significant because it offers a 'dirty laundry list' that reflects the biblical account but also includes an expanded account of their sins. Arrogant, unjust, and impious towards God: Josephus cites these three characteristics that arouse divine anger and ensure eventual punishment. But added to this list of Sodomite vices are two others: hating strangers and the mysterious 'Sodomite practices', which one can only infer refers to sexual behavior.

This quote from Josephus illustrates a conflation of a number of interpretive motifs that we saw mentioned before. Ezekiel's 'sin list' included arrogance and excessive wealth; Josephus here lists arrogance *as a result* of their great wealth. Also by citing 'Sodomite practices', it seems to mention sexual misdeeds, an interpretive motif that was also contained in *Testament of the Twelve Patriarchs* and *Jubilees*, though Josephus does not state that they abused strangers sexually, but uses the reflexive verb. The interesting new addition to the list that we have seen nowhere else is that 'they hated strangers', another way of saying that they were inhospitable. It is worth mentioning that *1 Clement*, a Christian source that also dates from the first century, states that Lot was saved from the conflagration because of his hospitality and his piety (φιλοξενία and εὐσέβεια). Though Clement does not state this explicitly, his interpretation suggests that Lot possessed these traits in strong contrast to the Sodomites around him, who were inhospitable and idolatrous, which thus echoes two motifs that Josephus mentions. As a historian and chronicler of biblical events, Josephus buries the exegesis by which he arrived at this summary list of iniquities. How did he come to the conclusion that the Sodomites were wealthy or that they hated strangers? Josephus states unequivocally and without exegetical explanation.

I should make explicit at this point that I am working under the assumption that during the Second Temple period a body of interpretation was developing about the Bible. It would have been passed down primarily orally, but some of it was preserved in writing in books of the pseudepigrapha in the form of shared interpretive motifs. To come to an understanding of how Josephus may have arrived at this list of sins, it is useful to look at some rabbinic interpretation that preserved (and no doubt elaborated on) some of the same body of interpretative tradition on which Josephus relied. Some of these points are mentioned in the biblical literature, others, in particular the notion that the Sodomites 'hated strangers' as a general characteristic, appear for the first time.

Here it would be helpful to draw upon the insights of James Kugel about two assumptions that governed ancient rabbinic interpretation, and midrash in particular. One is that midrash is 'first and foremost biblical exegesis, an attempt to make sense of a more than occasionally difficult and fragmentary text'.[10] Midrash is careful verse by verse commentary that frequently focuses on grammatical difficulties or gaps in the narrative for sources of meaning. The second is that 'the very act of exegesis celebrates the canon, the unity and univocality of all of Scripture'.[11] Ancient exegetes presumed that the Torah was revelation made of whole cloth, so that all parts could be safely inter-related in order to derive meaning from it. To quote another rabbi, there is no before or after in Torah. Temporal sequence is subsumed under the assumption of one cohesive perfected revelation in the text. These two points are important in understanding how the various verses in the Bible relating to Sodom were interpreted and their meanings harmonized.

If we move then to consider some midrash, we can see how an explicit exegetical connection is made among divergent biblical verses in order to yield such a conflation of interpretive motifs as cited by Josephus. There is a treasure trove of interpretive material that could help us here, aggadic traditions found in the Targums and also various midrashic collections, but *Pirqe deRabbi Eliezer* is one source that is particularly revealing about the interpretive development of the

10. James L. Kugel, *In Potiphar's House: The Intepretive Life of Biblical Texts* (New York: HarperCollins, 1990), p. 6.

11. James L. Kugel, 'Two Introductions to Midrash', *Prooftexts* 3 (1983), pp. 131-55 (138).

Sodomites' sin. Although the editing of this midrashic compilation probably occurred in the seventh or eighth century, it is recognized to contain much earlier traditions. *Pirqe deRabbi Eliezer* devotes an entire chapter to the episode at Sodom, in which we can see writ large, not only the specific sins of the Sodomites that Josephus mentioned in one short paragraph, but also the exegetical moves that the rabbis made in coming up with such an interpretation. That is to say, it points to the difficulties in the biblical text—grammatical irregularities and gaps in the narrative—that functioned as the irritating grains of sand that caused the rabbis to come up with their interpretive pearls.

T. Desmond Alexander has mentioned the significance of this work in connecting the interpretive tradition of Lot's hospitality to his portrayal as righteous in 2 Peter.[12] It is equally important as a source for understanding how the Sodomites came to be condemned for their lack of hospitality.

The interpretation of the sin of Sodom in *Pirqe deRabbi Eliezer* draws together and interrelates three verses that refer to the evil-doings of the Sodomites, Gen. 13.13, Gen. 18.21, and Ezek. 16.49. Genesis 13.13 occurs in the context of the separation of Lot from Abraham that is described in that chapter. The text states that Lot chose the well-watered and fertile Jordan valley to live, an area like the garden of Eden, in the vicinity of Sodom. Yet the Bible also mentions at that point, almost as a parenthetical statement: 'And the people of Sodom were very wicked and sinful before the Lord'. So on that basis, early exegetes assumed, first, that the Sodomites who lived there must be well-off because they lived in such an agriculturally rich and fruitful area, and second, that the wickedness mentioned at this point must have some connection to the fact. So in *Pirqe deRabbi Eliezer*, Rabbi Ze'era is quoted as saying that the men of Sodom were wealthy men of prosperity, because they lived on good and fruitful land. It was moreover inferred from this, reading this verse in light of Ezek. 16.49, that their wickedness had something to do with the fact that

---

12. T. Desmond Alexander, 'Lot's Hospitality: A Clue to His Righeousness', *JBL* 104 (1985), pp. 289-91. Other scholars have examined the evolution of Lot as a revered holy man of Israel. Indeed, Marcel Simon argued that at the beginning of the Christian era, Jews had already been venerating tombs of the patriarchs and prophets. Among the usual list of Israel's greats for which Simon finds evidence of veneration, he also mentions the 'cult' of Saint Lot. See his article, 'Les Saints d'Israël dans la dévotion de l'Eglise Ancienne', *RHPR* 34 (1954), pp. 98-127.

they abused the privileges of their wealth by oppressing the poor. Ezekiel 16.49 is then quoted to specify some of the ways the Sodomites were wicked: 'Here, this is the iniquity of your sister Sodom: arrogance, fullness of bread, and prosperous ease was in her and in her daughters; neither did she strengthen the hand of the poor and needy'.

The translation of Gen. 13.13 in *Targum Onqelos* also reflects this view by making some additions to the Masoretic text. It reads: 'The people of Sodom were very wicked *with their wealth* and sinful *with their bodies* before the Lord'.

After quoting Ezek. 16.49, *Pirqe deRabbi Eliezer* then offers a particularly ingenious interpretation. On the basis of one small grammatical irregularity in Gen. 18.21, they make a connection between the Sodomites' abuse of the poor and their lack of hospitality. The first half of v. 21 reads 'Let me go down and see if they are doing everything according to *her cry* that comes up before me'—הכצעקתה. Among the textual difficulties of v. 21, it contains one word that was particularly troublesome for the rabbis. The word for 'her cry' ends with the third feminine suffix. The Old Greek, *Targum Onqelos*, and the *versio Arabica* all have changed the third feminine singular suffix to the third masculine plural in order to give the sense of 'the cry against them', that is, an outcry against the Sodomites. English translations, of course, eliminate the question of gender entirely. The King James, for instance, reads: 'I will go down now, and see whether they have done altogether according to the cry of it which is come unto me; and if not, I will know'.

But fortunately, the rabbis were not fluent in the King's English, and so this small grammatical nugget they found in the Hebrew proved the source of a creative interpretation. The verse refers to *her* cry—who was 'she'? Of course, the *peshat*—the plain sense answer—would be that because 'city', עיר in Hebrew, is feminine, *her* cry refers to the city's cry. But the rabbis came up with some good *derash* on the basis of this word, lending a much more interesting significance to this female ending.

In *Pirqe deRabbi Eliezer*, Rabbi Jehudah gave this suggestion: The Sodomites had a law that forbade anyone from strengthening the hand of the poor or needy with a loaf of bread or offering hospitality to strangers, under penalty of burning. One young woman in Sodom, Lot's daughter, happened to transgress this law by offering some bread to a poor stranger, and so she was brought to trial. At that point *her cry* for justice went up before the Lord—הכצעקתה. *Targum Pseudo-Jonathan* also echoes this interpretation in its construal of Gen. 18.21:

> And the Lord said to the ministering angels, the cry of Sodom and Gemorrah, because *they oppress the poor* and *decree that whoever gives a morsel to the needy shall be burned with fire* is therefore great, and their guilt exceedingly weighty. I will now appear, and see whether, like *the cry of a young woman torn away* that rises before me, they have completed their sins.

According to the rabbis, then, this formed part of the basis for the Sodomites' reputation for antagonism toward strangers and lack of hospitality. The inhabitants of Sodom possessed a combination of wicked tendencies, understood by interrelating the three important verses in Genesis and Ezekiel, that resulted in the visit of the two angels in Genesis 19. The Sodomites' subsequent behavior upon learning that Lot was being a good host to these strangers was confirmation to God that the cities of the plain deserved destruction. *Pirqe deRabbi Eliezer* reflects a fully developed interpretive tradition about Sodom, elements of which are also contained in the Targums, *Genesis Rabbah*, and the tractate *Sanhedrin*. But as the passage from Josephus makes apparent, the basic parts of this conflated interpretation about the sin of Sodom were already in place by the late first century of the common era. Josephus refers to the Sodomites as arrogant, wealthy, unjust, and idolatrous, and as hating strangers and abusing them.

Although Genesis 19 certainly portrays the inhabitants' behavior toward Lot's guests as abhorrent, it is nowhere suggested in the text itself specifically why the town was already slated for destruction in Genesis 18. Josephus and the tradition of Jewish interpretation supplied a specific list of offenses that were sufficient to seal their fate, and chief among them was this law against hospitality and generosity toward outsiders.

Sodom in the Gospel of Matthew

Having unpacked a bit of this rabbinic interpretation, we can now turn briefly to consider how it enriches understanding of the pericope from Matthew 10 that alludes to Sodom and Gomorrah. (This passage also appears, with minor variations, in Luke 10.) The context of the passage is Jesus' commissioning of the 12 disciples. In Mt. 10.5, Jesus sends them out with certain instructions about what to teach and where to go. He then also gives specific guidelines about where to stay when entering a town. If no one welcomes them, they are told to shake off the dust from their feet before leaving that house or town, in a symbolic rejection of that place. The last verse in the passage contains the formulaic sentence that occurs again in 11.24: 'Truly, I tell you, it will be more tolerable for the land of Sodom and Gomorrah on the day of judgment than for that town'.

Daniel Harrington suggests that this saying connects the discourse to Israel's history and also places the mission to Israel in an eschatological framework.[13] But his commentary and others often neglect to mention how this reference to Israel's history and the destruction of Sodom and Gomorrah might carry special weight for someone familiar with the interpretive tradition about Sodom's abhorrence of strangers.[14] Surely the original social milieu generally connected with Matthew's Gospel would have suggested a large number of people familiar with traditional biblical interpretation.[15]

In this context then, the allusion to Sodom and Gomorrah would carry special force. As Loader notes:

> The motifs of messengers (the number differs in the various texts), hospitality, rejection, punishment on the day of judgment...and comparison to Sodom and Gomorrah...are all present in these passages. We have further

---

13. Daniel Harrington, *The Gospel According to Matthew* (Collegeville, MN: Liturgical Press, 1983).

14. Cf. the comment of John P. Meier about the wrongdoing of the Sodomites: 'Sodom and Gomorrah showed disrespect to the angels, the Old Testament messengers of Yahweh; worse still is the disrespect shown to the apostles, the New Testament messengers of Christ' (*Matthew* [Wilmington, DE: Michael Glazier, 1980], p. 108). W.F. Albright and C.S. Mann note only a most general sense of disobedience conveyed by this reference to Sodom, 'The place is frequently used in the New Testament as a typical example of the doom reserved for communities that resist the divine will' (*Matthew* [AB, 26; Garden City, NY: Doubleday, 1971], p. 121).

15. Richard B. Hays points to this criterion, which he refers to as the test of 'availability', as one of a number of constraints that should be considered in separating an authentic intertextual allusion from a mere figment of an interpreter's imagination. See in particular his helpful section on 'Hearing Echoes: Seven Tests', in *Echoes of Scripture in the Letters of Paul* (New Haven: Yale University Press, 1989), pp. 29-32.

evidence in the New Testament that the motif of hospitality was expressed in terms of the Sodom story.[16]

The role of the disciples as emissaries of the messiah bearing special news is analogous to the role of the two messengers in Genesis 19 who arrive as strangers in a foreign town. In Matthew's portrayal, Jesus is sending out his disciples not to the Gentiles, or Samaritans, but to the 'lost sheep of the house of Israel'. Whereas the story of the Sodomites in Gen. 19.19 highlights the fact that the divine emissaries are sent to visit Lot who is sojourning among foreigners, here in an ironic twist, Jesus is sending his own emissaries to sojourn among 'Israelites'. All irony aside, the message is clear. In likening the possible fate of these towns who reject Jesus' apostles with the Sodomites who mistreated all strangers who came within their purview, Matthew makes the strongest possible condemnation of them. Like Sodom, that paragon of wickedness, their grim future in the coming age is determined. For those who knew well the sins and punishment associated with the Sodomites in first-century Jewish interpretation of this episode, this was forewarning indeed.

16. Loader, *A Tale of Two Cities*, p. 119.

ABRAHAM AND SARAH:
LITERARY TEXT AND THE RHETORICS OF REFLECTION

Paul Borgman

> Abraham to kill him
> Was distinctly told—
> Isaac was an Urchin—
> Abraham was old—
>
> Not a hesitation—
> Abraham complied—
> flattered by Obeisance
> Tyranny demurred—
>
> Isaac—to his children
> Lived to tell the tale—
> Moral—with a Mastiff
> Manners may prevail.

Emily Dickinson[1]

Behind Dickinson's tongue-in-cheek response to this notable scene from Abraham's story one detects a serious encounter with the text. Søren Kierkegaard muses about the same incident a volume's worth, with quite a different and in fact contradictory conclusion. The moral, for the poet, is that with a demanding God, maintaining the prescribed etiquette and manners is wise. But for the nineteenth-century philosopher, the troubling episode indicates that a knight of true faith such as Abraham may be called upon to defy accepted morals and manners.[2]

Which of the two hears the true voice of the text? What I hear when I try to let the text speak in its own voice is quite different from what either Dickinson or Kierkegaard has heard. Does the text have

1. Thomas H. Johnson (ed.), *The Complete Poems of Emily Dickinson* (Boston: Little, Brown & Co., 1890, 1960), pp. 571, 572 (poem #1317).

2. Søren Kierkegaard, *Fear and Trembling, and The Sickness Unto Death* (trans. Walter Lowrie; Princeton: Princeton University Press, 1969), p. 84.

anything like 'one voice', and if so, can any two people hear that one voice similarly? The answer would seem to be *no*, yet surely the reader from whatever community of readers wishes at some level to approach the ideal of listening as carefully as possible to the voice of the text. Analogously, we best receive another person's voice when we can detach ourselves, in our listening, from our own desires and projections. Yet a third party, listening well to that same voice, will hear differently, selecting this or that emphasis, sensitive to this or that nuance. Conversation between two—text and reader, person and person—has its own organic structures of forward movement.

Such a conversation has been going on between the Abraham narrative and its readers from the rabbinic tradition through modern scholarship. Listening carefully to this conversation, we can hear voices reflecting various communal needs and rhetorical purposes. Seemingly contradictory interpretations arise. Regarding episodes like the doublet of Sarah's sexual jeopardy, for example, Philo and Augustine praise Abraham while most modern scholarship questions the first patriarch's uprightness. A second example is a saying like '[Abram] believed the Lord; and the Lord reckoned it to him as righteousness': the canonical writers Paul and James seem to contradict each other in the way this passage is heard. Clement, early bishop of Rome, appears to agree with James's interpretation of the faith–works tension though his hearing and rhetorical purposes reflect different communal needs.

Listening well to conversations from the past requires the same careful attention to the conversationalist's text and context as we bring to the canonical text around which the conversation is focused. As theological historical narrative, the canonical text reveals its own rhetorical purposes/structure, a factor in evaluating the subsequent critical conversation. What were the primary concerns of the various reading/listening communities, and what were their characteristic modes of discourse and response, and how is the canonical text illumined by an answer to these questions?

The argument/persuasion mode of the rabbinic tradition presents Abraham as an exemplary rabbi, while an inheritor of this tradition like Philo portrays Abraham as an exemplary Greek contemplative. The epistolary mode of Paul, James, and Clement is more occasionally oriented: Paul's Abraham is an exemplar of faith-no-boasting for a community racked by petty divisiveness, while for James and Clement, Abraham is an exemplar of obedience/works in communities impoverished by acquisitiveness and schism. In the confessional/ apologia of Augustine (*City of God*) and Calvin (*Institutes of the Christian Religion*), Abraham is, respectively, the perfectly progressing Christian, or the Christian suffering escalating calamity. Modern biblical scholarship departs from its precursors both in polemics (no epistles, for example) and in textual assumptions (no coherently unified narrative). The latter makes difficult the idea of 'character' (continuous, conscious self-identity, development). The rhetoric of most modern scholarship presents Abraham more as collage than character.

In their views of Abraham, various rhetorics can be understood to a surprising extent as complementary. Understood as conversational dialectic, always with changing audiences, the critical tradition can be viewed less in terms of better or worse interpretation than as an organically growing history of thought illumining text, reflection, and communities.

To what extent, then, can differing views of a biblical narrative be mutually informing while illumining that text?

Philo and the Rabbinic Tradition: Teacher of Righteousness Explains Abraham

A member of the Jewish Diaspora and a contemporary of Jesus, Philo demonstrates in his response to the Abraham narrative a reliance on the rabbinic approach to the Torah as a repository of literal stories but more especially of buried mysteries. As a teacher of righteousness, Philo mediates the mysteries for communities seeking both practical rules for living and moral projects for the soul. He is a revealer of revelations.

Attentive to the literal narrative, Philo is more interested in the allegorical possibilities of various textual elements, including plot, character, and individual words or parts of words. Philo's platonism is consistent even in its approach to a text: allegorical moral philosophizing is ultimate food for the soul, even though the literal text must be considered as a stepping stone, just as the body gives way to the soul. This method of listening to a text at both literal but most especially allegorical levels became part of the early Christian tradition of responding to Scripture, starting with the Gospel and epistle writers.

That Abraham journeys is, for Philo, the key to both the literal text and the allegorical possibilities. The patriarch journeys from a life ruled by material considerations toward a releasing and purifying of his soul.

Both early and late in that literal journey, however, Abraham involves Sarah in a scheme which ensures his safety by making his wife sexually available to foreign men. Philo recognizes that questions arise concerning the moral character of Abraham. He begins his answer, in regards to the second instance of the sojourn in Abimelech's land of Gerar, by expressing disdain for 'the opinion of some who believe that the wise man [Abraham] was a betrayer of the laws of marriage'.[3]

The literal text suggests that Abraham uses a half-truth to trick the foreigners, thereby saving himself from lecherous murder. Philo anticipates the reader's question: 'Why does Abraham again say concerning his wife, "She is my sister"?' The answer:

> Always and everywhere it is a kind of counsel of homage, that among strangers he called his wife 'sister'. Wherefore anyone who says that this was done through levity of character with unwashed feet and with a changed countenance and with complete practice is deserving of condemnation. For they cannot reflect and bear in mind that no one is so stupid and silly even among those who go far in wrongdoing as to think that he in whom there is perfection would as it were, wish to remain in sinful transgression and to celebrate many times those things which when spoken only once bring shame and disgrace.

In fact, to call your wife 'sister' was to confer legal standing, 'a kind of counsel of homage'. But Philo's concern, ultimately, goes beyond solving textual enigmas at a literal level. There is, here, food for the soul, to be harvested through allegory.

> But let not such a streak of impiety come upon us as that we should think unworthy things of the patriarch, father and founder. For a most noble occasion of glorification are those things which are seen by nature. For the virtue-loving mind calls virtue 'sister' but not 'wife', because it seems to be not only a protector of wisdom as if of a wife but by calling it 'sister' it shows that eagerness and zeal for this are common to all who are genuine and sincere in their desire for excellence.[4]

Abraham's is a journey toward the true pleasures of the mind which loves virtue. Sarah symbolizes virtue, and *sister* is a more suitable trope than *wife* to express contemplative love. This land of Gerar,

---

3.   Philo, *Quaest. in Gen.* 4.61.
4.   Philo, *Quaest. in Gen.* 4.60.

furthermore, represents for Abraham 'God-loving thoughts' and in the spirit of God-loving thoughts, Abraham calls his consort 'sister' to better represent his zeal for 'virtue'. Abraham is demonstrating to the foreign king 'that eagerness and zeal for this [virtue] are common to all who are genuine and sincere in their desire for excellence', of whom Abraham is chief.

Abimelech, according to Philo, cannot quite grasp the righteousness of Abraham. 'Why, when Abimelech asked [Abraham], "What was in thy mind that thou didst this?", did he reply, "Because I thought that God was not in this place, and that I should be waylaid and slain"?' Philo answers the question this way:

> Not all the truth is to be told to all men, wherefore also now the wise man manages the whole (affair) with alteration and change of names. For he knew that as for his wife, she would not be corrupted. This, however, he does not admit but only what it was proper for his interrogators to hear, in order that they might be delighted by the fact that he seemed to be showing that region had a desire for piety and for respect toward strangers, and that they might be even more mindful of piety and hospitality.[5]

That is, Abraham flatters the king and his people, while cagily withholding his confidence that in any case, Sarah 'would not be corrupted'.

The context of Philo's own text, his working hypothesis of the story's dramatic coherence, illumines both his own seemingly idiosyncratic allegorizing of specific texts but also the Abraham text itself: we recognize, after all, that in some fundamental sense, the literal story does have a plot characterized by journeying. Not only is Abraham called upon to journey, the journey is, as Philo sees, at least in part a progressive perfecting of the inner person. Like any good reader of story, Philo starts at the story's beginning.

Philo's sense of the dramatically coherent whole is implied by the title he gives his discourse on Abraham's story, 'On the Migration of Abraham'.[6] Leave country, kindred, and father's house, says God to Abraham at the story's beginning; for Philo as for many good listeners to narrative, the end is in the beginning.

The precise order of what God tells Abram to leave is, for Philo, of crucial interest: Abraham is to migrate first of all from his homeland,

---

5. Philo, *Quaest. in Gen.* 4.67.
6. Translation from the Loeb Classical Library, vol. IV (trans. F.H. Colson and G.H. Whitaker; London: Heinemann, 1958), pp. 133-225.

then from his kindred, and finally from his father's house (Gen. 12.1). These become the three steps of the soul toward self-knowledge and God-knowledge:

> God begins the carrying out of His will to cleanse man's soul by giving it a starting-point for full salvation in its removal out of three localities, namely, body, sense perception, and speech. 'Land' or 'country' is a symbol of body, 'kindred' of sense perception, 'father's house' of speech.[7]

Abraham's leaving of homeland, kindred, and father's house, then, becomes a migration of the soul toward its destination and the story's end, in which all land, family, and domesticity give way to the soul's contemplation, in solitude, of a beatific vision. The 'where' of Abraham's destination becomes the goal of moral development. The story's plot moves not so much toward Abraham's settling down after a physical wandering as it is a drama of the soul's coming to know itself which enables the soul's rest in knowing God:

> The third stage [after the Chaldees, after Haran] is when, having opened up the road that leads from self, in hope thereby to come to discern the Universal Father, so hard to trace and unriddle, it will crown maybe the accurate self-knowledge it has gained with the knowledge of God Himself. It will stay no longer in Haran, the organs of sense, but withdraw into itself.[8]

I suggest that Philo's grasp of the literary text as a coherently ordered drama of the soul's journey helps to illumine the story of Abraham, however unfamiliar we modern readers are with the allegorical elaborations of individual pericopes or words out of context.[9] Conversely,

---

7. Philo, *Migr. Abr.* 1.2. 'Take up your abode, as I have said, in yourselves; leave behind you opinion, the country of the Chaldeans, and migrate to Haran, the place of sense-perception, which is understanding's bodily tenement. For the translation of Haran is "hole", and holes are figures of openings used by sense-perceptions: for eyes are, in a way, openings and lairs used by sight, ears by hearing, nostrils to receive scents, the throat for tasting, and the whole structure of the body for touch. Gain, therefore, by a further sojourn, a peaceful and unhurried familiarity with these...And when you have surveyed all your individual dwelling with absolute exactitude...bestir yourselves and seek for your departure hence [from Haran], for it is a call not to death but to immortality. You will be able to descry sure indications of this, even while held fast in the dens and caves of the body and of the objects of sense', Philo, *Migr. Abr.* 34.187-90.

8. Philo, *Migr. Abr.* 35.195.

9. In his careful analysis of Philo's interpretation of Abraham, Samuel Sandmel

an understanding of Philo's platonism and its appeal to his community of Alexandrian Jews illumines both his community of readers and his reading of Abraham as a Socratic pilgrim.

If I could enjoin Philo in this conversation I might want to suggest that a closer look at the doublet of Abraham's passing off of his wife as sister—at his literal level—reveals a moral development as he suggests, but from fumbling toward blamelessness rather than from perfection to perfection.

Paul, James, and Clement: Communal Needs and Immediate Epistolary Response

Both Paul's epistle to the Romans and James's letter 'to the twelve tribes in the Dispersion'[10] focus on a central judgment regarding Abraham's character, taken from the Hebrew narrative: 'And [Abraham] believed the Lord; and the Lord reckoned it to him as righteousness' (Gen. 15.6).[11] The patriarch's righteousness is viewed by Paul as a matter of faith, while James praises Abraham's uprightness as a

---

describes this tendency of the rabbinic method: 'The rabbinic exegesis, like the Philonic, pays little regard to the context. The verse itself, lifted completely out of its setting, serves the *darshan* for whatever purpose he might wish. The point of departure is the *darshan*'s immediate need or his immediate interest, and, accordingly, the rabbinic Abraham is a character associated with the problems and speculations not of patriarchal days but of rabbinic times. One could construct an almost complete picture of rabbinic theology and rabbinic attitudes from only the Abraham material.

'In rabbinic literature, in conformity with the elaborate exegetical method developed by the rabbis, the relevant Scriptural passages served as means of inferring extended and magnified conclusions explicit from the text, as well as new conclusions such are bound to Scripture only by the tenuous thread of exegetical method' ('Philo's Place in Judaism: A Study of Conceptions of Abraham in Jewish Literature', *HUCA* 26 [1955], pp. 197-98).

10. In James's salutation, 1.1.

11. This assessment of Abraham's character occurs after the patriarch had left family and homeland, and then Egypt, and finally Lot. The divine words leading to the judgment of righteousness are reassuring: 'Do not be afraid, Abram, I am your shield; your reward will be very great' (Gen. 15.1). Abraham then expresses concern about being childless, though pointing out to God that a slave has been designated as heir (15.2, 3). God's rejoinder negates this possibility, with a promise that Abraham's descendants will be as numerous as the stars overhead. Then we read that Abraham put his trust in the Lord, who in turn affirms Abraham as righteous, or in 'a right relationship with God'.

playing out of faithfulness. Clement, Bishop of Rome, understands Abraham's righteousness as obedience to the *paideia* of God. James's reading seems much closer to Clement's than to Paul's.

Following the rabbinic model, each writer included in his letter allegorical interpretations of Hebrew narratives. 'Now this is an allegory', Paul tells us about contrast between Hagar and Sarah and their respective offspring (Gal. 4.24). An allegorical or typological interpretation is almost always assumed by these early Christian readers, and their writing exhibits the characteristic rabbinic focus on narrative detail to make a moral point, often with seeming indifference or disregard for the literal context. But of course each assumed an overall narrative unity which allowed a sense of plot and theme and significant detail.

In their respective interpretations, Paul, James, and Clement choose different supporting details from Abraham's story to demonstrate not only the theme of the story but the lesson for the contemporary community as well.

Between James and Paul

One of the most noted episodes of Abraham's story in the history of its interpretation and even in its retelling (in medieval mystery plays, for example) is mentioned by James but not by Paul, namely, the willingness of Abraham to kill his son at God's request. This great deed—the three-day journey and the binding of his son and raising of the knife—is passed over by Paul: faith makes a person righteous, not works.

In his letter to the Church at Rome, Paul contends that deeds have nothing whatsoever to do with Abraham's righteousness.

> For if Abraham was justified by works, he has something to boast about, but not before God. For what does the scripture say? 'Abraham believed God, and it was reckoned to him as righteousness.' *Now to one who works, wages are not reckoned as a gift but as something due. But to one who without works trusts* him who justifies the ungodly, such faith is reckoned as righteousness (emphasis added; Rom. 4.2-5).

James, however, interprets Abraham's righteousness as integrally related with works:

> Was not our ancestor Abraham justified by works when he offered his son Isaac on the altar? You see that faith was active along with his works,

and faith was brought to completion by the works. Thus the scripture was fulfilled that says, 'Abraham believed God, and it was reckoned to him as righteousness', and he was called the friend of God. *You see that a person is justified by works and not by faith alone* (emphasis added; Jas 2.21-24).

For Paul, then, 'a person is justified by faith apart from works' (3.28) while for James 'a person is justified by works and not by faith alone'.

I hold that what seems contradictory between James and Paul regarding the Abraham text is actually complementary, if each specific judgment is viewed within the larger contexts of the respective writer's entire letter-text and community concerns.

In the major portion of his letter to the Church at Rome, Paul is concerned with an attitude of boasting which he feels distances Jewish Christians from Gentile Christians. The bad feeling between these two groups bothers Paul mightily at this time in his missionary efforts. Exploring the nature of the difficulty leads Paul, at the end of his epistle, to practical considerations for implementing peace between the Gentile Churches and the Church at Jerusalem: he himself will go, risking danger, to effect this unity.[12]

What, at heart, causes such a breach, occasioning such a passionate letter of appeal? Paul goes back to the story of father Abraham to help him explore this issue of jealousy, boasting, and divisiveness.

God accepts as righteous, Paul explains, those who trust in God's grace: 'Then what becomes of boasting?' he asks.[13] The apostle is wrestling with an attitude toward the law which measures one's righteousness before God on the basis of how well the law is kept. The result is the boasting of a self-righteousness. Pride or guilt—polar

---

12. 'His major preoccupation during this period—perhaps three or four years—has been the disastrous rift between the conservative Jerusalemite body of Christians and their Gentile brethren. Paul's work has lain almost entirely among Gentiles and he himself has been both misunderstood and opposed by many Jewish Christians. As a consequence of a conference in Jerusalem on this issue..., Paul sets about raising a sum of money, of undisclosed but obviously large proportions, among the Gentile churches for the relief of poverty at Jerusalem [see Rom. 15.25-29]. He hopes that this offering—so important symbolically that in spite of danger to his person he intends to deliver it himself—will heal the breach and bring peace to the church' (*The Interpreter's Bible* [New York: Abingdon Press, 1954], p. 359). On the conference, see Gal. 2.1-10. 'Acts has this same conference in mind in 15.1-29', comments John Knox, 'although it probably places it too early in Paul's ministry'.

13. Rom. 3.27.

possibilities of self-righteous obsession—indicate a poor understanding of our proper response to God.[14]

And what of Abraham's having obeyed? What of his 'works', so prominent in the interpretation of James? Witness, from earlier in Paul's epistle:

> [God] will repay according to each one's deeds; to those who by patiently doing good seek for glory and honor and immortality, he will give eternal life; while for those who are self-seeking and who obey not the truth but wickedness, there will be wrath and fury... *For it is not the hearers of the law who are righteous in God's sight, but the doers of the law who will be justified* (emphasis added; Rom. 2.7, 8, 13).

James's concern for divine repayment based on deeds, on doing the law, is similar in thought and even in language:

> Therefore rid yourselves of all sordidness and rank growth of wickedness, and welcome with meekness the implanted word that has the power to save your souls. *But be doers of the word, and not merely hearers who deceive themselves.* For if any are hearers of the word and not doers, they are like those who look at themselves in a mirror; for they look at themselves and, on going away, immediately forget what they were like (emphasis added; Jas 1.22-24).

With such a striking example of agreement between Paul and James as to the place of 'doers', what accounts for the apparent difference in tone if not substance in their respective readings of Abraham's righteousness?

Paul gleans from Abraham's story the narrative's emphasis on—its theme of—an attitude of trusting God which allows letting go of self-securing, self-promoting measures. Paul holds up the patriarch's faith, his posture of trust, a spirit which disallows smugness and self-righteousness. A person with such an attitude finds nothing to boast about; her humility is truly open to the divine word about what is to be done, and a commitment to doing it. 'Welcome with meekness the implanted word that has the power to save your souls.' These could have been the words of Paul in his letter to the Romans, but they are the words of James. And they are words which fit both interpretive views of Abraham: James emphasizes the fruit of such trust.

---

14. Paul's concern about the human tendency to point to an external—keeping the law, or even the presumed special status of being a non-Jew 'grafted' into God's family tree—runs either explicitly or implicitly through the entire epistle. See especially 1.30; 2.17; 2.23; 3.27; 11.18.

James is the more practical theologian: this is the word of God about unity and submission, so do it. Paul's approach is more psychological. What are the emotional results in measuring one's own righteousness against some external standard? What accounts for and what prevents boasting? In what does jealousy consist? What is the cure for this problem of the heart? The sin of boasting is an attitude or feeling of self-inflated importance at the expense of others and of God's grace.

Paul recommends an inward response of the heart, a turn of the will, of attitude. We can trust in God's loving acceptance of us in Christ, says Paul, and so let go of boasting and any tendency to make one's self look good at the ultimate expense of someone else. Accept God's goodness toward you, so bountifully expressed in Christ. Don't seek to measure yourself over against someone else by way of being better at keeping the law. After all, when you come right down to it, we all sin. No one, ultimately, climbs far enough out of the mire of self-seeking and name-preserving to achieve a righteousness acceptable to God. Accepting God's forgiveness and valuing of us renders worry about acceptability by our neighbors quite beside the point, and quite divisive. Abraham heard God speak and trusted, says Paul, and God counted this attitude as 'righteousness'—both 'right action'[15] and 'a right relationship with God'.[16] The heart of a right relationship, for Paul, is a relationship characterized by trust in God's unconditional acceptance of us through the work of Christ.

Paul wants unity of spirit,[17] and thinks that God has provided in Christ a way, finally, to achieve an end to human divisiveness. The

---

15. *The New Bible Dictionary* (Grand Rapids: Eerdmans, 1962), p. 1097.

16. Bruce Metzger and Roland Murphy (eds.), *The New Oxford Annotated Bible* (New York: Oxford University Press, 1991), p. 18.

17. 'The thematic exposition in [Romans] chs. 1-11 turns about the single question of the relationship between Jew and Gentile, with the necessary corollary, the place of the law in Christianity. From his other correspondence we would not suspect that this was *the* central concern of Paul's proclamation, for elsewhere only in Galatians does it become the dominant issue... Considering the circumstances of the Claudian expulsion, one can readily imagine that the relationships must have been very sensitive both between church and synagogue and between former Jew and former Gentile within the church. Paul's emphasis both on the unity of Jew and Gentile and on the abiding validity of God's promises to Israel would certainly have had immediate relevance to those relationships' (Wayne A. Meeks [ed.], *The Writings of St. Paul* [New York: W.W. Norton, 1972], pp. 66-67).

syndromes of self-righteousness and others-not-so-righteous are inevitable without trust in and a right relationship with God, says the apostle. Part of the context for understanding Paul's view of Abraham, here, is the apostle's own scrambling effort to fulfill the fine points of the law contrasted with his new-found freedom in trusting God's effort on his behalf. Paul's own experience of trust helps to shape what he sees in Abraham's story.

Abraham received ultimate approval from God for his trust, says Paul, and in like manner we can be freed from boasting since there is no need to gain the favorable notice of anyone else. Jew and Gentile can meet without any ranking order, because the law has been done away with as a measure which judges and differentiates. Paul's desire for such a unity of spirit, of attitude, becomes practical by the end of the epistle when he mentions the financial assistance given the Jewish Christians in Jerusalem by Gentile Christians, 'for if the Gentiles have come to share in their [the Jews'] spiritual blessings, they ought also to be of service to them in material things' (15.27).

Clement, Bishop of Rome: Abraham in the Letter to the Church at Corinth

Before the end of the first century after Christ, Clement writes to a church at Corinth torn by schism. Included is his perspective on the Abraham narrative, in the form of a plot review which begins and ends this way:

> Abraham, who was called 'the Friend', was found faithful in his obedience to the words of God. He in obedience went forth from his country and from his kindred and from his father's house, that by leaving behind a little country and a feeble kindred and a small house he might inherit the promises of God.

> Because of his faith and hospitality a son was given him in his old age, and in his obedience he offered him as a sacrifice to God on the mountain which he showed him.[18]

---

18. The rest of the text reads as follows: 'For God says to him, "Depart from thy land and from thy kindred and from thy father's house to the land which I shall show thee, and I will make thee a great nation, and I will bless thee, and I will magnify thy name, and thou shalt be blessed; and I will bless those that bless thee, and I will curse those that curse thee, and all the tribes of the earth shall be blessed in thee". And again, when he was separated from Lot, God said to him, "Lift up thine eyes

For Clement, Abraham is the shining example of a righteousness characterized by obedience and hospitality. In the rabbinic tradition, almost all of Abraham's actions demonstrate his excellence as the hospitable one: both in method and substance, Clement's address to the Church echoes the rabbinic approach even more than do the letters of Paul and James.

Several leaders in that Church at Corinth had been thrown out. Anarchy and schism were threatening. As an answer, Clement advocates acceptance of one's place, however lowly, in the community. *The First Epistle of Clement to the Corinithians*, influential and widely read, makes a plea for unity with the help of biblical examples of true faith and righteousness—or the conspicuous lack thereof. 'Let us obey [God's] excellent and glorious will', Clement writes, 'and let us turn to His pity, and abandon the vain toil and strife and jealousy which leads to death'.[19]

Just before his rendering of Abraham's story, Clement cites Enoch, 'who was found righteous in obedience' and Noah, who 'was found faithful in his service' (*1 Clem.* 9.3, 4). Immediately following we find one- or two-sentence comments on three more biblical characters: 'For his hospitality and piety Lot was saved out of Sodom' while his wife is condemned to becoming a pillar of salt because she 'changed her mind and did not remain in agreement with him [was dis-obedient]'[20] about leaving the scene of wrongdoing and destruction. And, 'For her faith and hospitality Rahab the harlot was saved'.[21]

Clement's Abraham does not obey a nebulous will of God. He learned the '*paideia* of God', as Clement puts it toward the end of his letter.[22] The Greek term *paideia* is used by Clement to indicate 'the oracles of the teaching of God'.[23] *Paideia* would have been a familiar

---

and look from the place where thou art now, to the North and to the South and to the East and to the West; for all the land which thou seest, to thee I will give it and to thy seed forever. And I will make thy seed as the dust of the earth. If a man can number the dust of the earth thy seed shall also be numbered". And again he says, "God led forth Abraham, and said to him, 'Look up to the Heaven and number the stars, if thou canst number them; so shall thy seed be'. And Abraham believed God, and it was counted unto him for righteousness"' (*1 Clem.* 10.1-7).

19. *1 Clem.* 9.1.
20. *1 Clem.* 11.1, 2.
21. *1 Clem.* 12.1.
22. *1 Clem.* 62.3.
23. As does the LCL edition cited.

concept to the bishop's audience in the Greek city of Corinth for whom moral and communal instruction was part of a tradition going back to Plato in the fifth and fourth centuries before Christ. For educated Greeks and Romans of Clement's time, *paideia* would have been accepted as that education which equips the individual to take his or her place in serving the larger community. For Clement, this community becomes the local Church. To counter the jealousy, envy, and partisanship tearing the Church of Corinth apart, Clement urges obedience according to Christian *paideia*.[24]

This epistolary purpose governs Clement's selection of Abraham as an example in the first place, undoubtedly influencing as well his choice of what constitutes the key events and major themes from the story.

1. The events are three, under one rubric: *Abraham responds obediently to God by leaving or separating himself* (a) from homeland and family, (b) from nephew Lot, and finally (c) from his son Isaac, whom Abraham 'offered...as a sacrifice to God on the mountain which he showed him'. Similar to Philo's sense of journey and leave-taking, Clement nicely surveys the story's entire plot, bearing witness to its unity.

2. For themes, Clement cites the action of God and the response of Abraham. God promises and challenges, while Abraham obeys, and trusts. The obedience of Abraham, for Clement, is characterized by faithfulness, faith, hospitality; his belief in God 'was counted unto him for righteousness'. The themes work together in Clement's view: God's promises/challenges represent the *paideia* of God while Abraham's response is that of the faithful learner. The spirit of such obedience is seen best, for Clement, in Abraham's hospitality, his willingness to entertain strangers. In this reading, Abraham had the faith to be schooled by God in entertaining the possibility of a world quite different from his own natural inclinations and affinities.

Clement's concern was that the Christians in Corinth should learn the excellence of *paideia* in order to solve their communal dissension and potential schism. Abraham's story seems a likely narrative to use for his rhetorical purpose of presenting a godly example of *paideia*. Here is a man who learned—was willing to be taught. And in learning, he believed God, and was obedient in works of hospitality and

24. A wonderfully lucid analysis of Clement's use of *paideia* in his epistle forms can be found in Werner Jaeger's *Early Christianity and Greek Paideia* (Cambridge, MA: Harvard University Press, 1961), II, pp. 12-25.

leave-taking. He illumines the text even as he illumines the prior conversation of Paul and James, revealing their complementariness.

Augustine and Calvin: From Epistle to Apologia

Like Philo centuries before him, Augustine illustrates the righteousness of Abraham as revealed in the doublet of Sarah's sexual jeopardy
following Abraham's scheme to save himself.

Philo's Abraham is a flawless but limited soul whose journeyings
lead 'home' to self-knowledge and perfection of soul. Similarly, the
early-fifth-century Abraham of Augustine, nearly flawless, progresses
primarily through the terrain of self-knowledge. And in shift of
rhetorical mode from the letter-writing of Paul, James, and Clement
to a more systematic apologia, the Bishop of Hippo is, like Philo,
attempting to sketch an entire moral landscape. As Bishop of Hippo,
Augustine's concern ranged from a Church here or there with its
problems this or that to the many Churches and concerns under his
jurisdiction.

Ten centuries later, John Calvin writes in a similar rhetorical mode,
as indicated by the title, *Institutes of the Christian Religion*. Like
Augustine, Calvin wishes to set forth a comprehensive view of what
Christians should know about the entire landscape of their faith. Each,
of course, was addressing problems and possibilities for the Christians
of his own respective age: their respective works reflect those broad
concerns.

'Let us now survey the progress of the city of God', says Augustine
in his great work *City of God*, 'from the era of the patriarch Abraham, from whose time it begins to be more conspicuous, and the
divine promises which are now fulfilled in Christ are more fully
revealed'.[25] Writing 400 years after the time of Christ, Augustine
portrays Abraham as an ideal citizen of the heavenly city, even in the
case of the patriarch's passing off of his wife as sister:

> Abraham proceeded thence and dwelt in the desert, and was compelled by
> pressure of famine to go on to Egypt. There he called his wife his sister,
> and told no lie. For she was this also, because she was near of blood;
> just as Lot, on account of the same nearness, being his brother's son, is
> called his brother. Now he did not deny that she was his wife, but held
> his peace about it, commiting to God the defense of his wife's chastity,

25. Augustine, *De Civ. Dei* 16.12.

> and providing as a man against human wiles; because *if he had not pro-vided against the danger as much as he could, he would have been tempt-ing God rather than trusting in Him* (emphasis added; *De Civ. Dei* 16.19).

But the text at this point seems to offer an opposing interpretation, that Abraham's trust in God is demonstrably imperfect: Abraham attempts here to save his own neck rather than trusting God for his life and name.

Abraham's scheming, further, appears to put Sarah at risk. But according to Augustine, Abraham knew that Sarah would be all right. She would not be in jeopardy, even though the text says that Pharaoh took Sarah as his woman (rendered 'wife' in most modern transla-tions). Sarah's situation was not a problem, because

> what Abraham had expected the Lord to do took place. For Pharaoh, king of Egypt, who had taken her to him as his wife, restored her to her hus-band on being severely plagued. And far be it from us to believe that she was defiled by lying with another; because it is much more credible that, by these great afflictions, Pharaoh was not permitted to do this (*De Civ. Dei* 16.19).

Or, perhaps the plagues were precisely the fate—the punishment—that Abraham knew these foreign men feared if they slept with another man's wife.

When Augustine comes to the repeated instance of Abraham's action, he accepts at face value the patriarch's defense for his actions: 'Then Abraham did again at Gerar, with Abimelech the king of that city, what he had done in Egypt about his wife, and received her back untouched in the same way. On this occasion, when the king rebuked Abraham for not saying she was his wife, and calling her his sister, he explained what he had been afraid of, and added this further, "And yet indeed she is my sister by my father's side, but not by the mother's"; for she was Abraham's sister by his own father, and so near of kin' (*De Civ. Dei.* 16.30). Or perhaps Abraham confesses, in effect, the half-truth used falsely, for personal gain and at his wife's expense. In the first instance, Abraham says not a word to the foreign king, while in the repeated instance he talks not only to the king but also to God on behalf of the king.

When dealing with the first of two scenes of another woman appar-ently at risk, the episodes involving Hagar, Augustine again portrays Abraham not only as absolved of any wrongdoing, but as honorable in his handling of concubine and wife:

> And when the pregnant bond woman despised her barren mistress, and Sarah, with womanly jealousy, rather laid the blame of this on her husband, even then Abraham showed that he was not a slavish lover, but a free begetter of children, and that in using Hagar he had guarded the chastity of Sarah his wife, and had gratified her will and not his own—had received her without seeking, had gone in to her without being attached, had impregnated without loving her—for he says, 'Behold thy maid is in thy hands: do with her as it pleaseth thee'; a man able to use women as a man should—his wife temperately, his handmaid compliantly, neither intemperately! (*De Civ. Dei* 16.25).

Or perhaps the text suggests that Abraham is a coward, protecting his own interest with Sarah at the expense of putting another woman at risk.

Augustine had a polemical interest in his *City of God*: he was inveighing against Pelagianism and charges that Christians were responsible for the overthrow of Rome. Within these rhetorical concerns, Augustine views Abraham as an ideal citizen of God's City, an example of God's overwhelming and pre-determining grace. Possibly: conversation that moves forward does so often by way of 'perhaps this, but perhaps that'. The most attentive readings are always colored, sometimes for better and sometimes for worse, by the reader's unwitting and decided points of view.

I take the point of view represented by the stated *possibly*, above: I think Abraham stumbles in the two cases of doublet involving a woman at risk. But I, as a literary critic, am able to converse with Augustine as with Philo because they assume the narrative as a connected and unified whole. For both Philo and Augustine, the story represents a pilgrim on a journey, a journey with beginning, middle, and end as in any narrative plot. Augustine's concern to exonerate the pilgrim alerts me to enigmatic and crucial junctures of that plot requiring further exploration.

In his lengthy *Institutes of the Christian Religion* John Calvin offers a perspective on the Abraham narrative which is also in the form of a plot review. Calvin is interested exclusively in the deprivations faced by Abraham:

> When [Abraham] is first called by God's command [Gen. 12.1], he is taken away from his country, parents, and friends, considered by men the sweetest things in life, as if God deliberately intended to strip him of all life's delights.

What more frightful thing can the human mind imagine than for a father to become the executioner of his own son? If Isaac had died of sickness, who would not have thought Abraham the most miserable of old men—given a son in jest—on whose account his grief of childlessness should be doubled? If he had been killed by some stranger, the calamity would have been much increased by the indignity. But for a son to be slaughtered by his own father's hand surpasses every sort of calamity. In short, throughout life he was so tossed and troubled that if anyone wished to paint a picture of a calamitous life, he could find no model more appropriate than Abraham's![26]

Calvin's Abraham suffers a calamitous life, from beginning to end. The story's point, for Calvin, is that 'infinite difficulties' make impossible, for the Christian pilgrim, any ordinary happiness in things temporal. Clement's Abraham, however, seems to experience little of such suffering and loss. This Abraham journeys from victory to victory on the basis of his obedience to the word of God. Brief observations on the respective contexts of these two overviews can begin to

26. The rest of the text reads as follows: 'As soon as he has reached the land in which he has been bidden to dwell, he is driven from it by famine [Gen. 12.10]. Seeking aid, he flees to a place where he has to prostitute his wife to save his life [Gen. 12.11-20], an act probably more bitter than many deaths. When he has returned to the land of his abode, he is again driven from it by famine. What sort of happiness is this—to dwell in a land where you often have to go hungry, even perish from hunger, unless you flee from it? He is reduced to the same straits in the land of Abimelech, so that to save his own head he has to suffer the loss of his wife [Gen. 20.1-18]. While in uncertainty he wanders about hither and thither for many years, he is compelled by the continual quarreling of his servants to dismiss his nephew whom he cherished as his own son [Gen. 13.5-9]. Doubtless he bore this separation as if he had undergone the amputation of a limb. Shortly thereafter, Abraham hears that his nephew has been taken captive by enemies [Gen. 14.14-16]. Wherever he goes, he finds barbarous neighbors who do not even let him drink water out of the wells that he had dug with great labor, for he would not have recovered the use of them from King Gerar had he not first been denied it [Gen. 21.25-31]. Now when he has reached a worn-out old age, he finds himself childless [Gen. 15.2]—the most unpleasant and bitter feature of age. Finally, beyond all hope, he begets Ishmael [Gen. 16.15], but the birth of this son costs him dear. For he is wearied by Sarah's reproaches, as if he, by encouraging the handmaid's arrogance, were himself the cause of domestic strife [Gen. 16.5]. Finally, Isaac is born [Gen. 21.2], but with this condition—Ishmael, the first born, is to be driven out and forsaken almost like an enemy [Gen. 21.9-21]. When Isaac alone is left, in whom the weary old age of the good man may repose, he is shortly after ordered to sacrifice him [Gen. 22.1, 2]' (*Christ. Religio. Instit.* 2.10.11).

explain why the two interpretations seem to be referring to two different stories, but also how the two views can be seen in an important sense as complementary.

The full title of John Calvin's *Institutes of the Christian Religion*, from which I have gleaned the author's synopsis of the Abraham story, concludes with *A Preface to the Most Christian King of France, in Which this Book is Presented to Him as a Confession of Faith*. Calvin has a confessional purpose which shapes much of what he writes. The *Institutes*, as scholar John T. McNeill points out, is a work 'offered to a persecuting king in behalf of the author's fellow believers'.[27] Calvin himself had been in flight for his safety and life even before the publication of the *Institutes*; suspects like Calvin 'were imprisoned and burnings took place from day to day'.[28] How like these appears Calvin's Abraham, who flees from the proverbial frying pan into the fire. As Abraham was for Clement the ideal for obedience, so Abraham for Calvin is the ideal for perseverance under fire.

Calvin's rendering of the Abraham narrative occurs in a chapter in which he wishes to suggest that the Old and New Testaments are similar, particularly in respect to the hope in each testament for eternal happiness as opposed to earthly delights. Abraham is the outstanding example in either the Old or New Testaments, for Calvin, of a faith perspective that rests in the hope and happiness of things that last rather than in things temporal. Our mortal life can be harsh and disappointing.[29] In the words that follow the Abraham review, Calvin offers a prefatory word on Abraham's son: 'Isaac is afflicted by lesser ills, but has scarcely even the least taste of sweetness'.

Calvin helps to alert me to narrative continuity, the rise in action to the ultimate 'calamity'. In the rabbinic tradition, this is the last of ten

27. 'Introduction', *Calvin: Institutes of the Christian Religion* (ed. John T. McNeill; trans. Ford Lewis Battles; Philadelphia: Westminster Press, 1960), p. xxxiii.

28. 'Introduction' to *Calvin: Institutes*, p. xxxi.

29. Just before the plot outline which I cited, Calvin begins with praise: 'We ought to esteem Abraham as one equal to a hundred thousand if we consider his faith, which is set before us as the best model of believing; to be children of God, we must be reckoned as members of his tribe [Gen. 12.3]. Now what could be more absurd than for Abraham to be the father of all believers [cf. Gen. 17.5] and yet not to possess even the remotest corner among them? But he cannot be removed from their number—not even from the very highest rank of honor—without wiping out the whole church' (*Christ. Religio. Instit.* 2.10.11).

tests. In these views, the crisis of Abraham's challenge to sacrifice his only and beloved son is, in fact, the story's crowning point. There is a plot, and it moves coherently toward a climax. By acknowledging this, one recognizes that there is a prior narrative context involving such crises, or tests, or challenges. Calvin's words indicate as much, even though there may be other important features of the narrative that help define the action. The story is a unified whole, say these various older commentators, reminding us that there is a plot, a dramatically unfolding context for what might appear as unrelated episodes.

Modern Scholarship: The Absence of Plot, a Problematic Abraham, an Inscrutable God

Biblical scholars Gerhard von Rad and Walter Brueggemann—to choose two whom I respect highly—represent a reading of the story quite different from all those offered above in at least two important respects: neither interpretive attempt is as obviously polemical, and neither assumes a unified and coherent narrative. Though von Rad and Brueggemann recognize the importance of considering the narrative as a whole, as it appears in its final canonical form, each treats the narrative in a more 'objective' manner, offering analysis of individual pericopes determined by the various historical sources. In effect, the final form of the text is broken up into bits and pieces: even the God of Abraham shifts divine identity from the first instance of patriarchal subterfuge to the repeated instance. Without one plot there can be no unity of character, for God or for Abraham.

With the Abraham story and with the two episodes of Sarah's sexual risk in particular, von Rad offers theological judgment based on certain episodes he deems morally superior, without determining the continuity—the integrity—of the narrative text as a whole.[30]

---

30. David Hopkins points out that von Rad viewed the sacrifice of Isaac in the context of the promise motif in Genesis (which I would argue is ironically too large a context to do justice to the immediate narrative, the Abraham narrative itself). But Hopkins applauds von Rad: 'Here von Rad stands over against the tendency of form criticism to atomize the biblical material. In his fundamental study of the Hexateuch, von Rad articulates the same passion. Both literary and form criticism have "led inevitably further and further away from the final form of the text as we have it". They have had a "profoundly disintegrating effect". Von Rad's counterpoise to this is his concern for the *Endstadium* of the *traditio*, the final stage of the tradition process...What von Rad claims of the Hexateuch as a whole must be carried through

Brueggemann, coming a bit later in time, is much more careful to trace connections among the various episodes, reflecting perhaps the fruitful results of literary critics like Robert Alter and Meir Sternberg and canonical scholars like Brevard Childs. But Brueggemann's primary method of analysis is to view essential episodes mostly in isolation from one another.

Both representative scholars view Abraham's actions in the doublet involving his wife at risk as morally questionable or even shabby. But these failures are random, with little final bearing on the divine will. In their reading, the inscrutable and powerful God overrides human error with mysterious majesty.

Gerhard von Rad

Following most biblical scholars, Gerhard von Rad notes the difference in tone between stories #1 and #2 of Abraham's passing off Sarah as his sister. He interprets that difference, not in terms of any progression or coherence in the larger story, but as indications, respectively, of the 'cruder' Yahwist source behind episode #1 and the more 'refined' Elohist tradition reflected in episode #2. The second telling (20.1-18), says von Rad, 'softens' features of the earlier Yahwistic version which emphasize the apparently gross behavior of Abraham and the unseemly consequences to his wife Sarah who becomes Pharaoh's wife.[31]

For von Rad, the different sources of each episode have their respective histories, and even theologies. What these two 'disturbing'

into exegesis: "For no stage in this work's long period of growth is really obsolete; something of each phase has been conserved and passed on as enduring until the Hexateuch attained its final form". These are not idle words, but, in fact, supply the undergirding of the traditio-historical research of which von Rad is progenitor. Yet for von Rad another set of words exerts equal energy: "Israel's kerygmatic picture (of her history) tends toward a theological maximum". This assessment of Israel's narrative intentions plays an extremely important role in von Rad's formulation of his tasks as an exegete. It pushes him as well in the direction of the theological maximum. His sole concern is the kerygma of the final text, the encountered text, and prehistory can only divert attention from such theological maximization' ('Between Promise and Fulfillment: Von Rad and the "Sacrifice of Abraham"', *BZ* 24 [1980], pp. 180-93 [184, 185]). I think Hopkins has pointed admirably to the tension which I call von Rad's rush to theological judgment which the following will demonstrate.

31. *Genesis: A Commentary* (trans. John H. Marks; Philadelphia: Westminster Press, 1961), pp. 222, 162-69, 220-25.

stories are doing in the whole narrative in the first place puzzles von
Rad, although he judges the theology of a unilaterally sovereign God,
as portrayed in the first episode, the superior theology.[32]

What is especially significant about von Rad's interpretation of each
episode of Abraham's deviousness is his recognition that more than
just a unit-by-unit analysis is needed to account for the inclusion of the
singular unit in the first place. About story #1 he acknowledges that,
in spite of the intrinsic 'offensiveness' of Abraham's action and in
spite of an earlier and simpler version of the unit that had no excur-
sion into Egypt, 'the Yahwist must have had all the more reason for
squeezing this block of material into the context here'—and even
more especially since the episode 'contrasts strangely with its relatively late insertion into the context, for among the three named variants[33] its whole style of representation is by far the most ancient and
difficult'.[34] By his own method, however, von Rad is limited in his
analysis of the context. Indeed, von Rad is aware of the problem:
'How does the interpreter proceed?' he asks, admitting uncertainty
about the narrative context while asserting its importance.[35]

Von Rad wonders: other versions—kinder to Abraham—were
available to the collector-compiler; this 'difficult' little story could
have been left out, moving quite smoothly from 12.9 to 13.2. Why
didn't the compiler skip this 'unrefined' story, asks von Rad. He
answers that this incident must be 'an example...of how the collectors
[of differing sources] occasionally give meaning to a narrative from
the overlapping whole'.[36] But what can be said, now, about this
'overlapping whole'? Von Rad says nothing, except to pronounce that
the narrative's strung-together 'units', or 'pericopes', demonstrate, in
a general way, God's univocal and unilateral providence. But perhaps
God's providence in this story does not operate in a vacuum of human
moral action. Perhaps God's promise is tied—at least in some minimal
sense—to human response.

Venturing beyond what his own methods allow, von Rad concludes
with a serious misrepresentation, I think, of the narrative's theology.
Looking at the story of Abraham as a collection of episodes minus a

32. *Genesis: A Commentary*, pp. 162, 164, 165, 221.
33. Including the Isaac version of the episode, 26.7-11.
34. *Genesis: A Commentary*, p. 163.
35. *Genesis: A Commentary*, p. 164.
36. *Genesis: A Commentary*, p. 164.

carefully developing dramatic coherence, von Rad suggests, naturally enough, a theology of God's univocal and unilateral sovereignty. Abraham's failures and successes appear random because the whole text lacks, in this view, a precise ordering of its parts. Perhaps the human side of response is, in reality, hopelessly 'spotty'. God, therefore, has to be 'the whole story'.

It can seem, says von Rad, that 'the bearer of promise himself [is] the greatest enemy of the promise...But though the narrative provokes these or similar reflections, they remain relatively secondary in the presence of Yahweh's activity'. He then concludes, significantly, with a hermeneutical humility which announces, in light of what we can't hope to understand, a theology of God's all-sufficient sovereignty.

> Our determination to understand is limited by Yahweh's power and mystery. The interpreter has to know about this limitation...That this material [the ancestress placed in jeopardy] is varied in three forms in the patriarchal history shows that Israel reflected on this saving intervention by God with special interest.[37]

For von Rad, how the human responds is, ultimately, not a deciding factor—if a factor at all—in the fulfilling of divine promise. This is a common enough theology, of course, but a theology not supported, I think, by the story of Abraham.[38]

'If Yahweh did not go astray in his work of sacred history because of the failure and guilt of the recipient of promise, then his word was really to be believed', claims von Rad.[39] What this theological judgment glosses over is the story's dramatic interest, perhaps its most important concern, with the delay of fulfillment to God's promise until Abraham perfects his response, based on trust in God's provision. The theology of the Abraham narrative includes, in addition to the initiating and providing nature of God, the indispensable role of

---

37. *Genesis: A Commentary*, pp. 164, 165.

38. Most biblical commentaries, reflecting the work of scholarship, assume very little continuity or connection among episodes. From *The Interpreter's Bible*, for example: 'That this story [of Abraham's faithlessness toward Sarah], so unflattering to Abraham, should have a place in Genesis is one of many evidences that for those who compiled the book the supreme interest was not any man, however great, but God...The final significance of the story of Abraham in Egypt is not that Abraham failed to be a hero; rather, it is in the fact that God's will is in control, whether those who are his instruments are for the moment worthy or unworthy' (I, pp. 582, 583).

39. *Genesis: A Commentary*, p. 165.

human response in the carrying forward of divine intention.

If, in fact, Abraham's failures are random in a rather fixed scenario of exemplary faith, then the human miscues are conveniently 'overridden' by the sovereignty of God. The logic of the narrative ordering, in this view, helps to determine such theology.

Walter Brueggemann

'When Abraham acts faithlessly, as he has obviously done [in risking Sarah's chastity for his own life], curse is released in the world'.[40] While Brueggemann acknowledges what seems obvious from a reading of both episodes together, he fails to locate these parallel accounts in a larger context in any systematic way.

'Even father Abraham must struggle for faithfulness', Brueggemann notes, anticipating the early failure of Abraham.[41] '12.10-20 [Sarah's jeopardy #1], quite in contrast to 12.1-9 [first visit between God and Abraham], presents Abraham as an anxious man, a man of unfaith. He is ready to secure his own survival because at this point he does not trust exclusively in the promise'.[42] But when commenting on the repeated instance, only the general 'softening' of Abraham's shabby action is cited, with no attempt to connect it substantively with the first, or with anything else in the story's narrative context:

> The material in 20.1-18 is recognized widely as an alternative version of the same themes in 12.10-20. Here, however, the theme has much less of the folklore flavor and much more self-conscious theological tone...It appears that the shaper of 20.1-18 had before him the older material which strangely presented Abraham caught in a bald lie. That material has now been reworked along other lines, making them less damaging to the reputation of Abraham.[43]

Abraham still acts poorly, but in a way 'less damaging to the reputation'. Such bit-by-bit examination—this episode, then that—with no attention to repetitive patterns, yields a theology which attributes inscrutability to God's power in overriding random human failure.

---

40. *Interpretation* is a series of biblical commentary designed, as the subtitle has it, 'For Teaching and Preaching'. Brueggemann is the author of the Genesis entry (Atlanta: John Knox Press, 1982), p. 129.

41. Brueggemann, *Genesis*, p. 125.

42. Brueggemann, *Genesis*, p. 126.

43. Brueggemann, *Genesis*, p. 177.

Brueggemann misses, for example, the dramatic effect of the text's delay of information regarding the foreign women's curse, above. And so he concludes that Isaac's birth is itself random and without purposeful ordering that can be understood in human terms.

> The birth of Isaac, the child of promise, is...reported in an understated account... It is an unsure and circuitous route to the fulfillment of the promise. As part of that circuitous route, the present narrative is a strange assortment of materials, the order of which appears to be unintentional.[44]

As we have seen, a narrative 'flashback' is hardly 'unintentional', and in this case the flashback to the curse of barrenness and its removal leads immediately in the text to Sarah's barrenness and its removal. 'The birth of the child is the fulfillment of all of the promises, the resolution of all of the anguish', Brueggemann concludes on this matter. 'And yet...one could almost miss the point...The fulfillment seems strangely anticlimactic after the troubled anticipation. This report seems oddly detached from what has gone before'.[45]

With this method of reading, then, Abraham's failures appear random but so do the acts of God, or at least random in the sense of any narrative coherence—as Brueggemann admits. One is left, theologically, with an inscrutable God and human beings who don't really change. Conclusion? 'The major themes of the narrative endure', asserts Brueggemann: 'the overriding faithfulness of God and the cowardly faithlessness of Israel'.[46]

'The overriding faithfulness of God': I think, rather, that God's faithfulness is measured in part by the divine willingness to wait, working with human frailty. The blessing of nations flows out of the blessing of the name and nation of Abraham, which follows from a closed womb opened, a wife restored to her husband, and the office of prophet learned.

Conclusion: My Agenda and Reading in a Context of Conversation Then and Now

Personal Agenda

Along with each of the conversationalists cited above, I too have an agenda which includes often unconscious perspectives from my own

44. Brueggemann, *Genesis*, p. 177.
45. Brueggemann, *Genesis*, p. 180.
46. Brueggemann, *Genesis*, p. 129.

cultural and linguistic environments. I wish to offer something worthwhile about the Abraham narrative to the ongoing conversation, and to do so I try to hear as much as I can of the text's full voice in part by discovering and taking account of hidden perspectives.

Certain aspects of my agenda are not so mysterious. For example, I assume the final form of the canonical text as worth my primary interest, since I love narratives and have a PhD in the study of them. Of course I recognize that the biblical narrative, as any narrative and especially those growing out of ancient oral cultures, has a fascinating and complex history of sources, compilation, redaction, and so forth. But I look for continuity rather than discontinuity in narratives that present themselves as unified dramas.

Secondly, I assume that the voice of this narrative text points to the voice of a God I seek. So I wish to get the voices straight.

Finally, I am sensitive because of my culture and my Christian communities to the plight of the oppressed, and particularly to the denigration of women. So the plight of Sarah's barrenness and the compounding of that loss of honor by her becoming another man's woman/wife arrests my moral attention. I notice that King Abimelech notices the same thing, and I am intrigued, and want to see if the larger context supports the possibility that Sarah's plight is central to the plot. And Abraham's role: even Philo and Augustine, who exonerate Abraham in this doublet, recognize the possibility of a contrary reading which implicates Abraham in chicanery of the lowest kind. I ask myself a question that the text itself may be posing: does Abraham have anything to learn?

The readings of Abraham's story by Clement, Calvin, Paul, and James are informed by extra-textual considerations: their own worlds of culture and Christian concern shape what they see in the story of Abraham. Realizing this state of affairs, two attitudes are open for me. (1) A text yields multiple and contrary interpretations, so I despair of hearing the voice of the text. (2) I can strain in my hearing toward that voice with the help of conversation heard circumspectly, looking for complementariness of readings. Recognition that the listener's world inevitably influences what is heard becomes an ingredient in the discipline of hearing more carefully a voice beyond my own. I want to hear that voice of the other rather than to be reconfiguring that voice according to my own desires and projections. Only then, I think, can I grow larger of soul.

My Reading of the Abraham Narrative: Directions
To Isaac, following Abraham's death, God appears with these words:

> I will make your offspring as numerous as the stars of heaven, and will
> give to your offspring all these lands; and all the nations of the earth shall
> gain blessing for themselves through your offspring, *because Abraham
> obeyed my voice and kept my charge*, my commandments, my statutes,
> and my laws (emphasis mine; Gen. 26.4).

The focus on Abraham's obedience in the readings of James and
Clement seems appropriate. The ultimate charge given Abraham is to
relinquish his hopes for a future, a name, in Isaac. He does, and
because he does, God fulfills the divine promises.

Providing for his own life and name at Sarah's expense, Abraham's
early failure led to a nation cursed, even as the earlier tower-builders
at Babel were cursed in providing for their own name.[47] Sarah is
cursed by becoming another man's woman/wife. And she remains
with her womb closed, a possible blessing under the circumstances of
sexual jeopardy.[48] Did Abraham come to feel his wife's curse as his
own? Did Abraham, knowing that through his name all the nations
were to be blessed, come to accept Egypt's curse as his own?

The dramatic scene is repeated, just before Sarah's womb is opened.
Again the scheme leads to a nation cursed—with barrenness. Sarah,
along with the foreign women, has been barren. But this time Abraham prays for his victim, and the women of the land have their
wombs opened. The narrative employs a flashback to provide the
information about the foreign women's barrenness and fertility, placing this surprising information in immediate juxtaposition with
Sarah's barrenness overcome with fertility and conception. I am willing to be surprised, and take note, looking again for connection to a
larger narrative context for this juxtaposition of infertilities overcome.

The story proper ends with Abraham's willingness to let go of his
own life, embodied in a son who is the sole guarantor of a name. In
the beginning, he was unwilling to risk himself, even though his wife

---

47. 'The close connection between blessing and name here [12.1-3] stands as an
opposition to the rejection of the tower people: "Let us build a city...that we may
make a name for ourselves"' (George W. Coats, *Genesis with an Introduction to
Narrative Literature* [1 vol.; Michigan: Eerdmans, 1983], p. 108).

48. 'One may ask how Sarai can bear Abram's promised seed if she is endangered in the harem of the pharaoh', comments Coats, *Genesis*, p. 111.

was placed in jeopardy. The story's climax comes full circle, then, and is the measure of Abraham's moral improvement.[49] Because you have done this, God says, I will do that.[50] A view of God based on this story—a theology of God's character—must include human response: here is a God who works out the divine will in conjunction with—not in contrast to—the morally improving human will.[51]

Abraham's story insists that God's pleasure is accomplished in and through the growing faithfulness of human response. That response is

49. From her reading of the narrative, Martha Rogers makes the nice connection between Abraham's trust in letting God be God, provider, and the possibility of human change: 'In allowing God to be God, and in giving up one's infantile omnipotence, one is actually more able to change. Without God, one is only capable of generating "more of the same" in one's behavior and thoughts... Abraham walked with God in this kind of ongoing relationship, as becomes clear if one follows the Genesis record; the evidence for continuing change in his life as a result of this feedback loop is apparent in the subsequent events' ('The Call of Abram: A Systems Theory Analysis', *Journal of Psychology and Theology* 9.2 [1981], pp. 111-27 [124]).

50. Gerald Bray states the case well: 'The importance of this condition of obedience, which is so clearly stated in Genesis 18–19, grows as time goes on... We must, therefore, conclude that the obligation of obedience was not optional, or supplementary to the promises made to Abraham. On the contrary, obedience to the law of God...would provide the basis for the social and religious context in which the promises would be fulfilled' ('The Promises Made to Abraham and the Destiny of Israel', *SBET* 7 [1989], pp. 69-87 [75]).

51. Claus Westermann speaks of the centrality of human response in any biblical theology based on these Old Testament narratives: 'If one understands the story told by the Old Testament as an interaction, then the human response becomes one of the three integral parts of the Old Testament and belongs to everything said in the Old Testament about God, from creation to apocalyptic. In all God says and does one needs to ask how people react, since all of God's acts and speaking is directed towards eliciting a response...The Old Testament presupposes that a person who has been commanded by God to do something is able to do it, and under normal circumstances would do it. When God commands Abraham "Go out..." and it is then reported that "Abraham went...", Abraham has thus complied with God's will.'

'With that', he concludes, 'we have expressed in a few broad lines what the Old Testament says about God. What the Old Testament says about God is a history developing between God and his creation, between God and humanity, between God and his people from creation to the end of the world. As in all stories of the world, there is on both sides action and reaction, word and response. The actions of God, the words of God, and the words and actions of people in response are the elements forming the constant basic structure of this history', *Elements of Old Testament Theology* (trans. Douglas W. Stott; Atlanta: John Knox Press, 1982), pp. 27, 28, 30-32.

nurtured by a God willing to wait on and work with the imperfect human will toward a perfection that is true blessedness.[52] If the clues of narrative repetition—as in a doublet—are heard, the narrative as a whole unfolds a divine character whose pleasure it is to press toward a global blessing by way of marital blessing, of sibling blessing, of family tribes blessed, and then a nation blessed. Such blessing will not begin, however, until human response approaches the blamelessness required by God (17.1). Not until, and because of:

> I will be with you [God says to Isaac], and will bless you; for to you and to your descendants I will give all these lands, and I will fulfill the oath that I swore to your father Abraham...And all the nations of the earth shall gain blessing for themselves through your offspring, *because Abraham obeyed my voice*...(emphasis added; Gen. 26.3-5).

Among God, Abraham, and Sarah there has been a growing intimacy, replete with formalities and outbursts recounted in seven visits with God. 'I will *indeed* bless you', God says to Abraham at the moment of dramatic resolve in visit seven (22.17). Completed for all three major participants in the plot is a graceful movement of faith and faithfulness represented by Abraham's improvement, Sarah's vindication, and God's promise reaffirmed in a framing formula of '*because Abraham obeyed*'.

Conversational Context: The Difference between Then and Now

In his *City of God*, Augustine insists on an Abraham whose responses are flawless, as does the early-first-century Jewish thinker Philo. Both interpretations contradict mine, but they also contradict each other's. Yet we three share an assumption about the story of Abraham that most modern scholarship does not, that the entire narrative as it

---

52. From an entirely different angle, Dixon Sutherland traces the moral improvement of Abraham through the story, with the sacrifice of Isaac the culminating point of that odyssey. Sutherland finds a pattern of repetition which emphasizes, at the chiastic heart of things, 'visions of confrontation between Yahweh and Abraham'. Overall, 'the pattern of arrangement does not enhance Abraham's character as *believer*'—although by story's end, with Abimelech and especially with Isaac, 'Abraham is presented as completely responsive to God's word'. As I have tried to show, Abraham comes to believe better by the time of his letting Sarah go to Abimelech. (In 'The Organization of the Abraham Promise Narratives', *ZAW* 95.3 [1983], pp. 337-43; citations above, p. 343).

appears in the canonical Scriptures is worthy of interpetation as a whole and coherent drama.

Only recently has there been a return among literary critics or canonically oriented scholars to the traditional assumption that Bible stories can be legitimately understood from the perspective of their final literary form.

In their epistles to fellow Christians in the first century after Christ, Abraham's story is referred to by Paul and James, and the non-canonical Clement, in terms that reveal their assumption that the Hebrew narrative is one whole and unified story. As such, it is capable of sustaining a theme. For the modern biblical scholar of the past two centuries, different historical sources lying behind the final story reveal distinct and often competing themes, allowing, as we shall see, theological preferences for, say, the 'Yahwist' over the 'Elohist' perspective, each competing in Abraham's story.

A further distinction separates most modern interpreters of the Abraham story from their predecessors. Most of the premoderns were polemical in the business of interpretation, reflecting on past stories and present events in order to further a certain argument or raise up a moral example or offer a more sure hope in an eschatological context. Many wrote letters which were urgent appeals. The fifth-century Augustine and the sixteenth-century John Calvin wrote more systematically and at greater length about matters pertaining to the Christian faith, but when reflecting on narratives from the Bible and Abraham in particular, each reveals his sense of the story being unified and coherent, but also an 'agenda' for persuading his audience.

The concern of our story—reflecting elders with an audience to be challenged or comforted—is missing, for the most part, from modern biblical scholarship and from my literary approach as well. With my ancient elders, however, I approach the entire text as a coherent narrative.

'The characteristic move' of the biblical scholar, as Robert Alter and Frank Kermode note in their *Literary Guide to the Bible*, 'was to infer the existence of some book that preceded the one we have—the lost documents that were combined to make Genesis as it has come down to us, the Aramaic Gospel, the lost "saying-source" used by Matthew and Luke, and so on'. In fact, Alter and Kermode are exercised about this dilemma: 'at this moment in cultural history there is an urgent need to try to learn how to read the Bible again'.[53] I share their concern, both in terms of 'cultural history' and the need to preserve what seems increasingly on the verge of being lost, but also with an eye on individuals and their capacity and will to understand their own stories, in the light of the biblical stories, as meaningful and 'connected'.

But what of the obvious 'bias' and distortion of the ancients? Moral agenda is easier to spot in writers like Paul, James, Clement, and Calvin because each is very open about his respective concerns. The first three are writing letters with clearly stated or understood purposes. Even Calvin's interest in the Abraham story can be explained by its context. Calvin has faced the temporal unhappiness of flight and possible torture. He himself says that his interpretation of Abraham's story will illustrate the fact 'that carnal prosperity and happiness did not constitute the goal set before the Jews to which they were to aspire' and that 'the hope of immortality' sustained them.[54] How well Abraham's story, from beginning to end, confirms that thesis! thinks Calvin aloud, letting the reader in on his thought process, his 'bias'.[55] With Calvin's concern to champion a protesting version of faith for the procuring of salvation over against what he perceived as the Church's doctrine of works, we might have expected a plot-version of Abraham paralleling the concerns of the apostle Paul. In fact, Calvin does share Paul's view of Abraham.[56] We understand the quality of Calvin's theology of adversity and hope better by appreciating his

53. Robert Alter and Frank Kermode, 'General Introduction' to *Literary Guide to the Bible* (Cambridge, MA: Harvard University Press, 1987), pp. 3, 4.

54. Calvin, *Christ. Religio. Instit.* 2.10.11.

55. 'First, we hold that carnal prosperity and happiness did not constitute the goal set before the Jews to which they were to aspire. Rather, they were adopted into the hope of immortality; and assurance of this adoption was certified to them by oracles, by the law, and by the prophets. Secondly, the covenant by which they were bound to the Lord was supported, not by their own merits, but solely by the mercy of the God who called them. Thirdly, they had and knew Christ as Mediator, through whom they were joined to God and were to share in his promises' (Calvin, *Christ. Religio. Instit.* 2.10.11).

56. 'Now, if faith excludes all boasting, works righteousness can in no way be associated with faith righteousness. In this sense he speaks so clearly in the fourth chapter of Romans that no place is left for cavils or shifts: "if Abraham", says Paul, "was justified by works, he has something to boast about". He adds, "Yet he has no reason to boast before God" [Rom. 4.2]. It follows, therefore, that he was not justified by works' (Calvin, *Christ. Religio. Instit.* 2.10.11).

options for interpreting the Abraham story as a whole dramatic piece.

We moderns can appear, for the most part, more objective. We have no concern but the text itself! Biblical scholars, theologians, and literary critics do not write letters, for example, as a context for our biblical interpretation. We wish truth about the text's history or about the history referred to by the text or about the literary dynamics of the canonical narrative in its final form.

Many of us, myself included, surely hope that our attempts as modern scholars can lead to true moral and religious training—the *paideia* of God as Clement urged directly through his biblical examples. Meanwhile, however, our 'bias'—our world of assumptions and concern—is there, shaping to some extent what we see in the text.

I can recognize the reality of Babel with its hermeneutical circles and overt agendas while working with disciplined care toward the goal of hearing the other's voice in its own tongue. And toward what end? Why bother with hearing well? The spirit which accepts, but wishes to overcome, the difficulty of hearing well another's voice is a powerful spirit that always goes beyond a truth-hearing to a truth-doing, hearing well in order to embrace more fully the best interests and vision of the person or text which I am straining to hear.

Conversational skill is required in listening to the biblical text and to the responses it has elicited. Discipline in the art of human conversation is presumably the same as that required for listening and responding to the voice of God, assumed by the faithful to be a living voice which depends on a context of conversation to be heard at all.

The Context of Conversation: A Final Case in Point

Historian Werner Jaeger brings together the three letter-writers of the first century, Paul, James, and Clement: 'Although Paul's insistence on faith remains unchanged in Clement's epistle, the special emphasis is on good works, as it is in the Epistle of James, which may belong to the same time and is so clearly polemical against Paul'.[57] As evidence of James's presumed polemic against—the contradicting of—Paul, Jaeger cites James's conclusion regarding Abraham: 'So faith by itself, if it has no works, is dead' (2.17). Jaeger sees Paul and Clement but not James as sharing complementary views of faith.

---

57. Jaeger, *Early Christianity*, pp. 15, 16.

I don't think Jaeger goes far enough, however, as suggested in a preliminary way by observations made earlier. Paul would agree with James and with Clement, I am suggesting, in regard to the relation between Abraham's trust and obedience. Interpretations must be judged from within their own contexts. This wider view of what James is saying in his letter is needed:

> The figure of James emerges in another early Christian context, which seems to be echoed in the letter, namely the dispute over 'faith and works'...James is not defending salvation through Christ against the Pauline understanding of 'works' as the efforts of non-Jewish Christians to conform to Jewish rites of circumcision, kosher food laws, and religious feasts. Paul would certainly agree that Christian life should be expressed by deeds of charity... James appears to be opposed to a distorted and sloganizing Paulinism, which influenced Christians to neglect their obligations to aid their poverty-stricken and suffering brothers and sisters.[58]

Paul and James are part of a conversation which includes the topic of Abraham. I think a closer examination of their respective epistles and of their interpretations of Abraham would reveal that in the larger context James's letter 'appears to be opposed to a distorted and sloganizing Paulinism' rather than 'so clearly polemical against Paul', as Jaeger suggests. For James and Paul—and Clement—Abraham is a doer of the word and not a hearer only. Paul emphasizes faith as an attitude, a disposition of the heart; James and Clement point to faith as action—faith 'brought to completion by the works' (Jas 2.22).

Obedience and faith/trust are prominent themes within the Genesis account of Abraham. When the interpretations of Paul, James, and Clement are taken together in their respective literary and historical contexts, they can be viewed as complementary in much the same way that the narrative themes of obedience and trust within the story of Abraham are mutually supportive.

Interpretations that appear contradictory, if understood in as wide a context as possible, can turn out to be complementary. The power of any interpretation to illumine a text depends in part on the illumination that comes from understanding the context of that interpretation.

---

58. *The New Oxford Annotated Bible*, p. 331.

THE SINGULAR PROPHET AND IDEALS OF TORAH: MIRIAM, AARON, AND MOSES IN EARLY RABBINIC TEXTS

Elaine A. Phillips

Introduction

Miriam and Aaron spoke against Moses concerning the Cushite woman whom he had married because he had married a Cushite woman and they said: 'Was it *only* with Moses the Lord has spoken? Has He not also spoken with us...?' (Num. 12.1, 2).

When readers encounter the challenge to Moses' authority by Miriam and Aaron (Num. 12), the initial questions are invariably: 'Why was Miriam punished and not Aaron?' and 'What connection is there between the Cushite wife and Moses' authority anyway?'. While answers to the first question can focus on the grammar of v. 1[1] or the perceived need to keep Aaron as priest free from any form of impurity, contemporary academics are left suggesting that the only viable response to both questions lies in positing the melding of several disparate sources. Thus, in the earliest strand of the narrative, Miriam alone challenged Moses for which she was punished with leprosy. This incident was later supplemented by a story about priestly contention from both Aaron and Miriam regarding the uniqueness of Moses the prophet. God responded by rebuking the two of them. George W. Coats refined this hypothetical process with a third level in which leg-

---

1.   The third feminine singular verbal form and the order of the names in v. 1 are said to indict her. Having said that, there is considerable discussion on those very grammar issues. When a clause has a compound subject, the normal procedure is for the verb form to agree with the noun closest to the verb (Ronald B. Allen, *Numbers* [*The Expositor's Bible Commentary*; 2 vols.; gen. ed. Frank E. Gaebelein; Grand Rapids: Zondervan, 1990], p. 799). See also Timothy Ashley, *The Book of Numbers* (NICOT; ed. R.K. Harrison; Grand Rapids: Eerdmans, 1993), p. 220. See also E. Kautzsch and A.E. Cowley, *Gesenius' Hebrew Grammar* (Oxford: Clarendon Press, 2nd English edn, 1910), §146f, g.

endary features were added to Moses' character so as to enhance his prophetic stature and the importance of the Torah of Moses.[2] Presumably, as the stories were joined, the process did not successfully smooth over the grammatical irregularities created by adding Aaron to the scene!

Questions that are intriguingly unanswered in the biblical narrative were engaged by early rabbinic exegetes as they read the text. Of particular interest are the motifs that appear in *Sifre baMidbar* (*SN*) and *Sifre Zuta* (*SZ*). They are reflected in brief in the Targums as well but I have chosen to limit my investigation to the exegetical texts. In the case of the exegetical midrashim, the significant controlling factor is the fundamental and acknowledged unity and complexity of Torah. Thus, treatment of any given episode in these contexts reflects the Sages' knowledge of and sensitivity to the larger picture of the biblical text.[3]

The 'Unambiguous' Message of the Biblical Text

As the biblical chapter unfolds, its compelling message is that Moses was the prophet and authority figure *par excellence*. After Miriam and Aaron explicitly challenged his singular position as God's prophet, claiming that God had also spoken through them (Num. 12.2), the major part of God's direct communication to them was his commendation of Moses as unique among His prophets (Num. 12.6-8).

2. George W. Coats, 'Humility and Honor: A Moses Legend in Numbers 12', in David J.A. Clines, David M. Gunn, Alan J. Hauser (eds.), *Art and Meaning: Rhetoric in Biblical Literature* (JSOTSup, 19; Sheffield: JSOT Press, 1982), pp. 97-98. The general consensus follows the analysis of Martin Noth, *Numbers: A Commentary* (Philadelphia: Westminster Press, 1968), pp. 92-93. The point of adding this material would have been, of course, to give credence to the Torah when it was being promulgated in the period of the monarchy. Enhancing the stature of Moses was a mechanism for accomplishing this.

3. I cite initially *SN* but draw on the material from *SZ* as it clarifies, changes, or supplements the emphases of the midrash. *SN* and *SZ* do vary in both their exegetical methods and thematic emphases and it is important to register the fact that *SZ* is primarily a reconstructed text. See H.L. Strack and G. Stemberger, *Introduction to the Talmud and Midrash* (trans. Markus Bockmuehl; Edinburgh: T. & T. Clark, 1991), pp. 269-72. On the knotty issue of dating these texts, see Strack and Stemberger, *Introduction*, pp. 292-94. When all is said and done, a good case can be made that the early exegetical midrashim were compiled in the last half of the third century CE.

The Messages in the Early Exegetical Midrashim

In a comprehensive survey of the rabbinic texts that shape and aug-
ment the biblical data about Miriam's role vis-à-vis her family,
Devora Steinmetz has proposed that, as the rabbis presented her,
Miriam was deeply concerned for family and royal continuity and
stability.[4] Steinmetz suggested that the authors of the midrashim on
Numbers may have already been predisposed to view Miriam in this
family context based on other exegeses. For example, Miriam per-
suaded her father, Amram, to remarry Jochabed after he had separated from her, an action he took in response to the edict of Pharoah
(*b. Soṭah* 12b; *Mekilta deRabbi Ishmael, Shirta* 10). The rabbis also
identified Miriam with the Azubah whom Caleb married, thus bringing her into the line of David (*b. Soṭah* 11b-12a). These interpretations, focusing on family preservation, influenced their reading of the
puzzling circumstances in Numbers 12.

There is value, however, in engaging the thematic emphases even
further. It is instructive to see how the exegetical community or
communities represented by *SN* and *SZ* managed the biblical data.
Notably, what was left ambiguous in the biblical text is explicated as
the issues of Numbers 11 and 12 are harmonized in a complex and intricate commentary. In the process of demonstrating these linkages in
Torah, the Sages constructed a message about ideals of Torah as particularly represented by the key characters, Miriam, Moses, and God.

How was this portrait from Numbers developed? First, the Cushite
woman was fundamentally assumed to be Zipporah, thus demonstrating that Moses did not take a second wife but remained monogamous:
'...*because of the Cushite woman...* Was she a Cushite? Was she not a
Midianite? For it is said, *And the priest of Midian had seven daughters*
(Exod. 2.16). Why then does Scripture refer to her as a Cushite?'
(*SN* 99).[5] The tasks, then, for the rabbis were to determine *why*

---

4.   Devora Steinmetz, 'A Portrait of Miriam in Rabbinic Midrash', *Prooftexts* 8
(1988), pp. 35-65. A significant part of this is the rabbis' linking Miriam with the
Davidic line. As a result, the issue of continuity becomes all that much more compelling. She is portrayed as intervening on more than one occasion in the lives of
family members in order to ensure that this continuity is sustained.

5.   This presumed identification also appears in several of the Targums:
Alejandro Díez Macho (ed.), *Neophyti 1: Targum Palestinense Ms de la Biblioteca
Vaticana.* IV. *Numeros* (4 vols.; Madrid: Consejo Superior de Investigaciones

Zipporah was called a Cushite and, more challenging, what the basis of the accusation of Miriam was. Characteristically, the rabbis drew both of these questions and their answers together. Initially, they explored the meaning of אדות in the expression, עַל־אדות 'because of the Cushite...'. This emphasis is much more focused in *SN* where three separate statements appear in response to this unusual term in order to make a case for Zipporah's beauty.

> ...*because of (עַל־אדות) the Cushite woman:*
> Scripture indicates that whoever saw her admitted to her beauty.[6]
> And so Scripture says, [*Haran*] *was also the father of Milcah and Iscah* (Gen 11.29). What is the meaning of Iscah? Everyone looked upon her beauty. So we see in the verse: *The princes of Pharaoh saw her and praised her to Pharaoh* (Gen 12.15).[7]
> R. Eliezer ben R. Yose HaGalili says, 'Her name was Zipporah: "Look and see how beautiful she is" '[8] (*SN* 99).

Having made that case with אדות, the Sages searched out corroborating biblical texts which would support the notion that 'Cushite' also meant distinctive, and, in Zipporah's case, distinctive in beauty. There are three of these prooftexts as well.[9] Further, that 'Cushite' is

---

Científicas, 1974); and the Paris and Vatican MSS in Michael L. Klein (ed.), *The Fragment-Targums of the Pentateuch* (2 vols.; Rome: Biblical Institute Press, 1980).

6. This is accomplished by using אדות, which shares consonants with the word מוֹדה meaning to 'admit'.

7. The keys to interpreting this lie in the parallel appearance of Iscah and Sarai in Gen. 11, the shared consonants of Iscah and the word meaning 'looked upon', and the tribute to Sarai's beauty in Gen. 12.

8. The words for 'look' and 'see' share consonants with the name of Zipporah. Leila Leah Bronner, *From Eve to Esther: Rabbinic Reconstructions of Biblical Women* (Louisville, KY: Westminster/John Knox Press, 1994), pp. 169-70, noted that the rabbis gave Miriam a husband, childen, and beauty in keeping with their perception of what an ideal woman should be. *SZ* briefly addresses the matter of beauty but only in the exegetical context of trying to figure out the significance of the plural ending on אדות. Other options are suggested as well but her beauty is not an emphasis.

9. These identifications are contrived as far as literal 'Cushites' go. In fact, texts have been chosen which specifically do *not* fit with Cush in a geographical sense but have been selected to make the point: Zipporah was distinctive just as each of the exemplars was distinctive and, as we read these, we see the exemplars were particularly not literal Cushites.

> The meaning is that just as a Cushite has skin different from others, so Zipporah was different from others in beauty, more beautiful than all other women.

mentioned twice in the biblical text was significant for the Sages. It meant that she was beautiful in looks and in deeds. Finally, to make sense of the entire narrative, the rabbis expanded the focus to include the events of ch. 11. When Miriam voiced the initial complaint about Moses' wife, it was because she had discovered from Zipporah that he was not engaging in פריה ורביה, an eminently important mandate for all of humankind.

Now, how did she know this? The story varies depending on the text and the tradent. In *SN* 99, there are two accounts. First, it is said that Miriam did some detective work. Noting that Zipporah was not wearing ornaments as were the other women, she asked why not and learned that Moses was not paying attention to such things. Realizing what that subtle message meant, she told Aaron and they both spoke against Moses. According to a second interpretation of Rabbi Nathan, Miriam happened to be present when *a young man ran and told Moses, 'Eldad and Medad are prophesying in the camp'* (Num. 11.27). When Zipporah heard the message, she said 'Woe for the wives of these men' and, again, Miriam put two and two together. According to *SZ*, on the other hand, Zipporah was more explicit.

> Rabbi Shimon says: As a matter of fact, Zipporah[10] began the matter and she spoke to Miriam and Miriam to Aaron and Aaron added to their words
>
> Likewise: *A shiggayon of David, which he sang to the Lord concerning the words of Cush the Benjaminite* (Ps. 7.10). [Here, the Hebrew of the Psalm title has changed Kish of the 1 Sam. 9 narrative to Cush.]
>
> Now was he a Cushite? The meaning is that just as a Cushite has skin different from others, so Saul was distinctive in his appearance, as it is said, *From his shoulders and upward he was taller than the entire people* (1 Sam. 9.2).
>
> Likewise: *Are you not like the sons of the Cushites to me, O children of Israel* (Amos 9.7).
>
> Now were they Cushites? The meaning is that just as a Cushite has skin different from others, so the Israelites are distinguished in the doing of religious duties, more so than all the nations of the world.
>
> Likewise: *And a servant of the king, a Cushite eunuch, heard...* (Jer. 38.7).
>
> Now was he a Cushite? The meaning is that just as a Cushite has skin different from others, so Baruch b. Neriah was distinguished in his deeds among all the members of the king's establishment [the text of Jeremiah does not explicitly identify Baruch with this Cushite, called a servant of the king] (*SN* 99).

10. The exegetical point here is that Miriam cannot be represented by the third feminine singular verb which commences the verse because her name was subsequently linked with Aaron's. Thus, it must have been Zipporah. It is possible that this is a reflection of the precise, more atomistic exegetical methods associated with the school of Akiva. The tendency is evident throughout the treatment of the biblical material in *SZ*.

and they discussed the matters and what were they discussing? They said: When the elders were appointed all Israel lit candles and they rejoiced because 70 elders went up to rulership. When Miriam saw the lights, she said, 'Blessed are these and blessed are their wives'. Zipporah said, 'Don't say blessed are their wives but woe to their wives because from the day that The Holy One Blessed Be He spoke with Moses your brother, he has not made love to me.' Immediately, Miriam went to Aaron and they were discussing the matter as it is said: *And she spoke, Miriam and Aaron against Moses concerning the matter of the (Cushite) wife*; concerning the matters of his separation from the woman (*SZ* 12.1).

Regardless of the version of the story, what had happened in Numbers 11 was seen as having a direct bearing on the factors presumably behind this development. Having established that Moses had an entirely desirable wife with whom he was not engaging in procreative activity, the question then was *why* did he choose to abstain? If other prophets and the patriarchs had not abstained, and the midrash explicitly makes that point several times,[11] why Moses? Was this an act of pride to demonstrate that he was holier than others? In posing the question of Miriam and Aaron in this context, the rabbis further brought together the seemingly disparate matters of the Cushite wife, Moses' authority, and the subsequent claim in the text for his humility (Num. 12.3). In the Sages' representation in *SZ*, the declaration that Moses was humble was a direct response to the accusation of Miriam and Aaron: 'They said: Moses is a proud man because The Holy One Blessed Be He did not speak only with him but already spoke with many prophets and with us and we have not separated from our wives as he has done as it is said: *Has The Lord spoken only with Moses?*' (*SZ* 12.1). Because the assumption of Miriam and Aaron that Moses was proud was not true, the answer for Moses' abstention had to be linked to his unique status: *With him I speak mouth to mouth*: 'Mouth to mouth I instructed him to give up procreation' (*SN* 103).[12] Only because Moses was the recipient of special communication from God had he given up that fundamental responsibility; it was not a matter of self-exaltation. In fact, humility, as the rabbis proceeded to demonstrate

11. In response to *Has the Lord spoken only through Moses?*, *SN* 100 continues: 'And is it not the case that also with the patriarchs did the Holy One Blessed Be He speak and they did not cease from procreation'. A second avowal appears in some texts: 'Has he not also spoken with us: And we have not ceased from פריה ורביה'.

12. The same thought is reiterated in *SZ* in response to *My servant*: 'Another interpretation: "My servant" means I told him to separate from his wife' (*SZ* 12.8).

at length, was a matter of Moses' temperament or way of thinking
(דעתו). Furthermore, it did not imply lack of courage, stature, or
wealth.[13]

The Sages carefully balanced the issues of propriety in family matters with a concern for justice. On the one hand, they acknowledged
that both God's rebuke of Miriam and Aaron and the punishment of
Miriam were appropriate. On the other hand, they made it eminently
clear that Miriam's initial concern was not from ill motives but out of
concern for the well-being of Moses and his family. At the same time,
however, they articulated a lesson regarding God's concern for obedience and justice even in the context of apparently good motives.

> Now it is an argument *kal vehomer*: If Miriam, who did not intend to
> speak against her brother for disgrace but for praise, and not to lessen
> procreation but to increase it, and who spoke only in private, yet she was
> punished; the one who intends to speak ill of his fellow and not in praise,
> to diminish and not to increase procreation, and speaks not in private but
> among others—how much the more so [will that one be punished]! (*SN*
> 99)[14]

13. This was a necessary exegetical move in order to bring this text into harmo-
nious relationship with other texts about Moses. *SN* 101 establishes the contrast
between way of thinking (דעתו) and other characteristics, demonstrating with biblical
texts that Moses was courageous and substantially wealthy.

> He was humble in his demeanor. You say that he was humble in his way of thinking
> (בדעתו). But perhaps he was humble [and cowardly] only in his conduct (בגופו)? Scrip-
> ture states, *And you will do to him as you did to Sihon, king of the Amorites* (Num.
> 21.34). He descended on Sihon and killed him; he descended on Og and killed him.
> Another matter: *Now the man Moses was very humble.*
>
> He was humble in his way of thinking. You say that he was humble in his way of
> thinking. But perhaps he was humble only in his wealth? Scripture says, *And the man
> Moses was very substantial* (Exod. 11.3). We find that sapphire of the tablets belonged
> to Moses, for it is said, *At that time the Lord said to me, 'Cut two tablets of stone for
> yourself like the first'* (Deut. 10.1). And elsewhere it says, *The tablets were the work of
> God* (Exod. 32.15), *They saw the God of Israel. Under his feet there was, as it were, a
> pavement of sapphire, clear blue as the very heavens* (Exod. 24.10). There is then an
> analogy between 'making' and 'making'. Just as in that case it was of sapphire, so here
> it was of sapphire.

SZ focuses more on the implications of individual words in this text and draws in
fewer prooftexts. Both midrashim rule the ministering angels out of the comparison
as they are not 'on the face of the earth' but do conclude that even Abraham, Isaac,
and Jacob were not as humble as Moses.

14. And characteristically, they enhanced that lesson by adding a parallel one,
drawn from another case of punishment by leprosy, that of Uzziah.

After initiating the accusation, Miriam became the silent recipient of both rebuke and punishment while Aaron and Moses asserted themselves as intercessors. Regarding Aaron's plea, the midrash follows closely the biblical text: He simply appealed to Moses.[15] When it comes to Moses, the Sages took the opportunity to present him as the exemplary person of prayer. In the first place, the use of לאמר in the context presents an occasion for indicating four instances when Moses was insistent with God and God answered even before Moses had finished his prayer (*SN* 105).[16]

Furthermore, the Sages found lessons on *how* to pray in the example of Moses.

> The disciples of R. Eliezer asked him: 'How long should a person draw out his prayer?'
> He said to them, 'Someone should not draw out his prayer more than did Moses, as it is said, *And I prostrated myself before the Lord as at the first for forty days and for forty nights* (Deut. 9.18)'.
> 'And how much should one cut his short prayer short?'
> He said to them, 'A person should not cut his prayer shorter than did Moses, as it is said,
> *Heal her, O God, I beseech you.*
> 'There is a time to cut prayer short, and there is a time to draw it out' (*SN* 105).

While this is a stock motif, that Moses would be the model for prayer is particularly fitting in this context. After all, the biblical text had just confirmed his singular position as the prophet who was on intimate terms with God.

As the rabbis conveyed their messages about Torah, family continuity, and character, they also drew conclusions about appropriate justice as evidenced in this incident. Here, the role model is the Holy One Blessed Be He. Notably, administration of justice followed only after the explanation, it was equitable, and God responded in

15. In fact, as the biblical text represents him, Aaron was characteristically a passive figure, seemingly molded by the personalities and events surrounding him. (See Exod. 32 and Lev. 10.) The irony in this narrative is that his role as high priest was supposed to be that of intermediary but the turn of events demonstrated that Moses indeed was his superior in that sphere as well.

16. The rhetorical patterns of the midrash include a declaration of Moses ('...and Moses spoke unto the Lord, saying...') rearticulated as a demand for a response: 'Answer me whether or not you are going to [do what I am about to ask]', followed by a text indicating that God did indeed answer immediately.

measure-for-measure fashion to Miriam's merit. First, God did not punish Miriam and Aaron until he had given the reasons for his action.

> *And the anger of the Lord was kindled against them, and he departed* (Num. 12.9):
>   After he informed them how they had gone wrong, then he made a decree of isolation against them.
>   And it is a matter of an argument *kal vehomer*: If He Who Spoke and the World Came into Being did not carry out his anger against flesh and blood before he had informed them of how they had gone wrong, a mortal should not carry out anger against someone before informing him of how he had gone wrong (*SN* 104).[17]

Secondly, in regard to equitable justice, the text of *SN* 105 delicately suggests that Aaron was also afflicted with the punishment of leprosy but in his case it only lasted momentarily because he had not initiated the talk against Moses.

> *And Aaron turned towards Miriam [and behold, she was leprous]*:
>   He turned away from his own leprosy.
>   R. Judah b Baterah says, 'Anyone who says that Aaron was afflicted with leprosy is destined to give a full accounting for saying so. If He Who Spoke and the World Came in Being concealed the matter, should you reveal it?'

SZ is again more explicit. On *...the anger of the Lord burned against them...* (Num. 12.9), the midrash says: 'Against both of them'. When the biblical text continues *And he went...*, that means: 'Immediately Aaron was healed'. *The cloud moved from over the tent* 'teaches that the cloud moved from over him [that is, Aaron]. Why did the verse expose Miriam and hint regarding Aaron? Because she began the matter.'[18]

Finally, God's justice was manifested in its characteristic measure-for-measure pattern. Because Miriam waited for Moses when he was a child, all Israel as well as the Divine Presence waited for her for

---

17. It should not escape our attention that the name of God as presented by the Sages in this context is eminently appropriate for the subject. The matter under discussion has to do with communication and they refer to God as He Who Spoke and the World Came into Being. We will see it again.

18. The fact is, Miriam's leprosy was also relatively short-lived. After Moses' prayer, she was apparently healed and then sent outside the camp for the seven days of waiting.

seven days. As is customary in the measure-for-measure formulations, the measures are balanced in kind but not degree. The benevolence of God is overwhelmingly evident.

> *...seven days, and the people did not set out on the march:*
> This teaches that by the measure that one metes out to others, one himself is measured as well.
> Miriam waited for Moses a single hour, as it is said, *And his sister stood off at a distance* (Exod. 2.4). Therefore, the Omnipresent delayed for her the Presence of God and the ark, the priests and the Levites and the Israelites and the seven clouds of glory, as it is said, *and the people did not set out on the march till Miriam was brought in again* (*SN* 106).

In addition to reassurances about justice, the Sages also made observations about *derekh eretz* based on the example of the One Who Spoke and the World Came into Being. In the matter of speech, God tactfully addressed Miriam and Aaron separately from Moses so that neither their shame nor his commendation would be spoken in Moses' presence.[19] Further, based on the polite שמע נא, the Sages drew additional lessons on speech etiquette.

> *And he said, 'Hear, I pray you, my words'.*
> The word 'I pray you' means only a request.
> And it is an argument *kal vehomer*: If He Who Spoke and the World Came into Being spoke with supplications, all the more so flesh and blood...
> R. Shimon b Yohai says, 'What is the meaning of the statement, "Hear, I pray you, my words"? Because they wanted to enter into the words of the Omnipresent, the Omnipresent said to them, "Wait until I am silent." All the more so that someone should not interrupt the words of his fellow' (*SN* 103).

Concluding Observations

Of interest are two distinct differences between modern treatments of this text and those of the early exegetes. First, while practically all contemporary scholarly works assume that this text as it stands reflects two or more levels of composition, the rabbinic treatment sustained the unity of the text. In fact, the Sages found answers to some of the

---

19. *And He summoned Aaron and Miriam and the two of them came out*
...Another interpretation: It is so that he [Moses] should not hear what was disgraceful to Aaron. Another interpretation: It was because people do not praise someone [Moses] to his face (*SN* 102).

puzzling features of this specific narrative by appealing to a continuity between the incidents in chs. 11 and 12 as well as additional facts known or imagined about the main characters. In their world view, Torah defines itself and its compelling issues by virtue of its unity and complexity. Its ideals are embodied in the characters in each narrative.

In this regard, there is a second tendency among modern commentators to denigrate the 'Cushite wife', whoever she was. This was not so among the rabbis. Not only was she assumed to be Zipporah to sustain the focus on monogamy but the Sages took pains to explain the designation 'Cushite' in the most positive terms. If anything, it was Moses who had a problem in that he did not apparently appreciate her comprehensive personal beauty!

Drawing together the thematic emphases, we find that central issues for the Sages had to do with family preservation and individual piety. Each of the major characters, including God, were presented as paradigmatic as the rabbis interpreted the biblical text. Moses illustrates the Torah ideals of monogamy, emphatic and appropriate prayer, measured humility, and even פריה ורביה as the rabbis dealt with the tension over his apparent lapses in that regard. Miriam was a model of concern for Moses and his family and particularly family continuity as evidenced by her focus on פריה ורביה. Even her errors were turned into examples from which to learn. Finally, as He intervened by word and deed, The Holy One Blessed Be He demonstrated the perfection of justice, mercy, and *derekh eretz*.

ISAIANIC MIDRASH AND THE EXODUS

George Wesley Buchanan

Introduction

Scholars all seem to agree that the book of Isaiah is an anthology rather than one uniform document, composed by one author. This is apparent because more than one period of history is reflected in the literature. There is at least a Second Isaiah, and perhaps a Third Isaiah, but even the first 39 chapters of Isaiah have not all been attributed to Isaiah of Jerusalem. Isaiah 35 seems to belong to the same period of history as Second Isaiah, and many scholars consider various other chapters as exilic or postexilic. By exilic, they mean Babylonian exilic, having forgotten all about the Assyrian captivity of the North Israelites. That was the captivity about which Isaiah himself prophesied.[1]

Isaiah himself seems not only to have written and prophesied but he also organized a school or sect which continued after him and added to the scribal activity of this position. No attempt will be made here to distinguish every line of Isaianic literature to determine whether Isaiah himself wrote it. I will refer to that which precedes the Babylonian exile as 'First Isaiah' whether it was written by Isaiah himself or not and try to show how Isaiah's midrashic method was continued throughout the school.

---

1. For questions of the unity of the book of Isaiah see G.T. Sheppard, 'The Anti-Assyrian Redaction and the Canonical Context of Isaiah 1–39', *JBL* 104 (1985), pp. 193-216; P.R. Ackroyd, 'Isaiah I–XII: Presentation of a Prophet', *Congress Volume: Göttingen, 1977* (VTSup, 29; Leiden: E.J. Brill, 1977), pp. 16-48; and his 'An Interpretation of the Babylonian Exile: A Study of 2 Kings 20, Isaiah 38–39', *SJT* 27 (1974), pp. 329-52; R.P. Carroll, 'Inner Traditions Shifts in Meaning in Isaiah 1–11', *ExpTim* 89 (1978), pp. 301-304; B.S. Childs, 'Isaiah', in his *Introduction to the Old Testament as Scripture* (Philadelphia: Fortress Press, 1979), pp. 311-38; and R.E. Clements, 'The Unity of the Book of Isaiah', *Int* 36 (1982), pp. 117-29.

The midrashic method of writing presumes there is a sacred literature that is doctrinally reliable. This literature has been accepted as
the word of the Lord. All later religious leaders are obligated to justify their prophesies by the text of this literature, just as a lawyer must
prove his or her case on the bases of the constitution and later legal
precedents. Isaiah and his school was one of the earliest to compose
prophesies on this basis. Isaiah used sources that he believed had some
sacred authority. In another context, while promising utter destruction
for Edom, Isaiah exhorted his readers to 'search (*deershoó*, דרשו)
from the book of Yahowah and read (*oókera-oó*, וקראו). Not one of
these will be left out' (Isa. 34.16). Unfortunately, we do not have
access to this source Isaiah used, but if we did, we would probably
find in the source the details that Isaiah's readers accepted as authoritative. If his readers had not accepted the Book of Yahowah as
authoritative, Isaiah could not have used it to prove his prophecy. The
Book of Yahowah evidently included curses like those in Isaiah 34,
and Isaiah was confident that every single curse would be carried out,
since it was God's word.

The word *darásh* (דרש), which Isaiah used to invite his readers to
check his documentation, is the very word later rabbis used in precisely the same way. It is from the root *darásh* that the word 'midrash'
is derived. Those who search the text and interpret it produce a
midrash or commentary on the sacred text. This is what Isaiah was
doing (Isa. 34.1-17). There are other prophecies in the Hebrew
Scripture against Edom (Jer. 49.7-22; Ezek. 25.12-14; 35; Amos
1.11-12; Obadiah; Mal. 1.2-5; Ps. 137; and Lam. 4.21-22), and some
of these may also have used this now unknown source, the Book of
Yahowah, but none seems to have the exact detail Isaiah 34 produced,
and none documents this source.

Although this methodology was extensively produced in medieval
Judaism and Christianity, unless all of this Isaianic literature can be
proved to have been composed by later authors, midrashic literature
was already an accepted literary genre as early as the seventh or
eighth century BC. This fact has not been widely recognized.

Exodus in First Isaiah

Since we are dealing with a literature about a literature, we will first
begin with the texts that were used in First Isaiah. The most important

of these was Exodus 15. This is a triumphant hymn about the deliverance of the Israelites from Egypt when they crossed the body of water where the Suez Canal now is. Whatever military maneuvers were involved in this escape, Israelites believed that the Lord Yahowah was their deliverer and savior, who overthrew the Egyptians and saved the Israelites.

Exodus 15

1. I will sing to Yahowah,[2] for he is greatly exalted.
     Horse and his rider he hurled into the sea.
2. My strength and my song is Yahowah;
     he will be my salvation.
3. Yahowah is a man of war, Yahowah is his name;
4. the chariots of Pharaoh and his army
     he hurled into the sea;
       his chosen officers were sunk into the Reed Sea.
5. Tiamat covered them;
     they went down into the depths like a stone.
6. Your right hand, Yahowah, marvelous in power!
     Your right hand, Yahowah, will shatter the enemy!
7. The greatness of your exaltation
     will destroy your adversaries;
       you will send forth your wrath;
         it will consume them like chaff.
8. With the breath of your nostrils the water piled up;
     the flood stood like a heap;
       Tiamat congealed in the heart of the sea.
9. The enemy said, 'I will pursue; I will overtake;
     I will divide the spoil!
       My desire will be filled from them.'
         I will draw my sword; my hand will possess them.
10. You blew with your wind; the sea covered it;
     they sank like lead in the mighty waters.
11. Who is like you among the gods, Yahowah?
     Who is like you, majestic in holiness?
       fearful so as to be praised, a miracle worker?
12. You stretched out with your right hand;
     the earth swallowed them.

2.   For a justification of this pronunciation, rather than the popular 'Yahweh', for the Tetragrammaton, see G.W. Buchanan, 'Some Unfinished Business with the Dead Sea Scrolls', in F. Garcia Martinez and E. Peuch (eds.), *Memorial Jean Carmignac* (Paris: Gabalda, 1988), pp. 411-20.

13. You led, in your mercy, this people you redeemed;
      you guided, in your strength, to your holy hill.
14. The people heard; they tremble!
      Anguish seized the inhabitants of Philistia;
15. Dismayed were the troops of Edom;
      terror seized the leaders of Moab;
         all the Canaanites melted away.
16. Terror and fear fell upon them;
      with the greatness of your arm
        they were still as a stone,
          until your people crossed over, Yahowah,
            until they crossed over, this people you acquired
               (Exod. 15.1-16).[3]

Psalm and Exodus 15

Exodus 15 was standard liturgy by the time Psalms 104–106 were written, because part of this extensive poem was based on that text. You can tell from the texts before you that the Psalmist not only told the story of the Exodus, but he took some of the very words from Exodus 15 and wove them into his poem, making a narrative midrash. This long historic poem shows the same kind of relationship to Genesis, Numbers, and Deuteronomy, but there is no history in the poem later than the story of Phineas and his encounter with Zimri and his new Midianite wife. Nothing is mentioned of the conquest of Canaan or the establishment of a kingdom. Most scholars think this is pre-exilic literature.[4]

Psalm 104	*Exodus 15*
I will sing to Yahowah with my life;	*I will sing praise* to *my God* while I exist!
I will sing to Yahowah	My strength and *my praise* is
Let my meditation please him;	
I will rejoice in *Yahowah*.	*Yahowah* (2).
Let sinners perish from the land,	
and the wicked be no more.	
Bless *Yahowah*, O my soul!	
Praise Yahowah (33-35).	

3. For an analysis of this poem itself, see G.W. Coats, 'The Song of the Sea', *CBQ* 31 (1969), pp. 1-17.
4. C.A. Briggs, J. Sarna, W.R. Taylor and W.S. McCullough, M.J. Dahood *et al.*

Psalm 105.1-4	Exodus 15
Give thanks to *Yahowah*; call out in his name! make known among *the peoples* his deeds;	I will *sing to Yahowah* (1) *The peoples* have heard; they tremble (14)
Sing to him! sing for joy to him!	I will *sing to Yahowah* (1)
Think of all his *miraculous deeds.* *Praise his holy name.* Let the heart rejoice, [you] who request *Yahowah.* Seek (*deershoó,* דרשו) *Yahowah* and his *strength* (1-4).	*a miracle worker* (11) *I will praise him* (2) My strength and my song is *Yahowah* (2)

First Isaiah

Isaiah 12	Exodus 15
I *give thanks* (Ps. 105.1) to you, *Yahowah*, because you were angry with me; your anger (*áhfuhkah,* אפך) *Yahowah* and his strength (1-4).	With the breath of your nostrils (*ahfáykah* אפיך) the water piled up (8)
Look! *God is my salvation* (Ps. 88.2); *I will* trust and not be afraid.	*he will be my salvation* (2)
For Yahowah is my strength and my song, Yahowah.	*My strength and my song is Yahowah* (2)
He has become my salvation	*He will be my salvation* (2)
You will draw *water* with joy	*The water piled* up (8)
from springs of *salvation.* You will say in that day, *Give thanks to Yahowah!*	he will be my *salvation* (2) *Yahowah is his name* (3)
Call out in *his name*; *make known among the peoples his* deeds (Ps. 105.1); Mention that *his name* is exalted	*Yahowah is his name* (3)
Sing to Yahowah (Ps. 105.2) *for he has acted gloriously.* *For he is greatly exalted* make this known in all the land.	I will *sing to Yahowah* (1, 20) *For he is greatly exalted* (1, 20)
Shout and sing for joy inhabitant of Zion, for great in your	*I will sing* to Yahowah (1) *inhabitants of* Philistia (14)

Isaiah 12	*Exodus 15*
midst is *the holy One* of Israel (Isa. 12).	... to your *holy* hill (13)
	majestic in *holiness* (11)

First Isaiah here seemed to be constantly and admittedly offering comfort by quoting from three poems he expected readers to recognize.[5] The brief quotation was expected to call their attention to the entire poem in each case.

1. From Ps. 88.2, he knew of another poet who believed that the Lord was angry with him. But even from that poet, he found an encouraging text: 'Look! God is my salvation'. That text prompted him to the resolution, 'I will trust and not be afraid'.

2. Then he turned to another text on salvation, and beginning a quote from Exod. 15.2, he interrupted the quote to remind Yahowah that he was still addressing this message to him. He seemed to be saying, 'Remember, Yahowah, this quote from Exodus 15, your very words, "Yahowah is my strength and my song"'. The use of the name Yahowah here, first as a part of a quotation and second in direct address, makes sense. Any interpretation that overlooks this quotation seems strange. The author seemed to be presenting his case before the Lord like a lawyer before a judge, reminding the judge of an earlier verdict that the judge himself had rendered which had gained for him a great deal of notoriety. Now confronted with a similar situation, the attorney wanted to call the judge's attention to that precedent and, by citing this report in Exodus 15, persuade him to act consistently and grant a similar verdict. Today, a modern attorney would call attention to the fact that the court in which he was pleading, and maybe even the judge himself, had rendered the verdict which the attorney cited from one of the law journals.

Another analogy for this peculiarity is in modern Jewish liturgy. When reading liturgy in which the directions are given for the people to respond with, 'Amen!' there was added, 'And [let the people] say,

---

5. P.R. Ackroyd, 'Isaiah I–XII', pp. 36-37 observed that Isa. 12 contained 'two short psalms or sections of psalms' (p. 36), and he also recognized some Exodus themes, but he did not identify the psalms or the midrash on Exod. 15 (p. 37). G.B. Gray, *A Critical and Exegetical Commentary on the Book of Isaiah* (New York: Charles Scribner's Sons, 1912), I, p. 231, noticed that this expression was like that in Exod. 15.1, but he reached no conclusions from this insight.

"Amen"' (*wuh imaroó amáyn* אמן ואמרו). Since these directions are now part of the liturgy, the people not only say 'Amen!' but they say, 'And [let the people] say "Amen!"'[6] This sort of peculiarity occurs only with a preserved text that is being quoted, as in the case of a court precedent or an earlier text, as in the case of Isaiah.

3. His third quotation was probably from Ps. 104.33–Ps. 105.3. Isaiah seems to have said, 'You will say in that day' (and I quote from Ps. 105):

> Give thanks to Yahowah; call out his name!
> make known among the people his deeds;
> Sing to him! sing for joy to him!
> Report all his miraculous deeds.
> Praise his holy name.
> Let the heart rejoice,
> [you] who seek Yahowah (Ps. 105.1-3).

If these words really stem from Isaiah, then Psalm 88, Psalms 104, 105, and Exodus 15 were evidently written by the eighth century BC in time for Isaiah to have used them. At a time when the author thought God was angry with him, he found reassurance in these texts, and he probably intended the reader to take from these brief quotes the lead to think of the rest of the poems involved. He felt as depressed as the poet who wrote Psalm 88, but the word, 'salvation', in that poem reminded him of Exodus 15 which confessed that God was his salvation, so Isaiah found encouragement and gave thanks to this God, who had been as victorious as Exodus 15 indicated. This ability to quote several passages of Scripture that are related to one subject was common among rabbis and New Testament authors.[7]

Early Jewish and Christian apologists also recognized text that had been used by later Scripture writers. For example, when Paul argued for the validity of the new contract the Lord had made with his people (2 Cor. 3-4), he had not only justified his case on the basis of Jer. 31.32, but he also used the text from Exodus (34.10-28) upon which Jeremiah had based his argument.[8] When the author of Acts 13 wanted

---

6. For example in the Kaddish, see S. Singer (ed.), *The Authorized Daily Prayer Book* (London: Eyre and Spottiswoode, 1960), p. 37.

7. See G.W. Buchanan, *Revelation and Redemption: Jewish Documents of Deliverance from the Fall of Jerusalem to the Death of Nahmanides* (Dillsboro: Western North Carolina Press, 1978), *passim*, Heb. 1.1-13.

8. See G.W. Buchanan, 'Paul and the Jews (II Corinthians 3.4–4.6 and

to tell of God's selection of David as king of Israel, he quoted from
Ps. 89.20, but he also supported his argument by quoting from 1 Sam.
13.14 and 2 Sam. 7.12 upon which the psalmist appealed for his
authority. The practice of supporting arguments using both earlier
midrashim and also the texts on which the midrashim based their narratives was not a new methodology for Paul and the author of Acts.
The First Isaianic author of Isaiah 12 seems to have used these psalm
texts and Exodus texts in the same way, hundreds of years before, but
it has not been generally recognized as a practice of the Hebrew
Scripture prophets.

　　Smith did not even notice that there was a relationship among these
various texts.[9] Skinner noticed them, but he reached no conclusions
from them about the early use of Scripture by Hebrew Scripture
authors.[10] Gray recognized the close similarity between Isaiah 12 and
Exodus 15,[11] but he overlooked Psalms 88, 104, and 105. He followed
Ewald, Lagarde, and others in concluding that this was not the work
of Isaiah but some author who wrote after the Babylonian captivity
and after Isaiah 40–66 had been published. Scott thought Isaiah 12
reflected some unknown psalms, but he did not recognize any biblical
psalms or Exodus 15.[12] Isaiah 12.2b does not occur in the Septuagint
and therefore raises the suspicion that this quotation from Exodus 15
is a later gloss. Although these are reasonable objections, there are a
few reasons for re-examining these conclusions. One is that the
Exodus 15 theme occurs in other related passages in the book of
Isaiah. For example Isa. 11.9-16:

Isaiah 11	*Exodus 15*
It will happen on that day,	Your right *arm*, Yahowah, noble in power; your right *hand, Yahowah*, shatters the enemy (6)
Yahowah *will extend his arm* a second time	*You extended your* right *arm*, the land swallowed them (12)

Romans 11.7–10)', in J.J. Petuchowski (ed.), *When Jews and Christians Meet* (New York: State University of New York Press, 1988), pp. 141-62.

　　9.　G.A. Smith, *The Book of Isaiah* (London: Hodder & Stoughton, n.d.), I, pp. 188-95.

　　10.　J. Skinner, *Isaiah* (Cambridge: Cambridge University Press, 1905), p. 103.

　　11.　Gray, *Isaiah*, I, p. 223.

　　12.　R.B.Y. Scott, 'The Book of Isaiah', *The Interpreter's Bible* V (New York: Abingdon Press, 1956), pp. 253-54.

Isaiah 11	*Exodus 15*
	with the greatness of your *arm* (16)
to acquire the remnant of *his people* who are left in Assyria, Egypt, Pathros, Ethiopia, Elam, Babylon, Hamath, and the islands of *the sea* (Isa. 11.11)	*this people you acquired* *this people* you redeemed (13)
They will fly down on the shoulder of *the Philistines* to the west; together they will plunder the people of the east. Against *Edom and Moab*	Anguish seized the inhabitants of *Philistia* (14) Then were dismayed the troops of *Edom*; terror seized the leaders of *Moab* (15)
they *will extend their hand.* The Ammonites will obey them.	*You extended your right hand*; the land swallowed them (11)
Yahowah will destroy the tongue of *the Sea* of Egypt; he *will wave his arm* over the river with a scorching *wind.* He will strike the seven rivers and enable [people] *to walk* [across] in sandals.	*Yahowah* returned over them the waters of *the sea* (19) You blew with your *wind*; *the sea* covered it (10) The children of Israel *walked* on the dry land in the midst of *the sea* (19)
There will be a highway (muhseeláh, מסלה*)* for the remnant of *his people* who have been left in Assyria [to return], just as it was for the Israelites on the day they went up from the land of Egypt (Isa. 11.14-16)	Until the people crossed over... *this people* you acquired (13) *this people* you redeemed (13)

By the time this Isaianic author composed these lines there were Jews and/or North Israelites not only in the promised land, but also in Assyria, Egypt, Pathros, Ethiopia, Elam, Babylon, Hamath, and the coastlands of the sea. This author thought the Lord would perform a second exodus, bringing these exiles from the four corners of the earth. When the Lord did this, hostility between the northern and southern kingdoms of Israel would vanish. The jealousy of Ephraim would turn away; those who injured Judah would be cut off. If this was not Isaiah, it was at least a Jew who wrote this, one with a condescending attitude towards Samaria. Ephraim would no longer be jealous of Judah, in his opinion, and Judah, correspondingly, would not torture Ephraim as it deserved. Their united forces would fly down on the shoulder of the Philistines, toward the sea, and unite to plunder the people of the East. They would together attack Moab and Edom, following the Exodus account of Israel terrorizing these peoples. The Ammonites would submit to them.

Yahowah would completely destroy the body of water now occupied by the Suez Canal. Like a fairy godmother with her wand, Yahowah would wave his hand over the (Great) River on the northern border of Lebanon[13] and, with his scorching wind, break it into seven creeks. Then people could walk over it in sandals, and there would be a highway for the remnant of his people from their exile in Assyria as there was for Israel in the day when they came up from the Land of Egypt with Moses and Aaron.

The author's mention of a 'second time' is clearly intended to compare the new event that he anticipated to the 'first time' Israelites came out of Egypt, when they crossed the 'Sea of Egypt' or the 'Red Sea' on dry ground. The author here expected history to repeat itself. As God had rescued his people from Egypt, so he would again rescue the North Israelites from their captivity in Assyria, Egypt, Babylonia, and other places where they had been sold as slaves by the Assyrians. On the one hand, God would dry up the water that formed a barrier in Egypt that prevented the sons of Israel from escaping from Egypt. He would also wave his hand over the (Great) River on the northern boundary of modern Lebanon, and it would dry up, magically. Then Diaspora Israelites from the North or from the South could cross these bodies of water in sandals. For the northern refugees, Isaiah expected that there would be a highway to return from Assyria, just as there had originally been from Egypt, even though no Scripture mentions such a highway.

At first glimpse it would seem that scholars, like Gray,[14] Scott,[15] Skinner[16] and others, who think Isa. 11.9-16 was written after the Babylonian captivity are probably correct, because Isa. 11.9-16 deals throughout both with Judah and with Ephraim after the kingdom had

---

13. For the identification of this 'River' see G.W. Buchanan, *The Consequences of the Covenant* (Leiden: E.J. Brill, 1970), pp. 91-109. Contra Scott, *Isaiah*, p. 252, who thought 'the river' involved was the Nile.

14. Gray, *Isaiah*, I, p. 233.

15. Scott, *Isaiah*, p. 251.

16. Skinner, *Isaiah*, p. 100.

been divided and there had been a dispersion both to Assyria and Babylonia. This would seem to require composition after the Babylonian dispersion in 586 BC, but Stohlmann[17] has made a strong case for holding that there was a third exile. This one was implemented by Sennacherib in 701 BC. Assyrian sources claim that Sennacherib took many citizens from Judah into exile during that campaign. Comparing Assyrian texts with biblical reports, Stohlmann concluded that the number 200,150 did not refer to the number of exiles, but to the number of Judeans Sennacherib took captive. Many of these were left in Judah, but some were also taken captive into Assyria. This does not require that Isaiah himself wrote these chapters after 701 BC, but that someone did, and that a date very much later than 701 is not required for its composition.

The text, however, nowhere says Jews were among the captives. Those who were to return were taken captive by the Assyrians, who probably took some captives back to Nineveh and sold the rest to other countries, like Egypt and Babylonia. Whoever this author was,[18] he was acquainted with Exodus 15. The poem was probably placed next to Isaiah 12, because the editor recognized the similarity of content and source. There is a strong tradition among biblical editors to classify materials and put laws together, psalms together, wisdom literature together, and history together. These editors further classified psalms into units of subject matter, and they organized prophets together according to some chronological or content principle.

Isaiah 12 has no direct statement requiring it to be the product of a period after the Babylonian exile. In order to prove that it is post-Babylonian-exilic, Isaiah 12 would have to be categorized as non-Isaianic according to style, and this is not absolute. Because this unit is determined partially by the literature quoted in it, it does not reflect only the style of the author. Since Isaiah is the one who admittedly used sources, like the Book of Yahowah, and since he encouraged contemporaries to do research and read these earlier authoritative sources, it seems reasonable to assume either that he had done so

17. S. Stohlmann, 'The Judaean Exile after 701 BCE', in W.W. Hallo, J.C. Moyer, and L.G. Perdu (eds.), *Scripture in Context II* (Winona Lake: Eisenbrauns, 1983), pp. 146-75.

18. M. Arnold, *Isaiah of Jerusalem* (London: Macmillan, 1883), p. 127, and Smith, *The Book of Isaiah*, I, pp. 194-95; both presume the author was Isaiah.

himself or that it was composed by his earlier disciples. In either case Isaiah 12 is a very much earlier piece of literature by someone in the Isaiah school.

Isaiah 27	*Exodus 15*
In that day Yahowah will visit with his harsh, great, and strong *sword* over *Leviathan*, the fleeing serpent, over *Leviathan* the twisting serpent, and he will murder the *dragons* that are *in the sea* (27.1)...	I will draw my *sword*; my hand will possess them (9)
In that day Yahowah will thresh the grain from the [Great] River (*Nahar il Kabir*)[19] until the River Egypt, and you will be harvested, one by one, children of Israel. *On that day a* great *trumpet will be blown* and those who were lost in *the land* of Assyria and those who have been pushed into *the land* of Egypt will come and worship Yahowah in the holy mount, in Jerusalem (27.12-13).	*Tiamat* congealed *in the* heart of *sea* (8) You shall send *a trumpet blast* on the seventh month, on the tenth of the month, *on the Day* of Atonement you shall send out the *trumpet* throughout all *your land...* It will be Jubilee for you, and you shall return each person to his native place, each person to his family (Lev. 25.9-10).

Commentary

Like Isaiah 11 and 12, the prose introduction and conclusion to Isaiah 27 anticipates the return of the North Israelites for a great jubilee celebration. When the Lord would sound a great trumpet all the North Israelites who had been taken by the Assyrians and probably sold to Egyptians, Babylonians, and other surrounding countries, would return. This was according to the rules of Sabbatical eschatology.[20] On the Jubilee years the captives would not only be returned but their land would be restored to the original owners. The most likely time for this to have been written is sometime before the first Jubilee following the Assyrian captivity—before 671 BC. There is nothing in any of these chapters that anticipates a Babylonian captivity of Southern Israelites.

19. The basis for this identification can be seen in Buchanan, *Consequences*, pp. 91-109.

20. On Sabbatical eschatology see Buchanan, *Consequences*, pp. 9-18.

Second Isaiah's Midrash

Typology

The general typology of Second Isaiah, relating the new exodus from Babylon to the old exodus from Egypt, is obvious, even to the casual reader.[21] The Genesis characters Abraham, Isaac, and Jacob are all mentioned by this prophet, and the creation themes are poetically dramatized. To Second Isaiah's imagination the Lord sits above the circle of the earth and stretches out the heavens like a curtain (Isa. 40.22; 44.24), but his knowledge was more than general and not only about Genesis; he also shows specific borrowing from Ps. 104.2. The announcement of Good News in Isaiah 61 is not only a Jubilee hymn, but it is also a midrash on Leviticus 25. The suffering servant was an antitype of the servant Moses who bore the sins of the people and therefore was not allowed to enter the promised land. Instead he made his death with the wicked Gentiles, encouraged that he could see his posterity enter the land of life. Like the ancient type,[22] in the new antitype Jews would proceed through the waters with the Lord before and behind the chosen people[23] just as the Lord's servant, Moses, had volunteered to do earlier.[24] The Lord would be present with his people again in the wilderness to provide food, water, and miracles needed for survival.[25] The Lord would again prevail against the enemies of Israel with an arm that was not too short to save.[26] Just as the Lord delivered the Hebrews on wings of eagles,[27] so the Jews would mount up with wings as eagles[28] to return to the promised land. A more specific kind of typology, however, is evident in the poetic midrash of Isaiah 35 and 42 on Isaiah 11 and Isaiah 42, 43, and 51 on Exodus 15.

21. See further C.C. Torrey, *The Second Isaiah* (New York: Charles Scribner's Sons, 1928), p. 379.

22. Exod. 14.19-20.

23. Isa. 43.2; 51.11; 52.12; 58.8; 63.12-14.

24. Exod. 32.32-35

25. Isa. 35.3-10; 40.10-11; 41.17-18; 43.16-20; 44.3-4; 48.28; 49.10; see also Deut. 26.8.

26. Exod. 15.3; Isa. 41.12; 42.13; 50.2; 54.14-17; 59.1.

27. Deut. 32.8-11.

28. Isa. 40.31.

Isaiah 35	*Isaiah 11 and Exodus 15*
There will be there a highway (*masloól,* מסלול) and a road; it shall be called the holy road (35.8)... *The redeemed* shall walk there, and the ransomed of *Yahowah will return* (35.9-10)	*There will be* a highway (*muhseeláh,* מסלה) for the remnant of his people *to return* who are left of the Assyrian [captives] (Isa. 11.16) You led in mercy this people you *redeemed* (Exod. 15.13).

Isaiah 40

A voice cries, 'In the wilderness prepare *the way* of Yahowah; make straight in the Arabah *a highway* (*muhseeláh,* מסלה) for our God (3).

Isaiah 43

Look! I am doing [something] new; now it will emerge. Do you not know it? I will even put in the wilderness *a road,* rivers in the desert (19).[29]

I will make all my mountains *a road,* and my *highways* (מסלתי) raised... (49.11).

Isaiah 62

Prepare *the way* of the people; build up, build up the highway (*hahmuhseeláh* המסלה), clear it of stones (10).

29. Scott, *Isaiah,* p. 495, correctly said, 'The motif of the way or road (*derekh*) is prominent in Second Isaiah. It is already sounded in the first strophe of the Prologue and it continues to the end (55.12-13)'. Scott did not, however, relate the highway of Second Isaiah to the highway of Isa. 11.

Isaiah 65	Isaiah 11
The wolf and the lamb *will graze* as one;	*The wolf will* live *with the* sheep; the leopard will lie with the kid; the calf, *the lion*, and the fatling together; and a small boy will lead them. The cow and the bear will eat; their offspring will lie down together;
the lion will eat straw like the cow; and dust will be the serpent's food.	*The lion will eat straw like the cow;* the suckling child will play over the hole of the asp, and the weaned child shall put his hand on the adder's den.
They will not hurt; they will not destroy in all my holy mountain says the Lord (25).[30]	*They will not hurt; they will not destroy in all my holy mountain* (6-9).

In Isaiah 11 and 27 some earlier prophet anticipated the return of the Northern Israelites who had been kept from the promised land ever since the Assyrian conquest of Samaria. Some were in Egypt, and others were in northern countries like Assyria and Babylonia. The Lord was expected to blow a great Jubilee trumpet and open up the Suez Canal and the river on the northern border of Lebanon. As on other Jubilees, this was a time of liberation. The captives would be set free and the land restored to its original owners. When the Lord fulfilled this Jubilee expectation, he was also counted on to prepare highways for the chosen people of North Israel to return. At a later time in Babylon a Jewish captive looked forward to a return to the promised land, going through the desert as Moses had, and having a specially prepared road built, like a Garden State Parkway, on which the redeemed Jews could return. This prophet not only had the whole history of the exodus and the wilderness wanderings at his fingertips, but he had also read Isaiah 11 which had been written earlier by some other Isaianic Jew. The expectation of a new road was not just some casual thought mentioned in Isaiah 35, but it was also a theme for Isaiah 40, 43, 49, and 62.

To be sure, the author of Second Isaiah was heavily dependent upon Exodus 15 and the whole theme of the exodus and wilderness

---

30. Scott, *Isaiah*, p. 757, thought that the author intentionally used the reference about the serpent and the dust to allude to Gen. 3.14, but he did not think of the similarity between Isa. 65.25 and Isa. 11.6-9 as a clue to indicate that the author of Isa. 65.25 used Isa. 11.6-9 midrashically in the same way.

experiences of the Hebrews who left Egypt, but he also obviously considered Isaiah 11 to be the valid word of God. Not only were the very words of Isaiah 11 used in reference to the anticipated highway, but from the same chapter is quoted the peaceful coexistence of people in the promised land.[31] Not only people but even the domestic animals and the wild beasts would live in peace. Lest anyone think that the author of Isaiah 65 coincidentally composed the very same words, the author of Isaiah 65 documented his quotation, 'Thus said Yahowah'. By this he meant he read it in earlier Scripture, where the word of God was reported. This is true Isaianic midrash.

Isaiah 42	*Exodus 15*
Sing to Yahowah a new song,	I will *sing to Yahowah* (1)
his praise from the ends of *the land,*	I will *praise* him (2)
	fearful so as to be *praised* (11)
	The land swallowed them (12)
[you] who *go down to the sea and*	*They went down into the* depths (5)
fill it, [you] coastlands and their	My desire *will be filled* (9)
inhabitants.[32] Let the wilderness and its	*inhabitants* of Philistia (14)
settlement raise their voices,[33] the	
villages Kedar *inhabits.*[34] Let *the*	
inhabitants of	*inhabitants of* Canaan (15)
Sela sing for joy,[35] from the top of	
the mountains, let them shout! Let them	
give *Yahowah* glory; let them make	Sing *to Yahowah* (1)
known in the coastlands his *praise!*	fearful so as to *be praised* (11)
Yahowah, like a mighty man, goes	*Yahowah* is
forth,	
like *a man of wars* he stirs up his fury.	*a man of war* (3)
He cries out; he shouts aloud!	
He becomes mighty against	shatter *the enemy* (6)
his enemies (Isa. 42.10-13).[36]	*The enemy* said (9)

31. Skinner, *Isaiah*, p. 260, noted that the image of the highway was found in other Isaianic passages but he did nothing to explain the relationship.

32. Since the verse begins with the second person plural, it is assumed that the same subject applied throughout the verse. Another possibility, however, is that the opening verb is an exhortation in the second person, followed by the third person plural imperatives afterward. This would read: 'Let those who go down to the sea and fill it, those coastlands and their inhabitants'. However this sentence was constructed, the intention was to exhort all areas of the land to rejoice and sing to

Exegetical Details

The Jewish poet's hope that Yahowah would overpower his enemies (Isa. 42.13) is a reminder of the Exodus hymn, 'Your right hand, Yahowah, will shatter the enemy' (Exod. 15.6). Just as the Lord would strike terror in the hearts of all the neighboring peoples at the time of the exodus from Egypt (Exod. 15.14-16), so Second Isaiah called upon all the peoples in Palestine to praise Yahowah for his military achievements (Isa. 42.10-13).[37]

Yahowah—those who go down to the sea, the coastlands, wilderness areas, Bedouin camps, or small settlements, those who live in the rocky caves or cities like Petra, and the mountains. For other exhortations to shout, see Isa. 49.13; 52.9-10; 54.1-2. P.-E. Bonnard (*Le second Isaie* [Paris: Gabalda, 1972], p. 130) has mistakenly assumed that the praise was also extended to the end of the earth and all nature.

33. These are Arabian settlements, paralleled by 'villages of Kedar'.

34. This group also includes small, unwalled Arab villages; Kedar was one of the sons of Ishmael, the ancestor of the Arabs. See Song 1.5; Isa. 60.7; Jer. 49.18, etc.

35. Sela was an Edomite town (2 Kgs 14.7), possibly identified with Petra. The word also means 'rock', however, and may mean the cave dwellers, generally. Since these caves are in the mountains, cave dwellers could readily shout from the top of the mountains.

36. The Lord is also pictured as a mighty warrior in Exod. 15.3; Deut. 10.17; Zeph. 3.17; Pss. 24.8 and 78.65. The close relationship between Isa. 42.10-13 and Exod. 15 has not been noticed by most scholars.

37. Professor James Sanders mentioned in his presidential address at the Society of Biblical Literature meeting in New Orleans in 1978 that he had found a passage in Second Isaiah which was midrash on Exod. 15 (J.A. Sanders, 'Text and Canon: Concepts and Method', *JBL* 98 [1979], pp. 5-29 [18]). At the very next hour, at the same meeting, in a seminar on midrash, my paper which had been published prior to the meeting in the *Seminary Papers* considered in detail the relationship of this same Isaiah passage to Exod. 15, along with two others and their respective Exodus texts ('The Word of God and the Apocalyptic Vision', *Society of Biblical Literature 1978 Seminar Papers* [Missoula: Scholars Press, 1978], pp. 183-92). This should not be considered a unique phenomenon. Intertextuality is a field that is 'white with harvest' (Jn 4.35). Professor Sanders and I have been working in this 'field' for many years, comparing notes, and encouraging others. The field is so large that we are not likely to run out of material. As soon as many people begin working in intertextuality, however, they are certain to duplicate insights, because the facts are very obvious. There should be no effort made to keep people out of the project so that a few can have the glory of the insights. As many as want should begin. We should rejoice when insights are made even if two or three people make the same discovery simultaneously, as Professor Sanders and I have done. There should be more interest given to the discovery than to the discoverer.

Isaiah 43	*Exodus 15 and Isaiah 11*
	You led in your mercy this people *you*
Thus says Yahowah, your *redeemer,*	*redeemed* (13)
the holy one of Israel, your king:	your *holy* dwelling (13)
'For your sakes I sent and brought down all the refugees of Babylon[38] and the pleasure boat of the Chaldeans. I am	
Yahowah, your holy One, creator of Israel,	majestic in *holiness* (11)
your *king,*' Thus says *Yahowah,* who provides *in the sea* a way;[39]	*Yahowah will be king* (17)
in the mighty waters,[40] a path, who	They sank like lead *in the mighty waters* (10)
brings out *the rider and horse, the* strong and the mighty together: they collapse, never rise; they will be extinguished; like [a] flax [wick] they will be snuffed out' (Isa. 43.14-17)[41]	*the horse and his rider* he hurled into the sea (1)
I will set in the wilderness *a road,* in the wilderness, rivers of water. The beasts of the field honor me; jackals and ostriches will respond; for I will supply in the wilderness water, rivers to provide drinking water for my chosen people[42]	There will be *a highway* (Isa. 11.6)
	until they cross over,
This people I formed will tell of my praise (Isa. 43.19-21).	*this people you acquired* (16)

38. Some change this to 'gates of Babylon'. So E.J. Kissane, *The Book of Isaiah* (Dublin: Brown and Nolan, 1943), II, p. 57. Others, like F. Delitzsch, *The Prophecies of Isaiah* (New York: Funk and Wagnalls, n.d.), I, p. 145, saw no reason for this. Torrey, *Second Isaiah,* p. 339, related the *barihim* of Isa. 43.14 to *Barehu* of Exod. 14.5. Isa. 43.2; 51.11; 52.12; Isa. 58.8 and 63.12-14 seems to allude to Exod. 14.19-20 as well as to Exod. 15, but Exod. 14 was not used nearly as much as Exod. 15. The allusion Second Isaiah seemed to make to Exod. 14.5 was done satirically, because it was the Hebrews who had been refugees from Egypt. From Babylon, however, the poet anticipated the Babylonians unsuccessfully trying to flee, both on land and by sea.

39. It would not have been necessary for Babylonians to cross any sea to get back through the Fertile Cresent to Palestine. It was the Egyptian exodus through the sea which formed a type as a basis for this antitype. Without a midrashic, typological concern for Exod. 15, the author would not have instinctively thought of the

Exegetical Notes

It is clear that the crossing of the body of water at the eastern border of Egypt was an old event that provided the poet with a type for his antitypal invocation and assurance that the Lord was about to do a new thing which was very much like the old things he had done before. The knowledge disclosed seems to be more general. Expressions like 'This people you redeemed' (*'am zoo ga-áltah,* עם זו גאלת) and 'This people you acquired' (*'am zoo kaneétah,* עם זו קנית) (Exod. 15.13, 16) seems reflected in Second Isaiah's 'this people I formed' (*'am zoo yatzárty,* עם זו יצרתי) (Isa. 43.21). The claim of Second Isaiah that 'Yahowah goes out like a mighty warrior; like a man of wars, he stirs up fury' (Isa. 42.13) recalls the affirmation that 'Yahowah is a man of war; Yahowah is his name' (Exod. 15.3).

Isaiah 51	*Exodus 15*
Awake! awake! *gird on strength, O arm of Yahowah*; awake, as in the days gone by, earlier generations! Are you not the one who shatters	Your *right hand, Yahowah,* marvelous in *power*; your *right hand*, Yahowah, will shatter the enemy (6)
	You stretched out your *right hand*; the land swallowed them (12)
	with the greatness of your *arm* they were still as a stone (16)

Babylonian Jews passing through the sea to get back to their homeland.

40. See Job 9.13; 26.12; Ps. 89.11. See also M. Jastrow, 'Tiamat', in *The Religion of Babylonian and Assyria* (Boston: Ginn & Co., 1898), *passim*.

41. Without noticing the midrashic qualities of Second Isaiah, many scholars have observed the relationship between Isa. 43.14-17 and Exod. 15. B. Duhm, *Das Buch Jesaia* (Göttingen: Vandenhoeck & Ruprecht, 1922), p. 326; Delitzsch, *Prophecies*, p. 145; Bonnard, *Le second Isaie*, p. 146; and Westermann, *Isaiah 40–66* (OTL; Philadelphia: Westminster Press, 1969), pp. 125-29. Westermann, however, thought 43.14-15 was a separate unit. He may not have thought this if he had noticed that the midrash continues to v. 17.

42. Kissane, *Isaiah*, p. 57, replaced *neharot* with *netibot*. Many replaced 'water' with 'a way'. The 'correction' would make more sense in tracing the journey from Babylon to Jerusalem, but the author of this psalm was composing a typology, based on the exodus from Egypt which did go through the water. Therefore the antitype was expected to do the same, even though it made no sense, practically.

Isaiah 51	Exodus 15
Rahab, stabbing the dragon? Are you not the	*Tiamat* covered them (5)
one who dries up *the sea, the waters*	*Yahowah* returned over them *the water of the sea* (19)
of great *Telhom?*	*Tiamat* congealed in the heart of the sea (8)
	You led in your mercy this people *you*
for the ransomed	*redeemed* (13)
to cross over (Isa. 51.9-10)?[43]	until your people *crossed over,* Yahowah, until they *crossed over* this people you acquired (16).

Conclusions

'The Song of the Sea' was evidently a poem that was used as a textual basis for the writings of Deuteronomy, Isaiah of Jerusalem or one of his early students, Second Isaiah, Jeremiah, some authors from among the Dead Sea composers, Psalm 74, and no one knows just how many more. The idea of a special highway being built from Assyria to Palestine for the return of the exiles was based on the exodus from Egypt. It was designed originally by some author who used Exodus 15 as his textual source. The road was never constructed, and there is no official record of the return of the Assyrian exiles, but that did not prevent Second Isaiah from making the same prediction in relationship to the Jewish return from the Babylonian exile. When he foresaw the imminent return of Jews to Jerusalem, he expected the new exodus would be like the old one: Jews would pass through the wilderness on the way, and all of the miracles that happened before would happen again. There would be water flowing in the wilderness; miracles of healing would take place, just as they had happened before. There would also be a special highway constructed for these redeemed, orthodox Jews to return to Zion (Isa. 35.5-10). The author of the

43. Kissane, *Isaiah*, p. 243; C. North, *The Second Isaiah* (Oxford: Clarendon Press, 1964), pp. 125-26; and Torrey, *The Second Isaiah*, p. 400, all noted dependency of Isa. 51.9-10 upon Exod. 15, but none saw that it was a midrash. H.M. Orlinsky, *Studies in the Second Part of the Book of Isaiah* (Leiden: E.J. Brill, 1967), p. 192, however, related these verses in Isaiah to the creation, rather than the exodus from Egypt. The redeemed are the Jews from Babylon (see Isa. 35.9).

Dead Sea fragment used the text to prove that the temple should be exclusively for the Lord's holy people, which surely did not include bastards, Ammonites, or Moabites.

This essay was designed to show how early midrash was employed in the Hebrew Scriptures. When intertextual scholars completely screen the entire Bible for these relationships we may be able to develop a Hebrew Bible in which all of these relationships are shown in bold-faced print with documentation in the margins the way the Nestle–Aland Greek New Testament is designed.[44] By then we may discover that current hypotheses, such as J, E, D, and P as well as M, L, and Q, no longer describe the literature possibilities accurately. Time will tell.

---

44. This project has already been undertaken by Edwin Mellen Press and the Mellen Biblical Commentary: *Intertextual*.

Part II

BIBLICAL INTERPRETATION IN THE SECOND TEMPLE PERIOD

Nehemiah 9 and the Scripturalization of Prayer in the Second Temple Period*

Judith H. Newman

The prayer in Nehemiah 9 is often grouped together with other exilic and postexilic prayers such as those in Daniel 9, Ezra 9, and Baruch 2–3 and characterized flatly by biblical scholars as a late Deuteronomistic confession. My intention in this essay is to demonstrate that the prayer in Nehemiah is much more than a Deuteronomistic confession, and in fact has a more complex relationship to Scripture than is usually perceived. This prayer stands toward the beginning of a long trajectory in the Second Temple period in which prayers show an increasing tendency toward 'scripturalization'. Of course this 'scripturalization' occurs throughout Second Temple books, in all genres and forms of the literature. The rise of interpretation of earlier written traditions during the exilic and postexilic periods has been discussed at length by many scholars.[1] Nevertheless, the special significance of the interpretive use of earlier Scripture *in prayers* has gone largely unnoticed. There is a particular reason to focus attention on the 'scripturalization of prayer'. The allusive, interpretive use of the Bible eventually becomes a fundamental trait of Jewish and Christian

---

* Originally presented at the Annual SBL Meeting, Chicago, 20 November 1994.

1. To name just a few more recent works: James L. Kugel, *In Potiphar's House: The Interpretive Life of Biblical Texts* (New York: HarperCollins, 1990); Michael Fishbane, *Biblical Interpretation in Ancient Israel* (New York: Oxford University Press, 1985); the articles on biblical interpretation at Qumran by Michael Fishbane and in the Apocrypha and Pseudepigrapha by Devorah Dimant in M.J. Mulder (ed.), *Mikra: Text, Translation, Reading and Interpretation of the Hebrew Bible in Ancient Judaism and Early Christianity* (CRINT, 2.1; Assen: Van Gorcum/ Philadelphia: Fortress Press, 1990); James L. Kugel and Rowan A. Greer, *Early Biblical Interpretation* (Philadelphia: Westminster Press, 1986) for a Jewish and Christian perspective.

liturgies. Focusing attention on how Scripture is used in Nehemiah 9 thus illuminates the origins of what eventally was to become a literary convention in the composition of liturgical materials.

An essential feature of the prayer's 'scripturalization' is its repre-sentation of Israel's past. The prayer traces a *selective* history of Israel from creation to the contemporary situation of subjugation by the Persian authorities. What is most significant about this prayer from our perspective is that Israel's history has been 'scripturalized', remembered through words and phrases recalled from all parts of the Bible. Written traditions—and presumably oral traditions—have become the means by which the past is recalled. The prayer has been referred to as Deuteronomistic. Major themes and numerous formu-lations in the prayer do show Deuteronomistic *influence*.[2] The main concern lies with the possession of the land and the importance of observing the commandments in order to maintain control of the land. 'The land' is mentioned seven times in the prayer, four times in con-junction with the promise to the ancestors.[3] The retelling of history in the prayer relates the same cyclical pattern that is found in the book of Judges: of disobedience of the people—divine forgiveness—repeated disobedience. Despite this Deuteronomistic flavor, the prayer nonethe-less suggests its own particularly postexilic sense of Torah. The author studiously avoids certain formulations that one might expect in a Deuteronomistic prayer, perhaps most conspicuously in that the term ברית, covenant, is never used in reference to the event between God and Israel at Sinai. In the description of the covenant in vv. 13-14, God simply 'gives' the ordinances and commandments to the people.[4] There are many other examples that point to deliberate exegetical and compositional decisions by a careful author.

Before proceeding with a closer examination of Nehemiah 9, let me clarify the term 'scripturalization'. Gary Anderson has discussed this sort of intense study of the text during the Second Temple period in

2. Characteristic Deuteronomistic formulations include אתת ומפתים, the 'signs and wonders' in Deut. 4.34; 6.22; 34.11, and the list of goods the Israelites inherited when they came into the land: ברת חצובים כרמים וזיתים, 'hewn cisterns, vineyards, and olive orchards', from Deut. 6.11.

3. Neh. 9.8, 15, 22, 23, 24, 25, 35.

4. Moshe Weinfeld, for one, has suggested that this is one of the earliest refer-ences that reflects the later rabbinic conception of the Torah as a 'gift' from God, *Deuteronomy and the Deuteronomic School* (New York: Oxford University Press, 1972), p. 43 n. 2.

reference to laws about sacrifice. The same intense scrutiny obtained for the whole of Torah. We will therefore borrow his succinct definition of this phenomenon as the *'learned reflection on a developing canon of textual material'*.[5] This paper will extend the definition to include the learned reflection that comes to generate entirely new texts. 'Learned' is a particularly appropriate adjective, because it is clear that the author of this prayer was steeped in biblical language, and the character of the biblical reminiscences suggests an author who had studied biblical texts and knew much of them by heart. 'Learned *reflection*' rings true because not only is the textual tradition tapped for phrases and quotes, but the text is reflected upon, in the sense that it is interpreted consciously for use in this particular prayer. The author has digested the text to the degree that it seems to have become a natural part of the author's linguistic repertoire for composing new texts. This reflection on earlier texts necessarily involves a conservative stance toward the textual material, conservative in the literal sense of the word, reflecting a desire to preserve what has been transmitted, though the subsequent transmission necessarily involves a reshaping of the text and transformation.

The 'scripturalization' or learned reflection on Scripture in Nehemiah 9 is evident in three ways: the prayer in fact contains scriptural references from all strata of the Pentateuch and other parts of the Bible (besides the book of Deuteronomy and the DtrH); there are certain interpretive elements found in the prayer that are not in the biblical text per se, thereby indicating that a certain degree of *interpretive* use of Scripture obtains in this prayer; and finally, the terms used to describe God also reflect a special kind of scripturalization—that is, the conscious reflection on earlier biblical material that also points to a development of the text specifically for liturgical purposes.

The first point is easily demonstrated: the prayer is rich in scriptural references, allusions, and citations from all strata of the Pentateuch. Let me provide some examples of Priestly material in the prayer since that will illustrate clearly that the author of our prayer has drawn on more than Deuteronomistic literature, and in fact shows an intimate acquaintance with a wide range of Israelite traditions.

5. Gary A. Anderson, 'Sacrifice and Sacrifical Offerings (OT)', *ABD*, V, pp. 870-86 (883).

- The historical review begins with an invocation to God as the creator. The reference in v. 6 to God's creation of 'heaven and its hosts' presumes the Priestly creation account in Gen. 2.1 in particular.

- The prayer as a whole has the Sinai theophany and law-giving at its heart, and observance of the law is a concern throughout the prayer, yet the only specific divine legal pre-scription mentioned in Nehemiah 9 is that Israel should observe the 'holy sabbath'. שבת קדש is a distinctive term, and found only once aside from Nehemiah, in Exod. 16.23, a passage from the Priestly traditions. Similar language, though not the exact term 'holy sabbath', is found in the Priestly creation account in Gen. 2.2-3 when God ceases from his work on the seventh day: וישבת ביום השביעי and hallows it, ויקדש אתו.[6] So too Ezekiel uses the same Priestly language in reference to consecrating the Sabbath (the use of קדש in the Piel).

- Yet another example lies in the prayer's reference to the divine covenant with Abraham. The wording in v. 7b: ושׂאת שׁמו אברהם belies knowledge of P's version of the covenant in Genesis 17 where Abraham's symbolic name change occurs.

Examples of such biblical wording abound and the interested reader can refer to the long though incomplete list of biblical references and looser biblical parallels found in Jacob Myers' Anchor Bible commentary on Ezra, Nehemiah for more on this.

The second way in which the prayer reflects the process of 'scripturalization' is in the appearance of interpretive elements in the prayer, which reflect some degree of studied reflection on earlier biblical traditions.

Though there are a number of elements in this prayer that reflect a proto-midrashic interpretation, one example should suffice to illustrate my point. Here is v. 6 of the prayer:

6. You are the Lord, you alone.
   You have made the heavens, the highest heavens and all their host,
   the earth and all that is upon it, the seas and all that is in them.
   You have given life to everything. The host of the heavens worships
   before you.

---

6. Cf. also the traditions of the Sinai narrative that refer to the Sabbath with this same notion of consecration, Exod. 20.8 and 31.12-18.

The final phrase of the verse is our focus: וּצְבָא הַשָּׁמַיִם לְךָ מִשְׁתַּחֲוִים—
'The host of the heavens worships before you'. I have just noted the
inclusion of Priestly material in this prayer. Verse 6 presupposes the
Priestly creation account of Gen. 1.1–2.4a, yet celestial beings worshipping the creator are not found in any part of the Priestly or Jah-
wistic creation accounts in Genesis 1–3. Rather, this image is the trace
of an interpretive tradition that the 'host of heaven', here meaning the
angels, was created for the purpose of praising God continuously. By
the postexilic period, this tradition was already well developed, but its
roots can be discerned in earlier biblical texts.

The reference to heavenly creatures surrounding God has hoary
ancient Near Eastern origins in the concept of a divine council. Ugaritic literature in particular contains descriptions of the divine retinue,
whose job is a *judicial* one—to assist the chief god 'El in rendering
judgments.[7] As it appears in this verse, however, the ancient Near
Eastern roots are completely obscured. These divine beings have been
transformed, so that the council is now a host of subservient and wor-
shipful beings whose premier task is to glorify God in response to the
divine act of creation. The interpretive transformation of the Ugaritic
divine council into the angelic hosts proclaiming the glory of God is
complex and cannot be detailed here. What is important to mention,
however, are some earlier and contemporaneous texts that depict this
presumed divine liturgy.

There are a number of biblical texts that contain references to the
angelic praise of God in connection with the creation. Psalm 148 calls
on all the created order to praise God, in the first verse calling on
those in the heavens. The second verse continues: 'Praise him, all his
angels; praise him all his host'. Psalm 103 contains a similar theme.
Although it does not state explicitly that the heavenly hosts have
praised God from creation, the psalmist does call upon the angels, his
hosts, his ministers, and all his works to join in the heavenly liturgy
and bless the Lord (vv. 20-22). God's so-called 'answer' to Job in
ch. 38 also contains a reference to this heavenly liturgy. In Job 38.7,

---

7. 1 Kgs 22.19-22 is one biblical example that stands close to the Ugaritic conception of the divine council. In this pericope, the prophet Michaiah ben Imlah
reports his vision of the heavenly throne to King Ahab and King Jehoshaphat. In that
case, צְבָא הַשָּׁמַיִם, the host of heaven, is not described as worshiping, מִשְׁתַּחֲוִים, God;
rather, they stand, עֹמֵד, before God who consults them about how to waylay King
Ahab. Ps. 82 also describes the scene of God holding court with the divine council.

God responds to Job's complaints with a question, asking Job where he was at the time of creation, when 'the stars of the morning sang together and all the sons of God raised a joyous sound'. Psalm 29 also contains an image of the בני אלים, the sons of God, worshiping the Creator. The later stages of the transformation, which occur mainly in later Second Temple literature, rely on the two prophetic call narratives that depict scenes of the divine throne, Isaiah 6 and Ezekiel 1.

The significance of this interpretive tradition in the context of our discussion of Nehemiah 9 is twofold.[8] The first point relates to the question of the 'Deuteronomistic' character of the prayer. By its recognition of angelic beings, the prayer departs from what might be called 'Deuteronomistic theology', which is strictly monotheistic, and opposes any kind of idolatry. A comment in this regard should also be made about the use of the Hebrew צבא השמים, the host of heaven, in this context. Of the 17 times this phrase appears in the Bible, 14 of them use the phrase in a negative context, in reference to idolatrous worship.[9] They appear primarily in the Deuteronomistic literature.[10] The transformation here is especially striking when compared to 2 Kgs 17.16, part of the passage describing the sins of the Israelites during the time of Ahaz, in which the Israelites are condemned for worshiping all the host of heaven.[11] The phrase in Nehemiah thus suggests a new use of this phrase; in a sense the host of heaven has been domesticated, robbed of its threatening role as an idolatrous temptation, and placed at the service of the Divine King himself.[12]

8. Moshe Weinfeld argues that in expositing Exod. 14 and 23, the author of Deut. 4 and 7 purposely omits the role of a mediating angel in the Exodus in keeping with the strict monotheism Deuteronomic theology embodies. Weinfeld suggests that Neh. 9 is one of what he calls late 'liturgical orations' in which the Deuteronomic emphasis on the exodus—election—covenant is supplemented with the creation motif (*Deuteronomy*, p. 34).

9. The 14 instances where the host of heaven appears as threat of idolatry: Deut. 4.19; 17.3; 2 Kgs 17.16; 21.3, 5; 23.4, 5; Isa. 34.4; Jer. 8.2; 19.13; 33.22; 2 Chron. 18.18; 33.3; Zeph. 1.5. One other is the occurrence in 1 Kgs 22, when Micaiah ben Imlah sees the heavenly court; the other is a reference in Dan. 8 that occurs in the context of Daniel's vision of a goat.

10. Other phrases for the divine council can be found in Ps. 89.7-8, בני אלים, 'sons of God', and סוד קדשים, 'council of holy ones'.

11. So too in 2 Kgs 21.3/2 Chron. 33.3, Manasseh is described as worshiping the host of heaven as his father Ahaz had done.

12. It is important to note the unique and subtle interpretive use of this image by the author. Elsewhere in this interpretive tradition, God is depicted as a king, the

The inclusion of this tradition is also significant because it indicates that the author of the prayer was aware of an interpretive motif that linked God's creation with an angelic liturgy. It is impossible to know exactly how well developed this interpretation was at the point when Nehemiah 9 was written. The references to the angelic liturgy from earlier and contemporaneous texts adduced above suggest that it was a well-known tradition by the time this author wrote. The reference in this account of the creation appears almost offhand, suggesting that it had already become a well-integrated part of the tradition by this point. I could compile a long list of texts, from the Apocrypha, from Qumran, from early Christian and rabbinic writings—all of which postdate Nehemiah 9—that contain more elaborate descriptions of the angelic praise than appears in this terse phrase in Nehemiah 9.[13] The

visions in Isa. 6 and Ezek. 1 are of the divine throne—royal imagery is an integral part of this tradition. Yet this royal element is missing from the creation account in v. 6. In fact, God is never referred to as king in the entire prayer. It seems that this royal theology has become an embarrassment to the author, perhaps in the absence of any clear successor to the Davidic throne and in the Jews' situation of subjugation to foreign kings in the postexilic period.

13. There are many other references to this interpretive tradition in Second Temple texts. The *Prayer of Manasseh*, which also describes God's role in creation, states toward the end that 'the host of heaven sings your praise'. Later Second Temple literature contains a more elaborate description of the angelic worship of God. The book of *Jubilees* presupposes an angelic hierarchy. According to *Jub.* 2.1-3, all of the different ranks of angels were created on the first day and their immediate response upon seeing the divine creation was to worship God: 'Then we saw his works and we blessed him and offered praise before him on account of all his works because he made seven great works on the first day'. The interpretive tradition of heavenly worship was also well known at Qumran, evidenced in the *Hodayot*, and in full-blown form in 11QShirShabb. The *Angelic Liturgy*, thought to date to the first century BCE, reflects an elaborate form of this tradition, which is based on imaginative interpretations of biblical passages that depict the heavenly throne. The liturgy contains the angelic songs of praise for God assigned to the first 13 sabbaths of the year, but it also contains obscure descriptions of the heavenly Temple, the divine throne chariot, and the different groups of beings participating in this collective praise. See Carol Newsom, *Songs of the Sabbath Sacrifice: A Critical Edition* (HSS, 27; Atlanta: Scholars Press, 1985).

This tradition became widely accepted in Christian and Gnostic circles as well. The introduction to the Magnificat in Lk. 2.13 reflects this background: 'And suddenly there was with the angel a multitude of the heavenly host, praising God and saying...' For more on this see Karl Erich Grözinger, *Musik und Gesang in der Theologie der frühen jüdischen Literatur* (Tübingen: Mohr Siebeck, 1982), Chapter 2.

point here is rather simply to indicate that Nehemiah 9 shows clear signs of familiarity with this tradition. This 'evidence' can be understood in one of two ways: either the author knew of much more elaborate traditions regarding the angelic liturgy and chose to include only this brief reference to it, or at the time Nehemiah 9 was composed, this interpretive tradition was still in its early, formative stages. But deciding this question need not detain us, because either way, the larger point is still valid: the author of Nehemiah 9 is sharing with the reader a 'learned reflection' on the text.

This is just one of the interpretive elements that can be seen in this prayer. Others that could be elaborated include an oblique reference in v. 8 to the testing of Abraham, and in v. 26, the interpretive tradition later seen in the New Testament that the Israelites persecuted and murdered 'the prophets'. There is also the trace of the idea in vv. 28 and 30 that later becomes an important part of rabbinic thinking about God, that God does not punish without warning.[14] None of these is an elaborate expansion on the text, like the midrashic elements that one finds in the books of *Jubilees* or *Pseudo-Philo*; nonetheless, their presence is important in giving us some idea about the process of scripturalization in the early postexilic period.

The third way in which I want to illustrate the appropriation of Scripture in Nehemiah 9 is in examining some of the terms used to describe God. Five verses in the prayer (9.17, 19, 27, 28, and 31) make reference to the divine self-disclosure passage that occurs in

Cf. also such liturgical poems as that from the collection of *Sa'adya Ga'on*, in which each word begins with a successive letter of the (Hebrew) alphabet: 'Blessed God, great of knowledge/prepared and wrought sun's brilliance // Formed skillfully glory for His Name/placed luminaries about His Might // Chiefs of holy throngs/ praising God endlessly/recount to God His holiness.' Translation from James L. Kugel, *The Idea of Biblical Poetry* (New Haven: Yale University Press, 1981), p. 312. The motif has continued to be a part of worship in Judaism and Christianity in which human participation in the divine liturgy is signaled by recitation of the Qedushah in traditional Jewish prayer and the Trishagion in traditional eucharistic liturgies.

14. The narrative sequence is as follows: in v. 28, God 'warns' the people to return to the Torah. So also in v. 30, God 'warns' the people through the prophets. They don't listen and in 30b the exile is mentioned as resulting from their obstinence. Sara Japhet views these references in Neh. 9 as the earliest mention of this idea that appears well developed in rabbinic literature; *The Ideology of the Book of Chronicles and Its Place in Biblical Thought* (Frankfurt: Peter Lang, 1989), p. 187.

Exod. 34.6-7 and occurs again, in what I think is a later tradition, in Num. 14.13-19. This use of Scripture differs from the sort of proto-midrashic use described above. Though the reuse of this language reflects an intense engagement with the biblical traditions, it is unlike the creative embroidery that resulted from harmonizing the irregular elements of a particular biblical narrative. Rather, the divine attributes' use in the prayer as a kind of refrain ties it more closely to later liturgical formulae.[15]

The most complete reference is the first one in the last half of Neh. 9.17b. It reads:

ואתה אלוה סליחת חנון ורחום ארך־אפים ורב־חסד ולא עזבתם

But you are a forgiving God, gracious and merciful, long-suffering and of abundant faithful love. And you did not abandon them.

The other references appear at intervals throughout the retelling of history in this prayer. The affirmation of divine mercy occurs as part of the larger pattern narrated in the retelling of history that recounts Israelite disobedience: the Israelites long to return to their slavery in Egypt, but God is *ready to forgive, gracious and merciful*, etc. (17).

---

15. Though it is beyond our scope here to delve into putative influences of this liturgical phrase and Neh. 9 on later Jewish and Christan liturgies, it is worth mentioning that Leon Liebreich has suggested that this prayer had a direct influence on the Sephardic liturgy for Yom Kippur. See his article, 'The Impact of Nehemiah 9.5-37 on the Liturgy of the Synagogue', *HUCA* 32 (1961), pp. 227-37. Ismar Elbogen also notes the widespread use of this passage already in biblical times as a significant step in the development of the liturgy. 'In particular, the Thirteen Attributes revealed to Moses when he received the second set of tablets (Exod. 34.6-7) are called סדר סליחה, "rite of forgiveness"; they belong to the ancient heritage and were very widespread, as shown by the frequency with which they are quoted in the Bible. "God showed Moses the order of prayer. He said to him, 'Whenever Israel sins, let them perform this rite before Me and I shall forgive them'; 'There is a covenant that the Thirteen Attributes do not return unanswered'" (Babylonian Talmud Rosh Hashanah 17b). This talmudic conception explains how the Thirteen Attributes became the nucleus of all prayers for atonement, so that they serve to this day as a refrain constantly repeated in all the seliḥot'. Elbogen, *Jewish Liturgy: A Comprehensive History* (trans. Raymond P. Scheindlin; Philadelphia: Jewish Publication Society, 5753/1993), pp. 177-78.

The liturgical setting and the role of the Levites in the narrative led von Rad to suggest that this prayer, which does in fact seem to be secondarily inserted into the book of Nehemiah, lived a double life as a part of a liturgical rite of confession or penitence.

They make a calf for themselves, but God in his *great mercies* did not abandon them (19). During the period of the judges, they threw the Torah behind their backs and killed the prophets, but God in his great *mercies* gave them saviors/judges to rescue them (27). During the period of kingship, they again rebelled, and God had *mercy* (28). The final affirmation of these divine attributes occurs at the very end of the historical review, after the Israelites had rebelled and been exiled from the land. Verse 31 reads:

> However, in your *great mercies*, you did not make an end of them and you did not destroy them, because you are a *gracious and merciful God*.
> This marks the transition in the prayer to the current period of distress, which is followed by a brief confession and a petition for help.

Two larger issues about the appropriation of the divine attribute formula as it appears in the prayer are worth noting. The first is that, in its most complete citation in v. 17, it appears out of chronological sequence when compared to its use in the book of Exodus. In Exodus, the narrative sequence of events while at Sinai is as follows: God makes the the first covenant with Moses and Moses receives one set of tablets (Exodus 19–31), the people rebel idolatrously by making the molten calf (Exodus 32), Moses seeks atonement for the people by offering a prayer and God accepts his request (Exodus 32–33), and this divine self-disclosure occurs in Exodus 34 as the second round of law-giving begins. In the chronological sequence of Nehemiah 9, however, the author's affirmation of the divine attributes of mercy *precedes* the episode of the molten calf. It comes in the middle of the longer section stretching from vv. 15-21 that describes the Israelites' wilderness wandering. The author of this prayer abandons strict adherence to the biblical sequence of events in order to present a certain cyclical scheme which continues throughout the historical review. In so doing, the author has taken liberties with Israelite history as it is presented in the book of Exodus in order to illustrate the main theological theme of the prayer: God's gracious providence in the face of continuing apostasy and disobedience on the part of Israel.

Another important feature of this interpretation is that the formula in its entirety as it appears in Exod. 34.6-7, and again in Num. 14.18-19 does not occur in Nehemiah 9. Only 34.6 is quoted, though with several slight modifications: the order of the adjectives חנון ורחום has been reversed. This is true in other exilic and postexilic appearances

of this phrase.[16] Exodus 34.6-7 occurs in conjunction with the revelation of the divine name so it begins with a twofold repetition of the
Tetragrammaton. In Neh. 9.17, God is affirmed as אלוה סליחות, a forgiving God. Another minor change is that the end of the clause in
Exod. 34.6 is ורב־חסד ואמת; Neh. 9.17 ends ורב־חסד ולא עזבתם. The
last two alterations serve to stress to an even greater extent the merciful aspects of God: God forgives and God did not abandon the
Israelites.

But the omission of the second half of the divine attribute formula
as found in the Pentateuch is more striking. God is not described here
as 'not clearing the guilty, but visiting the sins of the parents on the
children and the children's children to the third and fourth generation'. The notion of transgenerational punishment is missing. In contrast to tenth-century Israel and certain crazed twentieth-century
theorists, the author of Nehemiah 9 could not commit to the idea of
determinism through the gene pool.

Michael Fishbane has discussed the reuse of this attribute formula in
postexilic literature. Though he does not treat its appearance in
Nehemiah 9, his insights echo what I have observed here. He suggests,
quite plausibly, that the appearance of this clause, that is, the first part
of Exod. 34.6-7, in a number of other late biblical texts without the
punishment/reward clause is an aggadic reuse designed to emphasize
the gracious properties of God as opposed to divine judgment and
retribution. Given the alteration of the formulary in 17b to stress the
loyal/faithful character of God who will not forsake Israel, ולא עזבתם,
Fishbane's suggestion makes sense. This notion is also reinforced by at
least two other aspects of this prayer: the prayer emphasizes God's
inalienable gift of the land to the Israelites; and the punishment of
exile is downplayed so there is only the vaguest hint of life outside the
land in v. 30.

As was the case with the angelic liturgy, there are a number of
other late biblical texts that reflect an interpretive reuse of the divine
attribute formula. Fishbane has noted that many of these reflect
an emphasis on divine attributes of compassion.[17] (See for instance

16. Cf. also Joel 2.13, Jon. 4.2, Pss. 145.8; 11.4; 112.4, and 2 Chron. 30.9. It
is important to note however, that all postexilic literature does not follow this reversal. The Exod. 34 order obtains in 1QH 12.14; 16.16; 1QS 4.4, 5.

17. Fishbane mentions a number of psalms that seem to him to use this formulary
as an organizing principle: 40, 78, 79, 85, 99; *Biblical Interpretation*, p. 347. While I

2 Chron. 30.9, Joel 2.13, or Mic. 7.18-20.) But its appearance in prayers, including Nehemiah 9, Jonah's prayer in 4.2, and in such psalms as 86.15, 103.8, 145.8 and in partial form in the acrostic psalms 111 and 112, strongly suggests that from an early period this formula had become a stock phrase used in composing liturgical texts.

The internalization of 'the word of God' by this learned author of the postexilic period resulted in a composition that is permeated with textual references, allusions, and citations. Some of the uses of Scripture, as I have suggested above in the case of the divine attribute formula, seem to be conscious structural exegetical uses of earlier textual traditions. In other instances, the appropriation of Scripture seems less conscious and suggests an author who is simply using the language of Scripture as a native tongue. This use of the language of Scripture also marks a curious hermeneutical shift that was to come to mark the way in which Second Temple tradents used Scripture in prayer. What were once understood as God's words to humans (the theophany in Exodus 34) have become, by virtue of their new deployment, human words addressed to God. At a much later date, certainly by the time Christianity and Judaism went their separate ways, this kind of 'scripturalization' in the composition of prayers had become a convention that needed no justification. By the time of the authorship of Nehemiah, the 'scripturalization of prayer' had already begun.

disagree with his understanding that these psalms are somehow organized or structured around this formula in a conscious exegetical process, there was clearly a loose appropriation of some of the divine attribute terminology in these psalms.

THE DECALOGUE IN EARLY JUDAISM AND CHRISTIANITY

Richard A. Freund

Form and Content of the Commandments

The Ten Commandments are generally regarded by most authors of introductory books on religion as a basis for later Jewish and Christian formulations of morality.[1] Rarely do these authors or scholars of the Bible in general investigate the transmission of these so-called 'Ten Commandments' in the earliest text witnesses and manuscript traditions to determine whether the commandments themselves were as fixed in form and content as they seem to be in the minds of premoderns and moderns. In general, the commandments found in Exodus 20 and Deuteronomy 5 are treated by many ethicists as the basis for much discussion and ethical evaluation of how societies either achieve or approximate the formulations found there, especially in premodern religious ethics. Sometimes, the citation of the commandments in Western society is complicated by the differing formulations of the commandments found in the New Testament and early Church literature but rarely does this 'slight' inconvenience of differing formulations become itself subject of speculation. The textual differences between the two texts in Exodus and Deuteronomy and the New Testament and early Church citations of the Decalogue are generally noted by most modern biblical commentators, but in this chapter I will focus upon how an in-depth investigation of the textual differences between the formulations of some of the commandments and the development of these formulations can add much to our understanding of the meaning of the commandments and perhaps their importance for Second Temple Judaism and early Christianity.[2]

---

1. For example, Kyle M. Yates, Jr (gen. ed.), *The Religious World* (New York: Macmillan, 1988), p. 241.
2. There is an extensive literature analyzing the textual differences, their meanings

This chapter will explore different forms of biblical criticism which reveal different ethical meanings of the commandments. We will especially concentrate on the implications of biblical criticism for our understanding of ethical standards of the Bible and biblically derived ethics, and in particular how the changing and apparently fluid nature of the formulation of the Ten Commandments in ancient Jewish and Christian sources may reflect changing realities and ethical settings.

Modern Biblical Criticism and the Ten Commandments

Modern and especially recent biblical criticism employing the documentary hypothesis as its point of departure has pointed to different authors, settings, and raisons d'être for the different, almost parallel versions of the sacred history of the Hebrews found in the Hebrew Bible, especially in the first five books.[3] The different authors, settings and raisons d'être are most evident in the case of the Ten Commandments. Exodus 20.1-17 has been identified with the priestly author (P).[4]

In the so-called 'Covenant Code' in Exod. 20.18–23.33 another set of similar but much more extensive commandments are given which has been identified with the author who used the name of God as Elohim (E) in his accounts. In Exod. 34.1-35 another similar version of the commandments appears, this one identified with the author who used the Tetragrammaton (YHWH) or as the early biblical critics identified him, J. Finally, Deuteronomy 5.1-33 (D) is a similar, though not exact version of the same text found in Exod. 20.1-17 (P). At this point we will only investigate the openings of the four to demonstrate the similitude.

and the relationship between citations in other ancient works. A select bibliography includes the following:

a. C. Levin, 'Der Dekalog am Sinai', *VT* 35 (1985), pp. 165-91.
b. A. Phillips, 'Ancient Israel's Criminal Law', *JJS* 35 (1985), pp. 1-20.
c. J.J. Stamm and M.E. Andrew, *The Ten Commandments in Recent Research* (SBT Second Series, 2; London: SCM Press; Naperville: Allenson, 1967).
d. H.H. Rowley, 'Moses and the Decalogue', *BJRL* 34 (1951–52), pp. 81-118.

3. See for a review of the literature Richard E. Friedman's *Who Wrote the Bible?* (New York: Harper & Row, 1989).
4. Friedman, *Who Wrote the Bible?*, pp. 251 and 258-59.

Exod. 20.2-3 (P)	*Exod. 23.23-33 (E)*	*Exod. 34.11-17 (J)*	*Deut. 5.6-8 (D)*
2. I am the	23. When my angel goes	11. Observe what I command	6. I am the
Lord your God,	before you, and brings you	you this day. Behold I will drive	Lord your God,
who brought	in to the Amorites, and the	out before you the Amorites,	who brought
you out of the	Hittites, and the Perizzites	the Canaanites, the Hittites,	you out of the
land of Egypt,	and the Canaanites, the	the Perizzites, the Hivites and	land of Egypt,
out of the	Hivites, and the Jebusites,	the Jebusites. 12. Take heed to	out of the house
house of	and I blot them out. 24. You	yourself, lest you make a	of bondage.
bondage.	shall not bow down to their	covenant with the inhabitants	7. You shall
3. You shall	gods, nor serve them, nor do	of the land whither you go, lest	have no other
have no other	according to their works, but	it become for you a snare in	
	you shall utterly overthrow	the midst of you. 13. You shall	
	them and break their pillars	tear down their altars, and break	
	in pieces…32. You shall	their pillars, and cut down their	
	make no covenant with them	Asherim. 4. For you shall	
	or with their gods. 33. They	worship no other god…	
	shall not dwell in your land,		
	lest they make you sin		
	against me; for if you serve		
	their gods it will surely be a		
	snare to you.		

The similarity between the J and E account is marked by the language, style, and action suggested. In P and D here there are rather laconic prohibitions and reasons against idolatry, while J and E suggest that clear action must be taken. In the compared P and D sections one is advised not to worship other gods, apparently because God 'brought you out of the land of Egypt'. In the E and J accounts one must actively eliminate competing gods apparently because God will eliminate the resident populations making the worship of these gods superfluous.[5] P and D (in this section) have the prohibitions against idolatry without the necessary violence which is alluded to in E and J. E and J also appear to be less tolerant of religious diversity. The P and D accounts are exactly the same in both wording and placement of the first statement(s).

In the E and J accounts the wording and placement are similar but their order in the listed commandments/prohibitions is different. The order of the commandments in the P and D accounts is here the same,

---

5.   Also found in Deut. 7.1-5. Deuteronomy has the language of P and later especially J: '…But thus shall you deal with them: you shall break down their altars and dash in pieces their pillars, and hew down their Asherim, and burn their graven images with fire'.

but J and E seem to be following a different order of commandments. In the continuation of the P, E, J, and D accounts one finds the following:

Exod. 20.4 (P)	*Exod. 20.23 (E)*	*Exod. 34.7-17 (J)*	*Deut. 5.8-10 (D)*
4. You shall not make for yourself a graven image, or any likeness of anything that is in the heaven above, or that is in the earth beneath, or that is in the water under the earth; 5. you shall not bow down to them or serve them; for I the Lord your God am a jealous God, visiting the iniquity of the fathers upon the children to the third and fourth generation of those who hate me...	23. You shall not make gods of silver to be with me, nor shall you make for yourselves gods of gold.	7. ...visiting the iniquity of the fathers upon the children and children's children, to the third and fourth generation... 14. ...or you serve no other god, for the Lord, whose name is Jealous, is a a jealous God... 17. You shall make for yourself no molten gods.	8. You shall not make for yourself a graven image, or any likeness of anything that is in the heaven above, or that is in the earth beneath, or that in the water under the earth; 9. you shall not bow down to them or serve them; for I the Lord your God am a jealous God, visiting the iniquity of the fathers upon the children to the third and fourth generation of those who hate me...

Again, the P and D accounts agree. The E and J accounts contain similar information concerning the prohibition against the creating of idols but the language, style, and order of the material in E and J[6] is not similar to that of P and D. Again, P, D, and J share material ('jealous God' and 'visiting iniquity of fathers on children') although the order and language is not exact. J and E are assumed to be earlier than P and D, and the latter are therefore basing themselves on J and E. The unique material shared by P and D with J both here and in example #1 indicates that perhaps P and D quoted this directly from J.

More importantly, some modern biblical critics[7] who identify the *terminus ad quem* for P and D as the seventh to sixth century BCE, seem to recognize that the Decalogue was not in a static form even at this late date. Quite the contrary, in this period the ethical teaching of the Decalogue was questioned by at least two prophets. One finds, for

6. Friedman, *Who Wrote the Bible?*, pp. 48-49. There he identifies the language of J as a polemic against the molten calves of Jereboam in the north and E's more general language against 'gods of silver and gods of gold' as a religious polemic against the molten gold calves in the north and the plated golden cherubs in the Temple in Jerusalem.

7. Friedman, *Who Wrote the Bible?*, pp. 169-70.

example, that the prophet Ezekiel, quoting the tradition of P/D/J on the above cited 'visiting the iniquity of the fathers on the children' Decalogue tradition:

> The son shall not suffer for the iniquity of the father, nor the father for the son; the righteousness of the righteous shall be upon himself and the wickedness of the wicked shall be upon himself.
>
> (Ezek. 18.20; also see Jer. 31.30)

It appears that though the content of the Ten Commandments was known in the sixth century no one formulation was yet seen as canonized. Additionally, the fact that differently worded, arranged, and styled versions of the Decalogue were presented in almost synoptic fashion in succeeding chapters and books of the Bible leads one to the conclusion that the Decalogue was recognized to be more fluid than the written form captured by one author or another. The words spoken at Sinai were apparently more than the words registered by one author or another. The Decalogue was seen even as late as the authors of P and D to be the product of an ongoing and open-ended covenant. The content, style, and order of the Decalogue continued evolving long beyond the account of one author or another.

From the Sixth Century BCE to the First Century CE: Hellenistic Judaism's Contribution to the Commandments

Even though the Decalogue(s) which appear in Exod. 20.1-17 and Deut. 5.1-33 are remarkably similar, they contain minor changes in style and content in a number of areas, though no changes in order in the Hebrew Masoretic text. The minor changes in style and content found in the two versions have been discussed in a significant amount of literature.[8] Although the notion that there can be a 'minor change' is questionable when dealing with a sacred literature, the case of the Ten Commandments is unique because of the existence of two versions which by the sixth century BCE had reached what could be called a 'final form'. It is well known, for example, that the reasons given for the observance of the Sabbath in Exodus 20 are different from the reasons given in Deuteronomy 5. Exodus 20 states:

8. See the studies by A. Jepsen, 'Beiträge zur Auslegung und Geschichte des Dekalogs', *ZAW* 79 (1967), pp. 277-304; S.A. Cook, 'A Pre-Masoretic Biblical Papyrus', *Proceedings of the Society of Biblical Archaeology* 25 (1903), pp. 34-56; K.J. Thomas, 'Liturgical Citations in the Synoptics', *NTS* 22 (1975–76), pp. 205-14.

> Remember the Sabbath day to sanctify it...because in six days the Lord
> made the heavens and the earth...and He rested on the seventh day.
> Therefore the Lord blessed the Sabbath day and sanctified it.

This account gives the reason for Sabbath observance as based upon God's creation of the universe in six days. The Exodus commandments are following the P version of creation in Genesis 1 and therefore is assigned by some modern biblical critics to P authorship.[9] Deuteronomy 5, whose redaction has been attributed[10] to Jeremiah with the collaboration of Baruch the son of Neriyah in Egypt during the early years of the Babylonian exile, reflects a new sociopolitical and religious reason for Sabbath observance:

> Keep the Sabbath day to sanctify it...and you shall remember that you
> were a slave in the land of Egypt and the Lord your God brought you out
> from there with a strong hand and an outstretched arm. Therefore the Lord
> your God commanded you to observe the Sabbath day.

It seems that during the earliest period of the formulation of the commandments and their meanings the authors of the Bible saw them as a vehicle for expressing issues relevant to their setting. The Qumran Deuteronomy, or so-called 'All Souls Scroll', gives both of the reasons for observing the Sabbath (Exodus equals creation of universe and Deuteronomy equals redemption from Egypt), obviously in an attempt to appeal to those groups which knew both and found both meaningful and to avoid confusion.[11]

At a later period, the Samaritan text of Exodus actually added an entirely 'new' commandment which does not appear in any other textual traditions instructing the Israelites to build an altar on Mount Gerizim, obviously following what the Samaritan redactors saw as a legitimate process of interpretation evident in the earliest literary strata of the text.[12]

Order changes in certain commandments between the two versions, especially in translations of the Decalogue and ancient sources that purport to be citing the Decalogue, also give us insights into the unique nature of the Decalogue and its transmission. Despite the apparent agreement in the order of the commandments found in P and D in the

9. Friedman, *Who Wrote the Bible?*, pp. 258-59.

10. Friedman, *Who Wrote the Bible?*, Ch. 7, and especially pp. 113 and 188.

11. Friedman, *Who Wrote the Bible?*, p. 188 n. 22.

12. J.E. Sanderson, *An Exodus Scroll from Qumran* (HSS, 30; Atlanta: Scholars Press, 1987), pp. 235 and 318-20.

Masoretic text, after the sixth century BCE the Decalogue continued to be shaped. In this section we will deal with the order changes of commandments #6, 7 and 8 (Exod. 20.13-15; Deut. 5.17-19).

In Exod. 20.13-15 and Deut. 5.17-19, we have the same order and wording of commandments #6–8 in the Hebrew Bible:

A.   You shall not murder
B.   You shall not commit adultery
C.   You shall not steal

It is difficult to assess the reasons for this order of these three prohibitions since no explanation of the order is given in the text itself. The possibility that this order is the result of some influential literary precedent in ancient Near Eastern literature does not necessarily aid our investigation, since in a comparative text such as the Egyptian 'Protestation of Guiltlessness'[13] the order is: stealing murder, and adultery.[14] The apodictic formulation (found here) may also be unique in ancient Near Eastern comparative literature.[15] Within the text of the Hebrew Bible one finds allusions to the Decalogue[16] and there the order of these three prohibitions is mixed. In Hos. 4.2 one finds the order: murder, theft, and adultery, but in Jer. 7.9: theft, murder, and adultery.

In the Septuagint (LXX), the problem is complicated by the different readings and translations of Exodus and Deuteronomy, *but in the LXX readings of Exod. 20.13-15 and Deut. 5.17-19 we clearly have a different order for these three prohibitions!* In Exod. 20.13-15, the LXX reads:[17]

13. You shall not commit adultery.   14. You shall not steal.   15. You shall not murder.

13. *ANET*, pp. 34-36.
14. *ANET*, p. 35.
15. M. Dick, *Introduction to the Hebrew Bible* (Englewood Cliffs, NJ: Prentice-Hall, 1988), pp. 151-53.
16. It is important to note that in the Pentateuchal sources, the P document, Lev. 19, also includes a prohibition against theft (19.11) but does not include it in the same section along with prohibitions against murder or adultery. While this may imply a different ordering of the commandments in connection with the Holiness code document itself, its presence does not provide direct information for the ordering question being discussed here.
17. The manuscripts of these sections in LXX Exodus and Deuteronomy are also split on the order. Manuscripts A and F of LXX Exodus have the MT order.

In Deut. 5.17-19, the LXX order of these three prohibitions is according to the Hebrew Bible order of this section.[18] The question is: Why is the order of Exodus text inverted from the Hebrew version as well as the Deuteronomy LXX and Masoretic Text (MT)? The Aramaic translations of *Onqelos* and the *Palestinian*, with their consistent stylistic changes, follow the same order as the Hebrew texts of Exodus and Deuteronomy, as does the Qumran Deuteronomy scroll section (4QDeut[n]). Josephus[19] follows the Hebrew text order, but Philo does not. On two occasions,[20] Philo makes it clear that the order of the text is: adultery, murder, and stealing. The Nash Papyrus, containing an imperfect Decalogue, agrees with Philo. This may indicate an Alexandrian reading of the Decalogue which differs from the Palestinian version.[21]

The New Testament and Early Christian Literature

In early Christian literature (by way of manuscript readings), the changing order question continues. In the New Testament, there is no standard order for these three prohibitions even where it is clear that the writer is citing the Pentateuchal source(s).[22] The absence of the Decalogue in the *Gospel of Thomas*,[23] for example (and other Gnostic Gospel literature), is provocative but not unintelligible. It may indicate an attempt by this literature to eliminate formulistic and authoritative sayings found in the MT rather than indicating that the Decalogue did not have a place in the early Gospel literature. Again,

18. The Deuteronomy (B) manuscript has: adultery, murder, theft.

19. Josephus, *Ant.* 3.5.5.

20. Philo, *Dec.* 12, and then again, in characteristic style in *Spec. Leg.* 3.2, Philo gives homiletic/philosophical reasons for the placing of adultery first amongst the second set (6–10) of commandments.

21. This despite the fact that some have speculated that the Nash Papyrus (discovered in Egypt) derives from Babylonian Jewry. See S. Zeitlin, *Dead Sea Scrolls and Modern Scholarship*, pp. 83-84; also, G.R. Driver, *The Judaean Scrolls*, p. 410. The fact that 4QDeut[n], Josephus and the *Palestinian* and *Onqelos Targums* reflect one textual tradition (clearly of Palestinian origin) and Philo, Nash Papyrus, Clement of Alexandria, Origen (see below), and other non-Palestinian sources reflect another, is highly suggestive.

22. The Gospel accounts are citing a combination of the Decalogue and Lev. 19.

23. Although the *Gospel of Thomas*, for example, has in saying #25 the Lev. 19.18 citation: 'You shall love your neighbor as yourself...', it lacks the Decalogue.

however, one finds in the Synoptic Gospels' account of Jesus' advice to the rich, young man in Mt. 19.16-22; Mk 10.17-22; Lk. 18.18-23 that the order of the commandments may indicate a subtle commentary on the commandments:

Mt. 19.16-22	*Mk 10.17-22*	*Lk. 18.18-23*
17. And he said to him,	18. And Jesus said to him,	19. And Jesus said to him,
Why do you ask me what is good?	Why do you call me good?	Why do you call me good?
One there is who is good. If you	No one is good but God alone.	No one is good but God alone.
would enter life, keep the com-	You know the commandments:	You know the command-
mandments. He said to him:	Do not murder, Do not commit	ments: Do not commit
Which? And Jesus said: You	adultery, [24] Do not steal,	adultery, Do not murder, Do
shall not murder, You shall not	Do not bear false witness,	not steal, Do not bear false
commit adultery, You shall not	Do not defraud, Honor your	witness, Honor your father
steal, You shall not bear false	father and your mother.	and your mother.
witness, Honor your father and		
your mother, and You shall love		
your neighbor as yourself.		

What one immediately notices in these parallel accounts is the different order of the murder, adultery, and theft prohibitions found in the Lukan account versus the Matthew–Mark presentation. Furthermore, the additional 'Do not defraud' prohibition in Mark and the additional 'You shall love your neighbor as yourself' differentiates the Matthew tradition[25] from the Markan tradition on these commandments.

All three appear to be following a common Hebrew Bible source quotation of the Decalogue, with the fifth commandment (Exod. 20.12; Deut. 5.16) arranged after the ninth (Exod. 20.16; Deut. 5.20). Although the three Synoptic Gospel accounts are apparently linked by their overall arrangement of this section, they do appear to be (in their present state at least) independent of one another. The fact that Luke has the order as adultery, murder, theft, as opposed to the Matthew/Mark: murder, adultery, theft (as the MT/LXX of Deut. 5.17-19) raises the question again about the order of these commandments.

24. Manuscripts on Mark differ here. There seem to exist two manuscript traditions on this verse in Mark, one which follows the order of Matthew and the other which follows Luke. One manuscript has the most difficult: 'Do not commit adultery, Do not steal, Do not murder'.

25. The Matthew tradition on these three prohibitions does not always present them together; so Mt. 5.21-37 (murder, adultery, divorce, and swearing).

Luke's order does not agree with the order given in the LXX Exodus account (adultery, theft, murder) nor does it agree with the Matthew/ Mark (Deuteronomy MT/LXX) tradition.

In Rom. 13.9 Paul's order of the prohibitions agrees with the Lukan tradition in that it presents them as adultery, murder, theft. Unfortunately this order is not supported by other citations of these commandments in other Paul and Pauline literature (see n. 31 below), especially in Rom. 2.21-22, where a partial listing of the commandments gives theft and adultery (in that order). The Pauline and post-Pauline textual citations of the Decalogue do not seem to have referred directly to Matthew, Mark, Luke, or Paul for their references since 1 Tim. 1.9-11 and Jas 2.11 cite the order as murder, adultery, and theft and adultery and murder, respectively.[26]

The early Church Fathers continue the changing order question, sometimes apparently citing the Hebrew Bible order (Deuteronomy LXX) directly and other times citing one or another New Testament version which lists these commandments. The *Didache* (2.1-3), for example, lists the prohibitions in the following order:

1. Murder
2. Adultery
3. Pederasty
4. Fornication
5. Stealing
6. Magic
7. Witchcraft
8. Abortion
9. Coveting your neighbor's goods
10. Swearing
11. Bearing false witness
12. Speaking evil
13. Bearing a grudge.

Prohibitions 1, 2 and 5 (murder, adultery, theft—Mark/Matthew/MT order of Decalogue) are separated by #3 and 4: pederasty and fornication.[27] It should be pointed out that from the period of Paul and the

26. Jas 2.11 has a partial listing of these commandments but the order there is adultery and murder.

27. So too the *Constitutions of the Holy Apostles* 7.1.2 (apparently based on the

earliest Gospels onward these commandments in the New Testament and early Christian literature are complemented by other prohibitions and injunctions which are not found in any of the Hebrew Bible formulations.

Early Church Fathers[28] are divided. Clement of Alexandria has two versions. In his *Exhortation to the Heathen* he maintains a list which is partially consistent with the *Didache* text,[29] while in the *Stromata*,[30] he follows the Nash/Philo/Lukan reading. Tertullian[31] quotes inverted forms of the Mt. 19.17-20 version of the Decalogue which include the following order of commandments: (1) Love your neighbor as yourself; (2) You shall not murder; (3) You shall not commit adultery; (4) You shall not steal; (5) You shall not bear false witness; (6) Honor your father and your mother.

The use of the Matthew commandment order is not consistent in all early Church writers. One finds, for example, in Hippolytus's *The Refutation of All Heresies,* 5.15, the Lukan order of adultery, murder, and theft. The Latin and Greek versions of Origen's *De Principiis* 4.1.19 are split in their citation of Paul's teachings about these prohibitions, the Latin version quoting the Rom. 2.21-22 text (only quoting adultery and theft—in that order) and the Greek version quoting the Rom. 13.9 text which has murder, adultery, and theft. Four different orderings of these three prohibitions are the following:

Didache) lists murder, adultery, pederasty, fornication, and stealing (with additional commentary).

28. The confusion over the order and contents of the Ten Commandments continues into the fourth century with the Emperor Julian in his *Contra Galilaeos* citing another version of the commandments: '…That is a surprising law of Moses, I mean the famous decalogue: "Thou shalt not steal". "Thou shalt not kill". "Thou shalt not bear false witness…"' Cited from M. Stern, *Greek and Latin Authors on Jews and Judaism* (Jerusalem: The Israel Academy of Sciences and Humanities, 1980), II, pp. 519 and 535. Despite his obvious erudition in Christianity, Julian does not seem to know that these commandments appear in the New Testament.

29. Chapter 10: (1) Not to kill; (2) Not to commit adultery; (3) Not to commit pederasty; (4) Not to steal; (5) Not to bear false witness.

30. Book 6, chapter 16: Lists adultery, murder, and theft.

31. Tertullian, *An Answer to the Jews*, ch. 2; Also: *Against Marcion* 4.16 the order murder/adultery/ stealing is maintained. In these instances he is apparently either directly quoting the Matthew text or the Deuteronomy source since in *On Modesty*, ch. 5, he clearly lists them as adultery and murder! (See below.)

Exod. and Deut. MT	Exod. LXX^B	Rom.	Nash Papyrus, Philo
Matt.[32]–Mark	Origen (Latin)[33]	2.21-22[34]	Luke
Tertullian/*Didache* +			James,[35] Hippolytus,
additions,[36] 4QDeut.^{n}			Origen (Greek), Clement
Clement of Alexandria[37]			of Alexandria[38]
1 Tim. 1.8-11			Rom. 13.9
Josephus, Deut. LXX^A			Deuteronomy LXX^B
LXX^A Exodus			
1. Murder	1. Adultery	[1. Murder]	1. Adultery
2. Adultery	2. Theft	2. Theft	2. Murder
3. Theft	3. Murder	3. Adultery	3. Theft

The question is: How or why did these changes happen? The theories which I would like to put forward are the following.

First, it appears that the Hebrew may have preferred the descending alphabetical order of the three verb stems: (1) R(tz/h), (2) N(a/f), (3) G(n/b) and the LXX version of Deuteronomy maintains this same descending (Greek) alphabetical order of the verb stems: (1) Ph(oveo), (2) M(oicheo), (3) K(lepto). The Exodus LXX translator demonstrated elsewhere in the Exodus LXX translation that they were concerned with issues such as style and literary symmetry and consistency.[39] Although it is possible that there are linguistic reasons for the order, the order itself does also imply ethical prioritizing, if only for the reader. The fact that the LXX Exodus translator does not maintain the LXX Deuteronomy literary symmetry may indicate more concern with other criteria (ethical consistency between the commandments) rather than aesthetics in the formulation.

Secondly, it appears that in the minds of Philo and some of the early Christian writers the crime of adultery was connected with other sex

32. Partial agreement: Mt. 5.

33. Partial listing: adultery and theft.

34. Partial listing: theft and adultery.

35. Partial listing: adultery and murder. Many other partial citations could be given for Paul and Pauline literature which do not agree with the presented sequencing. So Rom. 1.29-31; Eph. 6.1-3; 1 Cor. 5-10, for example.

36. *Constitutions of the Holy Apostles.*

37. *Exhortation to the Heathen.*

38. *Stromata.*

39. This question was investigated in the chapter entitled: 'Biblical Ethics and Biblical Criticism: Why Not Both?', in my book *Understanding Jewish Ethics* (2 vols.; New York: Edwin Mellen Press, 1990), I, pp. 41-67.

offenses,[40] and reflects the view common in Roman law and society which made *adulterium iudicium domesticum*, or a crime affecting the entire family unit.[41] Additionally, adultery was connected in Jewish society with the crime of incest in some cases.[42] It is, therefore, perhaps understandable that it was placed directly after the fifth commandment (Exod. 20.12/Deut. 5.16) to 'Honor your father and your mother'.

The ordering of adultery and murder, respectively, is a connection which is made by both the Talmud[43] and the Church Fathers. Tertullian in his work *On Modesty* (ch. 5) clearly expresses the reasons for the linking of the two:

> That which results from the first is (in a sense) another first. And so adultery is bordering on idolatry. For idolatry, withal often cast as a reproach upon the people under the name of adultery and fornication, will be alike conjoined therewith in fate as in following—will be alike, co-heir therewith in condemnation as in coordination. Yet further: starting 'You shall not commit adultery' (the Law) continues, 'You shall not murder'. It honored adultery, of course, to which it gives the precedence over murder, in the very forefront of the most holy law, among the primary counts of the celestial edict, marking it with the inscription of the very principal sins. From its place you may discern the measure, from its rank the station, from its neighborhood the merit, of each thing. Even evil has a dignity, consisting in being stationed at the summit, or else in the centre, of the superlatively bad. I behold a certain pomp and circumstance of adultery: on the one side, Idolatry goes before and leads the way; on the other, Murder follows in company.

Thirdly, the reason for the Exodus LXX change may point to two different factors in the transmission history of the Decalogue and the LXX in particular. The order of these three prohibitions may be linked to the rather fluid nature of the Decalogue in the biblical and

---

40. Pederasty/fornication in *Didache/Constitutions* and in Philo, general sexual offenses prohibited in the New Testament, especially between forbidden family members. The inclusion of new offenses/prohibition/injunctions in the New Testament and early Christian literature versions of the 'Commandments' usually included sexual offenses.

41. Suetonius, *Caesars* (Tiberius), 35 (Augustus), 34. (Also: Cassius Dio, *Historia Romana* 54.30.4.)

42. *b. Sanh.* 50b-51a. This conclusion is supported and expanded in the chapter, 'Some Aspects of Jewish Sexual Ethics and Hellenism', in my *Understanding Jewish Ethics*, I, pp. 224-40.

43. *Sanh.* 74a.

perhaps the Hellenistic period. In the Hos. 4.2 and Jer. 7.9 citations, one finds that theft is listed as either first or second in their recitation of these prohibitions.

The influence of Hellenistic society, especially the sexual morality of the resident Greeks and Romans[44] may have led the LXX Exodus translator to manipulate an already fluid text according to the changing priorities of the readers; that is, placing adultery before theft. The LXX Exodus translator is especially sensitive to the ethical currents in the period as can be seen from the rather creative and ethically 'pregnant' reading of LXX Exod. 21.22-23[45] in comparison with the MT reading.[46] The LXX order (adultery/theft/murder) probably gave way to later homiletic concerns[47] (as is evident from the two different readings of Tertullian) which directly linked adultery and murder in both the mindset of the perpetrator and the severity of punishment, and relegated theft to an altogether different category.

Finally, it appears that the changes may represent an Alexandrian or non-Palestinian text tradition versus a Palestinian textual tradition, since the textual witnesses seem to break down into two major categories. Internally, the New Testament manuscripts of this section themselves show some disorder. This may also be attributed to different manuscript traditions in the New Testament text. The manuscripts of Mark are rather divided, probably resulting from later comparisons with Luke and the LXX tradition. One finds, for example, that instead of the Greek negating particle *ou* used in the LXX translations of Exodus and Deuteronomy, Mark and Luke use *mei* (not a direct reading of the LXX traditions of the Decalogue). Similarly, some of the oldest manuscripts of Mark maintain the Matthew tradition (murder/adultery/theft) but in other manuscripts have the Lukan order or a variant of adultery/murder/theft. The confusion is reflected in the works of modern biblical commentators who do not know how

44. On the increasing moral disintegration which gave rise to the *Lex Julia de Adulteriis* see: Dionysius of Halicarnassus, *Roman Antiquities* 2.25.

45. Additionally, Philo agrees with the LXX Exod. 20.13-15 and Exod. 21.22-23 readings, while Josephus does not, perhaps suggesting that the Palestinians and the Alexandrians had different textual traditions.

46. For a more complete analysis of this question, see the chapter entitled, 'The Ethics of Abortion in Hellenistic Judaism', in my *Understanding Jewish Ethics*, I, pp. 241-54.

47. Also in Philo, *Spec. Leg.* 3.2.

to describe the differing commandment lists in the New Testament.[48] The Syriac Peshitta tradition of Mark has a variation of the LXX Exodus tradition of adultery/theft/murder to further complicate matters.

The important change in the LXX traditions is the moving of adultery from the seventh commandment to the sixth commandment. The linking of the fifth commandment's content (familial responsibilities) with the prohibition of adultery (familial responsibility) seems to be the reason. Philo clearly establishes this as the raison d'être for this order. The LXX Exodus text, however, has a different order than both the LXX Deuteronomy and other textual witnesses of the LXX tradition. It appears that just as the LXX Exodus tradition presents a different ethical message by juxtaposing 'honoring parents' and 'adultery' rather than the MT sequence of 'honoring parents' and 'murder', so too the juxtaposition of the prohibitions of 'adultery' and 'stealing' in the LXX Exodus presents a different ethical consideration than the sequence of 'adultery' and 'murder' as found in the LXX Deuteronomy (or murder/adultery as in the MT).

The LXX Exodus may have been trying to make the point that adultery and stealing are ethically connected. The type of stealing being indicated by commandment #7 is not necessarily property or objects but rather people, especially someone else's wife. This would fit contextually with the #8 prohibition (murder) by continuing the theme of person-to-person crimes. My research in the LXX translation[49] has revealed that the translation is often more concerned with the aesthetic and conceptual positioning and sequencing of items than preserving a traditional reading. The New Testament order changes may suggest that the MT and LXX textual differences combined with important changing hermeneutical considerations in the individual texts may have given rise to differing orders and understandings of the Decalogue.

---

48. So, for example, J. Fitzmeyer in his commentary and notes to *The Gospel According to Luke* (AB, 28A), p. 1199, to Lk. 18.19-20 states: 'What is responsible for this divergence of order is not easy to say'.

49. In my book, *Understanding Jewish Ethics*, I, I provide ample exemplification of this phenomenon throughout the different chapters.

The Changing Ethical Status of Women as Reflected
in the Decalogue

In the continuation of the Decalogue (MT Exod. 20.14/LXX 20.17//MT Deut. 5.18/LXX 5.21) one again finds differences between the LXX order and the MT order for the tenth commandment. The MT Exodus states:

> You shall not covet your neighbor's house. You shall not covet your neighbor's wife, nor man-servant, nor his maid-servant, nor his ox, nor his ass, nor anything that is your neighbor's.

The LXX Exodus and Deuteronomy agree here:

> You shall not covet your neighbor's wife. You shall not covet your neighbor's house, nor his field, nor his man-servant, nor his maid-servant, nor his ox, nor his ass, nor his cattle, nor anything that is your neighbor's.

The wife/house order plus the added details all figure in the LXX Exodus and Deuteronomy accounts. Paul in Rom. 13.9-10 lists the Ten Commandments with changes and agrees with the LXX order of the wife/property and the MT Deuteronomy order without the details of property.

The MT Deuteronomy has the following:

> ...you shall not covet your neighbor's wife, neither shall you desire your neighbor's house, nor his field, nor his man-servant, nor his maid-servant, nor his ox, nor his ass, nor anything that is your neighbor's.

The MT Deuteronomy version is close to the LXX versions but lacks the additional 'cattle' and there is no recognition of a verb change in the Greek. The LXX Exodus text agrees with the LXX Deuteronomy and the MT Deuteronomy on one crucial point of sequencing which again presents a clear ethical consideration which is different than the MT Exodus. In the MT Exodus a wife is apparently considered part of a person's house as the prohibition sequence is '...not to covet a neighbor's house/wife'. In the LXX Exodus it appears that the translation availed itself of the Deuteronomy reading which creates a different ethical consideration (and perhaps even a different commandment).

In the Decalogue according to Roman Catholic tradition, derived from Augustine and followed by some Lutherans, for example, '...coveting one's neighbor's wife' is the ninth commandment and

'...coveting one's neighbor's house' is the tenth commandment.[50] This reading again demonstrates that internal literary consistency in the LXX is something quite important to the translator(s) of Exodus and Deuteronomy. More important, this section may represent an evolving ethical view of women in the ancient world. The view which included women as part of the husband's property expressed by Exodus was not expressed by Deuteronomy. This view moved from a reading which held that women were possessions of the husband/father to one which saw women as autonomous and not part of the property of the husband/father. The LXX translator brought Exodus into line with Deuteronomy's reading. This changing ethical view of women is supported by other studies of women in the ancient period.[51] More important, these different readings and changes may tell us about the changing status of women in P's, D's, and the LXX translator(s)'s societies.

Conclusions

The Decalogue is a simple, pithy way to refer to apodictic commands from an all-powerful and personal deity. In this way it is similar to other ancient Near Eastern law codes. The second person formulation does imply a closer relationship between the speaker and the reader than do the standard third person presentations found in many such listings. This formulation style may have contributed to the impression by authors of the various collections of Ten Commandments that the message was more than the sum of the individual parts. Specifically, the Decalogue may have been seen as a vehicle for the expression of relevant and immediate ethical, societal, or religious concerns. The large number of variations present in the Decalogue citations may indicate that the different authors/redactors did not view the manipulation or addition of one or more commandments or new meanings as violating the overall integrity of the text. Rather, the continuing patterns of variation may indicate an attitude towards the use of moral lists of this sort in the ancient world. The citations of differing orders and commandments by key Hebrew Bible and New

50. C.M. Laymon (ed.), *Interpreter's One-Volume Commentary on the Bible* (London: William Collins, 1972), p. 53.

51. S. Pomeroy, *Goddesses, Whores, Wives and Slaves* (New York: Schocken Press, 1976), pp. 57-60, 150-61, 227-30.

Testament figures such as Jeremiah, Jesus, and Paul and the later 'expanded' Church lists of commandments may imply that they saw the Sinaitic revelation as something more than a one-time appearance and declaration. Certainly the additions of D to P's Decalogue[52] includes considerations not in the Exodus Decalogue. And the P and D reformulation of earlier J and E materials implies literary and theological concerns for the form and content of the commandments. The latest interpretative layering by Jewish and Christian Medieval Bible Commentators may imply that they were following an ancient example of viewing the Decalogue as a general vehicle for an ongoing revelation of moral concerns rather than a fixed formulation of a single event at a single place.

52. According to Friedman, *Who Wrote the Bible?*, p. 210, and others, P is to be dated before D.

A RETELLING OF THE SONG AT THE SEA IN WISDOM 10.20-21*

Peter Enns

In Wisdom 10–19, Pseudo-Solomon rehearses the major events in Israel's past and reflects on the significance of that past for his readers. After recounting the deeds of Adam, Cain, Noah, Abraham, Lot, Jacob, and Joseph (10.1-14), he focuses his attention in the remaining chapters on the exodus from Egypt and the wilderness wanderings. He begins his discussion of the exodus with a succinct overview of Israel's Egypt experience in general (10.15-21), where he mentions, among other things, the plagues and the departure from Egypt. This passage concludes in vv. 20b-21 with the writer's comments on the Song at the Sea (Exodus 15), and reads as follows:

> καὶ ὕμνησαν, κύριε, τὸ ὄνομα τὸ ἅγιόν σου
> τήν τε ὑπέρμαχόν σου χεῖρα ᾔνεσαν <u>ὁμοθυμαδόν</u>·
> ὅτι ἡ σοφία ἤνοιξεν στόμα <u>κωφῶν</u>
> καὶ γλώσσας <u>νηπίων</u> ἔθηκεν τρανάς[1]

> They sang, O Lord, to your holy name.
> They praised *with one accord* your champion might,
> for Wisdom opened the mouth of the *dumb*
> and made the tongues of *babes* clear.

A reading of this passage leads one to make two rather obvious but important observations: (1) Pseudo-Solomon is in fact talking about

* A portion of this article was delivered at the Society of Biblical Literature annual meeting in Washington, DC on 22 November 1993. I am thankful to James A. Sanders for his kind and insightful comments. This article also represents a small portion of my doctoral dissertation completed under the direction of James L. Kugel and published as *Exodus Retold: Ancient Exegesis of the Departure from Egypt in Wis 10.15-21 and 19.1-9* (HSM, 57; Atlanta: Scholars Press, 1997), and has been previously published in *Bib* 76 (1995), pp. 1-24.

1. The Greek text is according to J. Ziegler's critical edition (*Sapientia Salomonis* [Septuaginta: Vetus Testamentum Graecum, 12.1; Göttingen: Vandenhoeck & Ruprecht, 1980]).

the Song at the Sea,[2] (2) what he says about the Song at the Sea does more than simply repeat the biblical text. Over these two points there is unanimous agreement, but differences in opinion arise over why the author treats the Song at the Sea the way he does.

Although answers to this question have not been entirely neglected in previous scholarship, most commentators have assigned to the exegetical aspect of the book a secondary role. Even those who have dealt in substantive fashion with Pseudo-Solomon's understanding of the biblical texts have tended to view him as an interpreter working in isolation; they imply that what he says about the Bible is, for better or for worse, largely his own creation.[3] As such, curious comments such

---

2.   Throughout Wis. 10.15-21, Pseudo-Solomon appears to maintain a strict adherence to the chronology of the Exodus narrative:

Wisdom 10	Exodus
16b	7.14–12.30 (plagues)
17a	12.31-36 (plundering the Egyptians)
17b-d	13.17-22 (way to the sea)
18-20a	14.1-31 (crossing the sea)
20b-21	15.1-21 (Song at the Sea).

3.   The most recent example of such an approach is Udo Schwenk-Bressler, *Sapientia Salomonis als ein Beispiel frühjüdischer Textauslegung: Die Auslegung des Buches Genesis, Exodus 1–15 und Teilen der Wüstentradition in Sap 10–19* (Beiträge zur Erforschung des Alten Testaments und des antiken Judentums, 32; Frankfurt am Main: Peter Lang, 1993). Despite what the title of this work might suggest, there is little to no substantive overlap with the method of this study. Schwenk-Bressler's monograph (a reworking of his 1991 Munich dissertation) is a comprehensive treatment of Pseudo-Solomon's interpretation of the biblical texts, but there is virtually no interaction with interpretive traditions to which Pseudo-Solomon might have had access. For Schwenk-Bressler, Pseudo-Solomon's comments on the exodus reflect his conscious adaptation (*Rückgriff*) of *biblical* themes and passages, rather than his adaptation, probably unconscious, of exegetical traditions current in his day. In other words, Pseudo-Solomon's 'shorthand' allusions (*Anspielungen*) are to specific biblical texts, and not to current interpretive traditions as I am arguing. Among the more prominent commentaries, four earlier works stand out in their detailed and substantive handling of the Book of Wisdom. These are the commentaries by C.L.W. Grimm, *Kurtzgefasstes exegetisches Handbuch zu den Apokryphen des Alten Testaments* (Sechste Lieferung; Leipzig: S. Hirzel, 1860); W. Deane, *The Book of Wisdom* (Oxford: Clarendon Press, 1881); P. Heinisch, *Das Buch der Weisheit* (EHAT, 24; Münster: Aschendorffsche Verlagsbuchhandlung, 1912); and A.T.S. Goodrick, *The Book of Wisdom* (New York: Macmillan, 1913). These works continue to be valuable sources of information, particularly concerning issues of translation, textual criticism, interaction with the

as those in 10.20-21 are often understood as mere flourishes or products of creative fancy. It is not to be questioned that these works are
representative of the rich reflection on the Wisdom of Solomon over
the years and are foundational to any further contribution. Nevertheless, the broader issues of Pseudo-Solomon's interpretation of Scripture, and more specifically the interpretive traditions to which he
certainly had access, are routinely either lacking in these commentaries or treated all too briefly.

Two recent commentaries stand out against this background: those
by C. Larcher[4] and David Winston.[5] Both of these works are important for this study, since, in addition to dealing thoroughly with the
issues that have occupied previous commentaries, they also draw
attention throughout to early Jewish interpretive traditions that parallel the Wisdom of Solomon. Winston's work is especially valuable in
that he seeks out parallels not only with early Jewish sources but with
Hellenistic philosophy as well, both of which are immediately relevant
for understanding the Wisdom of Solomon. Winston draws upon his
breadth of learning, and successfully and admirably locates the
Wisdom of Solomon in its literary and cultural milieu. Yet even these
two commentaries, it seems to me, have not gone far enough in discussing Pseudo-Solomon's interpretation of the Bible. Part of this has
to do with the limited space that can be allotted to any one verse in a
commentary on the whole of the Wisdom of Solomon. But beyond the
matter of available space lies what I take to be a difference in perspective between my study and even these two recent commentaries,
and it is perhaps wise to state this difference plainly at the outset.

history of scholarship at the time, and occasional reference to other sources of
antiquity that parallel the Wisdom of Solomon at a given point. J.A.F. Gregg (*The
Wisdom of Solomon* [Cambridge: Cambridge University Press, 1909]) mentions
'Palestinian *Midrashim*, or Commentaries' as a source for some of Pseudo-
Solomon's comments (pp. xiii, 95), but does not develop this to any significant
degree. J. Reider (*The Book of Wisdom* [New York: Harper & Row, 1957]) is one
of the few who occasionally makes a point to mention parallels to rabbinic exegetical
traditions, but his commentary offers nothing approaching a systematic handling of
this phenomenon.

   4.   C. Larcher, *Le livre de la sagesse ou la sagesse de Salomon* (3 vols.; Paris:
Librairie LeCoffre, 1983).

   5.   David Winstone, *The Wisdom of Solomon* (AB, 43; New York: Doubleday,
1979).

I believe that at the time that the Wisdom of Solomon was written,[6] there already existed an extensive and well-developed set of exegetical traditions concerning the Pentateuch in particular. Fragments and reflections of this exegetical corpus can be seen in still earlier Jewish works, particularly 'retellings' or condensations of biblical narratives found in such books as Judith, Ben Sira, *Jubilees, Biblical Antiquities* and others, while other parts of these interpretive traditions only surface fully in later rabbinic works. I believe that Pseudo-Solomon, although he was most probably a resident of the Greek city of Alexandria in Egypt,[7] was thoroughly versed in these ancient traditions (even to a greater extent than his apparent contemporary and neighbor, Philo), and it is they that provide the proper backdrop for understanding Pseudo-Solomon's exposition of Scripture. Furthermore, I have concluded with respect to 10.20-21 that these exegetical traditions are ultimately motivated by peculiarities in the biblical texts themselves, that is, by problems that bothered early interpreters in general and led them to offer 'explanations'.

What follows is an examination of Pseudo-Solomon's comments on the Song at the Sea in an attempt to document parallels to the Wisdom of Solomon in other sources, earlier and later, as well as to unfold the exegetical thinking that underlies what Pseudo-Solomon has to say. In doing so I hope to shift the discussion somewhat from Pseudo-Solomon's actual words to the interpretive traditions underlying them and the exegetical process that these traditions represent.

6.   Of all the opinions concerning the date of composition, Winston's is the most convincing (*Wisdom*, pp. 20-25; see also Goodrick, *Wisdom*, pp. 5-17). He dates the book to the first half of the first century CE, more specifically to the reign of Gaius 'Caligula' (37–41 CE), on the basis of (1) Pseudo-Solomon's extensive use of certain words and usages that do not appear in secular Greek literature before the first century, and (2) the 'desperate historical situation' that must have prompted Pseudo-Solomon's call to faith and his condemnation of the wicked (pp. 20-25). The date of composition, however, tells us very little concerning the antiquity of the exegetical traditions contained therein. Therefore, since the focus here is the interpretive traditions found in the Wisdom of Solomon, deciding on an absolute date is not a major concern. A summary of the arguments on the date of composition may be found in Betty Jean Lillie, 'A History of the Scholarship on the Wisdom of Solomon from the Nineteenth Century to Our Time' (PhD dissertation, Hebrew Union College, 1982), pp. 149-79.

7.   Pseudo-Solomon's home is routinely considered to be Alexandria, since his writing is 'steeped' in Middle Platonism, which was 'influential at that time in Alexandria' (Winston, *Wisdom*, p. 3; see also pp. 25-63).

The Israelites Sang 'With One Accord' at the Sea (10.20c)

At first glance, 10.20c as a whole does not appear to be of particular exegetical interest: *They praised with one accord your champion might*. The Song at the Sea was indeed a song of praise for God's deliverance, but 'with one accord' (ὁμοθυμαδόν) raises some suspicion. It seems like an insignificant flourish, but this is precisely the point. Since this is not explicit in the biblical text, and since it does not add to the discussion, one wonders why Pseudo-Solomon would bother to say it. The reason is that ὁμοθυμαδόν solves a particular 'problem' reflected in the MT, and the manner in which this problem is solved finds ample parallels elsewhere.

Exodus 15.1 introduces the Song at the Sea and begins, אז ישיר־משה ובני ישראל, 'Then Moses and the Israelites sang'. The subject is plural but the verb is singular (ישיר). This could have led early interpreters to envision the plural subject as somehow 'one' to correspond to the singular verb, and hence inspire a comment like 'they sang with one accord'. Taken in isolation, however, this is not a strong argument, since lack of subject–verb agreement is not uncommon in the Hebrew Bible, and it could rightly be questioned whether such a common occurrence would have motivated an 'explanation' by early interpreters.[8] But there is another grammatical problem more difficult to circumvent. The verse continues, ויאמרו לאמר, '*They* said (saying)'. This clause introduces the Song at the Sea, which is a song to be sung by 'Moses and the Israelites'. And, as expected, the verb is plural: ויאמרו. But what did *they* say? The song itself begins with a singular verb: '*I* will sing to YHWH' (אשירה ליהוה). The use of the singular verb אשירה with an implied plural subject would have presented a wonderful opportunity for early interpreters to offer some explanation. This, in addition to the juxtaposition of the singular ישיר to the plural subject משה ובני ישראל, poses an exegetical problem, and Pseudo-Solomon's '*they* sang with *one* accord' appears to be a documented witness to one manner of handling this difficulty.

It is perhaps worth emphasizing here that our concern should be what early interpreters might have found problematic in the biblical

---

8.   See, for example, Exod. 10.3, which closely parallels 15.1: 'Moses and Aaron came (ויבא) to Pharaoh and said (ויאמרו)...'. This type of incongruence is quite common.

text. The use of the singular 'I will sing' is hardly a problem for modern conventions (for example, hymns in the singular sung collectively), nor is it a problem within the Hebrew Bible itself (for example, the collective 'I' used in the psalms).[9] This should not, however, obstruct our view to the world of early biblical interpretation. The grammatical 'problem' discussed here, as we will see below, is just one example of similar grammatical phenomena that inspired explanations by early interpreters. It should also be mentioned that ancient interpreters offering an explanation for the singular verb in no way implies that the collective use of singulars was somehow strange to them. The point rather is that such a phenomenon afforded these interpreters an opportunity to engage the text.

Before proceeding to a discussion of some parallels in rabbinic sources to Pseudo-Solomon's comment, it is first worth considering 'with one accord' in light of the LXX and Targums. Both the singular יָשִׁיר and the plural יֹאמְרוּ are reflected in the LXX and targumic traditions. The singular אָשִׁירָה, however, is *plural* in the LXX and Targums.

Hebrew	LXX	Targ. Onq.	Tg. Ps.-J.
יָשִׁיר	ᾖσεν	שבח	שבח
יֹאמְרוּ	εἶπαν	אמרו	אמרין
אָשִׁירָה	αἴσωμεν	נשבח[10]	נשבחא[11]

At least one tentative conclusion to be drawn from these data is that the singular יָשִׁיר apparently did not pose a particular exegetical problem for the translators of the LXX or Targums, since they read the singular as well. Hence, יָשִׁיר, if it did play a role in Pseudo-Solomon's

---

9. See especially B. Childs, who sees the singular in Exod. 15.1 as a stylistic feature similar to the psalms (*The Book of Exodus* [Philadelphia: Westminster Press, 1974], pp. 249-50). Other modern explanations are offered by N. Sarna, who says that the singular verb אָשִׁירָה can only refer to Moses, but he does not attempt to reconcile this to יֹאמְרוּ (*Exodus* [Philadelphia: Jewish Publication Society of America, 1991], p. 77). Likewise, M. Noth calls the song at the sea a '"solo hymn" with a single speaker in the first person...', although this does not account for the plural elements (*Exodus: A Commentary* [Philadelphia: Westminster Press, 1962], p. 123). J. Hyatt says that the reference is to 'Moses, or the person taking Moses' role in the cult, or the personified community' (*Commentary on Exodus* [London: Oliphants, 1971], p. 164).

10. *Targ. Onq.* has a second verb נוֹדֵי, 'we will give thanks'.

11. Like *Targ. Onq.*, *Targ. Ps.-J.* has a second verb (נוֹדֵה) but in reverse order. *Targ. Neof.* and *Frag. Targ.* also have the plural.

interpretation 'with one accord', the evidence from the LXX and Targums suggests that role is arguably a secondary one. This is also suggested by the fact that יָשִׁיר receives some attention in rabbinic sources, but the problem most often discussed is not the number of the verb but the tense, past or future, especially as it is affected by אָז.[12] Yet the possibility that יָשִׁיר contributed to Pseudo-Solomon's exegesis should not be dismissed too quickly. There are some rabbinic texts that seem to support the notion that this singular provided at least part of the motivation for 'with one accord'. *Mekilta Shirata* 1.11-12 comments on Exod. 15.1 ('Moses and the Israelites') and says, 'Moses was considered equal to Israel [שָׁקוּל כְּיִשְׂרָאֵל]'[13] and Israel was considered equal to Moses [שְׁקוּלִין כְּמֹשֶׁה] when uttering the song'. It does not seem that the mere fact that Moses and the Israelites are mentioned side by side would be a sufficient motive for the *Mekilta*'s comment.[14] Rather, it is that 'Moses and the Israelites' are the subject of a singular verb. This same tradition is seen in the timeless anecdote found in *Cant. R.* 4.2.

> Rabbi was once expounding the Scripture and the congregation became drowsy. He wanted to rouse them so he said: 'One woman in Egypt brought forth six hundred thousand at one birth'. There was a certain disciple present named R. Ishmael son of R. Jose, who said to him: 'Who can that have been?' He replied: 'Jochebed who bore Moses, who was considered the equal of six hundred thousand [שֶׁשְּׁקוּל כְּנֶגֶד שִׁשִּׁים רִבּוֹא], the number of all Israel, as it says, "Then sang Moses and the children of Israel"' (Exod. 15.1).

Another tentative conclusion may be drawn from the data of the Targums and LXX; since the MT alone reads the singular אָשִׁירָה 'I will sing', this suggests that our author might in this case have been familiar with an exegetical tradition based specifically on a Hebrew textual tradition.[15] The difficulty with this conclusion, however, is that there

---

12. See *Exod. R.* 23.1-4 and *Mek. Shir.* 1.1-10. This tradition is not reflected in Wis. 10.20c.

13. See J. Goldin's translation 'on par with' (*The Song at the Sea* [New Haven: Yale University Press, 1971], p. 67). H.S. Horowitz and I.A. Rabin have מֹשֶׁה שָׁקוּל כְּנֶגֶד כָּל יִשְׂרָאֵל (*Mechilta D'Rabbi Ishmael* [Jerusalem: Bamberger & Wahrman, 1960], p. 116).

14. Larcher attributes 'with one accord' to this juxtaposition of 'Moses and the Israelites' in Exod. 15.1. He cites the choral tradition to substantiate his comment (*Sagesse*, 2.646-47) as does Reider (*Wisdom*, p. 139). See below and n. 17.

15. Pierre Grelot mentions this possibility as well, albeit in passing ('Sagesse 10,21 et le Targum de l'Exode', *Bib* 42 [1961], pp. 49-60 [49]).

is no Hebrew exegetical tradition that clearly treats the אשירה problem of 15.1 the same way. The typical (and ubiquitous) explanation in rabbinic literature is that the song was antiphonal: Moses sang first (hence the use of the first person in 15.1) and the Israelites responded by repeating the same words.[16] Some commentators see a reflex of this tradition in Pseudo-Solomon's ὁμοθυμαδόν. Despite the ubiquity of this tradition, however, it is very unlikely that ὁμοθυμαδόν refers to alternating choruses. Throughout the LXX, ὁμοθυμαδόν is used in the sense of simultaneous activity, not two parties (in this case choirs) alternating their activity.[17] Rather, Pseudo-Solomon's use of ὁμοθυμαδόν seems to be a clear statement to the contrary: they all sang at the same time. Hence, Pseudo-Solomon's 'with one accord' seems to be specifically aimed at solving the אשירה problem, but in a way not paralleled elsewhere in either earlier or later sources. Was it therefore Pseudo-Solomon's invention? This is far more difficult to determine, but I am inclined to conclude that 'with one accord' is the lone extant witness to an ancient tradition, particularly since the *manner* in which the singular is explained in 10.20c is found elsewhere to explain similar difficulties in biblical texts.

Examples of such an approach are legion. One example is *Mek. Besh.* 3.22-25, which comments on Exod. 14.10. The biblical text

16. Goldin mentions that the doubling of the verb (ויאמרו לאמר אמר) 'suggests to the sages that some kind of responsive...recitation took place when the Shirah was recited' (*The Song at the Sea*, p. 77). For other ways in which לאמר is handled, see James L. Kugel, *In Potiphar's House: The Interpretive Life of Biblical Texts* (San Francisco: HarperCollins, 1990), pp. 47-48. The tradition of alternating choirs is found in *Mek. Shir.* 1.87-99; *b. Soṭ.* 27b, 30b; *m. Soṭ.* 5.4; *Exod. R.* 23.9; *Memar Marqah* 2.7; *Vit. Mos.* 1.180 (cf. L. Ginzberg, *Legends of the Jews* [7 vols.; trans. H. Szold; Philadelphia: Jewish Publication Society of America, 15th edn, 1988], III, p. 34, VI, p. 12 n. 63). See also Larcher, *Sagesse,* 2.646; Reider, *Wisdom*, p. 139; Sarna, *Exodus*, p. 76; Goldin, *Song at the Sea*, pp. 77-79. Israel repeating the *singular*, however, still leaves us with the problem. According to *Memar Marqah* 2.7 (John MacDonald, *Memar Marqah: The Teaching of Marqah* [BZAW, 84; Berlin: Alfred Töpelmann, 1963]), Moses and the Israelites alternated the verses of the song. An overview of the different types of antiphony attributed to Moses and the Israelites here may be found in James L. Kugel, *The Idea of Biblical Poetry: Parallelism and its History* (New Haven: Yale University Press, 1981), pp. 116-19.

17. See Exod. 19.8; Job 2.11; 16.11; Jer. 5.5; Jdt. 4.1-2; 7.29; 13.17; 15.2, 5, 9. See also Acts 15.25. Also worth mentioning are three passages in Pseudo-Philo's *Biblical Antiquities* that describe other songs as sung in unison: Joshua's song in 21.9, Deborah's song in 32.1, and perhaps Hannah's song in 51.7.

reads, וְהִנֵּה מִצְרִים נֹסֵעַ אַחֲרֵיהֶם, 'The Egyptians were marching after them'. The *Mekilta* comments:

> It is not really written 'were marching' [נֹסְעִים] but 'was marching' [נֹסֵעַ]. This means that the Egyptians all formed squadrons, each marching like one man.[18]

The unexpected singular is explained in a manner analogous to what we find in Wis. 10.20c. Another relevant midrash is a comment on Gen. 49.6 found in *Gen. R.* 99.7. Gen. 49.6 reads 'For in their anger they slew a man [אִישׁ]'.[19] 'They' refers to Levi and Simeon. The 'man' they slew refers to the Shechemites who violated Dinah. The reference to the Shechemites as 'a man' is explained in *Gen. R.* 99.7 as follows:

> Did they then slay but one man? But it says, *And they slew every male* (Gen. 34.25)? But were not all of them as one man [כְאִישׁ אֶחָד] before the Holy One, blessed be He? Thus it says, *Behold* [הֵן], *the nations are but as a drop of a bucket* (Isa. 40.15). Now what does 'hen' mean? It is Greek, meaning one. Thus it says, *And you shall smite the Midianites as one man* (Judg. 6.16). Similarly, *The horse and his rider* [סוּס וְרֹכְבוֹ] *he has thrown into the sea* (Exod. 15.1), as though they were but one horse and his rider [כְּסוּס אֶחָד וְרוֹכְבוֹ].

Saying 'as one', or something similar, is a common rabbinic explanation of a singular form where the context demands a plural.[20] It is not

18. The verbal forms are participles. An alternative explanation is found in *Exod. R.* 21.5: the singular verb means that *Mizraim* refers not to the nation, but to Egypt's guardian angel. *Exod. R.* 21.5 extends this to include another part of Exod. 15.1 that exhibits a similar singular/plural problem: '*horse and rider* he has cast into the sea'. The singular there means that the horse and rider refer to Egypt's guardian angel. The same midrash is also found in *Exod. R.* 23.15 and *Deut. R.* 1.22.

19. See also James L. Kugel, 'The Story of Dinah in the *Testament of Levi*', *HTR* 85 (1992), pp. 1-34 (12-15). Kugel argues that the curious singular in Gen. 49.6 is also responsible for the tradition represented in *T. Levi* 6.4-5, that Levi and Simeon were each responsible for killing one man each (Simeon killed Hamor and Levi killed Shechem), and, presumably, the rest of the male populace was killed by the other brothers. Kugel cites Eusebius, *Praep. Evang.* 9.22.10-12 as evidence for this tradition.

20. Examples could be multiplied. A final example offered here concerns the dispute over Exod. 8.2 (And the frog came up [וַתַּעַל הַצְּפַרְדֵּעַ] and covered [וַתְּכַס] the land of Egypt) recorded in *b. Sanh.* 67b: R. Eleazar said: One frog (צְפַרְדֵּעַ אַחַת) bred (הִשְׁרִיצָה) and filled (מָלְאָה) the land. This is a matter disputed by Tannaim. R. Akiba said: There was one frog and it filled (מָלְאָה) all the land of Egypt. But R. Eleazar b. Azariah said to him, 'Akiba, what do you have to do with *Haggadah*? Stop your

overreaching to suggest that Pseudo-Solomon's ὁμοθυμαδὸν is evidence of a similar exegetical maneuver.

What increases this possibility is Pseudo-Solomon's own use of ὁμοθυμαδὸν in Wis. 18.5. Commenting on the Egyptians drowning in the sea he says,

> You destroyed them *with one accord* [ὁμοθυμαδὸν] in violent waters [ὕδατι σφοδρῷ].

Pseudo-Solomon says 'with one accord' here for the same reason he says it in 10.20c, to account for a singular where there ought to be a plural. The problem in the biblical text is Exod. 15.1, the same one addressed in *Gen. R.* 99.7 quoted above: 'horse and his rider (סוס ורכבו) you have cast into the sea'. Was there only one horse and one rider? No, but for Pseudo-Solomon, consistent with the analogous problem in 10.20c, the singular indicates that God threw them into the sea 'as one'. The same notion is found in *Mek. Shir.* 2.95-102: 'When the Israelites do the will of the Lord, their enemies are before them as but one horse and his rider'. All of this shows that, irrespective of the fact that an identical explanation for אשירה is not readily apparent, the clear presence of the same type of explanation elsewhere, in rabbinic literature as well as in Wis. 18.5, makes it very likely that Pseudo-Solomon is employing this explanation in dealing with אשירה. 'With one accord' is not merely a flourish, but evidence of an exegetical tradition that grappled with the biblical data.[21]

---

talking and devote your self to "Leprosies" and "Tents". One frog croaked for the others, and they came"'. An early witness to this 'one frog' tradition is a fragment of Artapanus' work (Eusebius, *Praep. Evang.* 9.27.32; see J. Charlesworth [ed.], *The Old Testament Pseudepigrapha* [Garden City, NY: Doubleday, 1983], II, p. 902; the date given is from 250 to 200 BCE [2.890]). See also J. Weingreen, *From Bible to Mishna: The Continuity of Tradition* (Manchester: Manchester University Press, 1976), p. 20.

21. Not only is 'horse and his rider' of Exod. 15.1 relevant to this discussion, but Exod. 14.25 as well. In the context of the Egyptians' retreat at the sea we read...ויאמר מצרים אנוסה. Another biblical passage that may have helped inspire this exegetical tradition in Isa. 43.17: המוציא רכב־וסוס חיל ועזוז יחדו. These same factors may have motivated the comment by Philo, that the Egyptians were destroyed 'one and all' (*Vit. Mos.* 1.180). The only other use of ὁμοθυμαδὸν in the book is 18.12, where our author comments on the fact that in the plague of death, the Egyptians died 'with one accord, all by one form of death' (ὁμοθυμαδὸν δὲ πάντες ἐν ἑνὶ ὀνόματι θανάτου). The relevant biblical passage may be Exod. 11.5: *every* first-born throughout *all* of Egypt, whether rich or poor, will die.

2. The 'Dumb' Sang at the Sea (10.21a)

That the dumb (κωφῶν) are said to sing at the sea is a most curious statement and, as far as I can see, Pseudo-Solomon is alone in making such a remark. He seems to be saying that those who sang the Song at the Sea were enabled to do so; the singers were previously 'dumb' before Wisdom intervened and made it possible for them to sing. The biblical motive for this statement is most often considered to be Moses' speech difficulty in Exod. 4.10 (כבד־פה וכבד לשׁון, ἰσχνόφωνος καὶ βραδύγλωσσος) and 6.12, 30 (ערל שׁפתים, ἄλογος).[22] Moses complains that he is not eloquent enough for the task God has given him: to confront the king of Egypt. In response, God arranges for Aaron to be Moses' 'prophet' to do the speaking for him (7.1, see also 4.16).

But there are seemingly insurmountable difficulties in adducing this episode as an explanation for Pseudo-Solomon's comment. First, and most important, Moses' speech problem in Exodus was overcome so that he and Aaron could confront Pharaoh by means of the plagues and ask for the release of the Israelites, not so that he could sing praise to YHWH at the sea. The entire episode of Moses' speech difficulty is really irrelevant. It is unclear in what specific sense Moses' mouth could be said to be opened (ἀνοίγω) at the sea in a way that it had not already been opened when he began talking to Pharaoh. Second, even assuming that this episode is relevant, Exodus still does not say that Moses was 'dumb'. He merely had some difficulty speaking (whatever that difficulty was). Third, 'dumb' is plural (κωφῶν), hence, Pseudo-Solomon is likely speaking of more than one person. Although it would be possible in the abstract to understand the plural as an example of an 'allusive plural',[23] the problem would still

22. This explanation is adopted in varying degrees by Winston, *Wisdom*, p. 222; Reider, *Wisdom*, p. 139; Larcher, *Sagesse*, II, p. 647; Deane, *Wisdom*, p. 168; J. Geyer, *The Wisdom of Solomon* (London: SCM Press, 1963), p. 100.

23. Winston defines the allusive plural as a plural 'by which one person is alluded to in the plural number' (*Wisdom*, p. 219). Pseudo-Solomon's use of the plural where a singular is clearly intended occurs in various places throughout the book. I argue elsewhere that, despite the presence of this phenomenon in the book as well as in Greek literature (see also P. Skehan, *Studies in Israelite Poetry and Wisdom* [CBQMS, 1; Washington, DC: Catholic Biblical Association, 1971], pp. 132-36), not all of Pseudo-Solomon's unexpected plurals should be automatically understood as a function of grammar (Enns, *Exodus Retold*, pp. 46-52).

remain: who would this one person be whose mouth was opened at the sea? Furthermore, the plural is a problem only if we assume that the referent is Moses and his speech difficulty, but, again, the context of this comment is the Song at the Sea.

Seeing these difficulties, some commentators have offered other solutions. One such attempt is to maintain the connection to Exodus 4 and 6, but to extend the reference to include the Israelites along with Moses, thus accounting for the plural κωφῶν. Reider, for example, says that κωφῶν 'clearly' refers to Moses and Exod. 4.10, 'though the plural includes others besides Moses'.[24] Goodrick, following F.W. Farrar,[25] says that Exod. 4.10 is 'ideally extended to all Israelites'.[26] But these approaches do not bring us any closer to solving the problem: (1) again, it is unclear why one would appeal to an incident in the early portion of the exodus narrative to explain Pseudo-Solomon's comment on the Song at the Sea; (2) although this accounts for the plural, we still have the same problem as above: Moses is not 'dumb' in Exodus 4 or 6; (3) if anything, this problem is not solved but compounded when including all Israel, for just as Exodus does not say that Moses was dumb, it certainly does not say that the Israelites suffered the same disability. It is still necessary to show in what way the Israelites were dumb, and not merely to state that Moses' situation is 'ideally extended' to the Israelites. To put it another way, no reason is given by these commentators to extend Moses' speech difficulty to the Israelites other than the attempt on their part to account for the difficult plural. Deane goes beyond the others in offering to explain in what way the Israelites were dumb: the Israelites, 'who through fear had not dared to sing to God in the house of bondage, now praised Him in a hymn of victory'.[27] Although this is a reasonable solution in the abstract, Deane assumes Pseudo-Solomon's statement is a fabrication.

Another solution, closer to the mark, is to have κωφῶν refer to the Israelites at the sea (not Moses and his speech problem), and to understand the word metaphorically. This approach has the twofold advantage of locating the problem at the Song at the Sea and of taking

---

24. Reider, *Wisdom*, p. 139.

25. F.W. Farrar, *The Wisdom of Solomon*, in *The Holy Bible, according to the Authorized Version* (ed. F.C. Cook; London: John Murray, 1888), pp. 403-534.

26. Goodrick, *Wisdom*, p. 238.

27. Deane, *Wisdom*, p. 168.

the plural literally. The difficulty I see, however, is that in understanding the plural literally, this approach also needs to understand 'dumb' metaphorically, since, at the sea, the Israelites were not actually dumb. Grimm argues that 'mouth of the dumb' refers to those who were previously ungifted (*Unbegabte*) for rhetoric (*Beredsamkeit*) or composing poetry (*Dichtergabe*), that is, the Israelites required some special help to compose such a beautiful song as Exodus 15. [28] Heinisch holds a similar view, explaining both κωφῶν and νηπίων in v. 21b as referring to the Israelites who were 'by nature incapable of praising God worthily', that is, it was *as if* they were dumb.[29] None of these solutions, however, really does justice to Pseudo-Solomon's words 'opened the mouth of the dumb'. The underlying assumption is that our author does not mean anything of interpretive consequence, that his comment is not really connected to the Song at the Sea in any concrete way. Since the remark is considered to be a free addition or flourish, not an example of interpretation, a metaphorical explanation is deemed sufficient.

Other solutions offered are those by G. Ziener, E.G. Clarke, and D. Georgi. Ziener understands v. 21 to refer to the rabbinic legend where angels raised the Israelite boys whom Pharaoh had thrown into the river in Exod. 1.22.[30] Although this is certainly relevant for νηπίων in v. 21b (discussed below), it does not help explain κωφῶν. Clarke[31] and Georgi[32] cite Isa. 35.6 as a parallel (τρανὴ ἔσται γλῶσσα μογιλάλων, 'those who speak with difficulty will speak

---

28. Grimm, *Handbuch*, p. 204. A similar explanation is given by Edwin Cone Bissell (*The Apocrypha of the Old Testament* [New York: Charles Scribner's Sons, 1880], p. 254).

29. Heinisch, *Weisheit*, p. 211. See also J. Fichtner, *Weisheit Salomos* (HAT, 2; Reihe 6; Tübingen: J.C.B. Mohr, 1938), p. 42, and E. Osty, *Le livre de la sagesse* (La Sainte Bible; Paris: Editions du Cerf, 1955), p. 880 n. h. Osty's solution is somewhat different. He sees Israel's dumbness as analogous to Moses' speech problem in Exod. 4 and 6. This would, however, necessitate reading 'infants' in v. 21b as a metaphor for the Israelites, an opinion that neither I nor Grelot ('Sagesse 10,21', p. 50) find convincing.

30. G. Ziener, *Das Buch der Weisheit* (Düsseldorf: Patmos, 1970), p. 70. See *Exod. R.* 23.8.

31. Ernest G. Clarke, *The Wisdom of Solomon* (Cambridge: Cambridge University Press, 1973), p. 72.

32. D. Georgi, *Weisheit Salomos* (JSHRZ, 3.4; Gütersloh: Gütersloher Verlagshaus/Gerd Mohn, 1980), p. 440.

clearly' [MT אלם לשון ותרן]), as does Grelot (who also adduces Isa. 32.4, 'the tongue of stammerers will speak fluently' [ולשון עלגים תמהר לדבר צחות]).[33] Although it is certainly possible that these passages were at one time brought to bear on the Song at the Sea (particularly in view of the wilderness imagery in Isa. 35.6b), 'stammering' (Isa. 32.4) and 'difficulty speaking' (Isa. 35.6) are quite different from being 'dumb'.[34] If Isa. 35.6 or 32.4 are responsible for Wis. 10.21a, why does Pseudo-Solomon say 'dumb', which these passages do not say, rather than 'stammering', which they do say?

It seems that another solution is in order. I suggest that Pseudo-Solomon's 'Wisdom opened the mouth of the dumb' is evidence of an exegetical tradition that dealt with a specific difficulty in the biblical text found in Exod. 14.14. Beginning in v. 10, where the Israelites see the Egyptians approaching, they complain to Moses (vv. 10-12). Moses responds that God will deliver them this day from Pharaoh and his army (v. 13). Verse 14 reads, 'YHWH will fight for you, ואתם תחרישון'. Some English versions translate this phrase somewhat vaguely: 'You have only to be still' (NRSV); 'You need only to be still' (NIV); 'Hold your peace' (NEB); 'while you keep silent' (NASB). But it seems that, rather than offering a word of comfort as these English translations imply, Moses is reprimanding the Israelites for their faithlessness despite God's deliverance from Egypt. The phrase should be translated 'keep still', or even better 'be quiet!' We could imagine the problem this might have created for an early interpreter of sacred Scripture. Moses—the mediator, the deliverer, the author of the Torah—said 'be quiet'. Yet, several verses later, without having been told that they may resume speaking, these very same people break out in song. How can this be other than by an act of God to open the mouth of the dumb?[35]

---

33. Grelot, 'Sagesse 10.21', p. 50. Fichtner holds the same opinion ('Der AT-Text der Sapientia Salomonis', *ZAW* 57 [1939], pp. 155-92 [177]). Larcher considers the connection to Isa. 35.6 to be 'incontestable' (*Etudes sur le livre de la sagesse* [Paris: Librairie LeCoffre, 1969], p. 88).

34. Schwenk-Bressler seems to have similar reservations about adducing Isa. 35.6 (*Sapientia Salomonis*, p. 106 n. 167).

35. W.R. Churton gives both Exod. 4.10 and 14.10-14 as cross-references to Wis. 10.21a (*The Uncanonical and Apocryphal Scriptures* [London: Whitaker, 1884], p. 244). Unfortunately, the nature of his commentary precluded any comment on the relevance of Exod. 14.10-14, but he likely had something similar in mind to what I am proposing. Of course, the imperfect could simply be understood as the future (cf. LXX ὑμεῖς σιγήσετε). This, however, would not substantially alter the

The advantage of this explanation over others that have been offered is that it locates Pseudo-Solomon's comment firmly in something that is happening in the context of the Song at the Sea, which is, after all, the topic of his discussion in Wis. 10.20-21. We actually have Israelites (thus accounting for the plural κωφῶν), and they are actually dumb, not simply suffering from a speech impediment or lacking gifts for composing poetry. After Moses tells the people to be quiet, they are obediently quiet for the remainder of ch. 14. Between 14.14 and 15.1, they do not utter a sound—Moses told them not to. One might even imagine a silent mass of humanity passing through the sea. But no sooner do they get to the other side than they open their mouth in song.

As mentioned above, it appears that Pseudo-Solomon's comment is the lone, extant witness to this tradition. This is no doubt at least part of the reason why there are such varied attempts at understanding this comment. And the absence of any clear parallel certainly militates against arriving at a definitive solution. Nevertheless, there is some evidence that lends support, if indirect, for the solution I have proposed. One such piece of evidence is *Cant. R.* 1.49. This midrash understands ואתם תחרישון of Exod. 14.14 as a strong reprimand. This is a matter of some importance, since my explanation of Pseudo-Solomon's comment is predicated upon understanding ואתם תחרישון in this way. The biblical text in view in *Cant. R.* 1.49 is Song 1.9, 'I have compared you (דמיתיך), my darling, to a mare harnessed to Pharaoh's chariots'. The mention of Pharaoh's chariots provides an obvious motive to associate this passage with the crossing of the sea in Exodus.[36] Our primary focus here is דמיתיך, the piel of דמה. *Cant. R.*

point. If Moses were simply telling the people what was going to be the case (rather than commanding them to be quiet), their subsequent singing would still require some explanation.

36. M. Pope presents in some detail the exegetical issues concerning Song 1.9 as well as the major currents in the history of interpretation of this passage (*Song of Songs: A New Translation with Introduction and Commentary* [AB, 7C; Garden City, NY: Doubleday, 1977], pp. 336-43. In particular, he attributes the origin of midrashic interpretations such as that seen in *Cant. R.* 1.49 to a misunderstanding (better, exploitation?) of the alleged first person suffix on the word לססתי (p. 337). Rather than a possessive pronoun, the *ḥîreq-yôd* ending is the *Hireq compaginis* (GKC §90k-m), thus being an indication of the construct form [Pope, *Song of Songs*, p. 338].) This word was misread as *my*, i.e. YHWH's, chariotry, that chariotry being none other than Israel itself. This would yield in Song 1.9 a comparison

1.49, like Wis. 10.21a, appears to make a great deal out of a relatively minor point in Exod. 14.14; it does so by exploiting the potential ambiguity of the root, which can mean 'to compare' (its meaning in Song 1.9[37]) or 'to be silent', and then applies the passage to Exod. 14.14. The midrash reads as follows:

> R. Eliezer said: Israel was like a king's daughter who had been carried away captive, and when her father made ready to ransom her she motioned to her captors, and said to them, 'I am yours and belong to you and will follow you'. Said her father to her: 'What! Do you think I am not able to deliver you? I will silence you [דומה דמיתיך]; be completely silent' [דומי בשתיקה]. So when Israel was camped on the Red Sea *and the Egyptians pursued after them, and overtook them encamping by the sea* (Exod. 14.9), the Israelites motioned to the Egyptians out of fear and said to them, 'We belong to you and are yours and will follow you'. Said the Holy One, blessed be He, to them: 'What! Do you think I am not able to deliver you? Be quiet'. The word דמיתיך here means שתקתיך, I made you silent. Hence it is written *The Lord will fight for you, and you shall be quiet* (Exod. 14.14).

This midrash exploits the semantic range of the root דמה and comes to a climax in the last few lines, where it explicitly tells us that it understands דמיתיך as 'I have made you silent' rather than 'I have compared you'. It then ties this in to Exod. 14.14. Any possible misunderstanding is obviated by the last two sentences of the midrash itself: 'The word דמיתיך here means שתקתיך, I made you silent'. This midrash reads דמיתיך as 'be silent' not simply because the verbal root allows it, but because it is clearly a comment on why Moses says 'be quiet' in Exod. 14.14: because the people rebelled by failing to trust in YHWH's deliverance. This they ought not to have done, and Moses responds appropriately. This is one clear example of a midrash that understands ואתם תחרישון in Exod. 14.14 as 'be quiet', an understanding that is reflected in Wis. 10.20c as well. It is not within the scope of *Cant. R.* 1.49 to reconcile this with Exod. 15.1, but Pseudo-Solomon's comment represents an exegetical tradition that handled the problem in the way described above.

A second, and perhaps more telling, example is found in *Mek. Besh.* 3.140-9 and, like Wis. 10.20c, provides an explicit tie between Exod. 14.14 and the Song at the Sea.

---

between Israel and the chariotry of Egypt, which finds an obvious connection in the exodus narrative, as we see in *Cant. R.* 1.49.

37. See also Pope, *Song of Songs*, p. 341.

> Shall the Lord perform miracles and mighty deeds for you and you be standing there silent [וֹשְׁוֹתְקִין]? The Israelites then said to Moses: Moses, our teacher, what is there for us to do? And he said to them: You should be exalting, glorifying and praising, uttering a song of praise, adoration and glorification to Him in whose hands are the fortunes of wars... At that moment the Israelites opened their mouths and recited the song.

The *Mekilta* understands Exod. 14.14 as a question: 'YHWH will fight for you, and you are keeping quiet?!' This is precisely the opposite interpretation of Exod. 14.14 to that found in *Cant. R.* 1.49 cited above.[38] Nevertheless, this midrash is relevant for our understanding of Pseudo-Solomon's comment. Although Pseudo-Solomon understands Exod. 14.14 as a reprimand ('don't speak') and the *Mekilta* understands it as a question ('why are you not speaking?'), they are both clearly connecting Exod. 14.14 with the Song at the Sea. For Pseudo-Solomon, the reprimand in Exod. 14.14 precludes any possibility of singing, and so divine aid is needed for the Israelites to open their mouths in song. For the *Mekilta*, Exod. 14.14 is not a reprimand, but a question for the purpose of encouraging the Israelites not to keep silent in the face of their glorious deliverance from Egypt. As such, the *Mekilta* offers an alternate explanation to Exod. 14.14. By understanding ואתם תחרישון as a question, the tension between Exod. 14.14 and 15.1 is resolved. In other words, both midrashim offer *opposite* explanations but for the *same* phenomenon. I conclude that Pseudo-Solomon's 'opened the mouth of the dumb' represents one solution to the contradiction between Exod. 14.14 and the Song at the Sea.

'Babes' also Sang at the Sea (10.21b)

There is a popular rabbinic tradition that has infants singing at the sea. Wisdom 10.21b seems to be an early witness to such a tradition.[39] Later, more elaborate witnesses to this midrash are found in a number of sources, including *Exod. R.* 23.8 and *Targ. Ps.-J.* to Exod. 15.2.[40] I quote *Exod. R.* 23.8 at length.

---

38. See also *Mek. Besh.* 3.135-6.
39. See Winston, *Wisdom*, pp. 222-23.
40. Other sources are *t. Soṭ.* 11b; *PRE* 42; *Pes. K.* 47; *y. Soṭ.* 20c; *b. Soṭ.* 30b. See also Ginzberg, *Legends*, II, pp. 257-58 (V, p. 394 n. 25) and III, pp. 33-34 (VI, pp. 12-13 nn. 61 and 64).

R. Judah said: Who was praising the Holy One, blessed be He? It was those babies whom Pharaoh had sought to cast into the Nile that sang praises to the Holy One, blessed be He, whom they recognized [מכירין] at the sea. Why was this? Because when Israel was in Egypt and an Israelite woman was about to give birth, she would go to the field and deliver there; and as soon as the child was born, she would forsake the youth and entrust him to the Holy One, blessed be He, saying, 'Lord of the Universe! I have done my part; now do Yours'. R. Johanan said: Immediately, the Holy One, blessed be He, would descend in his glory (as if it were possible to speak thus), cut their navel, and wash and anoint them, for so Ezekiel says, *But you were thrown out into the open field in neglect* (16.5), and as it is written, *on the day you were born your cord was not cut* (v. 4), and it is written, *I clothed you with richly colored fabric* (v. 10) and *I bathed you with water* (v. 9). He placed two pieces of flint in his hand, one of which fed the child with oil and the other with honey, as it says, *He nourished him with honey from a crag* (Deut. 32.13). They grew up in the field, for it says, *I made you grow like a plant of the field* (Ezek. 16.7); and as soon as they had grown up they would return to their parents' home. When they were asked, 'Who looked after you?' they replied, 'A fine handsome young man came down and attended to all our needs', as it says, *My beloved is white and ruddy, pre-eminent above ten thousand* (Cant. 5.10). When the Israelites came to the Sea, and their children with them, and the latter beheld the Holy One, blessed be He, at the Sea, they said to their parents: 'This is He who did all those things for us when we were in Egypt', as it says, 'This *is my God, and I will glorify Him* (Exod. 15.2)'.

The relevant portion of *Targ. Ps.-J.* to Exod. 15.2 begins about halfway through the verse and reads as follows:

From their mothers' breasts the children were pointing with their fingers to their fathers and said, 'This is our God who nourished us with honey from the rock and oil from the field, gave birth to us and left us there, and he sent the angel and he washed us and swaddled us. Now we will praise him, the God of our fathers, we will extol him.'

Pseudo-Solomon's statement 'made the tongues of babes clear' appears to be another, albeit succinct, witness to this popular midrash in which infants (according to the Targum they were at their mothers' breasts [תדיי אימהון]) join in the Song at the Sea. The fact that *Exod. R.* 23.8 and *Targ. Ps.-J.* to Exod. 15.2 (as well as the other sources) conclude by citing Exod. 15.2 clearly indicates that there is something in Exod. 15.2 that motivates their comments. What appears to be the specific motivating factor is the demonstrative זה. For these sources listed above, saying 'this' was apparently understood to involve an act of pointing (see especially the Targum), as if the babes were physically indicating God's presence.

What is crucial for our understanding the exegetical thinking behind this midrash is the factor of 'recognition' (הכיר) mentioned specifically in *Exod. R.* 23.8 and clearly implied in the Targum (see also *PRE* 42). Infants are said to be the ones who recognized God at the sea, and it is this recognition that gives them the right (so to speak) to point up to the sky and proclaim that *this* was indeed their God. After all, who else in the exodus narrative could have *recognized* YHWH other than those to whom he had previously descended, whose navel he had cut, and whom he had washed and anointed?[41] That the ability to recognize YHWH at the sea was a point of concern for early interpreters is seen also in *Mek. Shir.* 3.28-39. This midrash also comments on Exod. 15.2 but arrives at exactly the opposite conclusion, albeit for the same reason.

> R. Eliezer says: How can you say that a maid-servant saw at the sea what Isaiah and Ezekiel and all the rest of the prophets did not see? It says about them: 'through the prophets have I spoken in parables' (Hos. 12.11). And it is also written: 'The heavens were opened and I saw visions of God' (Ezek. 1.1). To give a parable for this, to what is it like? A king of flesh and blood enters a province surrounded by a circle of guards. His heroes stand to his right and to his left, soldiers before him and behind him. All the people ask, 'Which one is the king?' because he is of flesh and blood like they are. But, when the Holy One, blessed be He, revealed Himself at the sea, no one needed to ask 'Which one is the king?' But as soon as they saw Him they *recognized* Him [הכירוהו], and

---

41. A curious element to this tradition, and one that I have not seen discussed, is the fact that the babes who were delivered in Exod. 1 could not have been babes in Exod. 15. Too much time elapsed, 80 years in fact, since this is the age given for Moses at the time of the exodus (Exod. 7.7). This problem may be obviated, at least in part, if we assume that the edict was not rescinded and male infants were being thrown into the Nile for the entire 80 years. This view has at least implicit support, since the edict is never actually rescinded in Exodus. In this sense, the babes singing at the sea would be those who had been *most recently* delivered from Pharaoh's decree. If this is so, the 'babes at the sea' tradition would be an alternate tradition to the one that states that Pharaoh rescinded his edict after his astrologers told him that Moses had already been born (see *PRE* 48; *b. Soṭ.* 12b; *Jub.* 47.3; J. Cohen, *The Origins and Evolution of the Moses Nativity Story* (NumBS, 58; Leiden: E.J. Brill, 1993), p. 5 n. 2; p. 11; pp. 98-99; H. Gressmann, *Mose und seine Zeit: Ein Kommentar zu den Mose-sagen* [FRLANT, 18; Göttingen: Vandenhoeck & Ruprecht, 1913], pp. 1-16).

they all [כלן] opened their mouths and said: 'This is my God and I will glorify him'.

Although the *Mekilta* says that all the people (rather than just the children) recognized YHWH, the concern of this tradition is certainly the issue of how they, or anyone else, would have been able to identify God positively. The question that might have arisen in an early interpreter's mind is: 'How is it that someone can point [suggested by זה] to YHWH and make such a statement when YHWH had not yet appeared to anyone but Moses?' The answer the *Mekilta* gives is: 'Well, this would be a problem if we were dealing with a human king, but since it was God himself who appeared, there wasn't the slightest doubt in *anyone's* mind who it was!' *Exod. R.* 23.8 and others, however, deal with the 'recognition' problem differently: 'Those who pointed and recognized YHWH at the sea could only be those who had previously beheld him: the babes delivered from Pharaoh's edict'. The solutions differ, but the motive for both is the same.

What gave rise to this 'delivered babes' tradition is apparently the Ezekiel passage outlined in *Exod. R.* 23.8 and alluded to in the Targum.[42] Although Ezek. 16.1-7 is an allegory of God's care for unfaithful Jerusalem, it is not too difficult to see a midrashist exploiting the imagery of this passage and employing it to describe God's care for the actual infants who were the subjects of Pharaoh's decree. There are two specific factors that might have strengthened the connection between Ezekiel 16 and Exodus 1. The first is Exod. 1.7, which reads "וַתִּמָּלֵא הָאָרֶץ אֹתָם". From the point of view of Hebrew grammar, the nifal of מלא followed by the accusative is not at all

---

42. For a full treatment of the various scriptural allusions that are involved in this tradition, see Grelot, 'Sagesse 10,21', pp. 49-60. He also cites *b. Sot.* 1.6 (i.e. 11b), which brings together Deut. 32.13 and Ezek. 16.4-6, and introduces this to the context of Exod. 15 (54). To attribute the motive for Pseudo-Solomon's comment to Ps. 8.3 ('From the lips of children and babes you have ordained praise because of your enemies, to silence the foe and avenger'), as do Grelot ('Sagesse 10,21', p. 57) and Schwenk-Bressler (*Sapientia Salomonis*, p. 106), is very unlikely, however. Such an appeal to Ps. 8.3 as the basis of a *Stichwortverbindung* (p. 106 n. 165) is in my view something that is characteristic of later rabbinic notions of intertextuality. Ps. 8.3 was certainly introduced, but at a later point. I do not think that Pseudo-Solomon's exegetical reach was quite so wide as to include in his comment on the Song at the Sea a psalm that has no overt connection to the exodus. J. Cohen treats the understanding of these passages in rabbinic literature as they pertain to Pharaoh's edict (*Origins and Evolution*, pp. 110-15).

unusual.[43] Nevertheless, this fact should not exert undue influence in our understanding of the interpretive possibilities that early exegetes might have seen in this grammatical construction. An early interpreter could easily (and purposefully) have read the verb as a piel, וַתְּמַלֵּא״, thus yielding 'the earth filled them', or something similar. This is not merely a conjectural possibility. The LXX seems to document just such a reading of Exod. 1.7: ἐπλήθυνεν δὲ ἡ γῆ αὐτούς. Although the niphal of מלא plus the accusative is properly translated 'the earth was full of them' or 'was filled with them', such a translation of the LXX is difficult to justify. According to Liddell and Scott, πληθύνω is a causal of πληθύω, and means to make multiple or 'plurify'. Furthermore, this is the only place in the LXX where πληθύνω is used to translate the nifal of מלא (more often πίμπλημι, ἐμπίμπλημι, or πληθύω are used). Perhaps more significant is how πληθύνω is used elsewhere in Exodus 1. The clear use of the passive earlier in v. 7 (ἐπληθύνθησαν) militates against reading ἐπλήθυνεν as anything other than active. In v. 20, ἐπλήθυνεν is used intransitively: 'The people increased'. We have then in the last few words of LXX Exod. 1.7 an active (ἐπλήθυνεν) transitive (αὐτούς) verb, which yields the translation 'the earth *increased them*', or something similar.[44] The

---

43. Verbs that in the active voice take a double accusative retain an accusative in the passive voice. See G.F. Davies, *Israel in Egypt: Reading Exodus 1–2* (JSOTSup, 135; Sheffield: JSOT Press, 1992), p. 38, esp. n. 1. B. Waltke and M. O'Connor refer to such a construction as a 'complement accusative', and cite Exod. 1.7 as an example (*An Introduction to Biblical Hebrew Syntax* [Winona Lake: Eisenbrauns, 1990], p. 168). GKC §117z also adduces Exod. 1.7 as an example of this construction meaning 'to fill oneself with something' (see also §121d). Gen. 6.11 is also cited, although this is without the direct object marker. Gen. 21.8 is similar, but there the verbs is גמל. See also Num. 14.21. The same phenomenon occurs in Greek (e.g. M. Zerwick, *Biblical Greek* [Rome: Biblical Institute, 1963] p. 26).

44. See also the translations of the LXX by L.C.L. Brenton and C. Thomson. The former has 'the land multiplied them' (*The Septuagint Version, Greek and English* [reprint of 1844 edition; Grand Rapids: Zondervan, 1970) and the latter 'The land caused them to abound' (*The Old Covenant Commonly Called the Old Testament: Translated from the Septuagint* [2 vols.; London: Skeffington & Son, 1904]). J. Wevers comments on LXX Exod. 1.7 as follows: 'The final clause uses the transitive verb ἐπλήθυνεν with an accusative αὐτούς as though the verb were Hiphil [I am suggesting piel-P.E.], probably because of the Hebrew's אתם. Note the attempt of mss. 53' to improve the sense by their επληθυνθη αυτοι' (*Notes on the Greek Text of Exodus* [SBLSCS, 30; Atlanta: Scholars Press, 1990], p. 3). In the footnote to this statement, Wevers says, 'The clause is more exactly rendered by Aq and Sym

LXX translation of Exod. 1.7 may reflect an early attempt (whether original to the LXX or not is beside the point) to link the allegory of Ezek. 16.1-7 exegetically to Exodus 1. I suggest that the specific passage that would have linked Ezekiel 16 to Exod. 1.7 is Ezek. 16.7: 'I made you grow like a plant in the field' (השדה נתתיך רבבה כצמח).[45] If we understand ותמלא in Exod. 1.7 as an active verb, precisely what we see in the LXX, a connection between Ezek. 16.7 and Exod. 1.7 seems to present itself: the earth 'multiplies' the Israelites (Exod. 1.7) like plants growing in the field (Ezek. 16.7). Hence, an exegetical connection between the actual infants of Exodus 1 and those of Ezekiel 16 is established. A second exegetical element that serves to tie Ezekiel 16 to Exodus 1 is the use of ילד and שלך. The second half of Ezek. 16.5 reads: 'You were thrown (ותשלכי) into the field; you were neglected on the day of your birth (ביום הלדת)'. A similar fate befell the male children in Exod. 1.22: 'Every son who is born (הילוד) you will cast (תשליכהו) into the Nile'. It is beside the point that Ezek. 16.5 refers to a field whereas Exod. 1.22 refers to the Nile. The fact remains that exegetical traditions exist that connect the infants of Ezekiel 16 and those of Exodus 1, and שלך/ילד and the syntax of Exod. 1.7 may have served, or even been exploited, to strengthen that connection.

In any event, Pseudo-Solomon's terse statement 'made the tongues of babes clear' certainly reflects a tradition of infants singing at the sea. In this respect, this motif is distinct from the previous two, since a clearly documented tradition seems to form the proper backdrop for Pseudo-Solomon's statement. It is not clear, however, to what extent this tradition had developed in Pseudo-Solomon's day, that is, whether we can rightly say that the later full-blown version of the tradition in all its detail, as reflected in *Exod. R.* 23.8 and *Targ. Ps.-J.*, can be assumed to underlie Wis. 10.21b. Nevertheless, it seems certain that the tradition in some form must have existed in Pseudo-Solomon's exegetical world in order for Pseudo-Solomon to have commented as he did.

The existence of this tradition in the Wisdom of Solomon raises certain issues that can only be touched on here, but are worth raising nevertheless. Pseudo-Solomon's 'made the tongues of babes clear' is an early witness to a later, more elaborate tradition. What is striking

with καὶ ἐπληρώθη ἡ γῆ ἀπ' αὐτῶν'. There is clearly an awkwardness to the LXX.

45. LXX has πληθύνου (middle/passive imperative) for רבבה, which may provide a further lexical connection between Exod. 1.7 and Ezek. 16.7.

is the brevity of the allusion. One might call this a 'shorthand' reference to the tradition. This suggests that Pseudo-Solomon was thoroughly familiar with this tradition, so familiar that he can make a brief, even casual, reference to the tradition in the context of his exposition of the Song at the Sea. One might even say that this particular tradition was part of the common biblical discourse at the time, one that was known not only to him but to his readers as well.

Moreover, the setting of the Wisdom of Solomon should be kept in mind. We have an Alexandrian Jew, writing words of encouragement to an oppressed and beleaguered people in the throes of persecution.[46] And in order to support and inspire his readers to remain firm in the faith, he provides numerous examples from Scripture of how Wisdom remained steadfast in delivering God's people: Adam, Noah, Abraham, Lot, Jacob, Joseph (10.1-14), and most prominently the Israelites from Egypt (the primary topic of discussion in 10.15–19.22). Yet, it is remarkable that in recounting these biblical events and heroes, he does more than simply repeat Scripture. Rather, Scripture is thoroughly infused with these interpretive traditions at virtually every turn: Abraham is a contemporary of the Tower of Babel story (10.5; cf. *Bib. Ant.* 6-7); the Sodomites are condemned for their inhospitable treatment of their guests (19, 14; cf. Josephus, *Ant.* 1.194); the wicked acts of the 'arrogant giants' (Gen. 6.4) are responsible for the flood (14.6; cf. *3 Macc.* 2.4).[47] It seems that for Pseudo-Solomon, his retelling of Scripture includes these traditions to the extent that the incorporation of these traditions are merely a matter of reflex. In fact, even to speak of 'incorporation' may be inaccurate in that it implies a degree of conscious exegetical activity. It seems that Pseudo-Solomon is not actually conscious that his biblical exposition includes these extra-biblical traditions. Rather, he is merely retelling Scripture in the only way that might be expected of him. For him and his contemporaries, certain traditions about the Bible had simply become associated with the Bible itself, so that the biblical text and the interpretation of that text went hand in hand.

What provides corroborating evidence for such a view is the fact of the presence of contradictory traditions in the Wisdom of Solomon. One example is the cause of the flood: in 10.4 the culprit is Cain; in

---

46. Enns, *Exodus Retold*, pp. 139-42.

47. A more detailed discussion of these and other examples may be found in Enns, *Exodus Retold*, pp. 17-34.

14.6 it is the giants of Gen. 6.4. Another example concerns the 'babes' tradition discussed above. The tradition that underlies Wis. 10.21b is one that places the infants *of Exodus 1* at the sea in Exodus 15: those who were delivered at birth sing praise to God at the sea. Wisdom 18.5, however, says that Moses alone was delivered:

> They [the Egyptians] wishing to kill the children of the holy ones, and *one child had been exposed and rescued* (ἑνὸς ἐκτεθέντος τέκνου καὶ σωθέντος), as punishment you took away a multitude of their children and destroyed them all together in raging water.

Although all the male children were subject to Pharaoh's decree, Moses *alone* was rescued. The νηπία who are said to sing in 10.21b, perish in 18.5. The fact of the existence of contradictory traditions in the Wisdom of Solomon speaks for the unconscious manner in which Pseudo-Solomon has adopted these traditions. Had he been consciously and directly engaging the biblical texts, he would probably not have offered two explanations for the same phenomenon. Rather, he is merely relaying exegetical traditions, origins unknown to him, that have become closely associated with the biblical text to the extent that text and interpretation become blurred.[48]

Conclusion

Pseudo-Solomon's comments on the Song at the Sea are not to be understood in isolation. Rather, they are evidence of exegetical traditions that grappled with the biblical data. To support this thesis, I have attempted to draw the reader's attention not only to possible parallels to Pseudo-Solomon's comments, but to the exegetical thinking that underlies these traditions represented in Wis. 10.20-21. For early interpreters such as Pseudo-Solomon, sacred Scripture itself posed problems that needed to be solved. It is within this larger framework that 'with one accord', 'mouth of the dumb', and 'tongues of babes' ought to be understood. These are not careless comments or insignificant flourishes. Rather, they are witnesses to ancient exegetical traditions whose hermeneutic called for a closer reading of the biblical text than might sometimes be appreciated.

---

48. For further discussion of some of the implications of this phenomenon in the Wisdom of Solomon see my *Exodus Retold*, pp. 155-69.

THE FAMILY AS SCRIPTURAL AND SOCIAL CONSTRUCT IN TOBIT

Will Soll

Study of the Jewish family in the Hellenistic period is still in its infancy. One potential source for such study is the book of Tobit, rich in its portrayal of family life. The value of Tobit for social history consists in the breadth of its portrayal of many aspects of Jewish family life: from weddings to burials, from meals to sleeping arrangements, from farewell admonitions to poignant reunions, from the duties of children to the affection and the friction that exists between wife and husband. To be sure, these depictions are often somewhat caricatured and stereotypical, but in many ways that adds to their usefulness as a source for the author's ideals, ideals which admittedly to do not always square neatly with reality.

Two aspects of the Jewish family in Tobit are closely bound up with the use of Scripture in the book. The first involves the family and lineage. The second relates to the themes of endogamy and the inheritance of daughters. In both these areas, values that are by no means unique to Judaism intersect with a Jewish interpretation of Jewish Scripture.

The Family and Lineage

The English word 'family' can be used in many ways, but the picture it evokes most readily in current usage is that of the nuclear family: a mother and father and their children.[1] However, this definition can be controversial in a number of contemporary contexts. And it becomes even more problematic when we turn to Tobit. Our author simply had no word available to him that meant 'nuclear family'. The husband–wife and parent–child relationships were of course very important to

---

1. For example, the first definition in the *American Heritage Dictionary* (3rd edn, 1992) is 'a fundamental social group...typically consisting of a man and woman and their offspring'.

him, but they did not create an insular group. Instead, these relationships realized their full importance within a larger network.

These difficulties of definition underscore James Casey's point that the family is 'not necessarily defined by objective criteria like property or descent, but by a certain idea of itself'.[2] Rather than hold rigidly to a preconceived notion of the 'family' and plunder Tobit for data that fit it, it is more fruitful to begin by inquiring after the idea of the family that the book conveys.

Family identity and connections in Tobit are fundamentally expressed through the language of lineage. This does not, however, constitute an 'objective criterion', since much of this language is fairly general, fictional, or metaphorical. Rather, lineage is used to create an idea of the family that informs not only particular family relations but the sense of Jewish existence in a Gentile world.

The importance of kin and ancestors is stressed right from the outset. In 1.1, Tobit is provided with a genealogy and a tribe (Greek, φυλή; the tribe is also designated by the word οἶκος [lit. 'house'] in v. 5). We are then told (v. 3) that Tobit performed many charitable acts to his kinsmen (lit. ἀδελφοί, 'brothers') and his people (ἔθνη, in the sense of 'members of my family, my group'[3]). Tobit marries 'a member of [4] his own family' (Greek, πατρία) (1.9).

The picture of the family that emerges from just the first nine verses of the book gives us several interrelated layers of family, from immediate ancestors and the 'extended' family of uncles, aunts, and cousins, to the clan, the tribe, and, finally the nation. It is not always possible to distinguish these layers with linguistic or interpretive certainty; rather, the book tends to move toward as much integration and overlap as possible of these different senses of family. Note, however, that none of these terms specifically designates the 'nuclear' family.

The idea of 'family' in Tobit also forms an important point of connection with the traditional literature of the people. Tobit urges his son to 'marry a woman from the descendents of your ancestors...*for we are descendents of the prophets*' (4.12). 'Lineage' here becomes inseparable from a sense of the biblical text and its significance for the

2. James Casey, *The History of the Family: New Perspectives on the Past* (Oxford: Basil Blackwell, 1989), p. 7.

3. Frank Zimmerman, *The Book of Tobit* (New York: Harper, 1958), p. 46.

4. Literally, 'from the seed of'; the word 'seed' also occurs in the genealogy in 1.1.

community. In particular, Tobit has the patriarchs of Genesis in view: 'Remember, my son, that Noah, Abraham, Isaac, and Jacob, our ancestors of old, all took wives from among their kindred' (4.12). The inclusion of Noah in this list is interesting since he is the ancestor of all humanity, and nothing is said in Genesis about the genealogy of his wife. But in *Jubilees*, Noah is one of many ancient patriarchs to marry a close relative, in this case his cousin.

Another 'non-canonical' literary work (to use an anachronistic term) which nevertheless influences our author's sense of Scripture is *The Story of Ahiqar*, a popular Aramaic wisdom tale which framed two collections of proverbs. That a Near Eastern wisdom text has been adopted into a Jewish context parallels the debt of the biblical book of Proverbs to non-Israelite sources. But the book of Tobit takes this adoption a step further, as Ahiqar is brought into a Jewish family, becoming Tobit's nephew. The connection serves to locate Tobit more plausibly in the court affairs of Assyria, and also provides a contrast to the behavior of Tobias and Sarah in the person of Ahiqar's nephew, Nadab.[5]

One vignette from the book illustrates the importance of tribe and genealogy in everyday relations particularly well. It occurs when Tobias introduces Raphael to Tobit as a potential guide for the journey to Media.

> Then Tobit said to him, 'My brother, of what family and from what tribe are you? Tell me, brother'. He answered, 'Are you looking for a tribe and a family or for a man whom you will pay to go with your son?' And he said to him, 'I should like to know truthfully whose son you are, brother, and your name'. He replied, 'I am Azariah, the son of the great Hananiah, one of your relatives'. Then Tobit said to him, 'Welcome, and may God save you, brother. Do not be angry with me, brother, because I wished to learn the truth about your family. It turns out that you are a kinsman of mine, of a good and noble lineage. For I used to know Hananiah and Nathan, the sons of the great Shemaiah; they used to go with me to Jerusalem and worshipped with me there, and were not led astray. Your

---

5. Called 'Nadin' in the original Aramaic text of *Ahiqar*. For further reflection on the connection of Ahiqar and Tobit, see J.M. Lindenberger, 'Ahiqar: A New Translation and Introduction', in J.H. Charlesworth (ed.), *The Old Testament Pseudepigrapha* (2 vols.; ABRL; New York: Doubleday, 1983–85), II, pp. 488-90; and J.C. Greenfield, 'Ahiqar in the Book of Tobit', in M. Carrez, J. Doré, and P. Grelot (eds.), *De la Tôrah au Messie: Mélanges Henri Cazelles* (Paris: Desclée, 1981), pp. 329-36.

kinfolk are good men, and you are of good stock. Hearty welcome!
(5.11-14)

Raphael's initial reluctance to answer Tobit should not lead us to
believe that Tobit is being fussy or snobbish. Rather, the angel's question gives Tobit an opportunity to display his 'family values', values
which we can confidently ascribe to the author of the book as well.
Raphael's challenge is not a rebuke, but a kind of test which Tobit
passes.

This episode illustrates Casey's observation that, in preindustrial
societies, genealogy serves the functions currently given to educational
and professional credentials, and is therefore a matter of keen practical interest. 'Where a people lacks the organic unity of a modern society, men like to "situate" an individual before doing business with
him.'[6]

Yet there is an irony in this scene with Raphael: the angel is lying
through his apparent teeth. True, the deception is completely benign,
but the genealogy he offers is still objectively worthless. Tobit may be
stretching the truth as well. His assertion that Raphael's alleged father
and uncle used to go to worship with him to Jerusalem is at odds with
his earlier assertion that he *alone* went to Jerusalem whereas all the
rest of his kindred worshiped the calf at Dan (1.5-6).

It is fair to conclude that in this exchange very little actual information is given about ancestors or events. But the almost total lack of
objective veracity does not render this exchange ineffectual for
'situating' the two men in each other's eyes. Both show that they speak
the language of genealogy and therefore may plausibly claim to
embody the values implied in being a person of 'good family'.

In real Hellenistic Jewish life, such an exchange would probably
have provided more objective information, especially where parents
and grandparents were concerned. However, the more distant past and
the broader family units may well have been the subject of plausible
invention. The genealogies of preindustrial societies fundamentally
deal with values that are so important that if suitable pedigrees cannot
be discovered they must be invented. At bottom, the concept of lineage, to quote Casey, '…means simply purity or honour. A pride in
ancestors, and a reverence for them, were the ways in which that
purity was maintained.'[7] In such genealogical systems objective

6. Casey, *Family*, p. 22.
7. Casey, *Family*, p. 38.

information would have been subordinated to the moral content of the idea of genealogy.[8]

Take, for example, the term 'tribe' so often used in Tobit. While the earliest tribes were probably groups bound by common descent, by the time of the monarchy the term came to designate primarily people who lived in the same region. 'Tribal' identity would seem to be unascertainable in the postexilic Diaspora. Yet we know that, for some, such claims were meaningful; Paul boasts proudly of being a member of 'the tribe of Benjamin' (Phil. 3.5).

There may have been others in the Jewish community who viewed the claim to belong to a 'tribe' as affectation; their voices may be reflected in the sardonic response of Raphael, 'Are you looking for a tribe and a family or for a man whom you will pay to go with your son?' The book of Tobit, however, urges that such forms of identification be taken seriously, for they align the individual with the group, with certain values, and with the sacred story itself.

Endogamy and the Inheritance of Daughters

We have already referred to Tobit's instructions to Tobias to take a wife from his kindred. That a Jewish father should tell this to his son is hardly a surprise, though Tobit's anxiety on the subject does seem to indicate that at least some Jews in the Hellenistic Diaspora married Gentiles. What is surprising is the degree of close kinship advocated in the prospective wife, which is much closer than what is mandated by biblical or rabbinic law.

We will begin our discussion with Tobit's parting instructions to Tobias. There, it is difficult to tell exactly what degree of relationship Tobit advocates for a prospective spouse. He tells him not to marry a foreign woman who is not of his father's tribe (φυλή). He says that Abraham, Isaac, and Jacob all took wives from their kindred (lit. 'brothers', ἀδελφοί), and that Tobias too should love his kindred. With the example of the patriarchs, a close degree of prior kinship between husband and wife is hinted at, though not directly advocated.

---

8. Jews, of course, were by no means distinctive in their concern for genealogy. Sarah Pomeroy writes that some Greeks created fictitious genealogies in order, for example, to share the reputation of a particularly famous practitioner of a trade ('Some Greek Families: Production and Reproduction', in S.J.D. Cohen (ed.), *The Jewish Family in Antiquity* [BJS, 289; Atlanta: Scholars Press, 1993], p. 163).

Yet the reader has been prepared for Tobit's discourse with the statement, at the end of the preceding chapter, that 'it fell to Tobias to inherit her [Sarah] before all others who desired to take her' (3.17). While we are wincing at the extent to which Sarah is referred to in proprietary terms, we should not miss the narrator's emphasis: Tobias has a right to marry Sarah, and anyone else who would do so usurps that right. We learn from Raphael's later speech to Tobias that this right is based on closeness of kinship (6.12). This right is said to be so strong that Raguel cannot give Sarah to another without violating the law of Moses and incurring the death penalty (6.13).

Just how the author of Tobit arrives at these strictures is unclear, especially since none of the possibly relevant laws prescribes the death penalty. Zimmerman and Zeitlin attempt to derive the obligation from the law of 'levirate marriage', whereby the brother of a man who dies without a son has an obligation to marry the wife who is left, and 'the first son she bears shall succeed to the name of the brother who is left' (Deut. 25.5-10).[9] This is the only case in biblical law where one individual is obligated to marry another by virtue of a kinship relationship. But if levirate law applied to Tobias, the question would be how closely he is related to one of Sarah's dead 'husbands' rather than to Sarah or Raguel. Sarah is never described as a widow, and her marriages were not even consummated. Finally, the concern of levirate marriage to perpetuate the name of the dead husband is never invoked in Tobit.

More promising is the law in Num. 36.8-9, which reads

> Every daughter who possesses an inheritance in any tribe (מטה) of the Israelites shall marry one from the clan (משפחה) of her father's tribe, so that all Israelites may continue to possess their ancestral inheritance. No inheritance shall be transferred from one tribe to another; for each of the tribes of the Israelites shall retain its own inheritance.

The law closely parallels the situation in Tobit, especially if the author of Tobit took 'clan' to refer to a specific group within the tribe, and not as a way of referring to the tribe itself. Moreover, this law shares with Tobit a concern for the inheritance of a daughter. Sarah's status as an heiress is central to all of the discussions about whom she marries.

To appreciate the importance of Sarah's inheritance we can compare Tobit with Genesis 24, the quest for a wife for Isaac. In both

---

9. Zimmerman, *Tobit*, pp. 82-83.

cases the finding of a suitable bride involves a long journey to a close relation (closer, in fact, than those who lived nearby). In both cases, a trusted servant plays a crucial role. In both cases, the marriage is readily assented to without any kind of courtship, and is settled with an exchange of property. But it is at this point that a crucial difference occurs: the exchange of property goes in different directions in the two texts. In Genesis 24 Eleazar, representing the family of the future husband, gives gifts to Laban, representing the family of the future bride. This corresponds roughly to the biblical *mohar*, or bride-price (Gen. 34.12; Exod. 22.16-17). In Tobit, however, it is Raguel who provides Tobias with an ample dowry.

Casey argues that the difference between bride-price and dowry corresponds to the prevalence of exogamy and endogamy respectively. Among people such as the Chinese:

> organized into clans by descent, the basic rule of marriage is that of exogamy—that is, one should marry outside the group...The point seems to be that the patrilineal clan in China constituted a sufficiently defined and important group in its own right, united in the ritual worship of the ancestor...[T]he fear was that a union of cousins would create more limited and exclusive solidarities which would prejudice the health of the whole.[10]

Endogamy, by contrast, presumes that the daughter inherits property as well as the son. Islam provides a contrast to the Chinese in this respect. The egalitarian fraternity of 'true believers' created by Islam destroyed the religious base of the clan. But Islam adapted:

> the residual strength of clan feeling to the pressing demands of a developed economy, allowing daughters to inherit, but preferring them to keep their inheritance within the clan by marrying their father's brother's son. This is not a rule but a preference, a 'noble' or 'proper' thing to do, even though the reality of family strategy often rules it out in practice.[11]

This connection between exogamy and bride-price on the one hand, and endogamy and dowry on the other, is subject to a myriad of variations and modifications in various cultures. But the basic connection as described by Casey may help us make sense of what is going on in Tobit, where endogamy[12] is strongly linked to dowry. The dowry

10. Casey, *Family*, pp. 67-68.
11. Casey, *Family*, p. 68.
12. Note that here I am using endogamy in the sense generally preferred by anthropologiests: marriage to cousin or close kin. Sometimes in studies of postexilic Judaism, 'endogamy' is used for the practice of Jews marrying other Jews. This is a

Tobias receives is, in effect, a down-payment on Sarah's inheritance, the remainder of which will fall to them after the deaths of Raguel and Edna (8.21). Tobias is, in turn, beholden to Sarah's family as parents; his filial obligation extends to them (14.12-13).

The appeal of this arrangement to our author is twofold. We have already seen how eager he is to retain the language of tribal lineage with its moral content for the postexilic Diaspora even though the original social contexts that gave meaning to tribal identity had largely disappeared. In such circumstances, endogamy fortifies 'the residual strength of clan feeling' in a manner comparable to that which Casey adduced for west Asian Muslims. This arrangement also appeals to the author of Tobit for economic reasons. In a situation where the daughter inherits, the marriage arrangement idealized in Tobit means

very broad (though technically possible) use of the term endogamy, a kind of endogamy practiced by most ethnic groups. Using this broad definition, the Chinese and Muslims discussed by Casey would both be endogamous, as would most groups.

In the Hellenistic period, the Jewish men were distinguished not by their reluctance to marry outside the ethnic group but by their view that sex outside of marriage was πορνεία ('fornication'; see below). When the Stoic writer Tacitus attempts to justify his claim that Jews demonstrate unusual enmity towards humankind, he states that 'although as a race they are prone to lust, they abstain from intercourse with foreign women' (cited in M. Stern, *Greek and Latin Authors on Jews and Judaism* [Jerusalem: Jerusalem Academic Press, 1980], II, p. 26). But this should not be taken as a statement that the Jews were particularly exclusive where *marriage* was concerned. It is true that many Jewish families would not approve of their children marrying pagan Romans, but it is just as true that Tacitus would not approve of his children marrying Jews. The real difference is not in the attitude towards foreigners, but in the attitude towards sexual intercourse which, for the Jew, implies marriage. As further illumination of Tacitus's remark, Stern (*Greek and Latin Authors*, II, p. 20) cites a rabbinic parallel in which a Roman hegemon sent two alluringly dressed women to Rabbi Aqiba:

> He sat there in disgust and would not turn to them...The hegemon sent for him and asked: Now why didst thou not do with these women as men generally do with women? Are they not human beings like thyself? Did not he who created thee create them?

For the hegemon, the question is not why Aqiba does not marry these women, which the Roman could understand by analogy with his own culture, but why he does not simply enjoy them.

Tacitus's view that the Jews are nonetheless 'prone to lust' may reflect the absence of any limitation on sexual practice within marriage; for the Stoic origins of the view of sexual intercourse being only for procreation, see P. Veyne, 'The Roman Empire', in P. Veyne (ed.), *A History of Private Life* (trans. A. Goldhammer; Cambridge, MA: Belknap and Harvard University Press, 1987), pp. 36-49.

that the wealth of 'good' Jewish families is not diluted; rather, their resources are pooled.

Another way in which two families pool their resources in the merger of marriage is reflected in the rabbinic law, where the *kethubah* basically corresponds to what Goody calls the 'indirect dowry'. Like bridewealth, the indirect dowry is paid by the groom's kin. But unlike bridewealth, it ultimately goes to the bride herself and her new family. In many societies, indirect dowry balances dowry. In this way, financial burdens and honor concerns between two contracting families are balanced out.

But Tobit knows nothing of the indirect dowry. The book is similar in this respect to Josephus's portrait of marriage among Herodian family members, where he mentions several cases of dowry but no clear cases of indirect dowry.[13] I wonder if the *kethubah* traditions in the Mishnah reflect a greater influence of Roman law and customs.

Josephus is also closer to Tobit than to the rabbis on the subject of endogamy. Endogamy is not held up as an ideal in the Mishnah for those outside priestly families. But Josephus does recount numerous cases of endogamous marriage among the Herodians, which reflects the favorable light in which endogamy is portrayed in Tobit, Judith, and *Jubilees*. Tobit's view of the matter seems to me in many ways an aristocratic one, designed to preserve the wealth and traditions of prominent families.

One anomaly remains. If endogamy is related to dowry, why does Genesis 24 show great pains being taken to arrange an endogamous marriage? There, despite marrying a cousin, Abraham and Isaac (through Eleazar) pay a bride-price for Rebecca, and there is no inference that they are in any way further beholden to Rebecca's family. The answer must be found in the special circumstances of the Genesis narratives, where each family represents a nation. There, to marry outside the family is to marry outside the nation, so it behoves the patriarchs to marry close relatives.[14] But the implication of this

13. K.C. Hanson, 'The Herodians and Mediterranean Kinship. Part III: Economics', *BTB* 20 (1990), pp. 10-21 (15).

14. For more on the significance of cross-cousin marriage in Genesis, see P.K. McCarter, 'The Patriarchal Age', in H. Shanks (ed.), *Ancient Israel* (Englewood Cliffs, NJ: Prentice-Hall, 1988), IV, pp. 14-15; and R.A. Oden, 'Jacob as Father, Husband, and Nephew: Kinship Studies and the Patriarchal Narratives', *JBL* 102 (1983), pp. 189-205.

for subsequent generations could simply be taken to be 'marry one of your people', and indeed this has proved to be the more widespread interpretation in Judaism. The book of Tobit, however, shows that the story could be taken very literally as a model—more literally than originally intended—in a way that dovetails with the author's concern to preserve Jewish families and their wealth and values.

Study of the Jewish family in Tobit is an area where anthropology and the history of interpretation can be mutually enriching. It is true, I think, that the author of Tobit finds in Scripture what he wants and needs to find about family life. But Scripture is more than a pretext. If, as Casey says, the family is 'not necessarily defined by objective criteria like property or descent, but by a certain idea of itself', then, for the author of Tobit, Scripture was part and parcel of that idea.

A More Complete Semitic Background
for בר־אנשא, 'Son of Man'*

Randall Buth

During the last three decades there has been a lengthy linguistic discussion on the meaning of 'Son of Man'.[1] By now every New Testament scholar should know that 'son of man' is an Aramaic idiom that means 'a person'. (It is also, incidentally, a Hebrew idiom that means 'a person'.) This linguistic debate on the Son of Man has taken place from within a restricted sociolinguistic perspective. This paper will present a simple, though far-reaching change of perspective that can lead to a fruitful, prolonged debate in a new direction.

Survey of Background

This linguistic debate has centered on the meaning and function of בר־אנשא 'son of man' in Aramaic and possible relationships to the use of the phrase in the Greek Gospels. It has led us away from an older debate over whether Jesus spoke about a known apocalyptic figure or about someone other than himself.[2]

The debate has included questions like whether 'son of man' could

---

* This is a revision of a paper that was read at the Scripture in Early Judaism and Christianity section of the Society of Biblical Literature, November 1993.

1. Cf. I. Howard Marshall, 'The Synoptic "Son of Man" Sayings in the Light of Linguistic Study', in Thomas E. Schmidt and Moisés Silva (eds.), *To Tell the Mystery, Essays on New Testament Eschatology in Honor of Robert H. Gundry* (JSNTSup, 100; Sheffield: JSOT Press, 1994), pp. 72-94. For general bibliography on the Son of Man one may be referred to Douglas R.A. Hare, *The Son of Man Tradition* (Minneapolis: Fortress Press, 1990); John R. Donahue, 'Recent Studies on the Origin of "Son of Man" in the Gospels', *CBQ* 48 (1986), pp. 484-98; William O. Walker, 'The Son of Man: Some Recent Developments', *CBQ* 45 (1983), pp. 584-607.

2. R. Leivestad, 'Exit the Apocalyptic Son of Man', *NTS* 18 (1971–72), pp. 243-67.

be used as an exclusive surrogate for 'myself' or 'yourself'. Answers have ranged from 'never', 'maybe', 'possibly', to 'commonly'. Since later Aramaic texts reveal a different idiom, ההוא גברא ('that man') as the idiom for referring to oneself exclusively, most would agree that an Aramaic self-referencing 'son of man' saying should include more than the speaker, that is, 'me *and* others like me'.[3]

The meaning and use of the article 'the' with 'son of man', that is, בר־אנשא (with the article) versus בר־אנש (without the article) has been discussed in more than one study.[4]

The dating and validity of evidence have also attracted attention. Some give primary importance to Qumran with its curiously mixed spellings but without dropping the *aleph* of אנש. Others recognize the colloquial character of talmudic and midrashic contexts and find them illuminating despite the later spelling convention of writing ברנש without an *aleph*, or as one word.

3. This can be further differentiated into 'anyone, me included' versus 'one such as myself'. For further elaboration of restrictions within a self-referencing 'son of man' see Richard Bauckham, 'The Son of Man "A Man in my Position" or "someone"?' *JSNT* 23 (1985), pp. 23-33; Barnabas Lindars, 'Response to Richard Bauckham: The Idiomatic Use of bar enasha', *JSNT* 23 (1985), pp. 35-41; Maurice Casey, 'General, Generic and Indefinite: The Use of the Term "Son of Man" in Aramaic Sources and the Teaching of Jesus', *JSNT* 29 (1987), pp. 21-56.

4. It should be acknowledged that Western Aramaic retained distinctive usages of the definite article longer than Eastern Aramaic. Cf. E.Y.Kutscher, מחקרים בארמית הגלילית in Eduard Yehezkel Kutscher, *Hebrew and Aramaic Studies* (Jerusalem: Magnes, 1977), pp. 173, 176-77 (= *Studies in Galilean Aramaic* [trans. M. Sokoloff; Ramat-Gan: Bar-Ilan, 1976], pp. 7-8, 13). However, such a definite article is still not appropriate for marking a title with an idiom like 'son of man'. Articles with 'man' and 'son of man' are commonly 'generic'. For example, in Hebrew the Mishnah frequently uses ha-ish and ha-adam where English would prefer 'a man'. E.g. *Šebu.* 3.8 ועל האיש שהוא אשה ועל האשה שהיא איש where Herbert Danby translates (*The Mishnah* [London: Oxford University Press, 1933], p. 413) '[swearing—RB] of a man that he was a woman or of a woman that she was a man' or *Ab.* 1.6 והוי דן את כל האדן לכף זכות with 'and when thou judgest any man incline the balance in his favour' (Danby, *Mishnah*, p. 446). [The form *adan* for *adam* is a colloquial Mishnaic Hebrew form found about 40 out of 428 times in Codex Kaufmann.] The correction in 1QS 11.20 shows that a generic article with 'son of man' was probably an early phenomenon (Who can contain your glory? What therefore is a son of man בן אדם? [corrected to]...what therefore is 'the son of man' בן האדם [=a human].) Cf. also בני האדם at CDC 12.4 (Magen Broshi [ed.], *The Damascus Document Reconsidered* [Jerusalem: Israel Exploration Society, 1992], p. 33) and 1QH1.27 (Jacob Licht, מגילת ההודיות [Jerusalem: Bialik, 1957], p. 62).

One of the results of this debate has had wide influence. Most writers on the Gospels will now assume that in Aramaic 'son of man' *barnash* could not be used as a description of some visionary being from Daniel 7, a title as it were. At least one would not speak to a group of people and expect them to understand a Danielic reference unless some other information was pointedly taught and added to the context. And the Gospels do not record such a discussion or development.

The material in the Gospels raises serious questions. The Synoptics only use ὁ υἱὸς τοῦ ἀνθρώπου ('the son of the [particular] man'). Contrary to common semitic usage, many of the passages cannot be understood as potentially valid for more individuals than Jesus. Critical inquiry can assign such passages to a secondary status, developed by a Church community or the Gospel writers. Many have discussed the significance of this for the Gospels, of whom Maurice Casey has been especially prolific.[5] 'Son of man' sayings in the Gospels can be tested to see if they reflect this Aramaic idiom, to see if the saying is true 'for Jesus and for others like him'.

Recently, Casey has surveyed other approaches and pointed out where they have not properly addressed this basic Aramaic understanding. For example, Casey discusses Otto Betz,[6] who argues that Jesus used 'son of man' as a special self-reference, based on Daniel. Casey finds Betz's method unacceptable. Betz never deals with Aramaic reconstructions of the sayings. At Mk 2.10 Casey argues that Betz has not provided sufficient connecting links. I would agree with

---

5. P. Maurice Casey, 'The Son of Man Problem', *ZNW* 67 (1976), pp. 147-54; *idem, Son of Man: The Interpretation and Influence of Daniel 7* (London: SPCK, 1979); *idem*, 'General, Generic and Indefinite: The Use of the Term "Son of Man" in Aramaic Sources and in the Teaching of Jesus', *JSNT* 29 (1987), pp. 21-56; *idem*, 'Method in our Madness, and Madness in their Methods: Some Approaches to the Son of Man Problem in Recent Scholarship', *JSNT* 42 (1991), pp. 17-43; *idem, From Jewish Prophet to Gentile God* (Cambridge: Clarke, 1991); *idem*, 'Idiom and Translation: Some Aspects of the Son of Man Problem', *NTS* 41 (1995), pp. 164-82. Cf. Barnabas Lindars, *Jesus Son of Man* (London: SPCK, 1983) and Geza Vermes, 'The Use of נש בר/נשא בר in Jewish Aramaic', Appendix E in Matthew Black, *An Aramaic Approach to the Gospels and Acts* (Oxford: Oxford University Press, 3rd edn, 1967), pp. 310-28; *idem*, 'The Present State of the "Son of Man" Debate', *JJS* 29 (1978), pp. 123-34.

6. Otto Betz, *Jesus und das Danielbuch* (ANTJ, 6/II; Frankfurt am Main: Peter Lang, 1985); Casey, 'Madness', pp. 28-29.

Casey's criticism, yet I believe that Betz is closer contextually to what actually was going on. The important issue is this: Was it impossible/ improbable to refer to Daniel with Aramaic *bar-enash*? If so, Casey, Lindars, Vermes, and many others should be followed.

One last background point needs to be added: In spite of the development within the Greek Gospel tradition where the 'son of man' sayings are linked to Daniel 7, our early Church traditions ignore this link to Daniel 7. As early as Ignatius (*Ign. Eph.* 20.2) and the *Epistle of Barnabas* we have widely influential Church leaders pairing and contrasting 'son of man' with 'son of God' and interpreting 'son of man' as a title designating the humanity of Jesus. The Gospels' apparent emphasis on the humanity of Jesus becomes somewhat embarrassing for the Church with its theology of the incarnation. Contrary to their expectation, Jesus seems to spend all of his time emphasizing what everyone would have assumed, that he was a human, and ignoring what was important, that he was the son of God (cf. *Barn.* 12.10, 'See Jesus, not as son of man, but as Son of God').[7]

Interpretation of the son of man in the Gospels can be grouped into three approaches.

1.   Some have followed an apocalyptic position that assumes that within first-century Judaism Daniel 7 was already linked with a popular, apocalyptic–messianic expectation. This position has been extensively criticized in the last 30 years, in part due to the linguistic debate.[8] While this remains part of the

---

7.   Because of the recognition that Greek was also used widely in Galilee and Judea in the first century it would be good to state explicitly that Jesus most probably did not use Greek to develop the Greek phrase of the Gospels, ὁ υἱὸς τοῦ ἀνθρώπου. Greek does not fit the cultural milieu of subtle scriptural allusion and ὁ υἱὸς τοῦ ἀνθρώπου only produces something jarring and un-Greek, not a scripturally based title. Cf. Casey, 'Idiom and Translation', p. 178, 'A bilingual Jesus might have accepted this translation [ὁ υἱὸς τοῦ ἀνθρώπου for (א)שנ(א)רב—RB]. A Jesus who taught in Greek, however, would surely have expressed himself quite differently'. Casey's comment would have validity if Jesus was trying to say 'a person', as well as if he was trying to refer to the son of man in Dan. 7. The best that a Greek phrase could do would be to refer to the 90+ examples in Ezekiel. For a recent survey of Greek in Galilee see Stanley E. Porter, 'Jesus and the Use of Greek in Galilee', in Bruce Chilton and Craig A. Evans (eds.), *Studying the Historical Jesus* (NTTS, 19; Leiden: E.J. Brill, 1994), pp. 123-54.

8.   For more recent discussion, see J.J. Collins, 'The Son of Man in First Century Judaism', *NTS* 38 (1992), pp. 448-66; Thomas B. Slater, 'One Like a Son of

overall question of background to Jesus' sayings we will not discuss it in this chapter.

2. Many place primary importance on the context of the Son of Man sayings in the Gospels and conclude that somehow Jesus was responsible for the phrase and that he intended it as something special. Betz would be included here, also I. Howard Marshall,[9] among many.

3. Others place primary importance on the Aramaic language background of the phrase 'son of man' and use that for classifying historical sayings from secondary sayings attributed to Jesus. This is the approach of Vermes, Casey, and Lindars.

We will be looking at these last two approaches, the contextual versus the linguistic, and will argue that they can be fitted together. In the process, the linguistic approach will be seen to undergo considerable expansion.

From a Two-Dimensional Linguistic Framework to Three Dimensions

The above debate has taken place in a two-dimensional framework. This chapter will propose a three-dimensional framework. As can be expected, the wider framework turns out to provide a flexibility that dissolves some of the constraints in the above debate.

The two-dimensional framework is simply an interpretation based on two languages only, Greek and Aramaic. In that framework, the strange sayings in the Greek Gospels must be analyzed, and the Aramaic idiom 'son of man' must be analyzed.

The three-dimensional framework recognizes that three languages were in common use in first-century Judaism: Greek, Aramaic and Hebrew. Before discussing the significance of this for the Gospel material we will briefly look at some sociolinguistic conclusions and statements of several authors.

Man in First-Century CE Judaism', *NTS* 41 (1995), pp. 183-98; Adela Yarbro Collins, 'The Origin of the Designation of Jesus as "Son of Man"', *HTR* 80 (1987), pp. 391-407; and Douglas Hare, *The Son of Man Tradition*.

9.   In addition to Marshall's 1994 article see his 'The Son of Man and the Incarnation', *Ex Auditu* 7 (1992), pp. 29-43, and his book *The Origins of New Testament Christology* (Leicester: InterVarsity Press, 1976).

Hebrew in the First Century

Basically, Hebrew was a written language *and* a spoken language among some strata of Jewish society in the first century. The linguistic situation and the relationships between Greek, Aramaic, and Hebrew are complex. A short article is not the place to resurvey the evidence concerning first-century Hebrew. Rather, a few representative quotations will show that New Testament scholarship has a need to include this changing awareness of the language situation within its philological work.

James Barr writes:

> According to the [older] theory...the only Semitic speech used in actual life was Aramaic...The persistence of this view was encouraged by the separation between biblical and post-biblical studies; and it has been particularly influential through its effect upon New Testament studies.

> It is therefore important to realize that *this older view...is no longer held by experts in the field* [my emphasis]...Middle Hebrew rests upon a basis of colloquial spoken Hebrew. That this is so is no longer questioned by major workers in the field...When we consider the language situation of (say) the first century CE, it can no longer be assumed that the emphasis must lie on Aramaic to the exclusion of Hebrew. On the question, in what language the teaching of Jesus was given, an increasing number of scholars in recent years has considered Hebrew as a responsible hypothesis, though the evidence for Aramaic continues to be rather stronger.[10]

That is a fair assessment, but New Testament scholars must learn to interpret that within a multilingual framework, not within a monolingual framework.

Moshe Bar-Asher:[11]

> La recherche a démontré que l'hébreu a été parlé en Palestine jusqu'en l'an 200 environ; et personne ne conteste plus l'opinion selon laquelle l'hébreu conservé dans la littérature rabbinique est bien l'expression d'un parler vivant, usité dans différentes régions de Palestine.[12]

10. James Barr, 'Hebrew, Aramaic and Greek in the Hellenistic Age', in W.D. Davies and Louis Finkelstein (eds.), *The Cambridge History of Judaism*. II. *The Hellenistic Age* (Cambridge: Cambridge University Press, 1989), pp. 79-114 [82-83].

11. Bar-Asher is a leading scholar on Palestinian Aramaic and Mishnaic Hebrew. Much of his research is published in Hebrew and not frequently cited in New Testament studies.

12. 'Research has demonstrated that Hebrew was spoken in Palestine up to about

An interesting example of changing scholarly viewpoints is provided by John Emerton. In 1973 he wrote:

> However, despite the caution, I probably failed in 1961 to do justice to the weight and extent of the [rabbinic] evidence, and I now doubt whether it is plausible to question the authenticity of all the ordinary conversations in Hebrew on everyday matters that are recorded in rabbinical literature. It now seems to me that they render very probable the hypothesis that Hebrew was used as a vernacular by some Jews in the first two centuries AD.[13]

His fuller position should also be noted:

> Hebrew was probably used as a vernacular in Judea in the time of Jesus, but Aramaic was also used there and was in more general use in Galilee.[14]

Two outlines below reflect current scholarship on Mishnaic Hebrew and help to illustrate the complexity of the sociolinguistic situation.

1. Spolsky and Cooper differentiate language use by social groupings and list languages in assumed preference order for the period around 130 CE (italics added for emphasis).[15]

> Jews in the Diaspora:
> a. Egypt, Rome, Asia Minor   Greek.
> b. Babylon   Aramaic and *Hebrew*

200 CE, and no one any longer contests the view that the Hebrew preserved in rabbinic literature is truly the expression of a living speech, in common use in different regions of Palestine'. Moshe Bar-Asher, 'L'hébreu mishnique: esquisse d'une description', *Académie des Inscriptions et Belles-Lettres, Comptes rendus des séances de l'année 1990* (Paris: Diffusion de Boccard), pp. 199-237 (200).

One might point out someone like Klaus Beyer, *Die aramäische Texte vom Toten Meer* (Göttingen: Vandenhoeck & Ruprecht, 1984) as a counterexample to Bar-Asher or Barr. Beyer thinks that Hebrew died out as a spoken language around 400 BCE (*Aramäische Texte*, p. 49). Somewhat inconsistently, Beyer, quoting a Greek comment by Meleager of Gadara, allows that Phoenician continued in use in the area until the first century BCE (*Aramäische Texte*, p. 49), but he boldly argues that there was no room for colloquial Hebrew because Aramaic is attested throughout Palastine (*Aramäische Texte*, pp. 55-58). However, Beyer does not deal with the Hebrew evidence in its depth and diversity, so Bar-Asher's statement still accurately reflects the general consensus of experts in the field of Mishnaic Hebrew.

13. J. Emerton, 'The Problem of Vernacular Hebrew in the First Century AD and the Language of Jesus', *JTS* 24 (1973), pp. 1-23 [15].

14. J. Emerton, 'The Problem of Vernacular Hebrew', p. 21.

15. Bernard Spolsky and R.L. Cooper, *The Languages of Jerusalem* (Oxford: Clarendon Press, 1991), p. 26.

Non-Jews in Palestine:

a. Government officials	Greek and some Latin
b. Coastal cities (Greek colonies)	Greek
c. Elsewhere	Aramaic

Jews in Palestine:

a. Judean village	*Hebrew*, Aramaic
b. Galilee	Aramaic, *Hebrew*, Greek
c. Coastal cities	Greek, Aramaic, *Hebrew*
d. Jerusalem i. upper class	Greek, Aramaic, *Hebrew*
ii. lower class	Aramaic, *Hebrew*, Greek

2. Michael Wise includes some genre distinctions in his chart for the first century CE:[16]

Judean Villages
  A. Upper Classes
    High form—Standard Biblical Hebrew for most genres
      Standard Literary Aramaic, Greek for contracts, receipts
      Spoken Aramaic for letters
      Mishnaic Hebrew dialects for letters, contracts at times of
      nationalistic fervor
    Low form—*Mishnaic Hebrew*/Aramaic, Greek
  B. Lower Classes
    High form—Mostly illiterate
    Low form—*Mishnaic Hebrew*/Aramaic

Jerusalem
  A. Upper Classes
    High form—Standard Biblical Hebrew for most genres
      Standard Literary Aramaic for a few genres and ossuary inscriptions
      Spoken dialects of Mishnaic Hebrew and Aramaic for letters,
      contracts at certain times
      Mishnaic Hebrew for written halakhic discussions, temple record-keeping.
      Greek
    Low form—Aramaic, Greek
  B. Lower Classes
    High form—Mostly illiterate
    Low form—Aramaic, Greek, *Mishnaic Hebrew* dialects.

We might notice that the second chart does not deal with Galilee. Wise frankly admitted that we do not have enough evidence to definitely reconstruct the language situation.[17]

16. Michael O. Wise, 'Languages of Palestine', in J.B. Green and S. McKnight (eds.), *Dictionary of Christ and the Gospels* (Downer's Grove, IL: InterVarsity Press, 1992), p. 441.
17. 'There is simply not sufficient evidence to attempt such for Galilee, although

In a monographic treatment the many pieces of evidence for the above tables could be rehearsed and evaluated. Instead, we will look at one important story from the Mishnah, not to prove the above points but to serve as an example of the kind of evidence and problems that mishnaic researchers must deal with. The story is regularly cited in discussions on how long Hebrew was spoken colloquially. It is important to read the story itself in order to see that it is not tendential and only incidentally has anything to say about Hebrew. In the talmudic context the story is used to show that interpretation and exegesis must be based on the common and natural use of language. Five different examples are strung together in an Aramaic story framework. The first three examples have quotations from people speaking Hebrew. The last two examples are illustrated from Aramaic quotations. This story is thus neutral to the question of relationship between Hebrew and Aramaic. Academia may be interested in that question, but this story is only interested in showing that common speech, in either language, can lead to understanding.

b. Megillah 18a

קראה סירוגין יצא	If he reads it *serugin* he has fulfilled his duty.
לא הוו ידעי רבנן מאי סירוגין	The rabbis didn't know what was 'serugin'?
שמעוה לאמתא דבי רבי דקאמרה	They heard Rabbi's maid[18] saying to them
להו לרבנן דהוו עיילי	while they were entering the house

one can say that use and attitudes differed between the two regions [and, quite possibly, within Galilee, which was divided into two distinct cultures, Upper and Lower Galilee]' (Wise, 'Languages of Palestine', p. 441).

Additional questions of genre need to be added to the above charts and to the discussion: what languages were used by Galilean rabbis in the first century for public and private teaching? What languages were popularly used for parables in the first century, for sermons and moral exhortation, for halakhic discussion, and for prayer? New Testament scholars may be surprised at the amount of support for Hebrew in those genres. On the question of Galilee an important article is Shmuel Safrai, 'The Jewish Cultural Nature of Galilee in the First Century', *Immanuel* 24/25 (1990), pp. 147-86; cf. also, *idem*, 'Jesus and the Hasidim', *Jerusalem Perspective* 42-44 (1994), pp. 3-22 [especially 4]; *idem*, 'Spoken Languages in the Time of Jesus', *Jerusalem Perspective* 30 (1991), pp. 3-8. On synagogue practice during talmudic times, see Stephen D. Fraade, 'Rabbinic Views on the Practice of Targum and Multilingualism in the Jewish Galilee of the Third–Sixth Centuries', in Lee I. Levine (ed.), *The Galilee in Late Antiquity* (New York: Jewish Theological Seminary, 1992), pp. 253-86.

18. The maid of Judah ha-Nasi, compiler of the Mishnah, c. 200–220 CE.

פסקי פסקי לבי רבי

with interruptions,

עד מתי אתם נכנסין סירוגין סירוגין

'How long will you enter with
interruptions?'

לא הוו ידעי רבנן מאי חלוגלוגות

The rabbis didn't know 'Haloglogot'.

שמעוה לאמתא דבי רבי דאמרה ליה

They heard Rabbi's maid saying to 'that
man'

להההוא גברא דהוה קא מבדר פרפחיני

while he was sowing purslane,

עד סתי אתה ספור חלוגלוגך

'How long will you scatter your
Haloglogot?'

לא הוו ידעי רבנן מאי סלסלה זתרוממך

The rabbis did not know [Prov. 4.8].

שמעוה לאמתא דבי רבי דהוות אמרה

They heard Rabbi's housemaid

להההוא גברא דהוה מהפך במזייה

say to that man while he was turning his
hair,

אמרה ליה—עד מתי אתה מסלסל בשערך

'How long will you "twist" your hair?'

לא הוו ידעי רבנן מאי השלך על ה' יהבך

The rabbis did not know [Ps. 55.23].

אמר רבה בר בר חנה

Rabbah Bar Bar Hannah[19] said,

זימנא חדא הוה אזילנא בהדי ההוא טייעא

'Once I was walking with a certain Arab[20]

וקא דרינא טונא ואמר לי

while carrying[21] my bundle.[22] He said to
me,

שקול יהביך ושדי אגמלאי

'Take[23] your bundle[24] and toss[25] it on
my camel'.

לא הוו ידעי רבנן מאי

The rabbis did not know

וטאטאתיה במטאטא השמד

(Isa. 14.23)

שמעוה לאמתא דבי רבי דהוות

They heard Rabbi's maid

אמרה לחברתה

say to her colleague

שקולי טאטיתא וטאטי ביתא

'Take the broom[26] and sweep the house'.

This is admittedly a collection of traditional material and has been
recorded quite far away from its origin. The Galilean maid speaks
Hebrew with the rabbis and Aramaic with a fellow maid. What is

19. Rabbah Bar Bar Hanah was a 2–3 generation Babylonian Amora (= late third
century CE).

20. בהדי טייעא 'in the presence of a traveller/Arab' is Babylonian talmudic Aramaic [*BTA*].

21. דרינא 'I was carrying' is probably only *BTA*. Cf. Michael Sokoloff, *A Dictionary of Jewish Palestinian Aramaic* (Ramat Gan: Bar Ilan, 1990), p. 156.

22. טונא 'bundle' is *BTA*.

23. שקל is *BTA* (Sokoloff, *DJPA*, p. 565, doubts that it is Jewish Palestinian
[*JPA*], which prefers נסב.)

24. יהב 'load, burden' is *JPA* and *BTA*.

25. שדי 'toss, throw' is *JPA* and *BTA*.

26. טאטיתא 'broom' is not attested in *JPA*, perhaps accidentally.

clear is that she is portrayed as a bilingual. Perhaps the second maid was non-Jewish, but it is more likely to follow majority and see this as Aramaic becoming the first language around 200 CE in Galilee. Her knowledge of Hebrew was certainly not artificial if she knew a Hebrew vegetable/spice name that the rabbis didn't use, חלוגלוגות ('purslane').

The syntax and Aramaic style is slightly better in a parallel text, *Roš Haš.* 26b, while the context of *Meg.* 18a fits more closely. The first example explains an ambiguous Mishnah. It is difficult to believe that the rabbis did not know the meaning of סירוגין 'non-continuously', since it is part of the Mishnah. However, in context, did it refer to simple pauses or mixing the reading with something else (reading from another passage or perhaps translation)? The maid's words from daily life helped them fix the intended meaning of the halakha. The examples were all from daily life, explaining a rare word and explaining three Scripture passages (Prov. 4.8; Ps. 55.23; Isa. 24.23). Of incidental interest, we have a Babylonian rabbi speaking Aramaic with an Arab. Another problem is that the Aramaic of Rabbi's maid has been adapted to Babylonian.[27]

The Three-dimensional Approach

To summarize, Semitic studies have recognized Mishnaic Hebrew as a living language during Second Temple and New Testament times. New Testament scholarship, on the contrary, has tended to take a general conclusion, that is, that Aramaic was the most common language in Galilee, as a justification for treating the linguistic background of the Gospels monolingually. With regard to the Son of Man this can be quite misleading.

Let us look at the first example of a 'son of man' saying in Mark and Luke and consider a trilingual background:

Mk 2.10: ἵνα δὲ εἰδῆτε ὅτι ἐξουσίαν ἔχει ὁ υἱὸς τοῦ ἀνθρώπου ἀφιέναι ἁμαρτίας ἐπὶ τῆς γῆς—λέγει τῷ παραλυτικῷ,

The words are identical in all three Synoptic accounts, although there are differences in word order.[28]

---

27. A parallel reference is in *Ber. R.* 947.3 (MS V30, p. 140a-b) on 'broom' Isa. 14.23 *JPA* ממאטא.

28. The word order in Luke (ὁ υἱὸς τοῦ ἀνθρώπου ἐξουσίαν ἔχει ἐπὶ τῆς γῆς) connects 'on earth' with authority: 'the Son of Man has authority on earth'. [An object before the verb ἔχει 'to have' had become quite idiomatic in common Greek

We must deal with several layers. Mark (along with Matthew and Luke) uses the full form ὁ υἱὸς τοῦ ἀνθρώπου with two articles, which represents a final layer of Gospel tradition and a fixed phrase in the Synoptic Gospels. Becasue of this, Mark is probably assuming an accumulative meaning for the phrase which would include the tie-in to Daniel. This is more explicitly expanded in places like Mk 14.62.

What we need to ask is whether such an understanding makes sense within this story, by itself? The answer is 'Yes'. Both the mention of 'authority' and 'upon earth' have distinct communication purposes if Jesus based his phrase on Daniel 7. Daniel 7 is where all dominion, honor and rule is given to the Son of Man, that heavenly symbol/ representative of the people of God. ἐξουσία 'authority' in Mark is semantically close to שׁלטן 'ruling authority' and מלכו 'reign' in Daniel.[29] More importantly, a communicative purpose for 'upon earth' is found. While Daniel 7 takes place in heaven, Jesus needs to add the new information for his audience that this applies 'on earth' as well.

Now we come to the crucial question. Granted that a reference to Daniel would fit this context, how was it possible for Jesus to allude to Daniel and to provide for relevant communication for his audience? The answer is by referring to Daniel 7 in its original language, with Aramaic *bar-enasha*, in the middle of Hebrew speech.[30] The brief language switch would let the audience know that some other sense than the basic one was intended. It would have the effect of putting the phrase in quotation marks. In addition, Daniel 7 is the only place in Scripture where the Aramaic 'son of man' occurs. We must remember that we are watching an interaction between astute people who delighted in signaling meaning by allusions based on scriptural texts.

and should not be overly stressed.] Matthew is pragmatically similar to Luke since only the subject divides 'on earth' from the verbal core. The preferred manuscripts of Mark put 'on earth' at the end of the clause 'to forgive sins'. Logically, all sins are earthly so these Greek texts show salient information which is secondary to the main point 'having authority' and either applies to 'forgiving' or to the whole statement: 'The son of man has authority to forgive sins, on earth'. In both Mark and Luke–Matthew one finds 'on earth' as significant, new information implying a contrast with 'heavenly'.

29. The LXX uses ἐξουσία for שׁלטון at Eccl. 8.8. However, שׁלטון became associated with foreign governments in Mishnaic Hebrew so that רשׁות and סמיכות may be more probable underlying words.

30. The dialogue with the lawyers on halakha and theology would have had a high probability of having been in Hebrew in the first century. Cf. Safrai (n. 18).

The point is this: an Aramaic *bar-enasha*[31] in the midst of a Hebrew sentence will send the audience to Daniel 7 to further ponder the significance of Jesus' statement.

Now is it reasonable to assume that such a language switch could occur? Surely. Language shifts are common in later midrashic and talmudic material and they are attested earlier. Names, especially, are mixed in languages. For example, in the Hebrew Bar Kochba letters we have some Aramaic 'Bar' names.[32] And the Aramaic Bar Kochba letters even have an Aramaic name with a Hebrew title.[33]

While the above reconstruction can be criticized as speculation it is unreasonable to ignore the linguistic option. It would be even more speculative and presumptive to claim that Jesus could not have made use of the option and that *bar-enash* could not refer to Daniel. It would be unreasonable to claim that Jesus could only use son of man as a general description of what is true for a group of people.

What we need is a solution that best answers all of the incongruities. An Aramaic *bar-enasha* in Hebrew speech can do that. It represents a changing linguistic perspective, and if details fall into place and align themselves within that perspective, then that also helps to validate the new perspective.

The advantages of the above solution are threefold.

1. It proposes a rationale for the frozen Greek phrase 'the son of the (particular) man'. The underlying Aramaic was special and that special quality has been preserved in translation with an unnatural Greek title.

2. It provides a communication framework for Jesus. Jesus would not have been speaking impossibly obtusely.

3. It can help explain why the phrase fell into apparent disuse or misuse among early Greek Christian Churches. After translating *bar-enasha* into Greek there is no longer a contextual signal to Daniel. Son of man becomes interpreted as a foil to 'Son of God'.

---

31. I prefer *bar-enasha* with the article as a way of explaining the fixed Greek phrase in the synoptics. However, *bar-enash* would also have worked in this context since the language switch is giving the interpretive signal and not the article.

32. For example, משמעון בר כוסבא (Kutscher 1976: ה׳נ).

33. שמעון בר כוסבה הנסי על ישראל 'S. bar K., the leader of Israel' (Kutscher 1976: ל״ח). Here, a Hebrew title in an Aramaic context is the inverse of what is being proposed for Jesus: using an Aramaic term in a Hebrew context.

Corollaries and Further Questions

There are several possibilities for Jesus' use of son of man. It is possible that the Daniel reference was primary and that he always made use of an Aramaic language signal to make this clear.

It is also possible that he never made use of the mixed-language signal or that he only used 'son of man' in its normal sense of 'someone'. This last possibility strikes me as highly improbable because it produces a poor or clumsy explanation of how the Gospels end up with the strange Greek phrase 'the son of the man'.

Perhaps he sometimes used son of man as a quasi-title[34] referring to Daniel and that sometimes he used the phrase in the normal idiom, for 'somebody, a person'. In addition, some of the same-language son-of-man references[35] may have been purposely ambiguous and some of the Gospel references are probably redactional.[36] These considerations of variation beg of a subtlety for individual logia that requires a monograph, not an introductory article.

Finally, there is material here that is worth a re-evaluation of the son of man debate, from the foundations. It means that for Jesus to speak in Hebrew, whether occasionally, frequently or even regularly, will affect the way in which we construct historical theologies, because of the central place of 'son of man' in Jesus' words and in the Synoptic Gospel traditions. It is time for New Testament scholarship to recognize that the Danielic Son of Man encountered in the Greek Gospels can be derived from a Semitic reconstruction:[37]

e.g.
בשל שתדעו שא לבר-אנשא רשות על הארץ למחול על עוונות—...
למען אשר תדעו כי יש שלטון(?) לבר-אנשא על האדמה לסלוח לחטאים—...
כדי שתדעו שיש לבר-אנשא סמיכות(?) על הארץ לסלוח לעוונות—...

---

34. I qualify 'title' as quasi-title so as not to imply a pre-existent title in the first century. It would seem to have been a 'live' title, to borrow the distinction between live and dead metaphors.

35. I.e. בן(ה)אדם in Hebrew or בר אנש(א) in Aramaic.

36. E.g. Mt. 16.13 compared to Mk 8.27, Lk. 9.18. However, even with redaction, one cannot woodenly apply a principle like multiple attestation. Cf. David R. Jackson, 'The Priority of the Son of Man Sayings', *WTJ* 47 (1985), pp. 83-96.

37. Actual reconstruction of the Hebrew sentence in which the Aramaic *bar-enasha* would be used can vary according to how 'colloquial/mishnaic', how 'literary', or how mixed one makes the reconstruction.

THE VILIFICATION OF JEHOIAKIM
(A.K.A. ELIAKIM AND JOIAKIM) IN EARLY JUDAISM*

Steve Delamarter

Introduction

One of the tasks taken up by the exegetes of antiquity was to clarify the moral character of key biblical figures. This is the case, first and perhaps foremost, with the Chronicler's History. To the extent that one can refer to the Chronicler's History (CH) as exegesis of the Deuteronomistic History (DH),[1] this tendency is clear. The Chronicler's treatments of David, Solomon, Hezekiah, and Josiah, for instance, are well known.[2] In the cases of David and Solomon, certain moral

---

* Written originally for presentation at the consultation on 'Scripture in Early Judaism and Christianity' at the national meeting of the SBL in Anaheim, CA, November 1989. I wish to thank my colleagues at Western Evangelical Seminary, Gerald Wilson and Bill Vermillion, for helpful critiques of several points.

1. The position taken by T. Willi, *Die Chronik als Auslegung: Untersuchungen zur literarischen Gestaltung der historischen Überlieferung Israels* (FRLANT, 106; Göttingen: Vandenhoek & Ruprecht, 1972).

2. In addition to n. 1 above, see, for instance, Peter Ackroyd, 'The Chronicler as Exegete', *JSOT* 2 (1977), pp. 2-32; 'The Theology of the Chronicler', *LTQ* 8 (1973), pp. 101-16; Roddy Braun, 'The Message of Chronicles: Rally "Round the Temple"', *CTM* 42 (1971), pp. 502-14; 'Solomon, The Chosen Temple Builder', *JBL* 95.4 (1976), pp. 581-90; 'Solomonic Apologetic in Chronicles', *JBL* 92 (1973), pp. 503-16; Raymond Dillard, 'The Literary Structure of the Chronicler's Solomon Narrative', *JSOT* 30 (1984), pp. 85-93; Steven L. McKenzie, *The Chronicler's Use of the Deuteronomistic History* (Atlanta: Scholars Press, 1984); Rudolf Mosis, *Untersuchungen zur Theologie des chronistischen Geschichtswerkes* (Freiburger theologische Studien, 92; Freiburg, Basel, Wien: Herder, 1973); James Newsome, 'Toward a New Understanding of the Chronicler and his Purposes', *JBL* 94 (1975), pp. 201-17; Robert North, 'Theology of the Chronicler', *JBL* 82 (1963), pp. 369-81; H.G.M. Williamson, 'The Accession of Solomon in the Books of Chronicles', *VT* 26 (1976), pp. 351-61.

failures were overlooked, others were substantially edited and, in certain places, new and complimentary materials were added. Together, these exegetical moves served to sanitize the records of David and Solomon. The Chronicler also dealt with some of the lesser figures in Israel's history. For instance, the figure of Hezekiah was slightly elevated and that of Josiah slightly deflated, apparently to express a schema in which Hezekiah, not Josiah, represented the ideal king after David.[3]

This tendency to clarify the moral character of biblical figures— toward the good *or* toward the evil—was taken up with enthusiasm by later Greek tradents of the four books of Kingdoms. D.W. Gooding, for instance, produced a series of studies which analyzed Greek treatments of Solomon (whose character was further rehabilitated in a variety of ways)[4] and of Ahab, who was portrayed as merely weak-willed and hen-pecked by his evil wife Jezebel.[5] Likewise, the survey articles of J.W. Wevers[6] and H.S. Gehman[7] point out several more examples of this type of 'exegesis'. An outstanding example of competing attempts to clarify the character of a biblical figure is to be found in the two accounts dealing with Jeroboam's rise to power— accounts which flatly contradict one another but lie side by side in the final form of the Septuagint text of Kings.[8] The shorter (P) and longer

3. Cf. Frederick Moriarty, 'The Chronicler's Account of Hezekiah's Reform', *CBQ* 27 (1965), pp. 399-406.

4. D.W. Gooding, 'The Septuagint's Version of Solomon's Misconduct', *VT* 15 (1965), pp. 325-35; *idem*, 'The Shimei Duplicate and its Satellite Miscellanies in 3 Reigns II', *JSS* 13 (1968), pp. 76-92; *idem*, 'Text-Sequence and Translation-Revision in 3 Reigns IX 10–X 33', *VT* 19 (1969), pp. 448-69; and *idem, Relics of Ancient Exegesis: A Study in the Miscellanies in 3 Reigns 2* (Cambridge: Cambridge University Press, 1976).

5. Gooding, 'Ahab according to the Septuagint', *ZAW* 76 (1964), pp. 269-80.

6. J.W. Wevers, 'Exegetical Principles Underlying the Septuagint Text of 1 Kings ii 12–xxi 43', *OTS* 8 (1950), pp. 300-22; 'Principles of Interpretation Guiding the Fourth Translator of the Book of the Kingdoms', *CBQ* 14 (1952) pp. 40-56; and 'A Study in the Exegetical Principles Underlying the Greek Text of 2 Sm 11.2–1 Kings 2.11', *CBQ* 15 (1953), pp. 30-45.

7. H.S. Gehman, 'Exegetical Methods Employed by the Greek Translator of I Samuel', *JAOS* 70 (1950), pp. 292-96.

8. Moses Aberbach and Leivy Smolar, 'Jeroboam's Rise to Power', *JBL* 88 (1969), pp. 69-72; J. Debus, *Die Sünde Jerobeams* (FRLANT, 93; Göttingen: Vandenhoeck & Ruprecht, 1967), pp. 55-65; D.W. Gooding, 'The Septuagint's Rival

(M, T, S, V) editions of the encounter between David and Goliath seem to provide another example where later tradents (in this case apparently M, T, S, V) were working to clarify the details of a biblical story, including the moral fiber of the characters.[9]

The purpose of this study is to detail a few examples of this kind of exegesis with reference to a single king in the final years of the kingdom of Judah: Jehoiakim, also known as Eliakim or, in the Greek texts, Joiakim. As we will see, the figure of Jehoiakim has undergone substantial vilification in the extant literature of early Judaism. Sources for our study include 4 Kingdoms καιγε,[10] 4 Kingdoms Lucianic,[11] the supplements from 4 Kingdoms embedded in the text of 2 Paralipomena

Versions of Jeroboam's Rise to Power', *VT* 17 (1967), pp. 173-89; 'Jeroboam's Rise to Power: A Rejoinder', *JBL* 91 (1972), pp. 529-33; R.P. Gordon, 'The Second Septuagint Account of Jeroboam: History or Midrash', *VT* 25 (1975), pp. 368-93; 'Source Study in 1 Kings XII 24a-n', Transactions of the Glasgow University Oriental Society, 25 (1973–74 [1976]), pp. 59-70; R.W. Klein, 'Jeroboam's Rise to Power', *JBL* 89 (1970), pp. 217-18; 'Once More: "Jeroboam's Rise to Power"', *JBL* 92 (1973), pp. 583-84; E. Tov, *The Text-Critical Use of the Septuagint in Biblical Research* (Jerusalem: Simor, 1981), pp. 303-304.

    9.   D. Barthélemy, D. Gooding, J. Lust, and E. Tov, *The Story of David and Goliath, Textual and Literary Criticism* (OBO, 73; Freibourg and Göttingen, 1986); J. Lust, 'The Story of David and Goliath in Hebrew and Greek', *ETL* 59 (1983), pp. 5-25; S. Pisano, *Additions or Omissions in the Books of Samuel—The Significant Pluses and Minuses in the Massoretic, LXX and Qumran Texts* (OBO, 57; Freiburg and Göttingen, 1984); A. Rofé, 'The Battle of David and Goliath—Folklore, Theology, Eschatology', in J. Neusner, Baruch Levine, Ernest Frerichs and Caroline McCracken-Flesher (eds.), *Judaic Perspectives on Ancient Israel* (Philadelphia: Fortress Press, 1987), pp. 117-51; E. Tov, 'The Composition of 1 Samuel 16–18 in the Light of the Septuagint Version', in J. Tigay (ed.), *Empirical Models for Biblical Criticism* (Philadelphia: University of Pennsylvania Press, 1985); *Textual Criticism of the Hebrew Bible* (Minneapolis and Assen/Maastricht: Fortress Press and Van Gorcum, 1992), pp. 334-36.

    10.   There never was, apparently, an Old Greek account dealing with Jehoiakim or any of the other figures in 4 Kingdoms. The text that recounts these stories in extant 'Septuagint' manuscripts is not Old Greek, but from the so-called καιγε recension instead. The text in use is that in the Cambridge Larger.

    11.   Witnessed to in the family of texts boc₂e₂ and published in Lagarde's *Librorum veteris Testamenti Canonicorum* (Gottingae, 1883).

35 and 36,[12] as well as texts in 1 Esdras,[13] Josephus[14] and the Septuagint of Jeremiah.

Jehoiakim as the Co-Sponsor of God's Wrath (4 Kingdoms Lucianic 23.26-27; 2 Paralipomena 35.5c-d // Jeremiah 22.17)

The text of 2 Kgs 24.3-4 comments on the reasons for the invasion of hoards of pro-Babylonian forces against Judah:

> Surely this came upon Judah at the command of the Lord, to remove them out of his sight, for the sins of Manasseh, according to all that he had done, and also for the innocent blood that he had shed; for he filled Jerusalem with innocent blood, and the Lord would not pardon.[15]

According to the Deuteronomistic historian, this calamity came upon Judah because of the deeds of the king nearly half a century prior to this time. The idea of the transferability of guilt is very much at home in the thinking of the DH. Indeed, this is not the first time that the DH makes use of the sins of Manasseh as an explanation for the cause of evil in later times. The other notable occasion is in the account of Josiah's reign, when, after recounting an extraordinary list of his

---

12. The Greek title for 2 Chronicles. The text used is Brooke and McLean's *The Old Testament in Greek*, Volume II, Part III 'I and II Chronicles' (London: Cambridge University Press, 1932). The reader will note that the Greek translation of 2 Chronicles, known as 2 Paralipomena, contains plusses at various points—additional material imported from 2 Kings. These plusses are fascinating not only for how they affect the meaning of the 2 Paralipomena passage, but also because they appear to reflect a Greek text different from the standard Septuagint text of 2 Kings = 4 Kingdoms. Ralph Klein and Leslie Allen carried on a spirited exchange about the nature and origin of these pluses: Klein, 'New Evidence for an Old Recension of Reigns', *HTR* 60 (1967), pp. 93-105; Allen, 'Further Thoughts on an Old Recension of Reigns in Paralipomena', *HTR* 61 (1968), pp. 483-91; Klein, 'Supplements in the Paralipomena: A Rejoinder', *HTR* 61 (1968), pp. 492-95; Allen, *The Greek Chronicles* (Leiden: E.J. Brill, 1974), I, pp. 214-18.

13. The text used is *Septuagint: Vetus Testamentum Graecum Auctoritate Academiae Scientiarum Gottingensis editum*, vol. VIII, 1, Esdrae liber I, edited by Robert Hanhart (Göttingen: Vandenhoeck & Ruprecht, 1974).

14. The text used is *Josephus*, vol. VI, *Antiquities of the Jews*, Books IX–XI, with an English translation by Ralph Marcus (LCL, 326; Cambridge, MA: Harvard University Press, 1937, repr., 1978).

15. Unless otherwise noted, English quotations are from the RSV.

reforms[16] and recording a superlative evaluation of Josiah,[17] the text abruptly takes a turn for the worse:

> Still the Lord did not turn from the fierceness of his great wrath, by which his anger was kindled against Judah, because of all the provocations with which Manasseh had provoked him. And the Lord said, 'I will remove Judah also out of my sight, as I have removed Israel, and I will cast off this city which I have chosen, Jerusalem, and the house of which I said, My name shall be there'.[18]

The καιγε text of 4 Kingdoms—the text found in most Greek MSS— follows the MT quite closely. The Lucianic text, however, has an interesting variant. It says:

> The anger of the Lord was against Judah to remove him from his face on account of all the sins of Manasseh according to all that he did, and in the innocent blood which Joiakim shed and he filled Jerusalem with innocent blood.[19]

Jehoiakim is here indicted as the co-sponsor with Manasseh of the wrath of God!

The Lucianic account of this story is not alone in making this assertion. With slight variation, the same idea occurs in 2 Par. 36.5c-d:

> The anger of the Lord was against Judah to remove him from his face on account of Manasseh in all that he did, and in the innocent blood which Joiakim shed. He filled Jerusalem with innocent blood.[20]

The idea that Jehoiakim was responsible along with Manasseh for the downfall of Judah is no small matter. Where does it come from? Are we to suppose that the *Vorlage* of these texts represents a better Hebrew text and that the name of Jehoiakim had somehow fallen out of the MT? Or, should we rather suppose that the Lucianic text of

16. Nearly the whole of the account of Josiah's reign: 22.3–23.24.
17. 23.25.
18. 23.26-27.
19. 24.3-4: πλην θυμος κυριου ην επι τον Ιουδαν του αποστησαι αυτον απο προσωπου αυτου δια πασας τας αμαρτιας Μανασση κατα παντα οσα εποιησεν και εν τω αιματι τω αθωω ω εξεχεεν Ιωακειμ και ενεπλησε ταν Ιερουσαλημ αιματος αθωου (Lagarde's text; author's translation).
20. πλὴν θυμὸς κυρίου ἦν ἐπὶ Ἰούδαν, τοῦ ἀποστῆναι αὐτὸν ἀπὸ προσώπου αὐτοῦ διὰ Μανασσὴ ἐν πᾶσιν οἷς ἐποίησεν, καὶ ἐν αἵματι ἀθῴω ᾧ ἐξέχεεν Ἰωακείμ· ἐνέπλησεν τὴν Ἰερουσαλὴμ αἵματος ἀθῴου· (The Cambridge Larger; author's translation).

4 Kingdoms and that of 2 Paralipomena record an exegetical innova-
tion of later origin?

It is probably the latter option that is the case. The point of departure seems to have been the phrase having to do with the shedding of
'innocent blood'. The DH was clear that Manasseh had been guilty of
such acts, but makes no reference to such deeds on the part of
Jehoiakim. The book of Jeremiah, however, uses just this phrase—
shedding innocent blood—with reference to Jehoiakim. At 22.17, the
text says of Jehoiakim:

> But you have eyes and heart only for your dishonest gain, for shedding
> innocent blood,[21] and for practicing oppression and violence.

Can we not conclude that a common exegetical tradition stands behind
4 Kingdoms Lucianic and 2 Paralipomena? The exegetical tradition
itself appears to be based on the recurrence of the term 'innocent
blood' in 2 Kings and in Jeremiah. 2 Kings makes it clear that it is the
innocent blood shed by Manasseh that will bring about the downfall of
Judah and Jerusalem. Jeremiah 22.6-9, as well, makes it clear that
Jehoiakim's actions as king are contributing to the downfall of Judah
and Jerusalem:

> For thus says the Lord concerning the house of the king of Judah: 'You
> are as Gilead to me, as the summit of Lebanon, yet surely I will make you
> a desert, an uninhabited city. I will prepare destroyers against you, each
> with his weapons; and they shall cut down your choicest cedars, and cast
> them into the fire. And many nations will pass by this city, and every man
> will say to his neighbor, "Why has the Lord dealt thus with this great
> city?" And they will answer, "Because they forsook the covenant of the
> Lord their God, and worshiped other gods and served them"'.

And it is precisely in this context (v. 17) that Jehoiakim is accused of
shedding innocent blood.

For the later tradents, the signals all pointed in the same direction.
The boundaries between the texts became translucent and meaning
from the one (Jeremiah) can legitimately flow to the other (4 Kingdoms Lucianic and 2 Paralipomena).[22]

---

21. τὸ αἷμα τὸ ἀθῷον in the LXX.

22. This move is essentially what is described by one of the so-called
'hermeneutical rules' of later rabbinic Judaism.

Jehoiakim's Burial with Manasseh (4 Kingdoms Lucianic 24.6, 2 Paralipomena 36.8 // Jeremiah 22.18-19)

The concluding regnal resumé typical of the DH is used with reference to the end of Jehoiakim's reign. It makes no mention of his burial:

> Now the rest of the deeds of Jehoiakim, and all that he did, are they not written in the Book of the Chronicles of the Kings of Judah? So Jehoiakim slept with his fathers, and Jehoiachin his son reigned in his stead (2 Kgs 24.5-6).

Similarly, the Chronicler's typical concluding formula makes no mention of the burial of Jehoiakim in 2 Chron. 36.8:

> Now the rest of the acts of Jehoiakim, and the abominations which he did, and what was found against him, behold, they are written in the Book of the Kings of Israel and Judah; and Jehoiachin his son reigned in his stead.

While 4 Kingdoms καιγε mirrors the MT with no mention of the burial of Jehoiakim, 4 Kingdoms Lucianic contains a significant plus in 24.6: 'And Joiakim slept with his fathers and was buried in the garden of Oza (κήπῳ Οζα)'.

The Kingdoms material in 2 Paralipomena likewise contains such a plus. However, in this case, the toponymn is completely transliterated from a Hebrew original: 'And Joiakim slept with his fathers and was buried in Ganoza (Γανοζαη)'.

The obvious questions at this point are: Where did this material come from and why is it here? Historically speaking, if we were to assume the most for a moment, we might entertain the possibility that these two early Greek texts preserve a fragment of genuine historical information about Jehoiakim's burial place—information unknown from any other source. Such a scenario cannot be dismissed out of hand.

Assuming less about its historical authenticity, we might entertain a second theory, the possibility that later tradents were attempting to fill in what they perceived to be an incomplete form. According to this theory, we might suppose that they felt the need to mention the precise burial places of kings and that they provided such designations—whether or not such information was, in fact, available from actual historical sources. Were this the case, their work as tradents would not be directed at Jehoiakim personally with a desire to say anything in particular about him, but rather their work would be directed at the literary form with a desire to make it as complete as possible. This theory, however, has no other evidence to support it. The fact that no such additions appear anywhere else would indicate that this plus is aimed, one way or another, directly at Jehoiakim. But why? Even if the information stemmed from actual historical sources, why was it felt important to record it here?

The answer may be found, I believe, by taking a close look at the particular place mentioned in 2 Paralipomena: Ganozah. This is clearly a transliteration for the Hebrew גַּן־עֻזָּא[23] which is mentioned only two places in the Bible, at 2 Kgs 21.18 and 26. There, we find that Γανοζαη, or 'the Garden of Oza', was the burial place of Manasseh and Ammon. The motivation for recording Ganozah as Jehoiakim's burial place seems instantly transparent: even in death, Jehoiakim was in bad company.

One wonders again if our passage from Jeremiah did not have an influence on the formation of this tradition. The fuller text of that passage reads:

> But you have eyes and heart only for your dishonest gain, for shedding innocent blood, and for practicing oppression and violence. Therefore thus says the Lord concerning Jehoiakim the son of Josiah, king of Judah: 'They shall not lament for him, saying, "Ah my brother!" or "Ah sister!" They shall not lament for him, saying, "Ah lord!" or "Ah his majesty!" With the burial of an ass he shall be buried, dragged and cast forth beyond the gates of Jerusalem' (22.17-19).

This passage clearly sets forth a derogatory place of burial for Jehoiakim. And, there can be little doubt that it affected later ideas on the subject. By the time of Josephus, for instance, this prophecy had been woven as fact into the historical narrative:

> ...when the king of Babylonia brought an army against him, Joakeimos, in fear of what had been foretold by this prophet [Jeremiah], received him, thinking that he would suffer no harm, as he had neither shut him out nor made war on him. On entering the city, however, the Babylonian king did not keep his pledges but killed the most vigorous and best favoured of the inhabitants of Jerusalem together with King Joakeimos, whom he ordered to be cast out unburied before the walls and appointed his son Joachimos as king of the country and the city (*Ant.* 10.96-97).[24]

23. The LXX (καιγε) has κήπῳ Οζα in both places.

24. For treatments of the tradition in the rabbinic literature, see Ginzberg, *The Legends of the Jews*, IV, p. 285.

For the tradents in 4 Kingdoms Lucianic and 2 Paralipomena, the passage in Jeremiah suggested an ignominious death. They had apparently already reached the conclusion that Jehoiakim and Manasseh were cohorts in life; the passage in Jeremiah, perhaps, suggested to them that the two were cohorts in death.

Jehoiakim's Treatment of Zarius (2 Chronicles 36.4, 1 Esdras 1.36//Jeremiah 26.20-23)

1 Esdras records an interesting—and in many ways baffling—account at 1.36.[25] The closest parallel to it is in 2 Chron. 36.4. Neco deposed Jehoahaz, set Eliakim as king and changed his name to Jehoiakim. Then, the MT says, 'Neco took Jehoahaz his brother and carried him to Egypt'. The text of 1 Esdras follows the MT closely up until this last line where it has: 'Jehoiakim bound the nobles and seized his brother Zarius and brought him up out of Egypt'.[26]

The relationship between these two texts has puzzled scholars. One describes the text of 1 Esdras at this point as 'hopeless confusion arising from misreadings of the MT'.[27] Among the commentators, four problems are sensed. First, there is no mention in Chronicles or Kings of Jehoiakim arresting anyone. Second, the name of the person mentioned in Chronicles and Kings is Jehoahaz; in 1 Esdras it is Zarius. Third, Neco, the subject of the action in 2 Chronicles, is not mentioned at all. And, fourth, the text of 1 Esdras speaks of bringing someone out of Egypt rather than sending them to Egypt as in 2 Chronicles. Sensing all of these problems, J. Myers judges the text totally in error[28] and translates the passage: 'Moreover Jehoiakim imprisoned the chief men and arrested Zarios his brother whom he took along to Egypt'.[29] E. Kautzsch emends the text to speak of

---

25. Verse 38 in the Greek.

26. καὶ ἔδησεν Ἰωακειμ τοὺς μεγιστᾶνας Ζάριον δὲ τὸν ἀδελφὸν αὐτοῦ συλλαβὼν ἀνήγαγεν ἐξ Αἰγύπτου.

27. S.A. Cook, 'I Esdras', *Apocrypha and Pseudepigrapha of the Old Testament*. I. *Apocrypha* (ed. R.A. Charles; Oxford: Clarendon Press, 1913), p. 23.

28. J. Myers, *I & II Esdras* (AB, 42; Garden City, NY: Doubleday, 1974), p. 32 n. 36: 'A mistake for Jehoahaz. II Chron 36.4 says nothing of the arrest of the nobles but asserts that Jehoahaz was deported to Egypt'.

29. Myers, *I & II Esdras*, p. 30.

'Joahas' and his sojourn in Egypt.[30] Even Hatch and Redpath identify 'Zarius' with Joahaz.[31]

There is a passage in Jer. 26.20-23 (LXX 33.20-23) which tells of a prophet Uriah (אוּרִיָּהוּ) who fled from Jehoiakim to Egypt. Verses 22-23 say,

> Then King Jehoiakim sent to Egypt certain men, Elnathan the son of Achbor and others with him, and they fetched Uriah from Egypt and brought him to King Jehoiakim, who slew him with the sword and cast his dead body into the burial place of the common people.[32]

I would like to argue that the difficult text in 1 Esdras alludes not to the Jehoahaz, brother of Jehoiakim, mentioned in 2 Chronicles, but to the Uriah of Jeremiah 26.

Perhaps the greatest argument in favor of this avenue of investigation is, in the first place, that it attributes coherence to the text of 1 Esdras. To say that a text is a 'hopeless confusion arising from misreadings of the MT' is to assume the worst about tradents—authors, readers, and copyists—in antiquity. This is not a case where ambiguous syntax or unknown spellings produce an impossible text. Such exist, but this is not one of them. This is a text which, on its own terms, makes perfect sense. As one becomes familiar with tradents of antiquity—becomes aware of the obvious extent of their knowledge of the biblical text and sees the sometimes breathtaking economy with which texts can be reinterpreted—it seems more appropriate to begin by assuming the best about them. Instead of attributing 'hopeless confusion' to them, we might do better to describe ourselves as hopelessly confused by a text that doesn't conform to our expectations about the transmission of texts.

J. Myers considers the possibility that 1 Esdras may be alluding to

---

30. 'Joahas ist für den unverständlichen Namen Ζαράχης eingesetzt. Am Schluss ist nach 2 Chron. 36,4 und 2 Kün. 23,34 zu lesen ἀπήγαγεν εἰς Αἴγυπτον. Der griech. Text hat: er brachte ihn heraus aus Ägypten'. *Die Apokryphen und Pseudepigraphen des Alten Testaments* (Tübingen: J.C.B. Mohr, 1900), p. 5.

31. 'Ζαράκης in libr. apocr. 1 Es. 1,36 (38) (= יוֹאָחָז II Chron. 36,4)', E. Hatch, H.A. Redpath, *et al.*, *A Concordance to the Septuagint and the other Greek versions of the Old Testament* (3 vols.; Oxford: Clarendon Press, 1987; repr. Grand Rapids: Baker Book House, 1983), III, p. 65.

32. The LXX (33.22-23) has, καὶ ἐξαπέστειλεν ὁ βασιλεὺς ἄνδρας εἰς Αἴγυπτον καὶ ἐξηγάγοσαν αὐτὸν ἐκεῖθεν καὶ εἰσηγάγοσαν αὐτὸν πρὸς τὸν βασιλέα καὶ ἐπάταξεν αὐτὸν ἐν μαχαίρᾳ καὶ ἔρριψεν αὐτὸν εἰς τὸ μνῆμα υἱῶν λαοῦ αὐτοῦ.

the Jeremiah text but rejects the idea with the comment: 'in view of the context, it is scarcely possible that the writer had in the back of his mind the extradition of the prophet Uriah referred to in Jeremiah 26.23'.[33] It is not clear what Myers means by the word 'context' in his comment. If he means, 'in the context of the relationship between 1 Esdras and the MT of 2 Chronicles' his judgment seems absolutely right. But in the flow of the text of 1 Esdras, this information makes perfect sense: Jehoiakim comes to the throne and continues in the same kind of bad leadership as do his brothers and son. Specifically, he mistreats the leaders and maliciously pursues a prophet who has told the truth.

As a second argument—one on the level of more concrete evidence—one may note that 1 Esdras translates various names with Ζαραιας.[34]It is not difficult to see that the Hebrew אוּרִיָּהוּ could be among them. Contrariwise, it is difficult to see how the name Jehoahaz could have been rendered with Ζαραιας.

The third line of argument which strengthens this hypothesis is the pattern we have observed in which tradents have interpreted the texts of 2 Kings and 2 Chronicles in the light of information in the book of Jeremiah. We have already seen that other events in Jehoiakim's reign were reinterpreted in the light of Jeremianic material.[35] Indeed, since the accounts about Jehoiakim's reign in Kings and Chronicles are so sketchy, it seems only natural to do so.

Perhaps the most anomalous piece of evidence confronting our hypothesis is the designation of Ζαραιας as Jehoiakim's brother. If the use of the term 'brother' is limited to a literal sense, then the text must refer to Jehoahaz. However, it is possible for the term to be used in a figurative sense, as in Leviticus 19, Deuteronomy 15, 19, and 23, where instructions are given aimed at guaranteeing the fair treatment of fellow Israelites. The term is used explicitly in Deuteronomy 17

33. Myers, *I & II Esdras*, pp. 32-33.

34. Hatch, Redpath, *et al.*, *Concordance*, III, p. 65.

35. Those that find this hypothesis unconvincing will, no doubt, object that interpretation in the light of Jeremiah was not proved in the previous cases. Therefore, it hardly proves anything to assume as fact something unproven to prove yet another case: this begs the question. As true as this observation is, it constitutes a two-edged sword. The assumptions underlying alternative hypotheses have not been specified nor proved either. 1 Esdras' straightforward text at 1.36 (LXX, 38) can be judged a 'hopeless confusion' only if the a whole set of historical, textual, and translation assumptions are brought to bear.

where instructions regarding a king for Israel are discussed. There it says that 'you may not put a foreigner over you, who is not your brother' (v. 15). Indeed, in the context of 1 Esdras, such a use accords perfectly with the intent to vilify Jehoiakim. Jehoiakim's ruthless treatment of the prophet Uriah was all the more blameworthy in that it was a sin against a fellow Israelite.

This is, in fact, precisely the sense in which the writer of Esdras employs the term on several occasions. Two examples will suffice:

- The Levites are instructed to prepare the Passover 'in accordance with the directions of David king of Israel and the magnificence of Solomon his son. Stand in order in the temple according to the groupings of the fathers' houses of you Levites, who minister before your brethren the people of Israel' (1.5 [LXX v. 6]);

- The Levites, then, 'prepared the passover for themselves and for their brethren the priests, the sons of Aaron, because the priests were offering the fat until night; so the Levites prepared it for themselves and for their brethren the priests, the sons of Aaron. And the temple singers, the sons of Asaph, were in their place according to the arrangement made by David, and also Asaph, Zechariah, and Eddinus, who represented the king. The gatekeepers were at each gate; no one needed to depart from his duties, for their brethren the Levites prepared the passover for them' (1 Esdr. 1.13-16 [LXX 14-15]).[36]

Conclusions

In these ways, then, Jehoiakim's reputation was run through the mud in late antiquity and early Judaism. He was made the co-sponsor of God's wrath against Judah, his place of burial was put as Manasseh's tomb, and his foul treatment of the prophet Uriah was highlighted.

What, though, do these traditions tell us about the tradents and communities who forged and perpetuated them? In fact, they give us a good deal of insight into some of the dynamics at work in the canonical process,[37] that is, in the ongoing relationship between Scripture

36. See also, for instance, 5.3, 5.48 (LXX 47), 5.56 (LXX 54), etc.
37. I am indebted, of course, to my mentor, James A. Sanders, for my understanding of the nature of the canonical process.

and the communities who looked to them for identity and ethos.[38]

Generally, we see that the later communities of faith wrestled with the biblical text to make moral as well as historical sense of them. This wrestling produced a Greek text whose ethical statements and models were trustworthy and edifying to the Greek-speaking communities they served. But, clearly, these judgments about what was trustworthy and edifying stemmed from deep-seated assumptions about the nature of history itself, about how history did and did not—or should and should not—work. Ethics flowed, at least in part, from historiographical assumptions.

For instance, in one of our examples, we saw that the Greek editions follow the Chronicler away from the DH's doctrine of the transferability of guilt and toward a doctrine of immediate reward and retribution. Israel experienced military setback not only because of the deeds of a king 75 years earlier, but also because of the actions of the current monarch.

A second observation about the canonical process has to do with the tendency we observed for tradents to read the texts of Kings and Chronicles in the light of other Scriptures, especially Jeremiah. This may suggest that the task of producing an 'ethically clean' text was in part motivated by the need to harmonize ethical aspects of texts as well as their historical aspects. Jeremiah reports that Jehoiakim would undergo a demeaning burial. Thus, 4 Kingdoms and 2 Paralipomena can report that Jehoiakim was buried in the same tomb with Manasseh and Ammon.

The exegetical moves demonstrated in these texts reflect a set of convictions about how one goes about interpreting the biblical text. Modern interpreters would share with ancient interpreters the conviction that it is proper to compare texts in Kings, Chronicles, and Jeremiah that have to do with the same people and events. These texts, we believe, in one way or another bear witness to a single historical reality, though modern interpreters will be quick to note that each text

38. The term 'canonical process' is to be distinguished from the 'process of canonization'. The scholars who use these terms mean two very different things by them. The latter, more common, term has to do with the specific history surrounding the inclusion of various books into the official list of accepted Scriptures. The former, less widely understood, term has to do with the dynamics that are played out when people look to Scripture as canon. In various ways, these dynamics transcend any specific history and are at work any time and any place when Scripture is looked to as canon.

reflects its own perception about that reality and that the various texts may not share the same perception. But even we moderns will collate these perceptions to try to reconstruct some coherent view about the history. Tradents of antiquity were willing to extend this practice beyond general references to the same historical events. The occurrence of the same term, for instance 'innocent blood', in two passages bore witness, they believed, to a further historical and moral reality. In some way, the common moral judgment bore witness to a single historical reality. Thus, the later tradents produced texts that were not only historically coherent, so they believed, but morally coherent as well.

Ultimately, it must be noted, the value of such 'ethically clean' texts was eclipsed by the value of texts which exhibited a closer fidelity to the Masoretic text. Over time, believing communities began to develop an ontology of text.[39] By this term is meant a set of convictions about the nature and character of the biblical text such as its inspiration, its authority, its perfection right down to the very letters which made up the words. Such a set of convictions, once developed and articulated by religious communities, dictated to members of the community what were the proper and improper ways of handling (e.g. copying, translating) the biblical text. Exegetical and hermeneutical practices were circumscribed eventually by this ontology of text. These convictions produced not only the need for a new kind of Greek edition (for instance, those of καιγε and Aquila) which bore closer affinity to the proto-Masoretic text, but also spelled the beginning of the end for many of the translation techniques so prevalent in late antiquity. This did not mean that such interpretations could no longer be made—it only dictated where and in what forms they could be recorded. Indeed, this development in the view of Scripture seems to have been responsible for spawning several new genres in which such interpretations could be preserved.

Finally, these examples give us insight into the various, and often subtle, ways in which biblical texts were resignified.[40] I marvel at the

39. The term is Sanders's as articulated in 'Text and Canon: Concept and Method', *JBL* 98 (1979), pp. 5-29.

40. James Barr's *The Typology of Literalism in Ancient Biblical Translations* (MSU, 15; Göttingen: Vandenhoeck & Ruprecht, 1979), while extremely helpful on this general subject, seems more germane to texts of the type created in the first century CE and later, i.e. kaige and Aquila, etc. The earlier tradents (who produced the

economy with which some texts have undergone resignification. We have tended to conceive of ancient translators' work in the following manner: as texts were translated word by word into a receptor language, the selection of Greek words with narrower or broader semantic ranges than those in the *Vorlage* resulted in a text with slightly different nuances. To a certain extent, this undoubtedly happened. But this way of conceiving things is too narrow. For one thing, it reflects an overemphasis on translation as a linguistic exercise, as though the translation were driven exclusively by linguistic (grammatical, syntactical, and vocabulary/semantic) considerations. For another thing, it attributes an ineptitude to tradents of antiquity, namely, that they were unable to control the meaning of their finished text. I doubt that this is the best way to conceive what was going on. The text was read and conceptualized, and to some extent reconceptualized. A new understanding of the text was achieved. How, though, could they register this reconceptualization? The challenge was to use as much of the *Vorlage*'s words and syntactical relationships, etc., to make their new point. The wonder is not that these tradents did as much violence to the text as they did, but that they respected it as much as they did when they had so much themselves to contribute to the text. This seems, to me, to be a fundamentally different, yet appropriate, way to view the tradents of antiquity.

Old Greek, etc.) did not labor under a view of Scripture which forced them to deal fundamentally with forms of literalism.

Part III

INTERPRETATION IN THE RABBINIC AND PATRISTIC PERIOD

SANCTIFICATION OF THE (DIVINE) NAME:
TARGUM NEOFITI'S 'TRANSLATION' OF GENESIS 38.25-26

Esther M. Menn

In its translation of the story of Judah and Tamar (Genesis 38), *Targum Neofiti* interjects thematically charged elements of plot and dialogue at the climax of the biblical narrative (Gen. 38.25-26). This unexpected narrative expansion transforms the morally ambiguous account of David's genealogical origins into an illustration of the concept known as 'sanctification of the (divine) Name'—a rich concept that became equated with martyrdom during the course of its post-biblical development. In the following pages, I analyze the manner in which *Targum Neofiti* incorporates Genesis 38 into religious discussions central to vital, contemporary communities. One may therefore view my analysis of *Targum Neofiti*'s 'translation' of Gen. 38.25-26 here as a case study exploring the broader issue of how early Judaism creatively used biblical interpretation to express its distinctive identity, ideals, and values.

Although each of the Palestinian Targums contains a version of the narrative expansion found in *Targ. Neof.* Gen. 38.25-26,[1] *Targum*

---

1. The abbreviations for the Palestinian Targums are as follows:

    Targ. Neof.: *Targum Neofiti*, Alejandro Díez Macho (ed.), *Neophyti 1: Targum Palestinense MS de la Biblioteca Vaticana*. I. *Génesis* (Madrid and Barcelona: Consejo Superior de Investigaciones Científicas, 1968).
    Frag. Targ.: *Fragmentary Targum*, Michael L. Klein (ed.), *The Fragment Targums of the Pentateuch According to Their Extant Sources*. I. *Texts, Indices, and Introductory Essays* (Rome: Biblical Institute Press, 1980), including:
    Frag. Targ. P: *Fragmentary Targum*, Ms. Paris Hébr. 110.
    Frag. Targ. V: *Fragmentary Targum*, Ms. Vatican Ebr. 440.
    Gnz. Targs: Genizah Targums, Klein (ed.), *Genizah Manuscripts of Palestinian Targum to the Pentateuch*. I. (Cincinnati: Hebrew Union College Press, 1986), including:
    D: Cambridge MS T-S B 8.3, f. 2v.
    X: Oxford Bodleian Ms. Heb. c 75r (tosepta).
    FF: Cambridge MS T-S NS 184.81r, 182.2r (tosepta).
    E: Oxford Bodleian Ms. Heb. e 43, ff. 66r-67r.

Neofiti is an especially suitable text for this study. Since it offers an Aramaic rendition of the entire Torah, this Targum's translations and interpretations of other biblical passages can illuminate the material under consideration.[2] In addition, the version of Gen. 38.25-26 in *Targum Neofiti* is a particularly rich one. Not only does it contain the full range of motifs found in the other Palestinian Targums, it also alters traditional material to forward a distinctive presentation of the characters and events of Genesis 38 in terms of the concept 'sanctification of the Name'.[3]

> *Targ. Ps.-J.*: *Targum Pseudo-Jonathan*, E.G. Clark (ed.), *Targum Pseudo-Jonathan of the Pentateuch: Text and Concordance* (Hoboken, NJ: Ktav, 1984). Although this Targum has linguistic affinities with the Babylonian *Targum Onqelos*, it also contains a version of the narrative expansion found in the other Palestinian Targums.

In addition, the Babylonian *Targum Onqelos* will prove useful for comparative purposes:

> *Targ. Onq.*: *Targum Onqelos*, Alexander Sperber (ed.), *The Bible in Aramaic*. I. *The Pentateuch According to Targum Onkelos* (Leiden: E.J. Brill, 1959).
> *t. Targ. Onq.*: *Targum Onqelos Tosepta*, Sperber, *The Pentateuch*, also contains a version of the narrative expansion found in the Palestinian Targums.

For an introduction to targumic literature see Roger le Déaut, *Introduction à la littérature targumique*. I. (Rome: Istituto Biblico de Roma, 1966), and 'The Current State of Targumic Studies', *BTB* 4 (1974), pp. 3-32; Martin McNamara, 'Targums', in IDBSup (1976), pp. 856-61; and Díez Macho, *El Targum: Introduccíon a las Traducciones Aramicas de la Biblia* (Textos y Estudios 'Cardenal Cisneros', 21; Madrid: Consejo Superior de Investigaciones Científicas, 1979).

2.   Although *Targ. Ps.-J.* is also a complete Targum, its linguistic affinities to the Babylonian *Targ. Onq.* would complicate the discussion.

3.   Arguments of Díez Macho and other scholars concerning the antiquity of *Targ. Neof.* notwithstanding, its version of the narrative expansion in Gen. 38.25-26 is obviously late. Díez Macho, 'The Recently Discovered Palestinian Targum: Its Antiquity and Relationship with the Other Targums', VTSup 7 (1959), pp. 222-45, argues that *Targ. Neof.* is a 1504 manuscript copy of a basically pre-Christian work. In general, scholars who use *Targ. Neof.* to illuminate traditions recorded in the New Testament assign to it an early date, based on criteria including the presence of legal traditions contrary (and therefore supposedly prior) to mishnaic halakhah and of other early aggadic material. There is no proof, however, that what is anti-mishnaic is pre-mishnaic, and the presence of early traditions does not necessarily signify that an entire document is early, as Anthony D. York, 'The Dating of Targumic Literature', *JSJ* 5 (1974), pp. 49-62, demonstrates. The fact that the Aramaic in which it is written is later, from the third to fifth centuries according to Martin McNamara (*Targum Neofiti 1: Genesis* [ArBib, 1A; Collegeville: Liturgical Press, 1992], p. 3) indicates a later date of composition.

The differences between the biblical climax of Genesis 38 and *Targum Neofiti*'s rewritten version of it strike even the casual reader. The original version in Gen. 38.25-26 illustrates the understated literary style typical of biblical literature. Facing execution by burning for illegitimate sexual activity, Tamar produces proof of Judah's responsibility for her condition. Her father-in-law immediately revises his assessment of the situation and spares her life:

> As she was brought out, she sent to her father-in-law saying, 'By the man to whom these belong I have conceived'. And she said, 'Recognize, now, to whom this seal, cord, and staff belong'. And Judah recognized and said, 'She is more righteous than I because I did not give her to Shelah my son'. And he did not continue to know her again.

By contrast, *Targum Neofiti* dramatically augments the turning point of the narrative:

> Tamar *went out* to be burned in the fire, and she sought the three witnesses but did not find them. She raised her eyes to the heights and said, 'I beseech mercy from before you, LORD. You are he who answers the oppressed in the hour of their oppression. Answer me in this hour which is the hour of my distress, O God who answers the distressed, and illumine my eyes and give me the three witnesses. And I will raise up for you three righteous ones in the valley of Dura: Hananiah, Mishael, and

While a comparison between the narrative expansions of Gen. 38.25-26 in the Palestinian Targums suggests that many of their differences stem from distinctive oral presentations of the same material, it is most probable that Gnz. Targ. E is the earliest version of this expansion and *Targ. Neof.* and *Targ. Ps.-J.* are the latest (or at least the most developed). The relationship between the different Palestinian Targums has received much attention. For example, Renée Bloch's article, 'Note sur l'utilisation des fragments de la Geniza du Caire pour l'étude du Targum Palestinien', *Révue des études juives* NS 114 (1955), pp. 5-35, presents a textual comparison of *Targ. Onq., Targ. Ps.-J., Frag. Targ.* P, Gnz. Targs D and E, as well as the Peshitta, for Gen. 38.17-30. Through this study, she establishes that *Frag. Targ.* P and Gnz. Targs D and E are closest in language and content, and that *Targ. Onq.* and *Targ. Ps.-J.* have linguistic affinities, although *Targ. Ps.-J.* contains a version of the narrative expansion absent in *Targ. Onq.* The relationship between these Targums and *Targ. Neof.*, which was published by Díez Macho in 1968 after Bloch's study, is complicated. While in language *Targ. Neof.* Gen. 38.17-24 and 27-30 most resembles Gnz. Targs D and E, in a couple of places it differs and corresponds to *Targ. Onq.* and *Targ. Ps.-J.* Similarly, the version of the narrative expansion in *Targ. Neof.* Gen. 38.25-26 generally parallels those found in *Frag. Targ.* P and Gnz. Targs D and E, although it also contains significant features found elsewhere only in *Targ. Ps.-J.* The composite nature of *Targ. Neof.* suggests a relatively late date.

Azariah. When they go down into the burning fire, they will sanctify your holy Name'.

And immediately the LORD heard the voice of her prayer and said to Michael, 'Go down! Give them, his three witnesses, to her!' And her eyes were illumined and she saw them.

And she gave them into the hands of the judge[4] and *said* to him, '*The man to whom these belong—by him I am pregnant.* But as for me, even if I am burned I will not identify him. But my Witness,[5] who is between him and me, he will place in his heart (the willingness) to see them in this hour, and he will redeem me from this great judgment'.

Immediately Judah rose to his feet and said, 'I beseech you, brothers and men of my father's house, listen to me: It is better for me to burn in this world with extinguishable fire, so that I do not burn in the world to come which is the fire that consumes fire. It is better for me to be ashamed in this world which is a passing world,[6] so that I am not ashamed before my righteous fathers in the world to come. And listen to me, my brothers and my father's house: With the measure with which a man measures it will be measured to him, whether a good measure or a bad measure. And happy is every man whose deeds are revealed. Because I took the garment of Joseph, my brother, and dyed it with the blood of a goat and said to Jacob, "*Recognize, recognize, please,* is this your son's garment or not?" now to me it is said, "*The one to whom these, the signet-ring, the cord, and the staff, belong—by him I am pregnant*". Tamar my daughter-in-law is *innocent. By me* she is pregnant. Far be it from Tamar, my daughter-in-law—she is not pregnant with sons of prostitution!'

A voice[7] went out from heaven and said, 'Both of you are *innocent.* From before the LORD is the decree'.

And Judah recognized and said, 'Tamar my daughter-in-law is *innocent because*[8] *I did not marry her to Shelah, my son'. And he did not continue to know her again.*

4.   The text has a single 'judge' (דדיינא), which a scribe changed to a plural with an addition of a ' above the line (דדייניא). Díez Macho, *Neophyti 1*, p. 255.

5.   The Aramaic word שהדי could also be translated as 'the witnesses', or even possibly 'his witnesses', but clearly God is meant in the last part of the sentence.

6.   The text reads 'a created world' (עלם עבוד), but Díez Macho, *Neophyti 1*, p. 255, corrects it to 'a passing world' (עלם עביר), which corresponds to *Targ. Ps.-J.*

7.   *Targ. Neof.* has the spelling ברם קלא, which Díez Macho, *Neophyti 1*, p. 255, corrects to ברת קלא, literally, 'the daughter of the voice', as it appears in several other Palestinian Targum manuscripts.

8.   Díez Macho, *Neophyti 1*, p. 255, suggests reading the phrase בנין כך in *Targ. Neof.* as בנין כן, 'because' or 'therefore', as it appears in Gnz. Targ. E. For a discussion of this phrase see McNamara, *Targum Neofiti 1*, p. 178 n. 16.

Although this passage is far from a literal translation of the Hebrew text of Gen. 38.25-26, one can identify fragments of the biblical verses (italicized). These are recontextualized and sometimes radically revised within an expanded narrative context. To note just one example, the verb in the first phrase of the Aramaic passage, 'Tamar went out' (תמר נפקת), is an active form, replacing the passive Masoretic Hebrew verb in the first phrase of Gen. 38.25, 'She was brought out' (הוא מוצאת).[9]

Besides this and other paraphrastic translations, however, there is additional material for which the biblical verses cannot account. An additional movement in the plot, the loss of the three items of Judah's pledge, elicits an extended prayer from Tamar. Divine response through an angelic intermediary follows immediately. Tamar once more places her life in danger by refusing to shame her father-in-law. Judah responds immediately with a public address, in which he employs aphorisms to reveal his willingness to accept punishment for his misdeeds, confesses to not one but two sins, and clears Tamar of the charge against her. Both apparently would have been executed for their sexual relations, but a voice from heaven intervenes and declares their innocence.[10]

Yet even in its embellished version of the narrative, *Targum Neofiti* does not entirely abdicate the task of translation for creative composition. In addition to the words of Gen. 38.25-26, *Targum Neofiti* translates into Aramaic particular rabbinic traditions of exegesis that also

9. The extra-biblical material follows this loose translation of the first verb of Gen. 38.25. Targumic literature commonly incorporates additional material after translation of part of an actual biblical verse. Concerning this technique, see Avigdor Shinan, 'The Aggadah of the Palestinian Targums of the Pentateuch and Rabbinic Aggadah: Some Methodological Considerations', in D.R.G. Beattie and Martin McNamara (eds.), *The Aramaic Bible: Targums in Their Historical Context* (JSOTSup, 166; Sheffield: Sheffield Academic Press, 1994), p. 210. Similarly, the jarring return to the biblical text in Gen. 38.26 with Judah's anticlimactic recognition of the three items and his redundant declaration of Tamar's innocence signals the end of the expansive portion of the text. The narrative expansion in *Targ. Neof.* is thus entirely enveloped in scriptural citation, and the appearance of other biblical phrases in the passage maintains a verbal connection to the canonical text.

10. This basic structure is found in all the Palestinian Targums, although Gnz. Targ. D is broken at the end, Gnz. Targ. E lacks many elements from Judah's speech and the intervention of the heavenly voice, Gnz. Targs X and FF and *t. Targ. Onq.* lack Tamar's statement of willingness to burn rather than identify Judah, and the order of the elements in Judah's speech varies from Targum to Targum.

appear in other midrashic sources, including *Genesis Rabbah*, the *Tanhuma*, and the Babylonian Talmud. For example, the motif of the lost and found pledge items through which providence first enters the targumic expansion stems from a widespread alternate reading of the first verb in Gen. 38.25. Instead of 'she was brought out' (מוּצֵאת), a passive participle from the root 'to go out' (יצא), this alternate reading interprets the verb as 'she found' (מוֹצֵאת), an active participle from the root 'to find' (מצא). This alternate reading suggests that if Tamar found something, she must have lost it earlier.[11] Of course, translation obscures the pun-like verbal correspondence at the base of this exegetical tradition in Hebrew, since in Aramaic the verbs 'to go out' (נפק) and 'to find' (שכח), bear no resemblance. Only the narrative content of the tradition remains in *Targum Neofiti*.[12]

But even more intriguing than these two types of 'translation' is *Targum Neofiti*'s fundamental 'carrying across' of a problematic biblical narrative into a new semantic field designated by the phrase 'sanctification of the (divine) Name'. Tamar's prayer following the loss of the pledge items is an appropriate place to begin this discussion about *Targum Neofiti*'s thematic translation of Genesis 38, because its contents are articulated only in the Palestinian Targums:

> She raised her eyes to the heights and said, 'I beseech mercy from before you, LORD. You are he who answers the oppressed in the hour of their oppression. Answer me in this hour which is the hour of my distress, O God who answers the distressed, and illumine my eyes and give me the three witnesses. And I will raise up for you three righteous ones in the valley of Dura: Hananiah, Mishael, and Azariah. When they go down into the burning fire, they will sanctify your holy Name'.[13]

11. This assumption is clearly indicated in *Tanh.* Wayyešeb 9.17; *Gen. R.* 85.11; *b. Sot.* 10b; as well as later sources including *Yal. Šim'oni* Gen. 38.25 and *Midr. haGadol* Gen. 38.25.

12. Other motifs in *Targ. Neof.* stemming from exegetical traditions include Tamar's refusal to identify Judah, the patriarch's liability to the same punishment as his daughter-in-law, his voluntary confession, the reading of the events in Gen. 37 and 38 as cause and effect, and the absolving voice from heaven. I have discussed these motifs and their points of connection with the biblical text at length in my dissertation, 'Judah and Tamar (Genesis 38) in Ancient Jewish Exegesis: Studies in Literary Form and Hermeneutics' (University of Chicago, 1995), pp. 275-317.

13. All the Palestinian Targums note that Tamar raised her eyes to heaven and present a version of her prayer. Other rabbinic sources also depict Tamar as a prayerful person, but her intercession outside of the Palestinian Targums almost always takes place as she waits for Judah at the gate of Enaim. The introduction of a prayer

The addition of this prayer might not appear especially surprising, given the abundance of prayers composed to illustrate the piety of biblical characters, beginning with the Second Temple period and continuing into the rabbinic period.[14] The Targums, in fact, emphasize prayer to an even greater extent than many of the other types of literature containing midrashic material, and this emphasis reflects the liturgical context in which they first emerged and circulated.[15]

The recognition that the incorporation of a prayer corresponds to a general trend in targumic literature does not exhaust the significance of its specific contents for reconstructing the distinctive perspective of *Targum Neofiti* on Genesis 38, however. One of the most striking features of Tamar's prayer is the introduction of the biblical heroes from Daniel 3 in her vow, 'I will raise up for you three righteous ones in the valley of Dura: Hananiah, Mishael, and Azariah'.[16]

This particular projection into the biblical future is unexpected.

---

at this point in the narrative is justified in *Gen. R.* 85.7 by an explanation in the name of Rabbi (Judah ha Nasi, second-century Palestinian) of the phrase 'gate of Enaim' (פתח עינים). Since nowhere else in Scripture does this Hebrew phrase refer to a specific location, it is taken as an indication that Tamar lifted her 'eyes' (עינים) to the 'gate' (פתח) of heaven towards which all eyes appeal for help. In this source, Tamar prays for success in her deception of Judah: 'May it be your will that I do not go out empty from this house'. *Tanḥ.* Wayyešeb 9.17, and *y. Ket.* 13.1 contain similar versions of this prayer. Perhaps the motif of lifting the eyes to heaven which introduces Tamar's prayer in *Targ. Neof.* derives from this traditional understanding of the words 'gate of Enaim' (פתח עינים). If so, then this motif has been transferred in the Palestinian Targums to a later point when Tamar's life is endangered.

14. See for example the prayers of Esther and Mordecai in the Greek version of the book of Esther, and countless others introduced in so-called intertestamental and rabbinic literature. For a discussion of early Jewish prayer, see le Déaut, 'Aspects de l'intercession dans le Judaïsme ancien', *JSJ* 1 (1970), pp. 35-57, and Joseph Heinemann, *Prayer in the Talmud: Forms and Patterns* (SJ, 9; Berlin and New York: Walter de Gruyter, 1977).

15. See Avigdor Shinan, 'צלותהון ובעותהון'. תפילותיהן של ראשונים בראי התרגומים לתורה ["'Their Prayers and Intercessions'": Prayers of the Ancestors in Light of the Targums to the Torah'], *Sinai* 78 (1975), pp. 89-92 (in Hebrew). For further examples of prayer in the Targums, see McNamara, *Targum Neofiti 1*, pp. 40-41.

16. These are Daniel's companions in Babylon, designated in the story about Nebuchadnezzar's idol in the valley of Dura (Dan. 3) by their Babylonian names: Shadrach, Meshach, and Abednego. In all the Palestinian Targums, Tamar refers to these three men. Tradition regards Hananiah, Mishael, and Azariah as Judah (and Tamar's) descendants because they are described in Dan. 1.6 as Judeans—literally, 'some of the sons of Judah' (מבני יהודה).

Based on the thematic and linguistic similarities between Tamar's prayer and another prayer in *Targum Neofiti*, one might expect instead a reference to the great worthies of the past, Abraham and Isaac. Directly after the binding of Isaac, Abraham raises the issues of innocent suffering and divine response in a prayer for Isaac's descendants in *Targ. Neof.* Gen. 22.14:

> And now when his sons are in the hour of oppression, you shall remember the binding of Isaac, their father, and listen to the voice of their prayer and answer them and deliver them from all oppression, so that future generations that will arise after him shall say, 'On the mountain of the sanctuary of the LORD, where Abraham offered Isaac his son, on this mountain the glory of the Shekinah of the LORD was revealed to him'.[17]

Many of the thematic and verbal similarities in these two prayers, such as references to an 'hour of oppression' and entreaties for an 'answer' to prayer,[18] may be traced to the incorporation into both of phrases taken from the Seliḥot prayers used on the Day of Atonement, at times of distress, and on public fast days.[19] An Aramaic form of the Seliḥot prayer is very similar in wording especially to Tamar's

---

17. A version of Abraham's prayer after the binding of Isaac is found in all the extent Targums, according to le Déaut, 'Aspects de l'intercession', p. 41. It appears in other midrashic sources as well, including *Gen. R.* 56.10.

18. Reference to an 'hour of oppression' appears in both Abraham's prayer (בשעת עקתא) and Tamar's prayer (בשעת עקתהון). In addition, both prayers emphasize the moment of crisis with other expressions, including 'all oppression' (כל עקא, in Abraham's prayer) and 'this hour which is the hour of my distress' (בשעתא הדה דהיא שעת אננקי, in Tamar's prayer). Abraham's prayer for Isaac's descendants contains the requests that God 'listen to the voice of their prayer' (ושמע בקל צלותהון) and 'answer them' (ועני יתהון); these phrases are echoed in Tamar's address to the God 'who answers the oppressed' (דעני לעיקי) and 'who answers the distressed' (דעני לאננקי), and in her request that he 'answer me' (עני ית). The first line of Tamar's prayer, 'I beseech mercy from before you, Lord' (בבעו ברחמין מן קדמיך ייי), also opens Abraham's prayer in *Targ. Neof.* Gen. 22.14 (not quoted in its entirety above), although this line is a common introduction to prayer in *Targ. Neof.* For a discussion of the significance of the binding of Isaac in Jewish tradition, see Shalom Spiegel, *The Last Trial: On the Legends and Lore of the Command to Abraham to Offer Isaac as a Sacrifice: The Akedah* (trans. Judah Goldin; New York: Random House, Pantheon Books, 1967).

19. See B. Barry Levy, *Targum Neophyti 1: A Textual Study. I. Introduction, Genesis, Exodus* (Lanham, London, and New York: University Press of America, 1986), p. 229, and Heinemann, *Prayer in the Talmud*, pp. 150-54.

prayer: 'May he who answers the afflicted answer us'.[20] It is also interesting to note that the first petition in the Seliḥot prayer listed in the Mishnah (*Ta'an.* 2.4) makes reference to a prayer offered by Abraham. This opening petition begins: 'May he who answered Abraham our father on Mt. Moriah answer you and hear the voice of your cry this day'. This dependence on a form of prayer used in the synagogue emphasizes the liturgical context within which the Targums took shape.

More important for this discussion, however, the affinities in language between the two prayers in *Targum Neofiti* lead one to read them as a set and to speculate that perhaps Tamar exemplifies the distressed generations of the future to which Abraham refers in his prayer. If this is indeed the case, she calls upon God for deliverance through the merits of the ancestors Abraham and Isaac.[21] Yet, although Tamar's allusive prayer tacitly evokes the presence of Abraham and Isaac, her vow directs explicit attention not to the past, but to the future; moreover, her vow does not connect the story with the royal or messianic characters generally associated with Genesis 38, but rather with heroes from the Babylonian exile.[22] Because the introduction of Hananiah, Mishael, and Azariah is so unexpected, the valence of the events in Daniel 3 in Jewish thought provides the key to understanding *Targum Neofiti*'s portrayal of Tamar and the biblical chapter as a whole.

---

20. Heinemann, *Prayer in the Talmud*, p. 150.

21. For the concept of the merits of the fathers, see Ephraim E. Urbach, *The Sages: Their Concepts and Beliefs* (trans. Israel Abrahams; repr.; Cambridge: Harvard University Press, 1975 [1979]), pp. 496-508, especially pp. 502-507, which discusses the binding of Isaac.

22. The reference to Hananiah, Mishael, and Azariah does not in itself rule out the possibility that in one version of the tradition Tamar identifies a future source of merit that would spare her from death. This interpretation is indeed justified in the cases of Gnz. Targ. X and *t. Targ. Onq.* Each of these Targums portrays Tamar vowing that the three men 'will go down into the fire in my stead' (עַל דִּילִי). This remark implies that she understands them as her substitutes. Significantly, in some rabbinic sources Isaac and the three men at Dura are considered together as exemplars of faith and piety. In *Gen. R.* 56.11, for example, all four devote their lives to study after divine deliverance from death. *Targ. Neof.* develops the relationship between Tamar and her descendants differently, however. In this Targum, Tamar parallels the three men at Dura by sanctifying the divine Name in her own distinctive way.

Tamar uses a significant phrase to describe the three men at Dura in her prayer, when she promises God that they will 'sanctify your holy Name' (שמך קדישא ומקדשין) by descending into the fire.[23] 'Sanctification of the Name' (קידוש השם) is a term with a rich history of meaning.[24] In Tamar's vow in *Targum Neofiti*, the adjectival form of this expression describing the three men presupposes that specific, exemplary actions by humans, such as the descent of the three men into the fire, positively affect God's status and perhaps even his potency in the world. The Hebrew Bible does not employ the phrase 'sanctification of the Name' to describe this type of positive connection between human actions and the holiness of God. A form of this expression in which the subjects of the verb are humans appears only in Isa. 29.23, where God says that the offspring of Jacob 'will sanctify my Name' (יקדישו שמי). In this verse, however, the expression denotes a recognition of God's power to redeem rather than specific human deeds.[25] The single human action in the Pentateuch evaluated in terms of God's sanctification consists of Moses and Aaron's behavior at the waters of Meribah at Kadesh. This example is a negative one, however, for God chides Moses when he says, 'you did not sanctify me (לא קדשתם אותי) in the midst of the sons of Israel' (Deut. 32.51).[26] The lack of positive examples is significant, given the importance of the holiness of God and his Name in the Bible.[27] In biblical literature, especially in the

23. While all the Palestinian Targums depict Tamar vowing to raise up the three men at Dura, only *Targ. Neof.* and *Targ. Ps.-J.* specify that they will sanctify the divine Name.

24. For an overview of the history of this concept see Ithamar Gruenwald, קידוש השם: בירורו של מושג [Sanctification of the Name: Explanation of a Concept], *Molad* 24 (1967–68), pp. 476-84 (in Hebrew), and Samuel Safrai, קידוש השם בתורתם של התנאים [Sanctification of the Name in the Teachings of the Tannaim], *Zion* 44 (1979), pp. 28-42 (in Hebrew).

25. Similarly, the phrase 'the Lord of hosts you will sanctify' (את יהוה צבאות אותו תקדישו) in Isa. 8.13 designates recognition of God's status rather than specific human acts. *Targum Jonathan*'s rendition of Isa. 29.23 and Isa. 8.13, however, interprets Israel's sanctification as verbal acknowledgment of God's holiness, which does constitute the specific act of speech.

26. See also Num. 20.12 and 27.14 (in both verses להקדישני).

27. 'Holy' (קדוש) is a commonly used adjective describing God in many biblical passages, including Isa. 6.3, Lev. 19.2, and Ps. 22.4. God's Name is described as holy in Lev. 20.3; 22.2, 32; Amos 2.7; nine times in Ezekiel; 1 Chron. 16.10; Ps. 33.21; 103.1. In a number of other verses, God's Name itself is 'Holy One of Israel' (קדוש ישראל), as in Isa. 1.4; 5.19; etc. (a total of 25 times in Isaiah);

book of Ezekiel, God sanctifies his own Name and manifests his own holiness before Israel and the other nations of the world through displays of power.[28] Interestingly, while God alone enhances the sanctity of his Name, people desecrate his Name in numerous scriptural passages.[29] In these passages, 'desecration of the (divine) Name' (חילול הֹשם) occurs through specific human infractions of justice and violations of God's commandments which lessen his status, especially in the eyes of foreign nations.

In discussions traditionally associated with the tannaitic period (the first two centuries of the common era), however, the expression 'sanctification of the Name' appears not only in connection with the miracles and displays of power through which God enhances his own status, but also in connection with a variety of human actions which reflect positively on the divinity. During this period, the meaning of 'sanctification of the Name' is enlarged to include the opposite of the biblical expression 'desecration of the Name'. For example, human praise of the divine Name in a liturgical context constitutes 'sanctification of the Name' in traditions attributed to this period. In a discussion of the 'Additional Prayer' for the New Year, both the anonymous voice of the Mishnah and R. Akiba call the third blessing recited by the congregation the 'sanctification of the Name' (קדושת הֹשם).[30] 'Sanctification of the Name' by humans is also the goal in legal proceedings, according to a tradition attributed to R. Akiba. In an argument with R. Ishmael, he maintains that Jewish law should not be bent in cases involving Gentiles in order to acquit the Jewish party because the primary goal in these legal proceedings should be 'sanctification of the Name' (קידוש הֹשם).[31] The phrase 'sanctification of the Name' was also applied to the exemplary actions of biblical characters. For example, a tradition ascribed to R. Tarfon, a contemporary of R. Akiba, explains that the tribe of Judah merited the

Jer. 50.29; 51.5; Ps. 71.22; 78.41; 89.19; or 'Holy One of Jacob' (קדוש יעקב), as in Isa. 29.23.

28. God sanctifies his own Name and acts for the sake of his holy Name in Ezek. 36.22-23. See also Ezek. 20.44 and 39.25. God manifests his own holiness in Ezek. 20.41; 28.22, 25; 38.16; 39.27; Isa. 5.16; and Lev. 10.3.

29. See Lev. 18.21; 19.12; 20.3; 21.6; 22.2, 31-32; Ezek. 20.39; 36.16-20; Amos 2.7; Jer. 34.16; Mal. 1.12. Lev. 22.32 implies, however, that when people refrain from desecrating God's Name, his holiness is enhanced.

30. *m. Roš Haš.* 4.5.

31. *b. B. Qam.* 113a.

kingship because at the time of the exodus Nahshon led this tribe in jumping first into the waves of the sea before it had parted. God responded to Nahshon's eagerness to obey his command to enter the sea by saying, 'The one who sanctified my Name (מי שקדש את שמי) at the sea will come and rule over Israel'.[32]

The expression 'sanctification of the Name' eventually assumed yet another connotation in rabbinic literature. It came to designate the ultimate human testimony of faith: the willingness to die rather than repudiate religious beliefs and practices.[33] This meaning of the term gradually assumed dominance, until in the middle ages 'sanctification of the Name' became synonymous with martyrdom for the Jewish faith. The initial application of this expression to martyrdom may have been a response to the Hadrianic persecution following the failure of the Bar Kokhba revolt, which resulted in the deaths of R. Akiba and his ten companions, but the phenomenon of martyrdom itself was not new to Jewish history. Jews gave their lives for their religious commitment during the reign of Antiochus IV (Epiphanes) in the second century BCE and during the period of Roman rule leading up to and following the destruction of the Temple.[34] But the term 'sanctification

32. *Mek.* Bešallaḥ 6, Jacob Z. Lauterbach (ed.), *Mekilta de-Rabbi Ishmael* (repr.; Philadelphia: Jewish Publication Society of America, 1933 [1961]), I, p. 237. The same tradition appears in *t. Ber.* 4.18 and *Midr. Teh.* Ps. 76.2. At the root of this tradition is an exegetical tradition concerning Ps. 114.1, which reads, 'When Israel went out from Egypt, the house of Jacob from a people of strange speech, Judah became his sanctuary, Israel his dominion' (בצאת ישראל ממצרים בית יעקב מעם לעז היתה יהודה לקדשו ישראל ממשלותיו).

33. Willingness to die to fulfill God's command is implicit in Nahshon's action in the previous example, although the discussion in the *Mekilta* stresses his obedience and the reward that he receives. Similarly, in *Gen. R.* 43.2 R. Nehemiah (middle of the second century) states that Abraham was willing to fall in war against the foreign kings in Gen. 14 to sanctify the Name of the Holy One. Although Abraham does not ultimately die, this biblical character was willing to give his life in order to sanctify God's Name.

34. See the accounts in 1 Macc. 1.60-63; 2 Macc. 6–7; *4 Maccabees*; and Josephus, *Ant.* 12.255-56, for examples of martyrdom during the reign of Antiochus IV (Epiphanes). Especially significant is the recurrent story of the pious mother who encourages her sons to die rather than transgress the commandments. This motif is echoed in Tamar's vow, where she approvingly alludes to her descendants' willingness to enter the furnace rather than worship an idol. For willingness to die rather than transgress Jewish law during the Roman occupation see Josephus, *Apion* 1.43; 2.218-19, 233-35; and Philo, *Leg. Gai.* 117, 192, 215, 233-36. In addition, see the

of the Name' is never used to describe this type of principled death in literature before the Hadrianic persecution. Instead, one reads in the early references to martyrdom that pious Jews died so as 'not to desecrate the holy covenant' (μὴ βεβηλώσωσιν διαθήκην ἁγίαν)[35] or that 'they gave their souls for the commandments' (נותנין נפשם על המצות).[36] It is interesting to note that even in descriptions of the deaths of R. Akiba and his ten companions during the reign of Hadrian one does not always find the expression 'sanctification of the Name'. At times other, more traditional expressions appear, such as 'they devoted themselves to slaughter for the words of Torah' (מסרו עצמן לשחיטה על דברי תורה).[37]

One of the earliest uses of the expression 'sanctification of the Name' in connection with martyrdom is found in a passage associated with the name of R. Ishmael, R. Akiba's contemporary, in *Sipra*, an early commentary on Leviticus.[38] In this passage, R. Ishmael begins with an interpretation of the injunction in Lev. 18.5 to live through the commandments and moves to an interpretation of the connection

rabbinic sources discussed by Gruenwald, 'Sanctification of the Name', pp. 477-79.

35. 1 Macc. 1.63.

36. These are words attributed to R. Nathan, a fourth-generation tanna, in *Mek. Baḥodeš* 6 (Lauterbach [ed.], *Mekilta deRabbi Ishmael*, II, p. 247). For other examples of expressions used to describe martyrdom in earlier periods, see Gruenwald, 'Sanctification of the Name', pp. 477 and 479.

37. *b. Sanh.* 110b.

38. Two other passages employing the expression 'sanctification of the Name' to denote martyrdom appear in *Sipra*. In a passage commenting on Lev. 22.32 (Isaac Hirsch Weiss [ed.], *Sifra de-ve Rab he sefer Torat Kohanim* [Vienna: Jacob Schlossberg, 1862; repr.; New York: UM, 1946], p. 99), the divine statement, 'I will be sanctified' (ונקדשתי), introduces a gloss: 'Devote yourself and sanctify my name' (מסור את עצמך וקדש שמי). The expression 'to devote oneself' is a traditional designation for martyrdom, as noted above. Another anonymous tradition on the same page in the Weiss edition continues, 'On this condition did I bring you out of the land of Egypt: on the condition that you devote yourselves to sanctify my name' (שתמסרו עצמכם לקדש את שמי). Safrai, 'Sanctification of the Name', p. 31 n. 17, notes, however, that these expressions are lacking in Vatican Ms. 66, and cannot be considered original. For a similar expression, see *Cant. R.* 2.7, in which the words 'Give your soul for the sanctification of the Name' (תן נפשך על קידוש השם) appear in a discussion attributed to R. Hiyya (early third century) concerning the persecution under Hadrian. A version of R. Hiyya's discussion also appears in *Pes. K.* 11.14. Martyrdom during the Hadrianic persecution is also called 'sanctification of the Name' in *b. Ber.* 20a and *Midr. Teh.* 16.4.

between the holiness of God, the holiness of the people, and the observation of the commandments in Lev. 22.31-33. The discussion continues with material of special significance for discovering the larger interpretive background of the narrative expansion in *Targum Neofiti*, and for this reason I quote this passage in its entirety:

> 'Live through them' (Lev. 18.5), not die through them. R. Ishmael said, 'Where do you find in scripture that if they say to someone privately, "Worship idols or you will be killed!" he should worship and not be killed? Scripture says, "Live through them", not die through them. Does this imply that even if they speak to him publicly he should obey them? Scripture says, "You shall not profane my holy Name (את תחללו ולא קדשׁי שׁם), so that I may be sanctified (ונקדשׁתי)" (Lev. 22.32). If you sanctify my Name (שׁמי את אתם מקדישׁים), I myself will sanctify my Name through you'. Just as Hananiah, Mishael, and Azariah did. When all the nations of the world were stretched out before the image, they were standing, resembling palm trees (לתמרים דומים). Concerning them it is explained in the Writings, 'This is your stature: you are like the palm tree (לתמר דמתה)', etc. 'I will go up (אעלה) in the palm tree (בתמר) and seize its branches' (Song 7.8-9). I was exalted (מתעלה אני) through them in the eyes of the nations of the world, those denying the Torah. Today I am punishing those who hate them for them. Today I am reviving the dead for them. 'I am the LORD' (Lev. 18.5; 22.31, 32, 33). I am a judge who punishes and who is faithful in giving rewards.[39]

The basic intent of the first part of this passage ascribed to R. Ishmael is to limit Jewish suffering and death at the hands of foreign enemies while still preserving God's sanctity. To this end, R. Ishmael introduces a distinction between private and public compliance with pressure to pay homage to other gods. Most likely in reaction to the recent blood bath of the great Hadrianic persecution, he argues that under duress one is allowed to privately break commandments pertaining to idolatry, since the commandments were given to foster life and not to bring death. On the other hand, one must refrain from publicly worshipping idols even if this means that one will be martyred, because to comply would desecrate God's Name and detract from his status in the eyes of all those present. The contrast between private and public

---

39. *Sipra* Aḥare Mot 14 (Weiss [ed.], *Sifra de-ve Rab he sefer Torat Kohanim*, p. 76). The reference to God as judge in the final line of this passage recalls the court setting of the narrative expansion in *Targ. Neof.* The concepts of God's deliverance of the faithful and his desire to reward positive behavior in *Sipra* also have loose parallels in the Targum.

actions introduced here in the name of R. Ishmael appears elsewhere in reference to 'sanctification of the Name' in rabbinic literature. It may even be the case that *Targum Neofiti* alludes to this aspect of the rabbinic discussion through Tamar's refusal to publicly identify Judah, and through Judah's willingness to publicly confess his sins.[40]

Of special importance is *Sipra*'s association of the phrase 'sanctification of the Name' with the willingness to die rather than publicly defile the Name of God by practicing idolatry. Significantly, this association occurs in a paraphrase of Lev. 22.32, not in the actual biblical text. While the biblical verse forbids human desecration of God's Name so that God may be sanctified, the paraphrase of this verse which immediately follows positively enjoins human sanctification of God's Name, and it promises a corresponding reaction from God to sanctify his own Name through those who do so. With this paraphrase, there is a subtle transition from R. Ishmael's discussion of the proper response to actual threats to life triggered by recent historical tragedy to a discussion of a biblical example in which ultimately no one loses his life. In this example, Hananiah, Mishael, and Azariah's willingness to sanctify God's Name by accepting death rather than publicly worshiping Nebuchadnezzar's idol evokes a corresponding willingness on God's part to sanctify his own Name by miraculously delivering them in the presence of many people. The focus shifts from a real historical dilemma to a literary pattern of human devotion and divine intervention. This passage portrays both human and divine efforts to sanctify the Name in some detail, with the quotation of phrases from the Song of Songs serving as the point of transition between the descriptions of the actions of the three men and those of God.[41]

---

40. The public nature of Judah's confession is positively contrasted with the private nature of Joseph's refusal of Potiphar's wife's sexual advances in *b. Soṭ.* 10b, where both are explicitly described as sanctifying God's Name.

41. Safrai, 'Sanctification of the Name', p. 32, concludes that in this passage from *Sipra* 'the emphasis of "sanctification of the Name" lies on the acts of salvation that the Holy One Blessed be He does, just as he did in the story of Hananiah, Mishael, and Azariah'; however, his conclusion doesn't take seriously the dialectical relationship between human and divine actions to sanctify God's Name in this source. There are other rabbinic texts, including Louis Finkelstein (ed.), *Sipre Debarim* (Berlin: Jüdischer Kulturbund in Deutschland, 1939; repr. New York: Jewish Theological Seminary Press, 1969), pp. 342-43, and *y. Ber.* 9.1, that focus exclusively on God's miracle in saving the three men. This passage in *Sipra*,

It is not clear whether the paraphrase of Lev. 22.32 beginning with the expression 'If you sanctify my Name' and the presentation of the example based on Daniel 3 were originally associated with R. Ishmael, or whether they were later accretions to the discussion. In *b. Sanh.* 74a and in *b. 'Abod. Zar.* 27b, the distinction between private and public acquiescence to threats involving idol worship attributed to R. Ishmael concludes with the biblical quotation from Lev. 22.32, but it is possible that the discussion has been shortened to suit the halakhic purposes of these talmudic passages. The evidence of variant manuscripts is similarly not decisive in answering the question of whether or not the second half of this passage was originally associated with the figure of R. Ishmael.[42] Whatever the case, the important thing for this discussion is that at some point in the history of Jewish thought, whether during R. Ishmael's life or later, Hananiah, Mishael, and Azariah become archetypal exemplars of the human side of the concept 'sanctification of the Name'.[43]

It is no accident that the type of death which these three archetypes of 'sanctification of the Name' accept consists of burning. Fire has a special connection to God's holiness in the literature of the Hebrew Bible.[44] Theophanies, such as those at the burning bush and at Sinai, are frequently accompanied by fiery manifestations. The entire

---

however, begins with a discussion of when it is appropriate for Jews to die for religious convictions, and celebrates both human and divine sanctification of the Name.

42. See the discussion of the manuscript evidence in Safrai, 'Sanctification of the Name', p. 32.

43. The archetypal status of these three men is apparent elsewhere in rabbinic literature as well. They are described as sanctifying God's Name in *b. Pes.* 53b and in *Cant. R.* 7.8 (in which they are also listed as the three pillars on which the world is established, like Abraham, Isaac, and Jacob). When the question is raised in *y. Ber.* 9.1 of whether or not a blessing should be said at places where miracles have occurred to persons through whom the heavenly Name has been sanctified, Hananiah, Mishael, and Azaraiah appear as the examples of such persons. In pre-rabbinic literature as well, these three men figure prominently in speeches of encouragement given in times of persecution, although the term 'sanctification of the Name' does not appear. See, for example, *4 Macc.* 13.9; 16.21; and *3 Macc.* 6.6. The persistence of the status of these three men as archetypes of the concept of 'sanctification of the Name' in the sense of martyrdom may be seen in Maimonides' employment of them in his discussion of this concept in *Seper haMiṣwot* 9 and *Fundamental Principles of the Torah* 5.

44. See the discussion of the connection between God's holiness and fire in James Muilenburg, 'Holiness', *IDB*, II, pp. 616-25 (617-18).

sacrificial system which evokes the presence of God has fire at its center. It is the Seraphs, or 'fiery ones' who proclaim God's holiness in Isa. 6.2-3. The judgment of God is often depicted as accomplished through fire, and in fact God is called a 'consuming fire' in Deut. 4.24 and 9.3. An instance in which God sanctifies himself in Lev. 10.1-7 involves the deaths of Nadab and Abihu through a blast of divine fire at the dedication of the tent of meeting. Interestingly, some sources honor these two sons of Aaron because they contributed their lives for God's holiness.[45]

The archetypal nature of the narrative pattern found in Daniel 3, including its fire motif, may also be seen in its extension in the aggadah to other biblical characters, including the patriarch Abraham himself. In a number of sources, Abraham is depicted as willing to enter the burning 'furnace of the Chaldeans', which is a midrashic interpretation of the biblical phrase 'Ur of the Chaldeans' (אוּר כַּשְׂדִּים), rather than commit idolatry.[46] In at least one source, Abraham, like the three righteous men, is delivered by the angel Michael,[47] and this angelic intervention dramatizes the power of God before many people. Significantly, a number of sources describe Abraham's acceptance of a fiery death with the term 'sanctification of the Name',[48] and he is frequently coupled with the three men at Dura in discussions within the midrashic corpus.[49] *Targum Neofiti* reveals its awareness of this

45. In *Lev. R.* 12.2 Moses and Aaron marvel at the honor that God bestowed on Nadab and Abihu by choosing them to sanctify his house at its dedication. See also *b. Zebaḥ.* 115b.

46. See Louis Ginzberg, *The Legends of the Jews* (Philadelphia: Jewish Publication Society, 1925, 1953), V, pp. 212-15 nn. 33, 34, and 40, for sources describing Abraham's descent into the furnace.

47. The angel Michael assists both the three men and Abraham in *Gen. R.* 34.13. In other sources, however, the angel who aids the three men at Dura is Gabriel, the angel responsible for fire, not Michael nor God himself, as in the traditions concerning Abraham.

48. See, for example, *Gen. R.* 42.3, 7; 44.13.

49. See for example, *b. Pes.* 118a, in which a discussion of the words of Hananiah, Mishael, and Azariah as they went in and came out of the furnace digresses into a discussion of why God himself saved Abraham from the fire and then returns to a discussion of how Gabriel came to save the three men from the fire. See also the discussion in *Gen. R.* 34.9, in which God accepts the sacrifice of Noah because of the good smell of Abraham and Hananiah, Mishael, and Azariah as they came out of the fire. References to Abraham and the three men also appear side by side in *b. Sanh.* 93a. In this latter source, yet other biblical characters, the lying prophets Ahab and

aggadic assimilation of Abraham to Hananiah, Mishael, and Azariah when it presents the words of God to Abraham in Gen. 15.7 as 'I am the LORD who brought you out of the furnace of fire of the Chaldeans (אנה ייי דאפקת יתך מן אתון נורהון דכשדאי) to give you this land that you might inherit it'.[50]

Similarly, the narrative expansion in *Targ. Neof.* Gen. 38.25-26 assimilates Tamar and, to a lesser extent, Judah to the basic pattern of 'sanctification of the Name' exemplified by the three saints in Daniel 3. One of the most striking means through which it accomplishes this assimilation is through its emphasis on burning and fire throughout the narrative expansion. The motif of burning is already present in Gen. 38.24 in Judah's command to bring Tamar out 'and let her be burned' (ותשׂרף), and this specification of execution by burning may have been at least partially responsible for the original association of Genesis 38 with Daniel 3. But *Targum Neofiti* significantly amplifies the motif of burning. The first reference consists of the phrase at the opening of the narrative expansion, 'to be burned with fire' (למתוקדה בנורא), explaining why Tamar went out.[51] While this phrase may initially appear to be a redundant expansion of the second part of Judah's command in Gen. 38.24 to bring her out 'and let her be burned' (ותתוקד in *Targ. Neof.* Gen. 38.24), on further examination it proves to be much more than a superfluous embellishment.

For one thing, its inclusion of this expanded phrase signals that *Targum Neofiti* stands within an interpretive trajectory that understands Tamar's sentence in light of the biblical law in Lev. 21.9.[52]

Zedekiah of Jer. 29.21-22 and Joshua the High Priest of Zech. 3.1-2, are also cast into the furnace by Nebuchadnezzar, with less favorable outcomes. Besides biblical characters, R. Akiba and his companions are also compared to Hananiah, Mishael, and Azariah in *b. Sanh.* 110b, as righteous men who are burned for the sake of the Torah. Similarly, in *Gen. R.* 34.9 the martyrs of the Hadrianic persecution give off a pleasing savor, as do Abraham and the three men at Dura. The reference to a pleasing savor introduces imagery of the sacrificial cult into the discussion of those who sanctify God's Name by demonstrating a willingness to give their lives.

50. Other allusions to the tradition of Abraham and the Chaldean furnace appear in *Targ. Neof.* Gen. 11.28, 31; 16.5.

51. The complete phrase 'to be burned with fire' is found also in *Frag. Targ.*, Gnz. Targs D (although somewhat broken) and FF, and *t. Targ. Onq.* A shorter notice that she went out 'to be burned' is found in all the remaining manuscripts (*Targ. Ps.-J.* and Gnz. Targs X and E).

52. The association of Lev. 21.9 with Gen. 38 is also attested in *Gen. R.* 85.10

This biblical verse states, 'The daughter of a priest who defiles herself by engaging in illicit sex defiles her father. She shall be burnt with fire' (באש תשרף). The fact that the *Targum Neofiti*'s translation of the punishment specified in Lev. 21.9 (בנורא תתוקד) contains the same verb and noun that appear in the phrase at the beginning of the narrative expansion in Gen. 38.25-26 confirms the intentional link between the two biblical passages.[53] The original basis for this intertextual reading of narrative and law clearly lies in the common themes of 'illicit sex' (Hebrew root זנה) and execution by 'burning' (Hebrew niphal נשרף).[54] Once these biblical passages are brought together, however, their juxtaposition opens potential interpretive directions for the biblical narrative and its characters. For example, a number of sources present Judah as an exemplar of Torah obedience before Sinai when he orders that Tamar be burned in compliance with biblical law.[55] Other sources focus on the specification that the woman under discussion in the law is 'the daughter of a priest' and enhance Tamar's character by providing her with a famous priestly father, namely Shem, who was also known by the name Melchizedek.[56]

---

and *Tanḥ*. Wayyešeb 9.17, which attribute the tradition to R. Ephraim Miqsha'ah (second century), reporting R. Meir's words.

53. Translating and interpreting one biblical verse in light of another with which it has verbal or thematic links is a common practice in targumic literature. See Michael A. Klein, 'Associative and Complementary Translation in the Targumim', *Eretz-Israel* 16 (1982), pp. 134-40.

54. The fact that the verbal root in the expression 'desecration of the Name' (ילול השם) appears twice in Lev. 21.9 ('defiles herself', תחל; 'defiles her father', את אביה היא מחללת) is also suggestive, in light of *Targum Neofiti*'s interpretation of Gen. 38 as an example of its opposite, 'sanctification of the Name'.

55. See for example *Targ. Ps.-J.* Gen. 38.24; *Gen. R.* 85.10; and *Tanḥ*. Wayyešeb 9.17. Judah's order to burn Tamar in the biblical narrative may appear cruel and unusual in light of the fact that stoning is the form of execution specified in biblical law for sexual sins in Deut. 22.21, which contains the same word for sexual misconduct which appears in Gen. 38 (Hebrew root, זנה), and in Deut. 22.24. Burning is prescribed in Lev. 20.14, however. Judah is also depicted as an early keeper of Torah when he observes the levirate law in *Gen. R.* 85.5; *Lev. R.* 2.10; *Cant. R.* 1.2.5; and *Pes. K.* 12.1.

56. Examples of texts which name Shem as Tamar's father include *Targ. Ps.-J.* Gen. 38.6; *Tanḥ*. Wayyešeb 9.17; *Gen. R.* 85.10; and *Ruth R.* 8.1 (which does not consider this genealogy in a positive light). The equation of Shem with Melchizedek, the priest of the Most High God and king of Salem, is a common one in rabbinic literature and is recorded also in *Targ. Neof.* Gen. 14.18. The traditions which

While the mere presence of the phrase from Lev. 21.9 may trigger memory of these interpretive traditions, the primary significance of the phrase 'to be burned by fire' lies elsewhere in *Targum Neofiti*. In this Targum the phrase introduces a central theme of the passage which unites its component sections. A quick review of the narrative expansion locates the next appearance of the words 'burning' and 'fire' at the conclusion of Tamar's prayer. Here she vows that she will produce three saints who will go down 'into the burning fire' (בנורא יקידתא) if her prayer for divine assistance is answered.[57] This phrase, which once again contains the same words that appear in *Targ. Neof.* Lev. 21.9, is also almost identical to the last part of an Aramaic phrase that recurs throughout Daniel 3. This phrase is 'the furnace of burning fire' (אתון נורא יקדתא, Dan. 3.6, 11, 15, 17, 20, 21, 26), which describes Nebuchadnezzar's instrument of death into which Shadrach, Meshach, and Abednego willingly enter rather than worship the idol. It is remarkable how the final editor of the narrative expansion in *Targum Neofiti* has clipped this phrase from Daniel 3 of its first word, 'furnace' (אתון), to exaggerate the verbal similarities between the fates of Tamar and the three men at Dura.[58]

Reference to burning next appears in Tamar's address to the judge, where she states 'As for me, even if I am burned (יקדה) I will not identify him'. The explicit use of the word 'fire' (נורא) found in the two earlier occurrences of the motif of burning is missing in this

---

portray Shem/Melchizedek, whose midrashic development is too extensive to discuss here (see Ginzberg, *Legends*, V, p. 187 n. 51; pp. 209-10 n. 13; and pp. 225-26 n. 102), as Tamar's father provide her and the Davidic line with a royal and priestly maternal pedigree. In addition, the tradition of Tamar's priestly parentage justifies Judah's command that she return to her father's house when widowed (see Lev. 22.13). It also assimilates Judah's character to that of Joseph in the biblical narrative by depicting him as producing two sons with a priest's daughter just as his younger brother does.

57. The exact phrase describing the three men's descent 'into the burning fire' occurs only in *Targ. Neof.* Different expressions alluding to their entrance into the furnace are found in *Targ. Ps.-J.*, Gnz. Targs X and FF, and *t. Targ. Onq.* In *Frag. Targ.* and Gnz. Targs D and E Tamar names the three men without specifying what they would do.

58. In *Targ. Ps.-J.*, Tamar refers to 'the furnace of fire' (לאתון נורא) from Dan. 3, and in Gnz. Targ. FF, she employs the whole phrase 'the furnace of burning fire' (אתון נורא יק[דהא) from that chapter. These Targums make the reference to Dan. 3 more explicit, whereas *Targ. Neof.* emphasizes the shared fate of Tamar and the three men at Dura.

statement. But the correspondence between Tamar and the three men
at Dura already carefully established twice through exact verbal correspondence is reinforced in yet another way here. Tamar's readiness
to burn echoes Shadrach, Meshach, and Abednego's readiness to burn
in Dan. 3.16-18. In the biblical passage these men express their willingness to enter the furnace rather than worship the golden image,
whether or not their God chooses to deliver them. They emphasize
their active choice and personal risk in entering the furnace. In
Targum Neofiti, Tamar also expresses her willingness to burn rather
than violate an ethical principle.[59] Looking back at the opening of the
narrative expansion, one finds that Tamar's active choice to burn
rather than humiliate her father-in-law is expressed in its very opening words, through the transformation of the passive Masoretic reading, 'She was brought out' (הִוא מוּצֵאת), to the active targumic reading,
'Tamar went out' (תמר נפקת).[60] Through Tamar's principled acceptance of death, the punitive burning prescribed as a means of execution for sexual immorality by Judah in Gen. 38.24 and by the law of
the priest's daughter in Lev. 21.9 takes on a different valence in
Targum Neofiti. It becomes the means through which Tamar, like her
pious descendants in Babylon after her, proves that she is a person of
integrity, who would rather accept an unjust sentence than violate a
central ethical principle.

The final appearance of the motif of burning occurs in Judah's confession before the court. Judah states in an introductory aphorism to

---

59. Whereas the biblical narrative assumes that the pledge itself will identify
Judah, rabbinic interpretation focuses on the fact that Tamar never explicitly mentions
her father-in-law's name. For example, *b. Soṭ.* 10b registers surprise at this omission: 'She should have told (the messenger his name)!' This source also emphasizes
Tamar's silence when it applies the superscription of Ps. 56 to her, calling her a
'silent dove' (יונת אלם) when she loses the pledges. *b. Soṭ.* 10b may be associating
the word 'dove' (יונה) with the Hebrew root 'to oppress' (ינה). If this is the case, then
the theme of innocent suffering expressed in Tamar's prayer in *Targ. Neof.* is present also in this source. Note that in *Cant. R.* 2.14 the interpretation of the line 'My
dove in the clefts of the rock' as Israel entrapped by the Egyptians at the sea may
stem from the verbal similarity between the Hebrew words 'dove' (יונה) and the root
'to oppress' (ינה).

60. A number of Targums besides *Targ. Neof.* have this active reading, including
Frag. Targ. and Gnz. Targs D, FF (partially broken at this point), and E. A more literal translation retaining a passive verb is found in *Targ. Ps.-J.*, *Gnz. Targ.* X, and
t. Targ. Onq.

his family members, 'It is better for me to burn (יְקַד) in this world with extinguishable fire (בְּאֶשָׁא טְפֵיא), so that I do not burn (נִיקוּד) in the world to come which is the fire which consumes fire (אֶשָׁא אָכְלָ[א] אֶשָׁא)'.[61] This aphorism provides a fitting final appearance of the motif, despite the fact that the word for 'fire' (אֶשָׁא) differs from the word for 'fire' (נוּרָא) used earlier in connection with Tamar.[62] Underlying Judah's confession in court and his acceptance of death by burning lie two post-biblical interpretive assumptions. One is that even after Tamar produced the pledge items Judah's identity remains unknown, and so he is free either to remain quiet or to confess.[63] A second interpretive assumption is that as the party responsible for Tamar's pregnancy Judah will share her fate if he confesses.[64] His immediate confession with its expression of willingness to die a fiery death in *Targum Neofiti* is therefore a pious action.

Admittedly, the correspondence between Judah and the three exemplars of the concept 'sanctification of the Name' is complicated by the fact that in *Targum Neofiti* he merely accepts just punishment

61. All the Targums contain this aphorism, but only *Targ. Neof.* presents it as Judah's first words to the court.

62. A statement attributed to Ben Zoma (second-century Palestinian), associated with Judah's confession in a passage in *Exod. R.* Mišpaṭim 30.15 contains vocabulary similar to that in the two aphorisms in *Targ. Neof.*: 'If you have been put to shame in this world, you will not be put to shame before God in the world to come, for he is a consuming fire. Why is this? Because the shame of this world is nothing compared to the shame of standing before him in the world to come'. Ben Zoma's statement appears to be the source of Judah's aphorisms in the Palestinian Targums. The phrase 'consuming fire' (אֵשׁ אוֹכְלָה) which appears in Ben Zoma's statement and in *Targ. Neof.* Gen. 38.25-26 in an expanded Aramaic form, 'fire which consumes fire' (אֶשָׁא אָכְלָ[א] אֶשָׁא), is from Deut. 4.24 and 9.3, in which the phrase 'consuming fire' (אֵשׁ אֹכְלָה) describes God.

63. In the biblical story, the pledge is apparently irrefutable evidence of the patriarch's paternity. Once Tamar produces it, Judah immediately compares her favorably with himself and admits his failure to arrange a marriage with Shelah.

64. The assumption that Judah would be liable for punishment is also absent in the biblical narrative itself, in which the patriarch is free as head of the family to reverse his earlier decree concerning Tamar's fate. A number of biblical laws, however, stipulate that both the man and woman are to be executed for sexual misconduct. Of special interest in this connection is the law in Lev. 20.12: 'Any man who lies with his daughter-in-law, both of them shall certainly be put to death. They have done an abominable thing. Their blood is upon them'. Clear statements that both should be punished for their sin may be found in *Gen. R.* 85.11 and *Midr. haGadol* Gen. 38.25.

for his sins. The strong traditional interpretation of Judah as an exemplar of penitent confession conflicts with *Targum Neofiti*'s project of portraying the characters of Genesis 38 in light of the events of Daniel 3.[65] Despite this fundamental conflict, Judah's opening aphorism emphasizes that he, like Tamar and the three men, is willing to die in flames.

But although both Tamar and Judah express their willingness to burn, ultimately they are spared through a type of divine intervention entirely lacking in the biblical narrative.[66] The heavenly voice[67]

65. For an example of the portrayal of Judah's confession, see *Gen. R.* 71.5, in which he and a number of his family members (including Leah, David, and Daniel) are renowned for their confessions and praises. (Both words come from the same Hebrew root ידה.) In this and other sources, Judah's biblical evaluation 'She is more righteous than I' (Gen. 38.26) is quoted as the basis for his reputation as a confessing sinner. Judah's confession gains him various rewards in different sources. It is singled out as the reason why Judah's brothers praise him in Gen. 49.8, according to *Tanh.* Wayehi 12.12 and *Gen. R.* 97, New Version. It is described as the means through which Judah gained life in the world to come in *Num. R.*, Naso 9.17, and *Gen. R.* 97, New Version. It is regarded as the decisive factor through which Judah's offspring merited the kingship of the people in *Exod. R.* 30.19, although other sources (including *Mek.* Bešallaḥ 6; *t. Ber.* 4.18; and *Midr. Teh.* Ps. 76.2) object to this association by noting that confession only suffices to remove the guilt of the crime. Judah's confession is specified as the reason that the messianic lineage may be traced to this tribe in *Tanh.* Wayehi 12.12. It also explains why this tribe remained so long in the land where they settled in *y. Meg.* 4.11, based on a reading of Job 15.18-19, and why they were victorious in war over their enemies in *Gen. R.* 97, New Version. It is portrayed as the reason Judah's descendants were spared from death in the exile in *Gen.R.* 97, New Version; *b. Soṭ.* 10b; and *Tanh.* Wayyešeb 9.17, where Daniel is also spared. See also *Num. R.*, Naso 13.4, and *Exod. R.* 16.4. It is associated with the fact that the Jewish people are called by his name in *Tanh.* Wayehi 12.12; *Gen. R.* 98.6; and *Midr. haGadol* Gen. 49.8. Finally, Judah's confession merits the honor of having the four letters of the Tetragrammaton in his name in *b. Soṭ.* 10b. For further discussion, see C.E. Hayes, 'The Midrashic Career of the Confession of Judah (Genesis 38.26)', parts 1 and 2, *VT* 45 (1995), pp. 62-81.

66. In Gen. 38 itself, God appears only twice early in the narrative, in order to slay Judah's eldest two sons for their wickedness (Gen. 38.7 and 10). The rest of the biblical narrative lacks explicit reference to divine activity.

67. Literally, the voice is 'a daughter of a voice' (בת קול in Hebrew, ברת קלא generally in the Palestinian Targums). The motif of the divine voice is found in all of the Palestinian Targums except Gnz. Targ. E. The voice appears elsewhere in *Targ. Neof.*, for example in the story of the binding of Isaac (*Targ. Neof.* Gen. 22.10) which as noted above contains a prayer with similar thematic elements to Tamar's

acquitting Tamar and Judah and sparing them from a fiery death ('Both of you are innocent. From before the LORD is the decree') is a traditional motif incorporated, rather than invented, by *Targum Neofiti*.[68] Its presence nevertheless recreates Genesis 38 as a story of divine providence illustrating God's power to deliver those who piously surrender their lives, similar to Daniel 3.

Even before the voice actually sounds from heaven, Tamar introduces the motif of divine intervention when she expresses confidence that God will deliver her: 'But my Witness, who is between him and me, He will place in his heart (the willingness) to see them in this hour, and He will redeem me from this great judgment'. This verbal expression of faith in the power of God to save once again recalls the story of Hananiah, Mishael, and Azariah. In Dan. 3.17 these three men also express the possibility that their God might save them, although they are not as certain as Tamar that he will choose to intervene. It is worth noting that the expression 'my Witness' (שׂהדי), which Tamar uses to describe God in her statement of confidence, and the term 'witnesses' (שׂהדי), which earlier specifies the three items of the pledge, themselves evoke the concept of willingness to die for one's beliefs central to 'sanctification of the Name'. Not only in Greek is a

---

prayer, and also in *Targ. Neof.* Gen 27.33 and *Targ. Neof.* Num. 21.6.

68. The voice's double assertion results from a dramatic reassignment and expansion of Judah's first two words upon seeing the pledge in Gen. 38.26, 'She is more righteous than I' (צדקה ממני). (Significantly, the Palestinian Targums and other rabbinic commentaries entirely eliminate Judah's positive comparison of Tamar's actions with his own, most likely because it applauds Tamar's morally dubious behavior and reflects negatively on the patriarch himself.) The decree that 'Both of you are innocent' (תריכון זכיין) loosely corresponds to the Hebrew word 'she is righteous' (צדקה), although the Targum pluralizes the utterance and chooses a translation that emphasizes the legal nature of the scene. The assertion that 'From before the LORD is the decree' (מן קדם ייי הוה פתגמא) is a paraphrase of the prepositional phrase 'from me' (ממני) in the biblical text. In a number of sources outside the Palestinian Targums as well, the phrase 'from me' is reassigned to either the holy spirit or a divine voice claiming responsibility for the events in Gen. 38. These sources include *Gen. R.* 85.12; *Deut. R.*, 'Eqeb, Saul Liebermann (ed.), *Midraš Debarim Rabbah* (Jerusalem: Wahrmann Books, 2nd edn, 1964), p. 72; *Eccl. R.* 10.16; *b. Mak.* 23b; and *Midr. Teh.* 72.2. A voice is also heard at the conclusion of Judah's words in Gen. 38.26 in *b. Soṭ.* 10b, but the words attributed to it are different. For the rabbinic tradition that a heavenly voice intervened in three court cases in biblical times, including this one (Shem's court), Samuel's court, and Saul's court, see *Gen. R.* 85.12; *Eccl. R.* 10.16; *Midr. Teh.* 72.2; and *b. Mak.* 23b.

'martyr' (μάρτῦς) a 'witness' of faith through voluntary death, but also in rabbinic thought Hananiah, Mishael, and Azariah 'witness' (מעידין) to God's power through their descent into the furnace.[69]

Through its alignment of the characters of Genesis 38 with the three archetypes of 'sanctification of the Name' that appear in Tamar's vow, *Targum Neofiti* translates the biblical narrative in terms of larger cultural and religious discussions. In particular, these discussions concern the absolute claims of certain moral principles, the relative value of human life on this earth, and the power of God to deliver those who trust in him. It is true, however, that the correspondence between Tamar and Judah and the three men at Dura created in this narrative expansion is not as complete as that between Abraham and these men in aggadic literature. For example, hostile foreigners and the theme of idolatry are absent from *Targum Neofiti's* depiction of Genesis 38. These differences may be explained at least in part by the fact that the Targum is working within and around pre-existing biblical material and traditional exegetical motifs, rather than creating an independent legend such as the legend of Abraham's descent into the Chaldean furnace.

Evidence from the larger exegetical sphere of rabbinic Judaism confirms that the characters and events of Genesis 38 were indeed once interpreted in light of the concept 'sanctification of the Name' exemplified by Daniel 3. In fact, the passage from *Sipra* cited above contains one such piece of evidence at the point in the passage where

---

69. *Deut. R.*, 'Eqeb, Liebermann (ed.), *Midraš Debarim Rabbah*, p. 74, contains God's description of Hananiah, Mishael, and Azariah as 'those who witness (מעידין) for me, that I saved them from the fire'.

In addition, the Palestinian Targums' replacement of the biblical term 'pledge' (ערבון), designating security for Judah's debt to Tamar, with the term 'witnesses' (שהד/סהדי) accomplishes an important semantic shift from the business world of prostitution to the legal world of courts and justice depicted in the narrative expansion. Among other things, this shift relieves Judah of the appearance of an arbitrary patriarch who sentences his daughter-in-law to death without even questioning her, since the term 'witnesses' suggests due process. Three witness are one more than the two generally required to establish a point of fact in court, although here the witnesses are inanimate items. The number of witnesses in *Targ. Neof.* Gen. 38.25 is clearly based on the number of pledge items in the biblical story, but the number three has the additional function here of linking Gen. 38 with Dan. 3, which features three 'witnesses'.

phrases from Song of Songs appear in the discussion about the three
men at Dura:

> If you sanctify my Name (מקדישים אתם את שמי), I myself will sanctify
> my Name through you. Just as Hananiah, Mishael, and Azariah did.
> When all the nations of the world were stretched out before the image,
> they were standing, resembling palm trees (דומים לתמרים). Concerning
> them it is explained in the Writings, 'This is your stature: you are like the
> palm tree (דמתה לתמר)', etc. 'I will go up (אעלה) in the palm tree (בתמר)
> and seize its branches' (Song 7.8-9). I was exalted (אני מתעלה) through
> them in the eyes of the nations of the world, those denying the Torah.
> Today I am punishing those who hate them for them. Today I am reviving
> the dead for them. 'I am the LORD' (Lev. 18.5; 22.31, 32, 33). I am a
> judge who punishes and who is faithful in giving rewards.

The biblical material from Song of Songs quoted in this passage from
Sipra contains two references to a 'palm tree' (תמר), which is also
Tamar's name in Hebrew. The passage interprets the Hebrew word
'tamar' (תמר) in Song 7.8-9 literally as 'palm tree', judging from its
use of the plural form 'palm trees' (תמרים) in its figurative description
of the three men's erect posture before the idol immediately preceding
the scriptural quotations. But the curious interjection of these phrases
containing the word 'tamar' from Song of Songs into the context of
the discussion of 'sanctification of the Name' is highly suggestive. It
motivates a search for further evidence within the midrashic corpus
for an interpretation of them which directly compares Hananiah,
Mishael, and Azariah with the biblical character Tamar.

An explicit comparison of these characters appears in *Canticles
Rabbah*. Following an extended elaboration of the story of the three
men in Daniel 3, a brief alternate interpretation of the first part of
Song 7.8 appears:

> 'This is your stature: You are like Tamar' (דמתה לתמר, Song 7.8). Just as
> Tamar (תמר) was condemned to be burned (נגזרה עליה שריפה) but wasn't
> burned (ולא נשרפה), these (Hananiah, Mishael, and Azariah) were con-
> demned to be burned (נגזר עליהם שריפה) but weren't burned (ולא נשרפו).[70]

70. *Cant. R.* 7.8, *Midraš Rabbah 'al Ḥamišah Ḥummešе Torah weḤameš
Megillot* (Vilna: Romm, 1884–87), II, p. 75. The connection between Tamar and the
three saints in this tradition is confirmed in an interpretation in *Cant. R.* 7.9, which
reads, ' "Let your breasts be as clusters of the vine" (Song 7.9). This refers to Perez
and Zerah. Just as Perez and Zerah were condemned to be burned but weren't
burned, so these (three men) were condemned to be burned but weren't burned'.
Cant. R. 7.8-9 is the only source besides the Palestinian Targums that explicitly

This passage compares Tamar and the three men on the basis of the similarities between their stories. It must be admitted, however, that this tradition points only to their shared condemnation to be burned and its reversal, and not explicitly to any common willingness to be burned to sanctify God's Name.

The paragraph directly preceding this passage in *Canticles Rabbah*, however, emphasizes even more than Daniel 3 itself that Hananiah, Mishael, and Azariah actively decide to sacrifice their lives. In the midrashic portrayal of the events on the plain of Dura in this source, the prophet Ezekiel informs God that the three men 'desire to give their lives for the sanctification of your Name' (מבקשים ליתן נפשם על קדושת שמך). Ezekiel then inquires if the deity plans to save their lives. To test the three men, God replies that he will not intervene. But Hananiah, Mishael, and Azariah nevertheless proclaim their determination to follow through with their plan: 'Whether he stands by us or does not stand by us, we are giving our lives for the sanctification of his Name' (אנו נותנין נפשותינו על קדושת שמו).[71]

This strong presentation of the three men's willingness to burn for the purpose of exalting God colors the comparison between Hananiah, Mishael, and Azariah and Tamar that directly follows. Reading the passage in this context, one cannot help but conclude that Tamar's condemnation to be burned must also have involved some sort of laudable behavior that sanctified the divine Name. It is tempting to reconstruct a hypothetical reading of the phrases from Song 7.8-9 associated with Daniel 3 in *Sipra* that also alludes to Tamar's enhancement of God's status. These biblical phrases may have once been understood in the following manner: 'This is your (Hananiah, Mishael, and Azariah's) stature: You are like Tamar (דמתה לתמר)...I was exalted (אעלה) by Tamar (בתמר) and grasp her branches'. In this hypothetical reading, the word 'I will go up' (אעלה) in Song 7.9 is interpreted 'I was exalted' (אני מתעלה) as in the explanation in *Sipra*. The means through which God is exalted, however, is not the three men symbolized by the palm tree as in *Sipra*, but Tamar herself. In this reading, Tamar's 'branches' signify her three descendants in Babylon, whom God 'grasps' to save from the fire. There is, in fact, another source which interprets the word 'branches' as Hananiah, Mishael, and Azariah.[72]

---

associates the three saints with Tamar and not with Judah.

71. *Cant. R.* 7.8 (Vilna edition, II, p. 74).

72. See *b. Sanh.* 93a, in which this interpretation is attributed to R. Samuel b.

This reading of phrases from Song of Songs, although unsubstantiated by any extant interpretive record, might have contributed to the developing link between Tamar and the three men. Once this link between characters became established, the strong association of Hananiah, Mishael, and Azariah with the concept 'sanctification of the Name' would in turn begin to shape Tamar's exaltation of God into a corresponding example of 'sanctification of the Name'.

Some late sources, including *Midraš haGadol*, heighten the similarities between the stories of Tamar and the three men at Dura noted in *Canticles Rabbah* in a dramatic way. Focusing once more on the versatile first verb of Gen. 38.25, *Midraš haGadol* presents the following tradition:

> Another interpretation of 'She was brought out' (היא מוצאת): Don't read 'she was brought out' (מוצאת), but 'she was set on fire' (מוצָּת), as the wording in 'He kindled (ויצת) a fire in Zion' (Lam. 4.11). According to this interpretation, she was being burned (בשריפה).[73]

This interpretation identifies the root of the first word of Gen. 38.25 as 'to kindle' (יצת), rather than 'to go out' (יצא') as in the Masoretic text. The effect of this interpretation is to align the character of Tamar more closely with the three archetypes of 'sanctification of the Name' by describing her physical contact with fire. She, like Hananiah, Mishael, and Azariah, actually enters a fire.[74]

This midrashic intensification of the biblical narrative finds confirmation in a list of teachings attributed to R. Zutra that immediately follows in *Midrash haGadol*. This list concludes with the didactic statement:

> It is better that a person fall into the midst of the furnace of fire (שיפול לתוך כבשן האש) than embarrass his neighbor in public (ילבין פני הבירו ברבים). How do we know this? From the example of Tamar. As it is written, 'She was brought out' (or 'she was set on fire').[75]

Nahmani in the name of R. Jonathan; however, this passage interprets the palm tree as all of Israel, not as Tamar.

73. *Midr. haGadol* Gen. 38.25. The same tradition is also presented in *Leqah Tob* Gen. 38.25.

74. The heightened danger to Tamar's life in this late source parallels what happens to Isaac in late sources, where he is actually slain by Abraham. See Spiegel, *Last Trial*.

75. A version of the list of teachings attributed to R. Zutra appears also in *b. Ber.* 43b. The particular didactic statement quoted here may be found also in *b. Soṭ.* 10b;

The citation of this statement in close proximity with the earlier inter-pretation of the Hebrew word 'she was brought out' (מוצאת) as 'she was set on fire' (מוצת) reinforces the idea that Tamar actually entered fire rather than humiliate her father-in-law.[76] In addition, the descrip-tion of the pious person exemplified by Tamar, who chooses to 'fall into the midst of the furnace of fire' (שיפול לתוך כבשן האש), reinfor-ces the association between Tamar and the three men at Dura, who similarly 'fell into the midst of the furnace of burning fire' (נפלו לגוא אתון נורא יקדתא) in Dan. 3.23.[77]

Unfortunately, however, the particular expression 'sanctification of the Name' commonly associated with Hananiah, Mishael, and Azariah is never directly associated with Tamar in the sources examined thus far. But there is another source which does employ the phrase 'sanctification of the Name' in its portrayal of Tamar's actions in Gen-esis 38. This source is a seventh-century poem written by the liturgi-cal poet Yannai, who typically takes biblical events as his subject matter. Yannai's depiction of Tamar as a proselyte who risks her life to align herself with the people of Israel through bearing Judah's off-spring differs significantly from the depiction in *Targum Neofiti*; nev-ertheless, his poem confirms that the expression 'sanctification of the Name' was associated with this biblical character in the Palestinian milieu. In his poem, Yannai praises Tamar through an extended play on the Hebrew verbal root meaning 'to be holy' (קדש):

Holy (הַקְּדוֹשָׁה) Tamar sanctified the Name (קִידְּשָׁה שֵׁם) when she longed for consecrated (קְדוֹשָׁה) seed. She dissembled and became a cult prostitute (קְדֵשָׁה) and her Holy One (קְדוֹשָׁה) made her way successful.[78]

b. Ket. 67b; *b. B. Meṣ.* 59a; *b. Ber.* 43b; and *Yal. Šim'oni* Gen. 38.25. See also Urbach, *Sages*, p. 253.

76. This statement also reveals another resonance in rabbinic exegesis between Gen. 38 and the biblical law in Lev. 21.9 concerning the priest's wayward daughter. Before specifying the sentence of death by burning, the levitical law states that 'The daughter of a priest who defiles herself by engaging in illicit sex defiles her father' (אֶת אֲבִיהָ הִיא מְחַלֶּלֶת). The interpretive tradition extends the concern for the status of the father in this law to Tamar's concern for the reputation of her father-in-law.

77. The biblical allusion is obvious, despite the fact that the statement in *Midr. haGadol* is in Hebrew instead of in Aramaic as is the text of Dan. 3.

78. Menahem Zulay (ed.), *Piyyute Yannai: Liturgical Poems of Yannai, Collected from Geniza Manuscripts and Other Sources* (Berlin: Schocken and Jewish Publish-ing Company, 1938), p. 54.

Clearly in his eulogy Yannai develops a complicated pun on the biblical term 'cult prostitute' or 'priestess' (קְדֵשָׁה) which appears in
Hirah's question about Tamar's whereabouts to the local men in Gen.
38.21 and in his report to Judah in Gen. 38.22. In its biblical usage,
this term corresponds to an Akkadian title for a type of priestess
(*qadištu*).[79] But the root 'to be holy' (קדשׁ) at the base of the noun describing Tamar in Gen. 38.21 and 22 has multiple semantic associations
in Hebrew, as Yannai's liturgical poem illustrates. In one of his variations on the root, Yannai claims that Tamar herself 'sanctified the
Name' (קִידְּשָׁה שֵׁם). She may therefore be considered an exemplar of
this concept, although the precise range of its meaning in Yannai's
thought remains unclear.

It may be that the semantic associations of the verbal root 'to be
holy' (קדשׁ) applied to Tamar in Genesis 38 contributed to the development of the biblical narrative in terms of the concept 'sanctification
of the Name'. Another factor may have been the application of the
root 'to be righteous' (צדק) to Tamar by Judah in Gen. 38.26, when
he declares 'She is more righteous than I' (צדקה ממני). Those who
sanctify God's Name are commonly called 'righteous ones' (צדיקים) in
rabbinic literature.[80] Significantly, the roots 'to be holy' (קדשׁ) and 'to
be righteous' (צדק) applied to the figure of Tamar in Genesis 38 are
never applied to this figure in *Targum Neofiti*. In this Targum, the
same word for 'prostitute' (נפקת בר) used earlier in its translation of
Gen. 38.15 is used in Gen. 38.21 and 22,[81] and Judah declares Tamar
'innocent' (זכאה) rather than 'righteous' as in the Hebrew version. The
two roots 'to be holy' (קדשׁ) and 'to be righteous' (צדק) reappear in
Tamar's vow as descriptions of Hananiah, Mishael, and Azariah, who
are the 'righteous ones' (צדיקין) destined to sanctify the holy Name
(ומקדשׁין שׁמך קדישׁא).[82]

79. The traditional interpretation of the term קְדֵשָׁה as 'cult prostitute' has recently
been re-examined by Joan Goodnick Westenholz, 'Tamar, Qedeša, Qadištu, and
Sacred Prostitution in Mesopotamia', *HTR* 82 (1989), pp. 245-65.

80. For example, Hananiah, Mishael, Azariah, R. Akiba, and his companions are
called 'righteous ones' in *b. Sanh.* 110b. Hananiah, Mishael, Azariah, and Abraham
are called 'righteous ones' in *b. Pes.* 118a. Joshua the High Priest, who enters a furnace and emerges alive in a midrashic story in *b. Sanh.* 93a, is also called a
'righteous one'.

81. By contrast, the biblical narrative uses the common word 'prostitute' (זונה) in
Gen. 38.15 and the word 'cult prostitute' or 'priestess' (קדשׁה) in Gen. 38.21 and 22.

82. All the other Palestinian Targums call the three men 'righteous ones', except

One final problematic aspect of the understanding of Tamar as an exemplar of the concept 'sanctification of the Name' emerges in light of the evolving discussion within Judaism of when one should surrender one's life rather than transgress certain commandments. According to the passage from *Sipra* quoted above, R. Ishmael proposed that one need lay down one's life only when coerced into publicly worshipping idols. The example of the three men at Dura who 'sanctified the Name' by refusing to bow down to the golden statue before the assembled people fits well into his discussion. An alternate ruling was more stringent, however, in that it eliminated the distinction between private and public actions and specified two additional commandments that one should not transgress, even at the cost of one's life. According to the tradition found in *b. Sanh.* 74a, by a majority vote in Lod it was resolved:

> Concerning transgression of any law of the Torah, if they say to a man, 'Transgress, so that you will not be killed', he should transgress and not be killed, except for idolatry, incest, and shedding blood (ושפיכות דמים).

Targum Neofiti demonstrates its awareness of this ruling when it charges the people of Sodom with three sins in its version of Gen. 13.13:

> And the people of Sodom were evil, each man towards his neighbor, and they were very guilty of incest, of shedding blood (ובשפיכות אדמייה), and of idolatry before the Lord.[83]

In view of the placement of incest among the three weightiest transgressions it becomes difficult to understand Tamar's character positively, since in the biblical story she deliberately seeks sexual union with her father-in-law.[84] *Targum Neofiti* and other rabbinic sources

---

for *Targ. Ps.-J.*, which calls them 'holy ones' (קדישא).

83. Similarly, a marginal note in *Targ. Neof.* describes how Laban cleansed his house of these three great sins in preparation for receiving Jacob as his guest in Gen. 24.31: 'I have cleansed the house. I have cleansed (it) for worship. I have set it in order from three harsh works that stood within it: from idolatry, from incest, and from shedding innocent blood (שפיכות דם זכאי). And I have set a place in order for the camels'.

84. Rabbinic interpretations of Gen. 38 do not emphasize the biblical prohibition against incest with a daughter-in-law ('You shall not reveal the nakedness of your daughter-in-law', ערות כלתך לא תגלה) in Lev. 18.15, although the fact that Tamar is Judah's daughter-in-law constitutes such an important part of the story that I Chron. 2.4 specifies their affinity. In Ruth 4.12, 18-22 Tamar receives positive evaluation as

therefore take a drastic measure to preserve Tamar's reputation. Rather than evade the issue, they meet it head on and present Tamar not as a shirker of the minimum standards set at Lod, but as a keeper of a high moral standard who would willingly die even to prevent her father-in-law's humiliation. The focus on her zeal for this ethical principle functions as a kind of sleight of hand, preventing too much reflection on her voluntary transgression of one of the three commandments that one should never transgress.

Later sources, such as *Midraš haGadol*, recognize this problematic aspect of the biblical text and of the midrashic interpretation of Tamar in light of discussions about when one should die rather than transgress a commandment. In a discussion appearing in conjunction with the traditions quoted earlier concerning Tamar's entrance into the fire,[85] this source moralizes the list of three commandments and argues that embarrassing one's neighbor is actually among the three greatest sins—perhaps the only sin through which one forfeits all hope for a part in the world to come.[86] *Midraš haGadol* introduces a teaching attributed to R. Nahman b. Isaac at this point in the discussion: 'Everyone who causes his neighbor to blush with words (כל המלבין פני חבירו בדברים) is the same as one who sheds blood (שופך דמים)'.[87] Through R. Nahman's equation of embarrassment of one's neighbor and murder, Tamar is once more drawn into the sphere of discussion concerning 'sanctification of the Name'. Tamar's refusal to identify the father of her unborn children becomes the equivalent of a refusal to commit murder. She is therefore equal to one who refuses to transgress one of the three great commandments designated through the vote at Lod (shedding blood), just as the three men at Dura refuse

the ancestress of the Davidic line, but her status as Judah's daughter-in-law is never explicitly mentioned.

85. *Midr. haGadol* Gen. 38.25, quoted above, p. 233.

86. Adultery and calling people names are the other two listed in *Midr. haGadol* Gen. 38.25. This same list of three sins is also found in the Talmud, for example in *b. B. Meṣ.* 59a.

87. This tradition is also recorded in *b. B. Meṣ.* 58b and *Yal. Šim'oni* Gen. 38.25.

Note that the expression 'everyone who causes his neighbor to blush with words' (כל המלבין פני חבירו בדברים) basically corresponds to the expression in the statement attributed to R. Zutra that it is better to fall into a furnace (as Tamar did) than 'embarrass one's neighbor in public' (ילבין פני חבירו ברבים) in *Midr. haGadol* Gen. 38.25.

to transgress another of these three (idolatry).[88] The discussion in *Midraš haGadol* therefore confirms the hypothesis that *Targum Neofiti* follows a larger exegetical trend when it recreates Tamar's character in keeping with the larger cultural values expressed by the phrase 'sanctification of the Name'.

As far as the figure of Judah is concerned, his assimilation to the narrative pattern of his three descendants at Dura is less developed than Tamar's in *Targum Neofiti*, but other sources draw the connection much more forcefully.[89] At least one source explicitly states that Judah sanctified the divine Name when he confessed his involvement with Tamar. After discussing the addition of a letter to Joseph's name as a reward for his sanctification of the Name in private when he refused the sexual advances of Potiphar's wife, *b. Soṭ* 10b continues with a discussion of Gen. 38.26:

> Judah, who sanctified the heavenly Name (ש"ש שדקש) in public merited that the whole of his name should be called after the Name of the Holy One Blessed be He. When he confessed and said, 'She is more righteous than I', a voice issued forth and said, 'You rescued Tamar and her two sons from the fire. By your life, I will rescue through your merit three of your descendants from the fire'. Who are they? Hananiah, Mishael and Azariah.[90]

In this passage, Judah's sanctification of the Name through confession results in the honor of bearing the letters of the Tetragrammaton in his own name. The emphasis here is on Judah's willingness to save Tamar and her sons through acceptance of responsibility for her pregnancy, in contrast to the emphasis in *Targum Neofiti* on Judah's willingness to burn alongside her for his wrongdoing. But despite this difference, this passage demonstrates that a linkage between Judah's confession, the three men at Dura, and the concept 'sanctification of the Name' existed in the larger exegetical sphere of Palestinian Judaism.

88. Significantly, in the concluding section of Philo's work *De Virtutibus*, Tamar (220-22) follows Abraham (211-19) as an example of true nobility because of her rejection of idolatry. Willingness to burn is not part of Philo's presentation of either of these characters, however.

89. For example, see *b. Soṭ* 10b, *Exod. R.* 16.4; *Num. R.* 13.4; *Deut. R.*, 'Eqeb, Liebermann (ed.), p. 74; *Gen. R.* 97, New Version.

90. This teaching is given in the name of R. Hanin b. Bizna in the name of R. Simeon the Pious.

As demonstrated above, *Targum Neofiti* and other rabbinic sources bring Genesis 38 into the semantic circle of 'sanctification of the Name' by portraying especially Tamar, but to a lesser extent also Judah, as parallel figures to the three archetypes of this concept, Hananiah, Mishael, and Azariah. The development of this theme in *Targum Neofiti* transforms Tamar and Judah from the morally ambiguous characters of the biblical narrative to conscientious individuals who exemplify the most principled adherence to ethical standards through their willingness to give their lives. This development shifts attention from the royal ancestors' alarming involvement with deception, prostitution, incest, and perversion of justice, and resignifies Judah and Tamar as exemplars of post-biblical piety and morality, worthy of emulation by those standing in the shadow of biblical tradition. The divine intervention concluding the narrative expansion also corresponds to the pattern set by Daniel 3 and transforms Genesis 38 into a story illustrating God's power to deliver the faithful. The story thus becomes a dignified and inspiring chapter in Israelite history and a meaningful paradigm for human piety and behavior under duress.

At the conclusion of this discussion, it is worthwhile to pause for a moment to consider the liturgical setting of the recitation of the Targum and to reflect on the curious instructions found in *m. Meg.* 4.10 concerning translation of Genesis 38 into Aramaic in this context. This passage in the Mishnah, which contains a list of sensitive biblical passages and special stipulations concerning their liturgical reading and translation, presents the 'story of Tamar' after another tale of incest, namely the 'story of Reuben'. But unlike the tale of Reuben and Bilhah which is to be read in Hebrew but left untranslated, the Mishnah specifies that 'the story of Tamar is to be read and translated'.

Since according to other passages, including *m. Meg.* 4.4, verse by verse alternation of reading from the Torah and oral translation into Aramaic is portrayed as the norm in the synagogue liturgy, these explicit instructions to proceed as usual in the case of Genesis 38 are puzzling. Perhaps they indicate that at an earlier time Genesis 38, like the report of Reuben's sexual relations with Bilhah in Gen. 35.22, was only read but not translated because of the unseemly nature of its contents.[91] It is tantalizing to imagine that the inclusion of positive

91. P.S. Alexander, 'The Rabbinic Lists of Forbidden Targumim', *JJS* 27

interpretative material in the translation of this chapter, such as that found in the expansion in *Targum Neofiti*, secured the meaning of the text and thereby altered the attitude towards public presentation of a Targum to Genesis 38.[92]

While it not certain that the Aramaic version contained in *Targum Neofiti* was actually used in synagogue services,[93] one can easily understand why such an expanded translation would have been desirable in this context. With the presentation of the narrative expansion in the silence after the reading of the Hebrew text of Gen. 38.25 and 26, those listening would be guided in understanding the chapter in a manner concordant with contemporary moral and religious sensibilities and ideals. The requirement that the biblical text be accompanied by its Targum would therefore serve as a guarantee that the story would not be misunderstood. Or perhaps more precisely, it would guarantee that it would be properly misunderstood as conveying edifying truths worthy of Scripture.

(1976), pp. 177-91 (181-82), notes that the category of passages that are to be read and interpreted is redundant and indicates an earlier, more restrictive phase. But he suggests that by the tannaitic period this sort of restriction was no longer necessary, perhaps because of developments in the history of interpretation of this material. In the discussion of the woman accused of adultery in *Num. R.* 9.17 the affairs of Reuben with Bilhah and of Judah with Tamar are both described as 'things which neither she nor all the families of her father's house deserve to hear', possibly alluding to this earlier phase in which Gen. 38 and Gen. 35.22 were included in the same proscribed category.

92. No doubt the prominence of traditions portraying Judah as an exemplar of penitent confession attested in the Babylonian Talmud's version of the list of forbidden readings in *b. Meg.* 25a also played a role in this process.

93. Klein, 'Not to Be Translated in Public—לא מתרגם בציבורא' *JJS* 39 (1988), pp. 80-91, discusses evidence from the margins and bodies of targumic manuscripts, including *Targ. Neof.*, that suggests liturgical use. Similarly, Diéz Macho, *Neophyti 1*, p. 59, maintains that addresses to an audience in *Targ. Neof.*, such as 'O, my people', and 'O, sons of Israel', indicate the liturgical context of the synagogue.

HANNAH'S LATER SONGS:
A STUDY IN COMPARATIVE METHODS OF INTERPRETATION

Joan E. Cook

The period of formative Judaism and early Christianity was a time of dynamic interchange between the Scriptures and the people. The resulting literature is the product of several different processes of interpretation and appropriation. This study analyzes three later versions of the Song of Hannah (1 Sam. 2.1-10): in Pseudo-Philo's *Liber Antiquitatum Biblicarum (Bib. Ant.)*, *Targum (Targ.) of the Prophets*, and the Magnificat (Lk. 1.46-55); to illustrate the ways in which the first- and second-century communities of the Common Era reappropriated their foundational documents to express the concerns and beliefs of their own day.

The two Jewish works, *Bib. Ant.* and *Targ. of the Prophets*, follow similar midrashic processes of translating and adding words and phrases to the biblical text. The changes sometimes involve only a word or phrase, but result in dramatic shifts in the meaning of specific verses and of the entire passage. The Lukan text reformulates the biblical work in a more complex way, by telescoping various elements of the narrative and refocusing their meaning. These interpretive processes will be examined after a look at the biblical version.

The Biblical Version

The biblical Song of Hannah is a hymn sung by Hannah at the Shiloh shrine on the occasion of her dedication of her son Samuel to the Lord. She had promised to give back the son she requested from the Lord to remove her barrenness. The words of the hymn do not directly address her particular situation, but rather praise the God who reverses the fortunes of all, upsets the status quo, and offers particular protection to the more vulnerable members of society. Hannah sings a carefully crafted praise of divine attributes (vv. 2-3), divine guidance (vv. 4-5), and divine deeds (vv. 6b-8, 10) with a climactic statement of God's goal and rationale in vv. 8c-9. The Song expresses the specific concerns of an agricultural and pastoral society in the Galilean hills: the enemies are hunger, barrenness, and poverty. Likewise it expresses the conviction that those who rely on the Deity will be protected and rewarded with reversals of fortune in their daily life.

The Song interacts in several ways with its narrative and historical contexts. It appears within the narrative of the birth of Samuel, the transitional event that set in motion the foundation of the Israelite monarchy. Hannah's barrenness links her with Sarah and all the 'barren mothers' of Israel through whom the divine promise of offspring was carried forward. The setting maintains the cultic tie to the Ark of the Covenant, which was housed at the time in the Shiloh shrine where Hannah prayed. But Hannah emerges in a singular way because of the ways in which the narrative departs from the three models of the type of the barren mother: competition, promise, and request.[1] Regarding the competition model, like Sarah and Hagar, Rachel and Leah, Hannah had a rival, Peninnah; but unlike the others, Hannah did not respond to the taunts of her jealous rival (1.6). Neither was Hannah side-tracked by Eli, who mistook her praying lips for drunkenness (vv. 13-14).

Hannah's actions in relation to the promise model further illustrate her uniqueness: she made, rather than received, the promise to return her requested son to the Lord (v. 11). The doubts typically expressed in this model came from Eli, who questioned Hannah's entry to the shrine in what he took to be her drunken condition.

The narrative varies the request model as well: Hannah addresses God herself to ask for a son. Typically either the wife asked her husband as in Rachel's case (Gen. 30.1) or the husband petitioned God as with Isaac and Rebekah (Gen. 25.21). These departures from the barren mother type highlight Hannah's determination to bear a son and her conviction that the Lord was her only hope.

Hannah's actions in the narrative affirm her pivotal role in the transition to monarchy. After Samuel was weaned she returned with him to the Shiloh shrine, leaving him in Eli's care in fulfillment of her

---

1. For a detailed description of the type and its models, see Joan E. Cook, 'The Song of Hannah: Text and Contexts' (unpublished dissertation, Vanderbilt University, 1989), pp. 133-51.

vow. While at the shrine she praised the God who exercises dominion over all. The monarchy her son Samuel would later institute would concretize divine protection of the vulnerable in the person of the king.

But the nascent monarchy had to struggle to balance the powers and duties of the king with those of priest and prophet. Eli's lack of hospitality to Hannah on her first visit to the Shiloh shrine, and his lack of understanding of Hannah's purpose and actions at the shrine, create tension regarding the office and role of the priesthood. The narrative develops the tension further in its description of the corruption of Eli's sons (2.12-17) and of Samuel's increasing favor in the divine eyes (v. 26). Samuel anointed Saul and David in a priestly ritual (10.1; 16.13). And throughout the reigns of the two kings the struggles over who would perform priestly duties illustrate the kingdom's efforts to balance the powers of priest and king (1 Sam. 13.8-14; 2 Sam. 6.12-13).

Samuel's own resistance to the people's initial request for a king, and his opposition to the divine decision to replace Saul as king, serve to define the prophet's role in the monarchy. As intermediary between the people and God Samuel voiced requests and positions with which he personally disagreed, and carried out divine directions that he found disagreeable. These events illustrate the struggle to balance powers within the nascent monarchy, and the divine dominion that prevailed.

At the end of the Samuel corpus, David's Song of Thanks (2 Samuel 22) acknowledges that the divine king was Israel's ultimate leader, and his final testament (2 Sam. 23.1-7) offers the reflections of a God-fearing and righteous king whose personal life and political dynasty were guided by the divine spirit.[2] These words of Hannah at the beginning, and of David at the end, envelop the Samuel corpus and the early monarchy within the programmatic theme of divine dominion over the people, through the specific instrumentality of the kings anointed by Hannah's son.

The believing community in late eighth- and seventh-century Judah wrestled with the issue of trust in divine dominion in the face of Assyrian expansion. During that time the Song of Hannah and the Samuel corpus served to bolster the people's conviction that the

---

2. Walter Harrelson, 'Creative Spirit in the Old Testament: A Study of the Last Words of David (2 Sam. 23.1-7)', in D. Durkin (ed.), *Sin, Salvation, and the Spirit* (Collegeville: Liturgical Press, 1979), p. 131.

monarchy was a divinely sanctioned institution. The kings served as divine regents, but the Lord would continue to reign in the manner described by Hannah's praise. And the people were urged to depend on the divine king to protect them from military and political threats by Assyria and from the various maneuvers of the smaller powers who tried to resist the Assyrian onslaught.[3]

This discussion of the biblical Song of Hannah and its narrative and historical contexts offers a backdrop against which to examine the three later works.

Targum of the Prophets

In *Targum of the Prophets*, Samuel offers a close translation of the biblical text into Aramaic, except for a few poetic passages which the translators expanded in midrashic paraphrase.[4] These expansions affect the Song of Hannah in 1 Samuel 2 and David's Words in 2 Samuel 22–23. The fidelity of the narrative to the biblical text renders unnecessary any extensive comment about the narrative context of the Song. This analysis will therefore focus on the targumic Song, its historical context, and its theological content.

The words of the targumic Song clearly take the biblical poem as their point of departure.

> 1. *And Hannah prayed* in a spirit of prophecy *and said*: 'Now Samuel my son is to be a prophet on behalf of Israel. In his days they will be saved from the hand of the Philistines, and by his hands signs and mighty deeds will be done for them. Therefore my heart is strong in the portion that *the Lord* has given to me. And also Heman, the son of Joel, the son of my son Samuel who is to arise—he and his fourteen sons are to be speaking in song by means of lyres and lutes with their brothers the Levites to give praise in the house of the sanctuary. Therefore my *horn is exalted* in the gift that the Lord has appointed for me. And also concerning the marvelous revenge that will be against the Philistines who are to bring the ark on a new cart, and with it the guilt offering. Therefore the assembly of Israel will say: "Let my mouth be open to speak great things *against my enemies, for I rejoice in your saving power*"'. 2. Concerning Sennacherib the king of Assyria—she prophesied and said that he and all his armies would come up against Jerusalem, and a great sign would be worked on

---

3. For details about the provenance of the Song, see Cook, 'The Song of Hannah', pp. 45-60.
4. Jacob Neusner, *What is Midrash?* (Philadelphia: Fortress Press, 1987), p. 7.

him; there the corpses of his camp would fall. Therefore all the nations, peoples, and language groups will confess and say: '*There is not one* who is *holy* except *the Lord, for there is no one apart from you*'; and your people will say: 'There is no one who is strong except our God'. 3. Concerning Nebuchadnezzar the king of Babylon—she prophesied and said: 'You Chaldeans and all the peoples who are to rule in Israel, do not say many boastful things. *Let not* blasphemies *go forth from your mouth*, for the all-knowing *God is the Lord* and upon all his works he fixes judgment. And also to you he is to repay the revenge of your sins'. 4. Concerning the kingdoms of Greece—she prophesied and said: '*The bows of the* Greek *warriors will be broken*; and those of the house of the Hasmonean who were weak—mighty deeds will be done for them'. 5. Concerning the sons of Haman—she prophesied and said: 'Those who were *filled up on bread* and growing in wealth and abounding in money have become poor; they have returned to working as laborers for bread, the food of their mouth. Mordecai and Esther who were needy became rich and forgot their poverty; they returned to being free persons. So Jerusalem, which was like *a barren woman*, is to be filled with her exiled people. And Rome, which was filled with great numbers of people—her armies will cease to be; she will be desolate and destroyed'. 6. All these are the mighty works of the Lord, who is powerful in the world. *He puts to death* and speaks so as to make alive; *he brings down to Sheol*, and he is also ready *to bring up* in eternal life. 7. *The Lord makes poor and makes rich; he humbles, also he exalts.* 8. *He raises up the poor from the dust, from the dunghill he exalts the needy one*, to make them dwell with the righteous ones, *the chiefs* of the world; and he bequeathes to them *thrones of glory*, for before the Lord the deeds of the sons of men are revealed. He has established Gehenna below for the wicked ones. And the just ones—those doing his good pleasure, he has established the world for them. 9. *He will keep* away from Gehenna the bodies of his servants, the righteous ones. And *the wicked ones* will walk about in Gehenna *in the darkness*, to make it known that there is no one in whom there is strength having claim for the day of judgment. 10. *The Lord will shatter the enemies* who rise up to do harm to his people. The Lord blasts down *upon them* from *the heavens* with a loud voice. He will exact just revenge from Gog and the army of the violent nations who come with him from *the ends of the earth. And he will give power to his king and will magnify* the kingdom of *his anointed one*.[5]

The targumic Song includes almost all the biblical words, which are italicized above. But it makes several kinds of substitutions and

5. D.J. Harrington and A.J. Saldarini, *Targum Jonathan of the Former Prophets* (ArBib, 10, Wilmington: Glazier, 1987), pp. 105-106.

expansions that significantly alter the genre and themes of the Song.[6] Several changes are relatively simple and straightforward; for example, in a few instances the Targum substitutes adjectives for nouns or concepts for symbols, retaining the biblical meaning of the phrase. The biblical 'there is no Rock like our God' in v. 2 becomes 'There is no one who is strong except our God'. In v. 3 the biblical 'for the Lord is a God of knowledge' becomes in the Targum 'for the all-knowing God is the Lord'. The biblical 'the Most High will thunder in heaven' becomes 'The Lord blasts down upon them from the heavens with a loud voice' in v. 10. In v. 9 the biblical 'feet' of those in Gehenna becomes 'bodies', thus eliminating the synecdoche. The example from v. 10 illustrates a shift toward more cumbersome wording, but a different example shows a paraphrase from more to less awkward: 'Talk no more so very proudly, let not arrogance come from your mouth' in the biblical versions becomes the targumic 'Let not blasphemies go forth from your mouth' (v. 3).

Several simple substitutions and additions have theological implications. For example, v. 6 adds the verb 'speaks', changing the kind of divine intervention from action to word. And v. 9 substitutes 'righteous' for 'faithful', specifying the nature of fidelity.

In several instances lengthy additions particularize the meaning of indefinite or general nouns or phrases. This type of expansion dramatically affects the meaning of the Song and divides it into two thematic units, vv. 1-5 and 7-10, with v. 1 introducing the whole and v. 6 forming the transition between them.

Verse 1 adds 'in a spirit of prophecy' to the biblical 'and Hannah prayed', setting the tone for the predictive additions that follow. It further elaborates, 'Now Samuel my son is to be a prophet on behalf of Israel'. The Song thus announces Samuel's future role and provides the reason why Hannah sings at his dedication. The addition 'And also Heman, the son of Joel, the son of my son Samuel who is to arise—he and his fourteen sons are to be speaking in song by means of lyres and lutes with their brothers the Levites to give praise in the house of the sanctuary' provides further detail about Samuel's descendants (see 1 Chron. 6.33; 15.16-17; 25.4-8; 2 Chron. 5.12-13).

---

6.   Targumic translation techniques are discussed in Harrington and Saldarini, *Targum Jonathan*, pp. 4-13. In some instances they differ from those in *Targ.* 1 Sam. 2.1-10 and *Targ.* 2 Sam. 22–23, suggesting multiple authorship.

The biblical Song uses the word 'enemies' in v. 1; in vv. 1-5 the targumic version inserts references to the Philistines, Sennacherib the king of Assyria, Nebuchadnezzar the king of Babylon, the kingdoms of Greece and the sons of Haman, Mordecai and Esther, and Rome. It adds specific details about the enmity of each toward Israel, describing them as future events: the Philistines would 'bring the ark on a new cart, and with it the guilt offering'; Sennacherib's armies 'would come up against Jerusalem, and a great sign would be worked on him; there the corpses of his camp would fall'. Nebuchadnezzar would 'rule in Israel'; among the kingdoms of Greece the Song refers to 'the house of the Hasmoneans who were weak'.

In vv. 1-4 the Targum then uses the biblical words to foretell the consequences that would befall the enemies. In v. 1 the biblical words are spoken by the assembly of Israel against the Philistines. Verse 2 puts the biblical words in the mouths of 'all the nations, peoples, and language groups' who praise God for destroying the Assyrian armies (see Dan. 3.4). Verse 3 uses the biblical words to admonish the Babylonians. The biblical words in v. 4 predict the defeat of the Greeks, and in v. 5 they describe conditions before the enemy's defeat: the sons of Haman were 'filled up on bread' while Jerusalem 'was like a barren woman'. These expansions create a prediction by Hannah of divine protection of Israel throughout the ages of its history.[7]

The transitional v. 6 in the targumic version first summarizes vv. 1-5, then adds the words 'ready' and 'eternal' in the second half: 'He is also ready to bring up in eternal life'. These simple words actually shift the temporal focus of the second half of the Song from time to eternity. They then develop the apocalyptic allusion introduced in the first half by the references to the ages in Israel's history. Further additions describe the final judgment, the terms by which all will be judged, and the eternal consequences of reward and punishment.

In v. 8 the biblical 'sit with princes and inherit a seat of honor' expands to 'dwell with the righteous ones, the chiefs of the world; and he reserves for them thrones of glory, for before the Lord the deeds of the sons of men are revealed. He has established Gehenna below for the wicked ones. And the just ones—those doing his good pleasure,

---

7. Several centuries later *Gen. R.* 44.17 (on Gen. 15.12) recounts that Abraham foresaw the monarchies of Babylonia, Media, Greece, and Edom (Rome). See Neusner, *What is Midrash?*, p. 62.

he has established the world for them'. The expansion identifies the biblical 'princes' as the 'righteous ones'. It then specifies that the biblical 'seat of honor' is the 'thrones of glory', the world, the place of reward for the just, who are those who follow the divine will. The expansion broadens the spatial realm beyond the biblical earthly world, specifying that Gehenna is made for the wicked.

Verse 9 further develops the eschatological theme by expanding the biblical words to develop the topics of Gehenna and the day of judgment. It alludes to the eliminated 'feet', specifying that 'the wicked ones will walk about in Gehenna, in the darkness'. The biblical darkness is thus given a specific location. And the expansions focus on Gehenna to contrast the righteous and the wicked. The targumic version reads, 'He will keep away from Gehenna the bodies of his servants, the righteous ones' before stating that the wicked will walk in it. By locating the action in relation to Gehenna the targumic version reinforces the shift from this life to the next. It continues in that vein by stating the divine purpose, 'to make it known that there is no one in whom there is strength having claim for the day of judgment'. The expansion affirms the futility of personal strength or self-sufficiency. And it specifies the moment of reckoning as the 'day of judgment'.

Verse 10 elaborates on that decisive moment. It first identifies the biblical divine enemies as those 'who rise up to do harm to his people'. Verses 1-5 name the enemies in six ages of Israel; here the Targum refers to 'Gog and the army of the violent nations who come with him from the ends of the earth'. Rather than the burial announced in Ezek. 39.11-16 for the apocalyptic foe, the targumic version declares simply, 'He will exact just revenge from Gog'.

These changes and additions to the words of the poem change its genre from hymn to apocalypse. Structurally the expansions divide the Song into two parts, of which the first foretells specific periods and events in Israel's history and the second predicts and describes the final judgment and its consequences. Thematically the expanded poem particularizes and broadens the scope of divine dominion. Geographically it expands to include both Israel and Gehenna, and temporally it broadens to encompass both this life and the next.

The divine guidance throughout Israel's past and present which the Song affirms, and the divine guidance in the future for which the Song expresses hope, suggest its provenance within a community ravaged by destruction and demoralization. Such a group would have reason to look back on its history and affirm God's guidance throughout, in the hope that divine guidance on their behalf would extend to their immediate and long-term future.[8]

In its historical context the expanded Song reminds the reader of the Lord's continuing protection of the community during the most vulnerable episodes of its past. And it offers an eternal reward as a reason to remain faithful, during a period when temporal reasons were scarce.

Pseudo-Philo's Liber Antiquitatum Biblicarum

Pseudo-Philo's treatment of the biblical Song and its surrounding narrative follows a similar process of adding words and phrases. But it differs from *Targ. of the Prophets* in several ways that result in a significantly changed text. Pseudo-Philo's *Bib. Ant.* retains the narrative context and poetic style of the biblical Song, so as to be recognizable as Hannah's words at the dedication of her son. But unlike the Targum, it retains only a few of the actual biblical words. Much is eliminated and much is added to the poem and surrounding narrative. The result is a dramatically broadened and well-integrated whole. The following analysis of the text will illustrate the midrashic process and its resulting shifts in form and meaning.[9]

In *Bib. Ant.* the Song appears in 51.3-6. The phrases that follow the biblical version are italicized below, and the lines have been numbered for reference.

1. 3. 'Come to my voice, all you nations,
2. and pay attention to my speech, all you kingdoms,
3. because my mouth has been opened that I should speak

8. The Community within which the targumic Song was created is virtually impossible to pinpoint. The Targum itself is thought to have been composed over a period of centuries beginning around 135 CE in Palestine and eventually in Babylonia. But the Song could well have been interpreted and inserted independently, either before or during that period. Daniel Harrington ('The Apocalypse of Hannah: Targum Jonathan of 1 Samuel 2.1-10', in D.M. Golomb [ed.], *Working with No Data* [Winona Lake: Eisenbrauns, 1987], p. 152) sets its date of composition between 70 CE and the fall of the Roman Empire.

9. It has been suggested that the variations represent diverse oral traditions in circulation at the time. See Charles Perot, Pierre-Maurice Bogaert, and Daniel J. Harrington, *Pseudo-Philon: Les antiquités bibliques* (SC, 2; Paris: Cerf, 1976), pp. 25-26.

4.	and my lips have been commanded to sing a hymn to the Lord.
5.	Drip, my breasts, and tell your testimonies, because you have been commanded to give milk.
6.	For he who is milked from you will be raised up,
7.	and the people will be enlightened by his words,
8.	and he will show to the nations the statutes,
9.	and his horn will be exalted very high.
10.	4. And so I will speak my words openly,
11.	because from me will arise the ordinance of the Lord,
12.	and all men will find the truth.
13.	*Do not hurry* to *say great things*
14.	*or to bring forth from your mouth lofty* words,
15.	but delight in glorifying (God).
16.	For when the light from which wisdom is to be born will go forth,
17.	not those who possess many things will be said to be rich,
18.	nor those who have borne in abundance will be called mothers.
19.	*For the sterile one has been satisfied in childbearing,*
20.	*but she who had many children has been emptied.*
21.	5. Because *the Lord kills* in judgment,
22.	*and brings to life* in mercy.
23.	For them who are *wicked* in this world he kills,
24.	and he brings *the just* to life when he wishes.
25.	Now *the wicked* he will shut up in darkness,
26.	but he will save his light for the just.
27.	And when *the wicked* have died, then they will perish.
28.	And when *the just* go to sleep, then they will be freed.
29.	Now so will every judgment endure,
30.	until he who restrains will be revealed.
31.	6. Speak, speak, Hannah, and do not be silent.
32.	Sing a hymn, daughter of Batuel,
33.	about the miracles that God has performed with you.
34.	Who is Hannah that a prophet is born from her?
35.	Or who is the daughter of Batuel that she should bear *the light to the peoples?*
36.	Rise up, you also, Elkanah, and gird your loins.
37.	Sing a hymn about the wonders of the Lord.
38.	Because Asaph prophesied in the wilderness about your son, saying,
39.	'Moses and Aaron were among his priests,
40.	and Samuel was there among them'.
41.	Behold the word has been fulfilled,
42.	and the prophecy has come to pass.
43.	And these words will endure
44.	until they give *the horn to his anointed one*
45.	and *power* be present at the throne of his *king*.

46.   And let my son stay here and serve
47.   until he be made a light for this nation'.[10]

Throughout the poem Hannah addresses the people, herself, Elkanah, and Eli in the form of a testament. She does not directly address God, but refers at several points to divine praise. She asserts, 'My lips have been commanded to sing a hymn to the Lord' (*Bib. Ant.* 51.3); she urges the people, 'delight in glorifying God' (v. 4); she invites herself, 'Sing a hymn, daughter of Batuel', then urges Elkanah, 'Sing a hymn about the wonders of the Lord' (v. 6).

The Song divides into two parts, the first figurative (vv. 3-5) and the second literal (v. 6). In the first part Hannah speaks as mother of the giver of light and law, and in the second as mother of priest and prophet. Her words introduce Samuel to the people, and become the vehicle through which leadership passes to her son.

Her opening words in lines 1-4 invite all to listen because she speaks with the authority of Eli's command. She then relates her message to her new maternal status in line 5, by which not only her mouth but also her breasts are opened to nourish her son.[11]

Hannah announces that Samuel, 'the ordinance of the Lord', will enlighten the people and 'show to the nations the statutes', identifying him as a prophet. In Deborah's words, '[The Lord] established for you the Law and commanded you through the prophets' (*Bib. Ant.* 30.5). Samuel, the 'ordinance of the Lord', will show the people how to live so that 'all men will find the truth'. The Song appeals to the minds and hearts of its hearers, giving, in lines 6-11, information and affirmation of divine guidance through the instrumentality of Samuel.

The testament quotes briefly from the biblical Song with a warning against arrogance, alternatively advising 'but delight in glorifying God' (v. 4).

In lines 16-18 the poem refers again to Samuel, giver of light, the source of wisdom; then it alludes to the biblical announcement that the status quo will be overturned, and wealth and motherhood will be redefined. A quotation from the biblical Song (lines 19-20) supports the announcement and affirms the divine action in Hannah's changed circumstances.

10. D.J. Harrington, 'Pseudo-Philo', in J.H. Charlesworth (ed.), *The Old Testament Pseudepigrapha* (2 vols.; New York: Doubleday, 1983–85), II, pp. 365-66.

11. Milk and wisdom are linked elsewhere in intertestamental literature; cf. *Odes* 8.14.

The following section expands the meaning of the biblical hymn by developing the motifs 'wicked' and 'just' in a lesson about divine rewards and punishments: death and darkness will befall the wicked, and the just will receive life, light, and freedom. To the words 'the Lord kills' Pseudo-Philo adds 'in judgment' and to 'and brings to life' he adds 'in mercy', then follows in lines 23-28 with three pairs of oppositions between the divine treatment of the just and of the wicked. The poem then announces the duration of the divine judgments in lines 29-30. This section expands the scope of light and law: not only do they offer guidance during life, but they form the basis for divine judgment at death. Both Hannah and Samuel have pivotal roles as teachers of the law and bearers of light.

The second part of the poem begins with Hannah's second invitation to herself to speak. Using literal language she names Samuel's ancestors, then celebrates the divine gift of a son who is prophet and light-bearer in lines 31-40.[12]

Hannah summarizes this section of the poem with the assertion, 'And these words will endure 'until they give *the horn to his anointed one* and *power* be present at the throne of his *king*'. Her words parallel the conclusion to the first part, 'Now so will every judgment endure, until he who restrains will be revealed'.

Hannah concludes her Song with her reason for bringing Samuel to Shiloh, 'And let my son stay here and serve until he be made a light for this nation'. For Pseudo-Philo there is no question of fulfilling a promise, because none had been made (cf. 1 Sam. 1.11, 28).

The instructional nature of a testament is evident in Hannah's lesson about death, judgment, reward, and punishment.[13] Her words are similar in that regard to those of the targumic Song: both use 1 Sam. 2.6 as their point of departure for eschatological teaching, and both broaden the scope of the biblical verse beyond this world in time and place.

The shift in meaning that results from the expansions to the Song is strengthened by the surrounding narrative (*Bib. Ant.* 49.1–51.7). The

12. Asaph is identified as Tohou, Elkanah's ancestor in *Pes. R.* 43.6-7; cf. W.G. Braude, *Pesikta Rabbati* (2 vols.; YJS, 18; London and New Haven: Yale University Press, 1968), II, pp. 765-66. Batuel is not mentioned in any other known source.

13. For a detailed discussion of the teaching found in the Song, see Joan E. Cook, 'Pseudo-Philo's Song of Hannah: Testament of a Mother in Israel', *JSP* 9 (1991), pp. 103-14 (108-11).

narrative retains the basic plot of the biblical version, but eliminates a few elements: Elkanah's genealogy (1 Sam. 1.1), Hannah's vow to return her requested son to the Lord (1.11), and the fulfillment of her vow (1.24-28).

In addition it adds other elements to the narrative, dividing the plot into four episodes: first, an *inclusio* and transition that recounts Elkanah's selection as judge and his refusal to accept the appointment (*Bib. Ant.* 49); second, the account of Hannah's request for a son and his birth and dedication by Hannah (50.1–51.3a); third, the Song of Hannah (51.3b-6); and fourth, the report of Samuel's anointing by the people (51.7). The narrative supports the setting and themes of the Song, with a more unified result than the targumic version.

The first episode highlights Samuel's bridge position between the judges and kings. It describes casting lots for a new judge until Elkanah was designated. The procedure recalls the first judge, Kenaz, whom the people chose by lot after Joshua's death. When Elkanah declined the appointment God promised that Elkanah's son would rule and prophesy (49.5-7). To the people's question about which of Peninnah's ten sons would be chosen, God responded that none of her sons could rule, but the son would be born from his sterile wife (*Bib. Ant.* 49.8).

The second episode follows closely the biblical account of Hannah, expanding on Peninnah's taunts, Elkanah's efforts to reassure Hannah, Hannah's prayer for a son, Eli's priestly reassurance, and the birth and dedication of Samuel.

In the biblical account Peninnah remained silent, but the narrator repeats that she provoked her rival wife, to irritate her on account of her sterility. *Liber Antiquitatum Biblicarum* quotes, 'What does it profit you that Elkanah your husband loves you, for you are a dry tree? And I know that my husband will love me, because he delights in the sight of my sons standing around him like a plantation of olive trees' (50.1). Elkanah reassured Hannah with questions similar to those in the biblical account, but *Bib. Ant.* eliminates the problematic fourth question about Hannah's love for him. He asked instead, 'Are not your ways of behaving better than the ten sons of Peninnah?' (50.3).

Hannah's prayer for a son differs sharply from her biblical vow to return the desired son to the Lord. *Liber Antiquitatum Biblicarum* recounts that Hannah requested a son as a reward for her righteousness, and prayed silently in her perceived unworthiness and to avoid further tormenting from Peninnah. She described children as wealth:

> Perhaps I am not worthy of be heard, and Peninnah will then be even more eager to taunt me as she does daily when she says, 'Where is your God in whom you trust?' And I know that neither she who has many sons is rich nor she who has few is poor, but whoever abounds in the will of God is rich. For who may know what I have prayed for? If they know that I am not heard in my prayer, they will blaspheme. And I will not have any witness except in my own soul, because my tears are the servant of my prayers (50.5).

Liber Antiquitatum Biblicarum expands Eli's priestly reassurance of Hannah from the biblical uncomprehending generic blessing to the invitation, 'Tell me why you are being taunted' (50.7). Hannah then responds by telling Eli of her desire for a son, to which he replies, 'Go, because I know for what you have prayed; your prayer has been heard' (50.7). In *Bib. Ant.* Eli did not inform Hannah of the promise already made to the people (50.8).

The account of Samuel's birth eliminates Elkanah altogether. Samuel's name is interpreted differently from the biblical account: instead of 'I have asked him of the Lord', it substitutes 'Mighty One', and in another departure from the biblical account specifies that God named the child. In Pseudo-Philo's account Hannah had not vowed to return Samuel to the Lord (cf. 1 Sam. 1.11); consequently his dedication was not described as fulfillment of it. *Liber Antiquitatum Biblicarum* reports,

> And when she had weaned him, she went up with him and brought gifts in her hands. And the child was very handsome, and the Lord was with him. And Hannah placed the boy before Eli and said to him, 'This is the desire I desired, and this is the request I have asked'. And Eli said to her, 'You have not asked alone, but the people have prayed for this. This is not your request alone, but it was promised previously to the tribes. And through this boy your womb has been justified so that you might provide advantage for the peoples and set up the milk of your breasts as a fountain for the twelve tribes' (51.1- 2).

At that point Hannah learned that Samuel's birth had been promised earlier to the people. Then Eli explained that the boy's birth made Hannah a teacher of wisdom. At his affirmation of her status, Hannah sang her Song.

The fourth episode takes place after Hannah's Song. After they (ambiguous antecedent) left Shiloh, the people brought Samuel to Eli at Shiloh, anointed the boy and expressed the hope, 'Let the prophet live among the people, and may he be a light to this nation for a long time!' (51.7).

The shift in meaning that the additions create can be clarified in relation to the three models of the barren mother type. In *Bib. Ant.* the plot fits the competition model insofar as Hannah, the favored wife, is childless; her husband Elkanah's rival wife bears a son and belittles Hannah; then Hannah bears a son through divine intervention. The request model is expanded in *Bib. Ant.* to include two requests: a public petition by the people to the judge and Hannah's private requests to God and Eli. The promise model in *Bib. Ant.* differs from the biblical account as well. Instead of reversing the model, *Bib. Ant.* gives more weight to the public aspect of the promise: God speaks directly to the people but Eli speaks to Hannah. God explicitly promises the people that a son will be born to Hannah, but Eli tells her merely that her prayer has been heard. In this way *Bib. Ant.* highlights the public aspect of the plot and assigns less weight to the private.

This analysis of the song and narrative illustrates several significant shifts in meaning. First, *Bib. Ant.* explicitly links the roles of mother and teacher, thus integrating Hannah's expanded Song into the narrative. Her words not only teach but also nourish the people, in keeping with her maternal relationship to Samuel and to all nations and kingdoms. And the scope of the life she gives expands to include death, judgment, reward, and punishment. The presentation of her testament at the Shiloh shrine affirms the public dimension of her role and her words.

Secondly, Hannah's testament passes leadership from herself to her son, and from Elkanah to his son, but more importantly from God to Samuel at the request of the people. Hannah is the human mouthpiece for the poem, the genre of which expresses the transferral of leadership.

Thirdly, Hannah's position shifts in relation to Eli. She breaks into song when Eli announces her new maternal status within the community. Eli withheld from her what he knew about the public promise of a son until after the private promise was fulfilled. Then he made known that the private promise was merely at the service of the public one. Samuel was only coincidentally an answer to Hannah's prayer; he had already been promised as the new leader and prophet.

Fourthly, the expanded version augments Eli's priestly authority and role in the transferral of leadership. The text explained how Eli had become a priest (50.3); Eli knew a son had already been promised to Hannah before she confided in him; when he invited Hannah to speak he informed her of the public dimension of Samuel's birth; and he witnessed Samuel's anointing by the people (51.7).

The Song and its surrounding narrative offered reassurance and hope to the Jewish community just prior to the destruction of the Temple in 70 CE.[14] It reminded them of divine guidance in a prior time of uncertainty, with the implicit assurance that God would see them through their current crisis. And it enlarged the people's perspective on the meaning of current events by situating them within the context of life after death.

The Gospel of Luke

The treatment of the Hannah corpus in Luke 1–2 is of a different sort than the other two adaptations considered here. It does not expand the story in straightforward additions to the text. Rather, it reorganizes elements of the biblical version into a new story that nevertheless maintains a clear relationship to the Samuel narrative. The shifts are comparable to the rearrangement of glass chips in a kaleidoscope when the lens is rotated. The basic elements remain, but in a different and more complex pattern than the earlier version. A look at the Magnificat (Lk. 1.46-55) and then its surrounding narrative will illustrate the method and meaning of the later version.

The Magnificat begins with the same structure and parallelism as the biblical version, then divides into three parts, of which the first concerns the speaker herself; the second, all people; and the third, Israel. Verses 48-49 explicitly acknowledge the divine favor bestowed on Mary and the consequent acclaim of her that will result (Lk. 1.47-49). A transitional verse asserts that the scope of divine mercy extends beyond Mary individually to include all God-fearing people (v. 50). The second part of the hymn celebrates specific divine deeds that reverse fortunes and improve the situation of the vulnerable, particularly the lowly and the hungry, while upsetting the proud, powerful,

---

14. For a detailed discussion of the provenance of *Biblical Antiquities*, see Harrington, 'Pseudo-Philo', pp. 299-300.

and rich (vv. 51-53). The final section recalls the divine promise to Israel's ancestors as the rationale for constant divine favor toward the people (vv. 54-55).

In the Lukan reconfiguration from simple to complex two other hymns appear in the Infancy Narrative. At John's circumcision his father Zechariah praised God in the context of the traditions and history of Israel: he referred to the divine promise to be the God of the people (1.68), David the king (v. 69), the prophets (v. 70), and the covenant with Abraham (vv. 72-73). Zechariah specified that the rationale for divine deeds is to enable the people to serve their God (vv. 74-75). Zechariah then addressed his infant son, commissioning him as a prophet to prepare the way of the Most High (vv. 76-77; see also Isa. 40.3). He concluded by proclaiming the dawn of a new era of light, life, and peace made possible by divine mercy (vv. 78-79).

At the dedication of Jesus in the Temple Simeon spoke of the infant Jesus as the personification of salvation for Israel and the world (2.29-32; see Isa. 42.6), in a statement resembling last words. Likewise the prophet Anna praised God at Jesus' dedication, but her words are not recorded (2.38).

The Lukan settings alternate among the Temple, Zechariah and Elizabeth's home, and Mary's home in a way similar to the Samuel narrative's alternation between the Shiloh shrine, where the Ark was housed and the people offered sacrifices, and Hannah and Elkanah's home. Mary sang her hymn, not at the Temple as did Simeon, but at the home of Elizabeth, where later Zechariah also sang. But the announcement of a son to be born came to Zechariah while he was in the Temple performing his priestly duties (Lk. 1.8-10). And while the Lukan account does not mention Mary speaking in the Temple, it does record her presence with Joseph and Jesus at his presentation. This alternation of settings between private and public places affirms the dual aspect of motherhood and sonship found in the Samuel corpus. The women give birth to sons in the family line, but in a larger sense give birth to a new era in history. That new era had a cultic dimension, highlighted by the public settings at the religious centers, Shiloh shrine and Jerusalem Temple.

Luke rearranges the times of singing as well. Mary's praise came prior to her son's birth in the presence of Elizabeth, while Zechariah and Simeon sang during the initiatory rituals for John and Jesus in the presence of other guests. Just as according to the Samuel corpus the birth of Samuel set in motion the transition to the foundation of the Israelite monarchy, in the Lukan corpus the birth of Jesus set in motion the foundation of the kingdom of God. And the words of the hymns link the events of Jesus' birth with those of the ancestors, as does the plot of the narrative, which also evolves from simple to complex.

A look at the plot in relation to the three models of the barren mother type highlights its similarity to the Hannah story, and reveals several variations as well. Like the competition model of the barren mother type, the Lukan narrative involves two wives: the elderly, barren Elizabeth (v. 7) and her relative Mary, a betrothed virgin (v. 27). Unlike the competition model, however, the relationship between the two women was cordial: Mary hurried to Elizabeth after learning of their mutual situation. In addition Luke's version includes two husbands: Zechariah the priest (Lk. 1.5) and Joseph, who was betrothed to Mary (v. 27). The Lukan story expands the promise model insofar as two sons were promised by Gabriel, one to Zechariah and one to Mary. Zechariah's son would be a Nazarite like Samuel (Lk. 1.15) and Mary's child would rule as David's successor (1.32-33). Both recipients expressed doubts: Zechariah on account of the advanced age of his wife Elizabeth and himself (1.18) and Mary because she was not yet married (v. 34). Zechariah was left mute for the duration of the pregnancy, then he regained the use of his voice at his son's circumcision and sang his song of praise (1.19-22, 68-79). But Mary responded willingly to the angel's reassurance, recalling Abraham's words of acceptance (Gen. 22.1, 7, 11; Lk. 1.38). The third barren mother model, the request, does not appear in Luke's narrative.

Besides the models of the barren mother type, other aspects of the narratives are comparable as well. All three stories are situated in specific historical settings, anchoring them in relation to particular political, social, economic, and religious conditions. The Lukan narrative relates the two births to the Roman Empire (Lk. 1.5), just as Samuel's birth is situated at the end of the period of judges and in relation to the capture of the Ark by the Philistines (1 Samuel 4).

In another similarity related to time, the narratives report that all three sons grew chronologically and in spirit: Samuel grew 'in stature and in favor with the Lord and with the people' (1 Sam. 2.26); John the Baptist 'grew and became strong in spirit' (Lk. 1.80); and Jesus 'grew and became strong, filled with wisdom; and the favor of God was upon him' (Lk. 2.40).

The stories use foils to highlight differences among the three sons: Samuel's righteousness contrasts with the corruption of the house of Eli (1 Sam. 2.11–4.22); and John the Baptist and Jesus are contrasted insofar as John the prophet prepared the way for the salvation Jesus would bring (Lk. 3.4-17).

The various reconfigurations of the poem and surrounding narrative shift the meaning of the Samuel corpus in significant ways. Both accounts announce the inbreaking of a new era through divine intervention. In Samuel's case, he founded the kingdom of Israel and anointed its first two kings. In Luke's Gospel John set the stage for the kingdom of God and Jesus founded it with his teaching and healing. These kingdoms represented new kinds of divine presence among the people. Samuel wrestled with the covenantal understanding that God was leader of the people. He came to terms with a new way of understanding the covenant: that God would rule through the mediation of a human king whose mandate of justice under divine guidance, with special concern for the vulnerable, was expressed in the Song of Hannah. Luke introduced a kingdom founded by Jesus apart from the political regime of the Roman Empire. Its mandate announced in the Magnificat, Benedictus, and Nunc Dimittis was similar to that announced in the Song of Hannah. And Luke's expanded number of characters increased the number of witnesses to the new kingdom.

But Luke shifted several concepts. One of these was the meaning of wealth and poverty. In the Samuel account, Hannah belonged to a family of some means: Elkanah had two wives, suggesting that he could afford to provide for both of them. Her offerings at the shrine were those of a person of means: a three-year-old bull (the Greek text reads 'three bulls'), an ephah of flour, and a skin of wine (1 Sam. 1.24). Hannah's Song proclaims an end to poverty by divine deed. While it is true that by the end of Solomon's reign poverty remained an aspect of the division of labor and the socioeconomic inequities of his regime (1 Kgs 9.15-28), those conditions ultimately provoked the rebellion which ended the united monarchy. And the eighth-century prophets condemned those inequities and the inherent in them oppression (e.g. Isa. 1.16-17; Amos 2.6-8; Mic. 2.1-2).

In Luke's account, on the other hand, while Elizabeth and Zechariah probably lived comfortably, with the social status associated with priesthood, Joseph's only identification was his Davidic lineage. Mary and Joseph's child was born in poverty, and their offering at his presentation was that of the poor: 'a pair of turtledoves or two young pigeons' (Lk. 2.24). Mary praised God who feeds the hungry and Zechariah spoke of redemption in the traditional sense, but throughout the remainder of the Lukan corpus poverty is praised as an ideal. Examples are the beatitude, 'Blessed are you who are poor, for yours is the kingdom of God' (Lk. 6.20; cf. Mt. 5.3); the requirements for discipleship (homelessness, rejection of family, rejection of the past [Lk. 9.57-62]); and the instructions to the seventy who preceded Jesus in his journeys to the towns: they were to take no purse, bag, or sandals (10.1-4). The Samuel account and Luke's Infancy Narrative announce the elimination of poverty in the kingdom of Israel, but Luke's description of the kingdom of God idealizes poverty as a dimension of faith.

Luke also reinterpreted the idea of motherhood. In Samuel and throughout the Hebrew Bible, motherhood itself implies obedience to God's gift of a child.[15] But Luke redefined motherhood and all definitions of status and identity in terms of obedience to God, rather than the traditional categories of age, family heritage, and gender (8.21).[16]

These examples of Luke's kaleidoscopic shifts suggest that he reconfigured elements of the Samuel narrative to relate explicitly and graphically the kingdom of God to the history and traditions of Israel. But he reconfigured them to teach about the inbreaking of a new era, the kingdom of God. The result is a shift from the simpler, earlier story to the more complex Infancy Narrative, with an accompanying blend of shifted values which carry the new meaning of the corpus.

A look at the original text in 1 Samuel and the three later interpretations of it makes possible several observations. First, each of the later versions follows a different interpretive process. The targumic version changes only the poetic text, and leaves the narrative intact. The changes involve adding words and phrases to the original, creating a different genre. The resulting apocalypse rehearses Israel's history and highlights divine guidance throughout and into the future. *Pseudo-Philo*'s account expands both poem and narrative, again

15. Phyllis Trible, *God and the Rhetoric of Sexuality* (Philadelphia: Fortress Press, 1978), p. 35.

16. J.B. Green, 'The Social Status of Mary in Luke 1,5–2,52: A Plea for Methodological Integration', *Bib* 73 (1992), pp. 457-72 (468).

adding words and phrases but eliminating others. The resulting poem becomes a testament given at the point of transition to monarchy. The entire passage develops Hannah's status and role, and also that of Eli. Luke's reconfiguration expands and rearranges the original, resulting in more complex poems and narrative. Thus each of the later interpretations evolved into a new entity with its own particular emphasis.

The different processes and results have several common points, however. First, they serve to affirm divine guidance of the people, particularly the more vulnerable members of society, at times of uncertainty and transition. Second, the surface setting of the first three remains eleventh-century Shiloh and its environs, while the actual settings are several centuries later: for Samuel, the developing monarchy with its tensions and failings; for *Bib. Ant.*, the threat of Roman takeover in 70 CE; and for the Targum, the tensions surrounding the Jewish revolts against Rome. Luke's surface setting shifts to Jerusalem and its surrounding towns during the life of Christ in the first half of the first century CE. Its actual setting is a generation later, in the aftermath of the Roman destruction of Jerusalem and the development of understanding of the kingdom of God. For the people in each of the settings the issue of divine guidance and protection was crucial to their existence as a covenant people.

Finally, the conviction that God cares for the vulnerable permeates all four accounts. Human leaders are challenged to rule in that spirit, and their tenure is evaluated in terms of it. Ultimately, however, the four works attest to the people's faith in the God who promises to see them through, and whose intervention throughout their history convinces them that it will continue in their present and future.

WHAT DOES RUTH HAVE TO DO WITH RAHAB? MIDRASH *RUTH RABBAH* AND THE MATTHEAN GENEALOGY OF JESUS

Larry L. Lyke

Introduction

Among the more curious elements of the genealogy of Jesus in Mt. 1.1-17 is the presence of the names of only three women: Tamar, Rahab, and Ruth.[1] How is one to explain the mention of these three women among the many who clearly played a part in the genealogy? In his commentary on the infancy narratives of Matthew and Luke, Raymond Brown cites the three standard explanations for the reference to these three women in Matthew 1.[2]

1.   On the problem of the spelling of Rahab in Mt. 1.5 see Jerome Quinn, 'Is Rhachab in Matt 1.5 Rahab of Jericho?', *Bib* 62 (1981), pp. 225-28, and Raymond Brown, 'Rachab in Matt 1.5 probably is Rahab of Jericho', *Bib* 63 (1982), pp. 79-80. A fourth woman, Bathsheba, is mentioned in the genealogy but her name does not occur, rather, she is referred to only as 'the wife of Uriah'. On the significance of this designation see M. Petit, 'Bethsabée dans la tradition juive jusqu'aux Talmudim', *Judaica* 47 (1991), pp. 209-23. Later we will have occasion to consider her role in Matthew's genealogy. Suffice it to say at this juncture that she represents a midpoint between the types of stories that we claim inform Matthew's infancy narrative. On the importance of genealogies in late Second Temple Judaism see Raymond Brown, *The Birth of the Messiah: A Commentary on the Infancy Narratives in the Gospels of Matthew and Luke* (New York: Doubleday, 1993), esp. pp. 64-66; Robert Wilson, *Genealogy and History in the Biblical World* (New Haven: Yale University Press, 1977); M.D. Johnson, *The Purpose of the Biblical Genealogies, with Special Reference to the Setting of the Genealogies of Jesus* (SNTSMS, 8; Cambridge: Cambridge University Press, 1969). For recent discussion of Matthew's genealogy see n. 2.

2.   Raymond Brown, *The Birth of the Messiah*, esp. pp. 71-74. Others have considered the significance of these three women as well but Brown represents the general consensus. See also W.D. Davies and Dale C. Allison, *The Gospel According to Saint Matthew* (ICC, 1; Edinburgh: T. & T. Clark, 1988), pp. 169-72. W.R. Albright and C.S. Mann (*Matthew* [AB, 26; New York: Doubleday, 1971], pp. 5-6)

First is the notion that the women mentioned here were all regarded as sinners: their inclusion foreshadows, for Matthew, Jesus' redemptive role vis-à-vis sinners.[3] Notably, the category of 'sinners' hardly fits all of these women. Furthermore, as Brown notes, each of these women was relatively highly esteemed at the turn of the Common Era.[4] As a result, 'there is little likelihood that Matthew's readers

simply argue that the 'evangelist's tradition saw these women (in their capacity as instruments of God's providence) as forerunners of Mary'. Two of the more recent commentaries on Matthew are J. Enoch Powell, *The Evolution of the Gospel* (New Haven: Yale University Press, 1994) and Margaret Davies, *Matthew* (Sheffield: JSOT Press, 1993). For the most recent feminist treatment of the four women of Matthew's genealogy see Jane Shaberg, *The Illegitimacy of Jesus: A Feminist Theological Interpretation of the Infancy Narratives* (Sheffield: Sheffield Academic Press, 1995). Three representative articles on the significance of the women in Matthew's genealogy are: S. Blanco Pacheco, 'Las mujeres en la genealogía mateana de Jesús', *EphMar* 43 (1993), pp. 9-28; J.P. Heil, 'The Narrative Roles of the Women in Matthew's Genealogy', *Bib* 72 (1991), pp. 538-45; and E.D. Freed, 'The Women in Matthew's Genealogy', *JSNT* 29 (1987), pp. 3-19. Pacheco argues that the presence of these three women is part of a carefully constructed network of associations meant to point out their remarkable entry into the line of Judah/David. In the end, they are to be seen as precursors to Mary. Heil also ascribes to Matthew an intricate plan in including these women that has the purpose of emphasizing Jesus' birth as the 'apex of Matthew's salvation-historical genealogy' (p. 545). Freed, like Heil and Pacheco, thinks that Matthew had a single purpose in including these women: to defend against Jewish notions that Jesus was illegitimate. All of the previous work on the genealogy presumes that there is essentially a single reason that Tamar, Rahab, Ruth, and 'the wife of Uriah' are mentioned therein. In the following we will elaborate why it is fruitless to seek a single reason for their inclusion.

On the genealogy as a whole see (in addition to preceding) J.M. Jones, 'Subverting the Textuality of Davidic Messianism: Matthew's Presentation of the Genealogy and the Davidic Title', *CBQ* 56 (1994), pp. 256-72; R.P. Nettlehorst, 'The Genealogy of Jesus', *JETS* 31 (1988), pp. 169-72; J.D. Kingsbury, *Matthew as Story* (Philadelphia: Fortress Press, 1986); H.C. Waetjan, 'The Genealogy as the Key to the Gospel according to Matthew', *JBL* 95 (1976), pp. 205-30. Jones covers well the recent treatment of the genealogy as a whole. In addition, he argues that Matthew's goal is to promulgate a 'narrative ideology' that 'ultimately subverts the textuality of Davidic messianism in so profound a way that it revises Jewish history' (p. 257, cf. p. 266). I agree that there is a certain 'subversive' quality to Matthew's genealogy, in particular due to its multiple intertextual associations with other Hebrew biblical texts, but herein I suggest that this quality is likely not intentional on Matthew's part.

3.   Brown, *The Birth of the Messiah*, p. 71.
4.   Brown, *The Birth of the Messiah*, p. 72.

would have understood the women as sinners'.[5]

The second explanation for the presence of these women's names in the genealogy is that they are regarded as foreigners and were included to show that Jesus' ancestors included Gentiles. All three of these women do, indeed, seem to be foreigners. Brown raises a crucial objection to this second explanation: one would expect these three women to comprise some kind of analogue to Mary's role in the genealogy. Brown points out that Mary was not a foreigner.[6]

The final explanation for the presence of the names of Tamar, Rahab, and Ruth in Matthew's genealogy is the one that finds widest acceptance today and is twofold:

(1)   There is something extraordinary or irregular in their union with their partners—a union which, though it may have been scandalous to outsiders, continued the blessed lineage of the Messiah;

(2)   The women showed initiative or played an important role in God's plan and so came to be considered the instrument of God's providence or of His Holy Spirit.[7]

This twofold understanding makes good sense from a canonical perspective: reading these women through the events of Mary's life would naturally lead one to concentrate on the 'irregular' nature of their unions. In the end, the difficulty in understanding the presence of these women in the genealogy stems from two related factors: (1) we do not know for sure the assumptions that lie behind their association; (2) as a result, they are consistently understood in relation to Mary.[8]

Fortunately, a text in *Midrash Ruth Rabbah* is highly useful in addressing these two factors. This midrash not only treats these three

---

5.   Brown, *The Birth of the Messiah*, p. 72.

6.   Brown, *The Birth of the Messiah*, p. 73. Of course, Brown's comment presumes, like nearly all discussions of the genealogy, that Matthew had complete control of his sources and all of the implications embodied therein. As will become clear below, Matthew appears to have lost sight of this 'foreign' element that characterizes these three women.

7.   Brown, *The Birth of the Messiah*, p. 73.

8.   As we will see below, it seems as though modern interpreters make the mistake of following Matthew's interpretation of Mary in reverse. That is to say that while Matthew and his contemporaries grappled with interpreting Mary's life through examples of great women in the Hebrew biblical tradition, modern interpreters attempt to understand these three Hebrew biblical woman through the life of Mary. The circularity is hermeneutically problematic, especially so long as it goes unaddressed.

women but also suggests that their stories fit a recurrent topos in the Hebrew Bible that goes far in explaining their association.[9] In the following we present the text of *Midrash Ruth R.* 2.1 with a translation and extended commentary in order better to understand the association of Tamar, Rahab, and Ruth. After doing so we shall return to the implications this text has for understanding the first chapter of Matthew.

רבי סימון בשם ריב"ל ורבי חמא אבוי דרבי יהושע בשם רבי לא נתן דברי הימים
אלא להדרש הה"ד (דברי הימים א' ד') בני שלה בן יהודה ער אבי לכה . אב ב"ד של
לכה . ולעדה אבי מרשה אב בית דין של מרשה . ומשפחות בית עבדת הבוץ זו
רחב הזונה שהטמינה המרגלים בבוץ הה"ד (יהושע ב') ותטמנם בפשתי העץ . א"ר
יהודה ברבי סימון בבוסמין היתה עסקה . לבית אשבע שנשבעו לה המרגלים
שנאמר (שם) ועתה השבעו נא לי בי"י . ויוקים שקיימו לה השבועה הה"ד (שם ו)
ויבואו הנערים המרגלים . ומה תלמוד לומר ואת כל משפחותיה הוציאו תני רשב"י
שאפי' היתה משפחתה מאתיים אנשים והלכו ונדבקו במאתים משפחות אחרות כולן
ניצולו בזכותה . ואת כל משפחתה לא נאמר אלא ואת כל משפחותיה . ואנשי כזבה
שכזובה במלך יריחו שנאמר (שם ב) והאמר כן באו אלי האנשים וגו' . ויואש שנתיאשה
מן החיים . ושרף . שתקנה עצמה לשרופין . אשר בעלו למואב שבאתה ונדבקה
בישראל ועלו מעשיה לאביה שבשמים . וישבי לחם שנדבקה בישראל שקבלו את
התורה שכתוב בה לכו לחמו בלחמי . והדברים עתיקים ר' איבו ור' יהודה בר'
סימון אומרים דברים הללו סתומין כאן מפורשין במקום אחר . המה היוצרים אלו
המרגלים הה"ד (שם) וישלח יהושע בן נון מן השטים וגו' . ר' יהודה ור' נחמיה
ח"א כלי נגרות היה בידם מרגלים חרש לאמר . ר' נחמיה אומר כלי קדרות היה
בידם מקדרין חרש לאמר . תני רשב"י חרש כמשמעו אמר להם עשו עצמכם חרשין
ואתם עומדים על רזיהם . ר"ש בן אלעזר אומר מתוך שאתם עושים עצמכם חרשים
אתם עומדים על אופניים שלהם . ויושבי נטעים שהיו בקיאין בנטיעה על שם שנא'
(במדבר יג) ויכרתו משם זמורה . וגדרה שהטמינה אותן אחרי הגדר שנאמר ותאמר
להם ההרה לכו . ויש אומרים ששרתה עליה רוח הקדש עד שלא נכנסו ישראל
לארץ . וכי מהיכן היתה יודעת שחוזרין לשלשת ימים מיכן ששרתה עליה רוח הקדש .
עם המלך במלאכתו ישבו שם מכאן אמרו עשרה כהנים נביאים עמדו מרחב הזונה .
ירמיה . חלקיה . שריה . מחסיה . הנמאל . שלום . ברוך . נריה . יחזקאל . בוזי .
ויש אומרים אף חולדה הנביאה מבני בניה של רחב הזונה היתה:[10]

Rabbi Simon in the name of Rabbi Joshua ben Levi and Rabbi Hama, father of Rabbi Hosea, in the name of Rabbi: 'Divre Hayyamim was given only to do midrash'. As it is written: '*The sons of Shelah son of Yehudah: Er father of Lekhah*' (1 Chron. 4.21). (This means Er) father of the Bet

9. Heil ('Narrative Roles') engages in detailed analysis of the Hebrew biblical texts associated with these three women as well but in the end, again, argues for Matthew's purposeful manipulation of the sources for a single purpose (see n. 2 above).

10. *Midrash Rabbah* (ed. Isaac Ze'ev Yadler; Jerusalem: Tiferet Zion, 1960), pp. 281-85 (Hebrew).

Din of Lekhah. '*Ladah father of Mareshah*' (v. 21). (This means Ladah) father of the Bet Din of Mareshah. '*And the families of the house of linen making*' (v. 21). This refers to Rahab the whore who hid the spies in the linen. As it is written: '*She hid them in the pile of linen/flax*' (Josh. 2.6). Rabbi Yehudah ben Simon said 'Her occupation was in spices'. '*At Bet Ashbea*' (1 Chron. 4.21). Since the spies swore to her. As it is said: '*Now swear to me by Ha Shem…*' (Josh. 2.12) '*And Yoqim*' (1 Chron. 4.22). Since they fulfilled the oath to her. As it is written: '*And the young spies came…*' (Josh. 6.23) And what does scripture (mean) by saying: '*And all her families they brought out*'? (v. 23) Rabbi Simeon ben Yochai taught that even if her family were 200 strong and they went and clung to 200 other families, all of them would be delivered through her merit since 'all her family' is not written but rather 'all her *families*'. '*And the men of Khozebah*' (1 Chron. 4.22). Since she lied to the king of Jericho. As it is said: '*She said, "The men did just come to me…"*' etc. (Josh. 2.4). '*And Joash*' (v. 22). Since she gave up (her) life. '*And Saraph*' (v. 22). Since she was ready to be burned. '*Who had married into Moab*' (v. 22). Since she came and clung to Israel her deeds went up to her father in the heavens. '*And Yashubi Lehem*' (v. 22). Since she clung to Israel who had accepted the Torah in which is written: '*Come, eat my bread*' (Prov. 9.5). '*And the matters/words are ancient*' (1 Chron. 4.22). Rabbi Aybo and Rabbi Yehudah ben Rabbi Simon say: 'These words are unclear here but are explained in another place'. '*They were potters*' (v. 23). These are the spies, as it is written: '*Joshua ben Nun sent from Shittim…*' (Josh. 2.1). Rabbi Yehudah and Rabbi Nehemiah (argued) and one said: 'Carpentry tools were in their hands' (As it says): '*Spies, carpenters, saying…*' Rabbi Nehemiah says 'Pottery vessels were in their hands'. (As it says): '*Makers of earthenware, saying…*' Rabbi Simeon ben Yochai taught 'Silently, just like it sounds'. He said to them: 'Make like you cannot talk and you will learn/keep their secrets'. Rabbi Simeon ben Eleazar says: 'From your making like you cannot talk you will learn their ways'. '*And inhabitants of Netaim*' (v. 23). Since they were experts with regard to horticulture. As it is said: '*They cut a branch from there*' (Num. 13.23). '*And Gederah*' (1 Chron. 4.23). Since she had hidden them behind the wall. As it says: '*She said to them: "Go to the mountains!"*' (Josh. 2.16). There are some who say that the Holy Spirit came to rest on her before Israel had even entered the land. How else could she have known that they were returning in three days? From the foregoing (it is clear) that the Holy Spirit had come to rest upon her. '*They lived there with the King (doing) his work*' (1 Chron. 4.23). From this they said: 'Ten priests who were also prophets arose from Rahab the whore: Jeremiah, Hilqaiah, Seraiah, Mahasiah, Hanma'el, Shallum, Barukh, Neriah, Yehezqiel, and Buzzi'. There are those who say even Huldah the prophetess was a descendent of Rahab the whore.

This passage from *Ruth Rabbah* comes at the end of several midrashim treating Ruth 1.1 and is the first of four midrashim (*Ruth R.* 2.1-4) that treat all or part of 1 Chron. 4.21-23, the text and translation of which follows:

²¹בְּנֵי שֵׁלָה בֶן־יְהוּדָה עֵר אֲבִי לֵכָה וְלַעְדָּה אֲבִי מָרֵשָׁה וּמִשְׁפְּחוֹת בֵּית־עֲבֹדַת הַבֻּץ לְבֵית אַשְׁבֵּעַ:

²²וְיוֹקִים וְאַנְשֵׁי כֹזֵבָא וְיוֹאָשׁ וְשָׂרָף אֲשֶׁר־בָּעֲלוּ לְמוֹאָב וְיָשֻׁבִי לָחֶם וְהַדְּבָרִים עַתִּיקִים:

²³הֵמָּה הַיּוֹצְרִים וְיֹשְׁבֵי נְטָעִים וּגְדֵרָה עִם־הַמֶּלֶךְ בִּמְלַאכְתּוֹ יָשְׁבוּ שָׁם:

²¹The sons of Shelah son of Yehudah: Er father of Lekhah, Ladah father of Mareshah, and the families of the house of linen making at Bet Ashbea; ²²and Yoqim and the men of Khozebah and Yoash, and Saraph, who had married into Moab and Yashubi Lehem. And the matters/words are ancient. ²³They were the potters and inhabitants of Netaim and Gederah; they lived there with the king (doing) his work.

The relationship between this Chronicles passage and Ruth 1.1 is not made explicit but it is likely the mention of Moab in each that initially triggers their association. The significance of this association and all its attendant thematic and theological presuppositions becomes clearer in light of the three midrashim that immediately follow ours. Detailed analysis of these other three midrashim is not practicable here, but a brief outline of their contents and significance is in order.

Ruth Rabbah 2.2–2.4

Ruth Rabbah 2.2 assumes that 1 Chron. 4.21-23 refers to David. The brief text in Chronicles presents a genealogy of Shelah, the only surviving son of Judah and his first wife. The *darshanim* apparently associate the genealogy of Judah's third son with the most important of the Judahites, David. This is curious given that at the end of the book of Ruth itself we learn that David's genealogy extends backward through Ruth and Boaz to Judah, not through Shelah, but through Perez, Judah's son by Tamar. In fact, 1 Chron. 2.3-17 traces David's genealogy from Perez as well. It seems unlikely that either the Chronicler or the interpreters actually think that David is a direct descendent of Shelah. So why the connection of the Chronicles passage, in a midrash on Ruth, with David? That Ruth represents a full-blown and self-conscious story about one of David's key ancestors, a Moabite, seems to be the only plausible answer.

The second midrash following ours, *Ruth R.* 2.3, limits its interpretation to just 1 Chron. 4.22 and 23. Eliminating the reference to

Shelah and Judah, this interpretation asserts that the Chronicles passage refers to Moses. In this instance, the relevance of the Chronicles passage to the book of Ruth is difficult to detect. No association between Moses and Ruth seems to be presupposed in this midrash.[11] This interpretation may have come to reside in our collection simply because it treated the same Chronicles passage as *Ruth R.* 2.1, 2, and 4. Given the nature of the editing of midrashic collections one can never be sure of the 'logic' of the placement of any particular midrash. What counts for our purposes is that we have another midrash that treats the passage in 1 Chronicles.

The third midrash that follows ours, *Ruth R.* 2.4, interprets only 1 Chron. 4.22 and assumes that the verse refers to Elimelekh. Taking advantage of the fact that the reference to Moab in the Chronicles passage is interpreted as an oblique reference to Elimelekh, the editor apparently supplies a transition from the midrashim on Ruth 1.1 (containing the first reference to Moab) to those on v. 2 where Elimelekh is first mentioned. Additionally, the interpretation in *Ruth R.* 2.4 serves to establish the interpretive value of the Chronicles passage by associating it not only with Ruth 1.1 but with v. 2 as well.

The forgoing establish that while it is not immediately evident why the genealogy of Shelah in 1 Chron. 2.21-23 should be invoked in interpreting the book of Ruth, there apparently was a rather widespread association of the two passages. This association seems to have been popular enough for *Ruth R.* 2.3, an interpretation that associates 1 Chron. 4.22 and 23 with Moses and apparently sheds little light on Ruth, to be included as well. Furthermore, the understanding in *Ruth R.* 2.2 that the Chronicles passage refers to David suggests that the interpreters were associating other texts with the book of Ruth as well. In particular, because David's genealogy at the end of Ruth (4.18-22) lists the descendants of Perez down to David, one is reminded of the story of Perez's birth in Genesis 38 where Shelah is mentioned four times. It seems likely that the authors of the midrashim associate 1 Chron. 4.21-23 with David through a kind of mental conflation of the genealogies of two of Judah's sons, Shelah and Perez.[12] It is this kind of conflation or associative logic that serves as

---

11. But see below (pp. 276-77) the discussion of Moses and the spies in *Ruth R.* 2.1.

12. Notably Shelah's name appears in the Hebrew Bible eight times: four times in Gen. 38 (vv. 5, 11, 14, and 26) and once each in Gen. 46.12, Num. 26.20 and

the avenue by which to understand the association of Tamar, Ruth, and Rahab in our midrash and in Matthew.

Returning to the midrash that is our focus, with *Ruth R.* 2.1 the rabbis presume that 1 Chron. 4.21-23 consistently makes reference to the events of Rahab's life in Joshua 2 and 6. This is, at first blush, remarkable. *Ruth Rabbah* 2.2, 3 associated the Chronicles passage with great men of the biblical tradition. Even if the reasons for the association of Moses with Ruth (through the Chronicles passage) are unclear, one can at least appreciate that because of his status he, like David, might be connected with almost any biblical text. With *Ruth R.* 2.4 we have seen that the connection of Elimelekh with the Chronicles passage acts as a transition from Ruth 1.1 (and the digression into 1 Chron. 4.21-23) to Ruth 1.2. So why associate 1 Chron. 4.21-23 with Rahab and Ruth? As it turns out, the rabbis' interpretation of Rahab's life through the Chronicles passage reveals numerous parallels with the events in the book of Ruth. The best way to appreciate their observations is simply to follow their interpretation and consider the implications of their associative logic.

Ruth Rabbah *on 1 Chronicles 4.21*

The interpretation that begins our passage is a straightforward attempt to deal with two rather obscure names in 1 Chron. 4.21. The interpreter takes for granted that Er and Ladah are personal names but assumes that Lekhah and Mareshah are cities and that anyone described as the 'father' of a city is more likely the head of the *Bet Din* (court) there than he who has engendered all its occupants. This interpretation ignores the possibility that Lekhah and Mareshah are persons or eponyms. Moreover, it is of considerable interest that, according to the Chronicler, Shelah named his first son Er. This may be the Chronicler's way of indicating that Shelah, unlike his brother Onan, fulfilled his levirate duty to his oldest brother Er. Deuteronomy 25.6 says that a man is obligated to marry his brother's widow and that the first son born from this new union must be counted as the son of the dead brother so that *his name* not disappear from Israel. By

---

1 Chron. 2.3 and 4.21. In the three occurrences between Gen. 38 and ours in 1 Chron. 4.21 Shelah's name always is accompanied by reference to Perez and mention of his son (Gen. 46 and Numbers) if not a full list of his descendants down to David.

naming his eldest son after Er, Shelah appears to fulfill the stipulation set forth in Deut. 25.6. On the basis of numerous legal strictures against a son's sleeping with his father's wife (Deut. 23.1; Lev. 18.8; 20.11, etc.), it is perhaps unlikely that the Chronicler assumed Shelah's son Er was born to Tamar. On the other hand, Tamar was promised that when Shelah grew up she would become his wife. Genesis 38 does not elaborate on the fate of either Shelah or Tamar. The Chronicler may well represent a tradition that understood that Judah fulfilled his obligation to Tamar by arranging her marriage to Shelah after all. All this is open to speculation, however, because Shelah's wife remains unnamed. At any rate, this hint in 1 Chron. 4.21 that Shelah may have fulfilled his levirate duty likely underlies the rabbis' association of the Chronicles passage, via Genesis 38, with the book of Ruth in which we have the only other narrative example of levirate law in action. We will continue to see numerous ways in which Genesis 38 is presupposed in the constellation of texts under consideration. Beyond what appears to be an association of Genesis 38 with Ruth, our first interpretation otherwise represents a fairly simple clarification of wording that is admittedly vague.

The next clause in v. 21, 'the families of the house of linen making', the rabbis say refers to Rahab. They make this association based on their reading of Josh. 2.6 where Rahab hides the spies בפשתי העץ. This interpretation takes advantage of the synonyms בוץ in 1 Chron. 4.21 and פשת in Josh. 2.6 and assumes that the reference to 'linen' in the former is an allusion to the latter. But the logic of this connection and how Rahab fits into the picture awaits further explanation. Rabbi Yehudah ben Simon's claim that Rahab's occupation was in spices can only be explained if one assumes he associates the word בוץ with בוס, the first three 'letters' of בוסמין. While this connection is imaginative and may explain how the spies were attracted to Rahab's house it does little to solidify the connection between Josh. 2.6 and 1 Chron. 4.21.

The association of 1 Chron. 4.21 with Rahab is strengthened with the interpretation of its last two words 'at Bet Ashbea'. The rabbis pun on the root of Ashbea, שבע, which is the root of the verb 'to make an oath' as well. And how can Rahab's house be understood as the 'house of oath'? Joshua 2.12 supplies a ready answer—it was in her house that Rahab sought and received an oath from the spies that her kindness (חסד) would be repaid when the Israelites returned to take Jericho. Indeed, this oath is fulfilled in Josh. 6.22-25 when Rahab and her household are saved and allowed to live among the Israelites.

So the first verse in 1 Chron. 4.21-23, at least on the surface, seems merely to introduce the genealogy of Shelah, Judah's third son, by giving the names of his two sons Er and Ladah along with the names of their respective offspring. Whether the names of these offspring represent individuals or groups is unclear. The final clause of 1 Chron. 4.21, 'and the families of the house of linen making at Bet Ashbea', in its plain sense hardly makes reference to Rahab. Yet, through verbal and thematic parallels between texts, the rabbis presuppose numerous ways in which 1 Chron. 4.21 can be read as commentary, simultaneously, on the book of Ruth, Genesis 38, and the story of Rahab.

Ruth Rabbah *on 1 Chronicles 4.22*

Verse 22 continues to supply the rabbis with associations with Rahab. The first word in v. 22, 'And Yoqim', the Rabbis take as an allusion to Josh. 6.23 where the spies came and fulfilled (קיימו) their oath by saving Rahab and her family from the destruction of Jericho.[13] A peculiarity in the text of Josh. 6.23 attracts the rabbis' attention. Why does the text say that her *families* were brought out instead of her family? Rabbi Simeon ben Yochai claims that Rahab, on account of her kindness, had gained such a surplus of merit that it was sufficient to have saved even more people. At this point in the midrash and in the text of Joshua, one might think that Rahab's merit was simply her kindness to the two spies. Rabbi Simeon's use of language, however, adumbrates an even more meritorious quality of Rahab that emerges more clearly later in the midrash. Rabbi Simeon says that had Rahab 'clung' נדבקה to other families they could have been saved as well. In the rabbis' understanding, it is precisely Rahab's willingness to 'cling' to Israel, rather than to her fellows in Jericho, that comprises her more fundamental merit. This point will emerge more clearly below where we shall see that Rahab's willingness to 'cling' to Israel is understood to be analogous to Ruth's.

---

13. Note that the verb employed here in the midrash (קיימו) is used to translate השבעו in *Targ. Ps.-J.* to Josh. 2.12. The latter is used in Josh 2.12 when Rahab extracts the oath from the two men that they would spare her and her family. In other words, the rabbis apparently see in the word Yoqim (ויקים) a reference not only to the salvation of Rahab and her family in 6.23 but also to the point at which she extracted the oath from the two Israelites in 2.12 (reading קיימו in the Aramaic).

According to the rabbis, the next three phrases of 1 Chron. 4.22 continue to verify Rahab's merit. The first phrase, 'And the men of Khozebah', is interpreted as an allusion to Rahab's lie (כזב) to the king of Jericho; this lie is particularly important since it was the means by which she prevented the king of Jericho from finding the spies. One wonders whether the rabbis have in mind the occurrence of the root כזב in Genesis 38 as well. There we are told that Judah was in Khezib (בכזיב) when his wife had Shelah. The coincidence of the name Shelah and the root כזב in 1 Chron. 4.21-23 and Genesis 38 could hardly escape the notice of the rabbis and therefore is quite likely in the back of their minds in this midrash. This likelihood is made more sure with a number of other associations that the rabbis make between the story of Rahab and Genesis 38 via our Chronicles passage.

The next two words of 1 Chron. 4.22, Joash (יואש) and Saraph (שרף), are taken to signal that Rahab risked (נתיאשה) her life because she was fully aware of the consequences of her actions: were she discovered she would have been burned (שרף) to death by the king. Nonetheless, she hid the spies on her roof. It is unclear why the rabbis assume Rahab would have been burned had she been caught, but it is of note that in Genesis 38 Tamar is almost burned when Judah learns that she has 'whored' and become pregnant. When Judah discovers that she is carrying his child(ren), he declares that she is more righteous than he and rescinds the punishment. The remarkable coalescence of a common set of vocabulary and imagery in Genesis 38 and Joshua 2 may well trigger the rabbis' association of the near burning of Tamar in Genesis 38 with Rahab's supposed near burning in Joshua. Consider that by acting as (or being) a whore Tamar and Rahab display their greatest merit by allowing what, on first blush, appears to be illicit penetration. It is this penetration that at once comprises their life-threatening failure and their most profound act of kindness or righteousness. Furthermore, both provide for the perpetuation of Israel when a pair of Israelites depart from each of them. In both cases this 'departure' is marked by a red cord (השני). In fact, *Midrash haGadol* preserves a tradition in which the two spies who came to Rahab's house were none other than Perez and Zerah.[14] It is the latter who gave the red cord, which was tied onto his wrist at birth, to Rahab. It is impossible to determine whether the rabbis had

14. See Louis Ginzberg, *The Legends of the Jews* (Philadelphia: Jewish Publication Society of America, 1968), II, p. 36.

Genesis 38 in mind when they claimed that Rahab risked burning by her act of kindness to Israel, but the complex set of analogies between the texts is highly suggestive and likely underlies their interpretation.

The next clause in v. 22 and the phrase immediately following it are especially important for revealing the midrashic significance of 1 Chron. 4.21-23 in the rabbis' minds. We have noted that the mention of Moab in v. 22 seems to be the main reason the Chronicles passage is associated with Ruth and secondarily with Rahab. In addition, with their understanding of 'who had married into Moab, and Yashubi Lehem', the rabbis reveal more important parallels between the story of Rahab and Ruth. We should note that what we have translated as 'who had married into Moab' (אשר בעלו למואב) could as easily be translated 'who ruled over Moab'. For reasons that will become clear below, it seems likely the rabbis read בעלו as 'they married'.

Because the rabbis understand Rahab to be linked to Moab by marriage, her decision to cling to Israel is especially fascinating. It must be acknowledged from the start that it is not entirely clear how the rabbis understand Rahab's relationship to the Moabites. On one reading, Rahab herself marries into Moab, her ethnic origin being unclear. On the other hand, the rabbis equally likely read 1 Chronicles to mean that Rahab's ancestors had married into Moab. On this reading Rahab is at least half Moabite and her 'conversion' quite analogous to Ruth's.

The phrase that so strongly associates Rahab with Moab provides a second and even better opportunity for the *darshanim*. The rabbis explain that the phrase 'who had married into Moab' also means that since Rahab had clung (נדבקה) to Israel her deeds went up to her father in the heavens. The phrase בעלו למואב is apparently read באו עלו לאב(יה) 'her deeds went up to (her) father'.[15] This is a creative way to read the text on several counts. Most importantly, we should understand that אב is used to refer to God. In Rahab's situation the midrash calls God 'her father'. The implication is that as a result of her 'clinging' to Israel, their God becomes hers. Indeed, it seems the two acts are essentially inseparable. Clearly the midrash is aware of the parallel with Ruth 1.14-16 where it says that Ruth clung (דבקה) to Naomi. Naomi tells Ruth to return to her god(s) as did her sister Orpah but Ruth protests, and in one of the most moving passages in

15. L. Rabbinowitz also makes this point (*Midrash Rabbah Ruth* [London: Soncino Press, 1939], p. 24 n. 1).

the Hebrew Bible she declares her loyalty to Naomi. The key to this declaration is Ruth's acceptance of Naomi's God as her own. The midrash understands בעלו למואב to refer to Rahab's meritorious acts, her 'clinging' to Israel and her acceptance of their God, which are analogous to the events in the first chapter of the book of Ruth. This reading is particularly insightful in that by maintaining that Rahab may have been even partially Moabite the midrash solidifies the connections between the stories of Rahab and Ruth. Moreover, it changes a clause in Chronicles that can also be read to signal Rahab's integration (by marriage) into Moab (cf. our first reading in the last paragraph) into an account of her joining with Israel and their God. This, in turn, further links Rahab's story to Ruth's.

The phrase that immediately follows the clause 'who had married into Moab' is 'and Yashubi Lehem'. The rabbis see in this phrase another reference to Rahab's 'clinging' to Israel. In particular, they understand the phrase to refer to Rahab who clung to Israel who had accepted the Torah in which it says 'Come, eat my bread'. The midrash here cites Prov. 9.5 in which 'lady' wisdom pleads with 'him who is without sense' to partake of her hospitality. This association with Proverbs is ingenious and works on several levels. On one reading the woman of Proverbs 9 represents Rahab who has extended hospitality to the two Israelites that have come to her. On a second and more important reading 'lady' wisdom represents Israel, the mate of God. It is both Israel and God who will extend the ultimate hospitality when they admit Rahab into the fold for her act of hospitality. On a third level, the midrash seems to take delight in the fact that 'lady' wisdom represents the Torah (in its largest sense) in which all these multiple intertextual references reside. Moreover, the citation of Prov. 9.5 suggests the reciprocity of Rahab's reward for the kindness shown to the two Israelite men.

The final clause in 1 Chron. 4.22 is difficult to understand. Even the interpreters themselves acknowledge that this is the case when R. Aybo and R. Yehudah say, 'These words are unclear here but are explained elsewhere'. *Ruth Rabbah* 2.2 and 3 take up this phrase in rather extensive explanations, but neither fits particularly well with the midrash in *Ruth R.* 2.1.

So, in 1 Chron. 4.22 the interpreters continue to see allusions to Rahab. With the exception of the final phrase in v. 22 the interpreters find a veiled reference to Rahab in nearly every word or phrase in the verse. What is ostensibly simply a list of Shelah's descendants provides ample opportunity for such midrashic interpretation because it is not without ambiguity. Is Yoqim an individual, an eponym for a clan or tribe or the name of a city? The same questions can be asked of Khozebah, Joash, and Seraph. With the clause בעלו למואב it is unclear whom the plural verb is to include as subject. The final two phrases in the verse pose equal difficulty. All this means that the 'plain sense' of 1 Chron. 4.22 is not especially easy to determine. All that can be said with surety is that these names represent descendants (whether individuals, groups, or cities) of Shelah. This ambiguity begs for the clarification that the rabbis are quick to provide. For them the verse consistently acts as a prooftext of Rahab's merit.

Ruth Rabbah *on 1 Chronicles 4.23*

With their interpretation of 1 Chron. 4.23 the rabbis no longer find allusions to Rahab's merit but still find references to her story in Joshua 2. They explain that 'they were potters' (היוצרים) refers to the two spies that Joshua sent out of Shittim. This and several related midrashim are based on a peculiarity of the phraseology in Josh. 2.1. The difficulty lay in the words מרגלים חרש לאמר. In particular, the rabbis concern themselves with the awkward use of חרש, which apparently has an adverbial force here and should be translated 'silently' or 'secretly'. If this is the case, and it seems likely, it is the only time this root appears as an adverb. This rare and awkward use is an open invitation to any self-respecting *darshan*. The reference to potters in 1 Chron. 4.23 is read as an allusion to Josh. 2.1 by vocalizing the root חרש to read 'pottery'. On this reading 1 Chron. 4.23 refers to the two spies who come חרש (as potters) to Rahab's house. Rabbi Yehudah, however, did not accept this reading and argued that the root should be read as the nominal form meaning 'artificer' or 'carpenter'. Rabbi Simeon ben Yochai and Simeon ben Eleazar argue for the adverbial value 'silently'. They both think that Joshua instructed them to act dumb in order to lull the locals into talking since they would assume dumb people would not be able to tell their secrets. While their elaboration of the meaning 'silently' stretches the plain sense of Josh. 2.1, that חרש here means 'silently' or 'secretly' is likely. Aside from the differences of opinion on 1 Chron. 4.23, we note that at least some interpreters of its first phrase saw in it a continuation of the commentary on the story of Rahab, and in particular, on the spies in that story.

The next phrase in v. 23, 'And the inhabitants of Netaim', is also understood as a reference to the spies in Joshua 2. The midrash understands Netaim (נטעים) to refer to the spies' expertise with plants (נטיעות). After a perusal of Joshua 2, however, one would be hard pressed to find evidence of this expertise. As one might expect, the prooftext that the midrash brings is not from Joshua 2, nor is it from anywhere in the book of Joshua. Rather, it comes from Num. 13.23, the context and characters of which the rabbis view as related to Joshua 2. In the Numbers passage Moses sends Kaleb and his gang of 11 spies to the promised land in order to determine what type of place it is. Moses instructs them to scout the land and to bring back some samples of its fruit. In 13.23 we find the prooftext cited in our midrash 'They cut a branch from there'. In context, they simply carry out Moses' command to bring back fruit from the place. The interpreters of our midrash, however, see in this Numbers passage a prefiguration of Joshua 2 and of the book of Ruth. The rabbis interpret Netaim in Chronicles to refer to the horticultural skill displayed by the spies in Numbers who function much like the spies in Joshua 2. The midrash assumes the spies in Joshua 2 share these horticultural skills with their predecessors. At a thematic level, the connection of these two stories is especially suggestive. It seems as though the rabbis have in mind that the spies who brought back a foreign branch to Moses prefigured the spies in Joshua who brought the foreigner Rahab out of Jericho to dwell among the Israelites. This analogy is especially attractive because it is much like the events in Ruth 1. Obviously Naomi is not a spy but like the spies in Joshua she is responsible for bringing a foreign woman, a 'Moabite', into the Israelite fold. This similarity between Ruth, Joshua 2 and 6, and Num. 13.17-23 makes it hard to believe it was not in the rabbis' minds when they brought Num. 13.2 as a prooftext. Moreover, note that the rabbis presuppose in this midrash fertility imagery that is as striking as it is suggestive.[16]

---

16. In the case of Numbers, the notion is that Israel, when the Israelites get there, will be a place where they can be fruitful and multiply. Again, with Ruth, her inclusion in the Israelite fold is so 'fruitful' that it continues the royal lineage. With Rahab, the midrash likely understands that this 'whore' will only become fruitful in a meaningful way now that she is brought into the Israelite nation.

Finally, we should note that through the conquest of Jericho and all of 'the land' the Israelites did indeed become inhabitants of the land in which resided those 'plants' from which Kaleb and his friends cut off the branch.

The next phrase in v. 23, 'and Gederah', the rabbis take as a reference to the wall in which Rahab lived and hid her spy friends. That Josh. 2.15 employs חומה for wall rather than the root גדר is of no consequence to the interpreters. As their prooftext the interpreters choose a clause from Josh. 2.16; 'Head for the hills lest the posse come upon you. Hide there three days until the posse has returned. Then you may go on your way!'. This prooftext serves two purposes. First, it follows the twofold reference in v. 15 to the wall in which Rahab lived, from which she had just let the spies down and from which she is currently speaking to them. In this way the prooftext obliquely reminds the reader that Gederah in 1 Chron. 4.23 is an allusion to the wall in which Rahab lived. Secondly, the prooftext also introduces the last issue to be addressed in the midrash: how to account for Rahab's almost prophetic qualities?

How did Rahab know to tell the spies to make for the hills and to hide there for three days until their pursuers returned to Jericho? As it happens, the 'posse' did return in three days. From these events emerges the speculation on the part of some rabbis that the Holy Spirit must have come to rest upon Rahab. There is no other explanation for her prognostication. The suspicion that Rahab had prophetic abilities is also suggested by the interpretation of the last clause of 1 Chron. 4.23, 'They lived there with the king (doing) his work', which the rabbis take to refer to Rahab's descendants, ten of whom they think were priests and prophets and may have included Huldah the prophetess. It is perhaps notable that the biblical text itself depicts Rahab, the Canaanite whore, in such light. One suspects, however, that the rabbis had in mind even more significant evidence that the Holy Spirit had rested on her. In particular, it seems likely that they viewed Rahab's acknowledging of YHWH as the only God and her acts of חסד with respect to Israel (Josh. 2.11 and 12) as ample evidence that the Holy Spirit had rested on her before Israel crossed over into the promised land.

To summarize briefly our investigation to this point: the midrash found in *Ruth R.* 2.1 begins with a text that seems essentially unrelated to the book of Ruth. The text of 1 Chron. 4.21-23 is brought into consideration due to a single verbal cue: the reference to Moab in v. 22. Otherwise, the Chronicles passage simply presents the only account in the Hebrew Bible of the descendants of Shelah, Judah's only surviving son by his first wife. Because this genealogical list includes names that appear either for the first or only time it is not clear whether some of them should be understood as individuals, groups, or even cities. The ambiguity surrounding these names and references makes the passage ideal for midrashic interpretation.

What makes our midrash especially intriguing is the association of 1 Chron. 4.21-23 with the book of Ruth and the story of Rahab in Josh. 2 and 6. We have seen how each phrase and clause of 1 Chron. 4.21-23 is midrashically linked to the events in the book of Joshua. Furthermore, although the midrash fails to make explicit how the story of Rahab relates to the book of Ruth, we have suggested numerous parallels between the two. In addition to these parallels, we have suggested that Genesis 38 seems to inform part of the hermeneutic employed in our midrash. In the following we will consider a few additional connections among the texts that form the backdrop for this midrash. While the rabbis almost never elaborate or comment directly on this intertextuality, they continually presuppose it.

First we need to elaborate on a key connection between the book of Ruth and the story of Rahab. After her husband dies, Ruth decides to 'cling' to Naomi (v. 14). This act is proleptically described by Naomi in v. 8 and later by Boaz in 3.10 as *hesed* (חסד). Notably, Rahab frames her request to be saved in terms of *hesed*. She asks that her act of *hesed* (protecting the spies) be reciprocated by an act of *hesed*, their saving of her and her family. This reciprocity is similar to that requested by Naomi for Ruth in 1.8 where she says 'May YHWH return the *hesed* you have shown me and my family'. Indeed, both Rahab's and Ruth's kindness are rewarded by their inclusion in Israel. Another point of contact between Ruth and Rahab: Ruth's act of attaching herself to Israel was accompanied by her acceptance of YHWH as her God; likewise, Rahab, before she requested clemency for her family, acknowledged that YHWH was the only God. Once she had been saved and absorbed into Israel in ch. 6, Israel became her people and YHWH her God.

Above we argued that Genesis 38 seems to be presupposed in the interpretation of the Chronicles passage and by extension the book of Ruth. That Shelah's first son is named Er in 1 Chron. 4.21 may indicate that either the Chronicler or the *darshanim* understood this to be in fulfillment of levirate obligations to his oldest brother Er. Because Genesis 38 and Ruth are our only narratives in which the levirate law is practiced, the Chronicles passage seems to function, at least in the minds of the interpreters, as commentary on both. Other parallels likely underlie the rabbis' association of Ruth and Genesis 38. When Naomi tells Ruth and Orpah to go back home, she says that she is too old to have sons that they might marry and even if she were to marry and have a son they should not have to wait so long. Naomi presupposes levirate obligations in this declaration. She is concerned with providing her daughters-in-law with another son to marry them. When Ruth decides to 'cling' to her mother-in-law she is, in theory, waiting for Naomi's third son to fulfill his levirate obligations. Tamar, in Genesis 38, also awaits a third son, Judah's son Shelah. In the case of Ruth, Naomi is unable to provide offspring and Boaz steps in for an unwilling redeemer. In Genesis 38 Judah, unwilling to provide his offspring, steps in as an unwitting 'redeemer'.

There are strong similarities between Ruth and the story of Rahab, as there are between Ruth and the story of Tamar. The similarities between the story of Tamar and that of Rahab are more limited but no less significant. Recall the discussion above (pp. 272-73) in which we noted the presence of the crimson thread at the birth of Perez and Zerah and in the window of Rahab. Both threads mark the emergence of a pair of men who are crucial to the perpetuation of Israel. This emergence follows on the illicit penetration that, ironically, marks Tamar's and Rahab's greatest acts of courage and compassion for Israel. Another element that connects Ruth with Genesis 38—and likely connects all three texts we have been discussing—is the theme of alien women who are integrated into the Israelite and biblical tradition. In addition, this integration comes on the heels of acts of extraordinary kindness or righteousness on the part of these women. These acts signal that the women have adopted the Israelite code of conduct and the God it presupposes. In the cases of Tamar and Ruth, these women became so central to the tradition that they figure in the genealogy of David himself. Nowhere in the Hebrew Bible does Rahab figure in David's genealogy. This makes even more fascinating Matthew's claim in 1.5 that Rahab is the mother of Boaz and thereby is integral to the Davidic genealogy. Having gained a fuller understanding of the associations between Tamar, Rahab, and Ruth in the

Hebrew Bible and rabbinic traditions, it is to Matthew's account that we must now return.

Ruth Rabbah, *Intertextuality, and Matthew*

At the outset of this article we set as our goal to clarify the association between the three women mentioned in Matthew's genealogy. Midrash *Ruth Rabbah* 2.1 is exceptionally useful in clarifying the connections between the three. The rabbis' understanding of the Hebrew biblical text reveals important associations that inhere in the text itself. Their ability to recognize and uncover the intertextual associations among the three stories at hand illumines the biblical material in important ways. In this instance, the rabbis' focus is limited to these three stories, for the most part because they see in them parade examples of conversion. That these three stories share innumerable intertextual associations with other biblical material is peripheral to their vision, focused as it is by their 'lens of conversion'. Among the unlimited intertext that one could detail in relation to the stories of Tamar, Rahab, and Ruth, their association with a topos I would label as 'woman with a cause' apparently forms the lens through which Matthew views these three women and the events of Mary's life.

Indeed, the stories of Tamar, Rahab, and Ruth comprise a subset of this larger topos found throughout Hebrew biblical literature. Among the numerous examples of this topos are the stories of Abigail in 1 Samuel 25, the Wise Woman of Tekoa in 2 Samuel 14, and Bath-sheba in 1 Kings 1 and 2 among others.[17] The most general point of these stories seems to be that a woman shows great kindness and fortitude in preserving or defending the life of a loved one. Of course, there are numerous versions and adaptations of this topos. For example, the book of Genesis also contains permutations of the topos in the accounts of Sarah and Rebekah in which the unusual nature of their conceiving and giving birth to their sons is foregrounded. Of the many forms that this topos takes, two general categories are of particular concern for understanding Matthew's genealogy.

---

17. Among the numerous texts that fit this topos or represent variations on it are, Est. 5 and 7, Gen. 21 and 27, 1 Kgs 3 and 2 Kgs 6, 1 Sam. 28, 1 Kgs 14, 2 Kgs 22, and several others. It is not necessary here to go into all the factors that suggest that these accounts belong to the topos nor is it possible herein to detail the subdivisions represented by them.

Before identifying and considering these two categories a word of caution is in order. While the categories can be understood to inhere in the Hebrew biblical text, one should not presume rigid and unyielding boundaries between them. Like the notion of topos, the notion of these categories must remain flexible enough to allow for multiple interrelationships with other texts throughout the Hebrew Bible. In the following we concentrate on two loose categories of the 'woman with a cause' topos distinguished by key diagnostic elements. These two categories, if nothing else, seem to define the interpretive trajectories followed by the rabbis and Matthew.

The first category of the 'woman with a cause' topos that informs Matthew's account comprises stories in which the survival and perpetuation of Israel is dependent on foreign women who do great acts of kindness by which they preserve the Israelite lineage and, thereby, become members of it. This version is represented by the stories of Tamar, Rahab, and Ruth. Notably, *Midrash Ruth Rabbah* has in view this same category and may well assume that Rahab is part of the Davidic lineage; at least that is the implication of her association with Tamar and Ruth.[18] At any rate, it clearly associates her with the tribe of Judah. Matthew, going a step further than *Midrash Ruth Rabbah*, makes clear that Rahab is as much a part of the Davidic lineage as are Tamar and Ruth. Moreover, it seems that for Matthew, Rahab joins Tamar and Ruth in the honored genealogy. Key to identifying this category of the 'woman with a cause' topos is the combination of foreignness of the woman and her part in the perpetuation of Israel or the Davidic lineage.

In contrast to the first category of the 'woman with a cause' topos that apparently informs Matthew 1, the second essentially ignores the Davidic lineage. This category is defined by those accounts in which a wondrous event is associated with the conception of the woman's child. In this group we would include not only Sarah, Rebekah, and Rachel but also Hannah and Samson's mother. While Matthew's genealogy remains essentially indifferent to this version, 1.18-25, the verses immediately following the genealogy, are closely associated with it. This category, especially the stories of Hannah and Samson's mother, seems to underlie the Lukan Infancy Narrative as well.[19]

18. See earlier (p. 267) where Shelah's and Judah's genealogies seem to be conflated by the *darshanim*.

19. Indeed, Luke's infancy narrative comprises an extended and complex set of

Notably, Sarah and Rebekah likely represent the most important types for these two Gospel writers. Sarah's son Isaac, especially through his near sacrifice depicted in the Akedah, becomes a typological precursor to Jesus. Clearly the mothers of Isaac and Jesus would be similarly associated. Likewise, Rebekah, as the mother of Jacob/Israel, would be seen as the prefiguration of Mary, the mother of the 'new' Israel. Significantly, modeled as as they are on the wondrous conceptions and births that are associated with these women, the miraculous events of Mt. 1.18-25 have little to do with the Davidic lineage.[20] This is the

overlapping variations on this category. For extended discussion see Brown, *The Birth of the Messiah*, pp. 256-392. For our purposes it is useful to raise only a few of the issues involved in order to highlight the dynamics of Matthew's genealogy. Luke's account of Elizabeth's barrenness and subsequent conception has much in common with the story in Judg. 13.1-25 where Samson's mother is approached by an 'angel of God' and given specific (Nazirite) instructions for the son she is about to bear. Her husband's (Manoah's) insistence on being informed leads to an encounter between him and the angel during which Manoah suggests he make an offering. Compare Lk. 1.5-25 where Zechariah, preparing to make an offering, is the first approached by 'an angel of God' and given essentially the same instructions (for the son, John the Baptist, that is about to be born to them) that are given to Samson's mother (and then to Manoah) in Judg. 13. Of course the events surrounding Jesus' birth are comparable to those surrounding Samuel's. In particular, Lk. 1.46-55, the Magnificat, has numerous associations with Hannah's prayer in 1 Sam. 2.1-10. While it looks as though the story of John's birth is modeled on Samson's (note the women associated with their death who cut off their hair/head) and Jesus' on Samuel's, the truth is likely more complicated. For example, the sequence in which the first son is eventually supplanted by the second appears to be a variation on so many of the stories of sons in Genesis including the sons of Sarah/Hagar and Rebekah. We should likely understand the influences on Luke's infancy narrative to be so diffuse and complicated, and his account dependent on such an amalgam of traditions, that no single model ought to be sought for his account(s). We cannot pursue this line of argument further here but in the course of the following discussion we will see that the same complex traditionary process likely informs Matthew's genealogy and infancy account.

20. It should be noted, however, that by citing Isa. 7.14 Matthew may attempt to reintroduce the notion of the Davidic line. Matthew apparently views this promise of the birth of a child to a virgin to be addressed to a Davidid. That is, he seems to think this promise is fulfilled in Mary. By associating this promise of a 'virgin' birth with the larger topos of women like Sarah *et al.*, Matthew seems to find the means to bring together the miraculous birth and Davidic lineage. Of course, he still faces the difficulty of the paternity of Jesus and whether he is a Davidid. Perhaps Matthew understands the Davidic nature of Jesus' paternity in light of Ps. 2.7 where YHWH announces to David: 'You are my son, Today I have begotten you'. If this is the

case with all of the accounts that belong to this category in the Hebrew Bible as well. Ironically, by stressing the miraculous nature of Jesus' birth, Matthew's account not only resonates with these Hebrew Bible precursors, it also, de facto, removes Mary's son from the male Davidic lineage.

Matthew's account in ch. 1 seems to depend (likely not consciously) on these two categories of the topos. In other words, Matthew, immersed as he is in the interpretive milieu of his time, has the cultural and literary competence that leads him to interpret the life of Mary in association with the stories of great women in the Hebrew Bible tradition.[21] The problem arises because, when applied to Jesus' infancy, the two categories on which he relies run at 'cross' purposes. All of this is to say that the traditions on which Matthew relies have their own trajectories that, when juxtaposed, run counter to any single purpose. In a manner consistent with his interpretive milieu, Matthew conflates these traditions. Raymond Brown, and those with whom he agrees, read Matthew 1 in a way that privileges 1.18-25 and its emphasis on the wondrous conception and birth of Jesus, at the expense of the category that dominates the genealogy itself. That is to say, on this reading, Brown *et al.* read the genealogy through the events depicted in 1.18-25. In such a reading, one loses sight of the divergent paths that these two categories represent. The 'unusual' nature of the unions of Tamar, Ruth, and Rahab shares little with the unusual circumstances surrounding Mary's.[22] Her circumstances, in

association in the back of Matthew's mind then Jesus, understood as the Son of God, is more a sibling of David than an ancestor.

21. In the tension between these two categories of the 'woman with a cause' topos, the mention of Uriah's wife (Bathsheba) can shed some needed light. Like Mary, Bathsheba is instrumental to perpetuating the Davidic lineage; indeed, as Bathsheba reproduces the first in the line, Mary produces the last (significant) member of the line. Moreover, Bathsheba represents an awkward mixing of the versions of the 'woman with a cause'. She is instrumental to the lineage of David, but unlike Tamar, Rahab, and Ruth is not foreign. Furthermore, Bathsheba looks much like Sarah and Rebekah in fighting for her favorite son's fortunes and securing his future. The oblique reference to Bathsheba may, therefore, signal that she represents for Matthew, consciously or not, a prototype of the conflation of various versions of 'women with a cause'.

22. The major exceptions to this are that Tamar, Bathsheba, and Mary can be understood to be 'sinners' with 'men' other than husbands and, as a result, Tamar and Bathsheba share with Mary the crucial question of the true paternity of their son.

turn, are much closer to the category of the 'woman with a cause' topos that is represented by Sarah, Rebekah, *et al.*[23] Rather than choose one of the three ways in which to understand the association among Tamar, Rahab, and Ruth suggested by Brown, we should acknowledge that each, in its own right, has explanatory power.

In the end, it seems likely that Matthew does not have a 'single' purpose in mind in his account of the origins of Jesus; at least if he did, it was soon refracted by the traditions on which he relies. In his reliance on the cultural idioms that underlie his conceptualization, Matthew's sources enrich his message. The two categories of the 'woman with a cause' topos have a (previous) life of their own that considerably complicates Matthew's account. It is impossible to tell the degree to which Matthew intends the associations that inhere in his traditions. The traditionary threads that he picks up maintain their manifold connections to earlier formulations. Woven into a new text, they retain earlier associations of which no later tradent (or interpreter) is likely fully to be aware.

I conclude by stressing that I am not suggesting that there is a genetic relationship between *Midrash Ruth Rabbah* and Matthew. Theirs is the common attempt to grapple with genealogical material in the effort more clearly to define their identity in relation to Davidic promises.[24] Most important is to recognize that no purely analytic logic underlies their use of Hebrew Bible traditions. Rather, *Midrash Ruth Rabbah* and Matthew are motivated by numerous, often inconsistent associations among the traditions they know. Theirs is an ingenious analogical and associative logic that at once perceives and depends on these multiple associations that comprise, deepen, and complicate Scripture.

23. The citation of Isa. 7.14 provides the only apparent link between the otherwise disparate categories of this topos.

24. On the significance of use of genealogies in Second Temple Judaism see above n. 1.

τέλειος ἄμωμος: THE INFLUENCE OF PALESTINIAN JEWISH
EXEGESIS ON THE INTERPRETATION OF EXODUS 12.5
IN ORIGEN'S *PERI PASCHA**

Ruth Anne Clements

Origen's commentary, *Peri Pascha (On Passover)*,[1] is a verse-by-verse
exegesis of Exod. 12.1-11, the text which institutes the laws of the
Passover sacrifice. *Peri Pascha*'s editors, Octave Guéraud and Pierre
Nautin, have dated the work to c. 245 CE, some 11 or 12 years after
Origen left Alexandria (perhaps in 234 CE) to take up residence in
Caesarea of Palestine.[2] The editors locate the work in the tradition of

---

*   The issues and texts discussed in this article receive more expansive treatment
in my doctoral dissertation, '*Peri Pascha*: Passover and the Displacement of Jewish
Interpretation within Origen's Exegesis' (Harvard University, 1997).
    1.   Critical edition (Greek text with French translation): Octave Guéraud and
Pierre Nautin (eds.), *Origène: Sur la Pâque* (Christianisme Antique, 2; Paris: Beau-
chesne, 1979). Giuseppe Sgherri published an Italian translation with critical notes:
Origene, Sulla Pasqua: Il Papiro di Tura (ed. Giuseppe Sgherri; Milan: Figlie di San
Paolo, 1989). Robert J. Daly published an English translation; his notes recapitulate
for English readers the critical findings of the French editors: *Origen: Treatise on the
Passover and Dialogue of Origen with Heraclides and his Fellow Bishops on the
Father, the Son, and the Soul* (Ancient Christian Writers, 54; New York/Mahwah,
NJ: Paulist Press, 1992). I have consulted Professor Daly's translation for this
article, but made my own translations of the passages which are featured here.
    2.   Guéraud and Nautin (eds.), *Sur la Pâque*, pp. 108-10. By its contents, *Peri
Pascha* appears to build on and carry further the discourse on Passover found in
book 10 of Origen's *Commentary on John (CJn)*, completed sometime between 234
and 238 CE. Book 10 of *CJn* contains the most extensive exposition of Origen's
views on the Passover apart from *Peri Pascha*. Although some exegetical features of
this exposition have an affinity with *Peri Pascha*, important differences obtain; the
most significant is the absence from the earlier work of the definitions of Πάσχα as
διάβασις, 'crossing over', which Origen adapted from Philo as his hermeneutical
lynchpin in *Peri Pascha* (see especially *Spec. Leg.* 2.145-47; *Congr.* 106; *Quaest. in*

a growing number of Christian 'paschal tractates', which began to appear in the late second century in response to issues related to the Quartodeciman controversy.[3] However, although it is undoubtedly the case that Origen knew and in certain respects opposed the Passover interpretation of his Christian predecessors, I suggest that the factors which precipitated *Peri Pascha* were more immediate, and can be located in the interactions between Christians and Jews in third-century Caesarea.

The purpose of this paper is to test the thesis that interpreting *Peri Pascha* in the light of the cultural situation of Jews and Christians in Caesarea will assist in solving some of the puzzles of this document, and that in turn the document itself contains rhetorical clues to the cultural situation which Origen sought to influence.[4] I will first delineate more generally some of the features of Jewish and Christian interaction in Caesarea. Then, I will examine elements of Origen's exegesis of Exod. 12.5, the description of the Passover lamb, elements

Exod. I.4). In fact, *Peri Pascha* was probably written after Origen had finished writing *CJn* altogether. Book 28 of *CJn* recapitulates at much condensed length the argument developed in book 10, and bears no mark of the argument evidenced in *Peri Pascha*. P. Nautin (*Origène: Sa vie et son oeuvre* [Paris: Beauchesne, 1977], pp. 411-12) suggests that Origen brought the *CJn* to a close in c. 248 CE, which might imply an even later dating for *Peri Pascha*. On the other hand, the apologia *Contra Celsum*, written perhaps in 248 or 249, contains in condensed language the central elements of the interpretation developed over the length of *Peri Pascha*, including the definition of Passover as διάβασις.

3.   Guéraud and Nautin (eds.), *Sur la Pâque*, pp. 96-100. Some of these tractates appear to have engaged the dispute about the dating of Easter; others, such as Melito's sermon, did not. Nautin sees Origen's redefinition of Πάσχα (see previous note), in explicit opposition to a popular Christian etymology of Πάσχα from πάσχειν, as the clearest evidence of his anti-Quartodeciman intentions. However, this same etymology is explicit or implied in most Christian writers of the period (see n. 40 below), a phenomenon which calls into question the notion of *Peri Pascha* as an explicitly 'anti-Quartodeciman' tractate. *Peri Pascha* itself contains no references to Christian celebration of Easter.

4.   As the forgoing sentence makes clear, I understand *Peri Pascha* as both a literary product of its cultural setting and a rhetorical instrument composed with the design of influencing that setting. That means that this document contains historical clues of at least two distinct types: (1) 'factual' information, passed along incidentally in the course of Origen's argument; and (2) 'rhetorical' clues, represented by choices of language, directions of argument, and occasionally by problematic aspects of the argument, which point to the social interactions underlying the composition of the document.

which show the influence of Palestinian Jewish exegetical traditions. In *Peri Pascha*, that influence can be felt in two ways: (1) in Origen's adaptation of an exegetical tradition which developed via the reading of the Hebrew biblical text (rather than the LXX); and (2) in his creation of an exegetical opposition between Isa. 53.7 and Exod. 12.5, an opposition uncharacteristic both of prior Christian exegesis and of the customary interpretation of Origen himself. In the first instance, Origen utilized a Palestinian Jewish exegetical trend to give an exegetical hook for his own somewhat unusual exposition of the Christian's sacrifice of the Passover. In the second instance, he sought to displace a Jewish exegetical claim to the fulfillment of biblical prophecy by substituting a Christian claim.

Third-Century Caesarea: Debates and Discussions

Third-century Caesarea was a highly cosmopolitan city, the metropolis of the province of Syria-Palestina, graced by monumental architecture and Hellenistic cultural institutions, with a thriving seaport which marketed both the products of the local countryside and goods which came from greater distances via overland trade routes.[5] Because Caesarea stood as the center of Roman provincial government from 6 CE, it had a large pagan population. Although the Jewish community was drastically reduced in 66 CE, at the culmination of some eight years of open conflict between Jews and pagans,[6] there was some continuing Jewish presence in Caesarea through the second century.[7]

At the beginning of the third century, Caesarea experienced an influx of population from the surrounding countryside, such that by the middle of the century, Jews, Christians, pagans, and Samaritans

5. In general, for information on Caesarea of this period, see Lee I. Levine, *Caesarea Under Roman Rule* (Leiden: E.J. Brill, 1975). See also John A. McGuckin, 'Caesarea Maritima as Origen Knew It', *Origeniana* 5 (1992), pp. 3-25.

6. Levine, *Caesarea*, pp. 29-30; see his n. 185 on the various suggestions for dating the beginning of open hostilities. Josephus says some 20,000 Jews were killed in the final battles in 66 CE, while all the rest were imprisoned; before that, many had fled the city altogether (*War* 2.14.4-5, 285-92; 2.18.1, 457).

7. Levine, *Caesarea*, pp. 44-45, develops a sketch of some features of Jewish life based on the scattered references found in rabbinic literature. Non-literary sources from this period give evidence of pagan and general civic life but say nothing explicit of Jews, Christians, or Samaritans.

were represented in approximately equal numbers.[8] Among the new-comers were rabbis, who as a class began to establish themselves in the urban centers of Palestine around the turn of the third century, under the influence and aegis of Rabbi Judah the Prince. Lee Levine puts the formation of the rabbinic academy in Caesarea in about 230 CE, only two or three years before Origen himself arrived on the scene.[9] As members of an economic and possibly a political elite, the rabbis may have wielded considerable influence among Caesarean Jews and vis-à-vis the government;[10] however, the extent of their religious influence, at least at the beginning of the century, is less clear.[11]

The primary local Jewish communal institution for towns throughout Palestine was the synagogue.[12] As the institution evolved, it was

8. Levine, *Caesarea*, pp. 46-47.

9. Levine, *Caesarea*, pp. 86-89; cf. pp. 65-68 on the new attractiveness of Caesarea for Jews and R. Judah's role in facilitating the move to Caesarea by rabbis and their adherents.

10. See Shaye Cohen, 'The Place of the Rabbi in Jewish Society of the Second Century', in Lee I. Levine (ed.), *The Galilee in Late Antiquity* (New York and Jerusalem: Jewish Theological Seminary, 1992), pp. 157-73, esp. pp. 169-73. On the Caesarean rabbis more explicitly, see Levine, *Caesarea*, pp. 68-69, 92-95.

11. Levine, *Caesarea*, Chapter 5, gives a picture of minimal contact and involvement between the rabbis and Caesarean Jews through the second century, with rabbis taking increasingly active roles in economic, legal and religious matters as the third century went on. In the diverse environment of Caesarea, the rabbis came to prominence particularly as preachers and as debaters with Christians, Samaritans, and non-rabbinic Jews; however, rabbinic stories about authorities even from the latter part of the century continue to show tensions between rabbinic religiosity and popular religious culture (see especially pp. 70-73). Cf. also M. Goodman, *State and Society in Roman Galilee, AD 132–212* (Totowa, NJ: Rowman & Allenheld, 1983), Chapter 7, 'Rabbinic Authority in Galilee', pp. 93-118, who makes the case that, in general, rabbinic religious authority, such as it was, was minimally felt from after the Bar Kochba revolt until the third century, and in the case of secular matters, did not make itself felt until much later in that century.

12. Or בית כנסת, 'house of assembly', in Mishnaic Hebrew. The Greek συναγωγή seems originally to have meant, 'the assembly of the people', as reflected in the LXX (e.g. Exod. 12.3), rather than a 'place of assembly' per se. This assembly probably dealt with community legal issues as well as religious matters, especially in the Diaspora; however, by the time of the Mishnah's codification (ca. 200 CE), 'the assembly', in whatever language, had come to designate the building designed for the community to assemble. See Lee I. Levine, 'The Sages and the Synagogue in Late Antiquity: The Evidence of the Galilee', in Levine (ed.), *The Galilee*, pp. 201-22.

very much a lay institution, controlled by local officials and patrons. Traditions in rabbinic literature which can be dated to the third century show minimal rabbinic involvement with the synagogue at the beginning of the century, and sometimes antagonism towards its practices, although positive involvement increased as the century went on. The main mode of direct rabbinic involvement seems to have been preaching.[13] A sizeable segment of the Caesarean Jewish community was Greek-speaking, read the Bible in Greek, and probably prayed in Greek.[14] Since the common language of both Jews and Christians was Greek, members of either group would have linguistic access to the preaching of both church and synagogue.[15]

13. Levine ('The Sages and the Synagogue', p. 209) suggests that the two rabbis most frequently involved in synagogue preaching were R. Yochanan (in Tiberias) and R. Abbahu of Caesarea. R. Yochanan was Origen's contemporary and spent a fair amount of time in Caesarea because his teacher, R. Hoshaiah, was there. Reuven Kimelman suggests that R. Yochanan and Origen were influenced by each other's interpretations of the Song of Songs; see Kimelman, 'Rabbi Yochanan and Origen on the Song of Songs: A Third Century Jewish–Christian Disputation', HTR 73 (1977), pp. 567-95. R. Abbahu was active in Caesarea just following the period of Origen's own activity. The בית מדרש, or academy, would have continued to be the main locus of rabbinic teaching (Levine, 'The Sages and the Synagogues', pp. 203-205). The academy should be understood as limited to, but not restricted to, the rabbis and their students. The audience for synagogue preaching would encompass the broader community.

14. Levine, Caesarea, pp. 70-71, summarizes the evidence of Jewish inscriptions written in Greek, and the allusions in rabbinic literature of the persistence of Greek as a language valid for synagogue worship. The Mishnah evaluates Greek positively over other 'vernacular' languages; in m. Meg. 1.8, for example, Rabban Simeon ben Gamaliel singles out Greek as the only language besides Hebrew in which it is permissible to write the Torah. A talmudic story (y. Soṭ. 7.1, 21b) indicates the persistence of Greek as the liturgical language of the Caesarean synagogues in the latter part of the third century.

15. It is possible that we should understand Caesarean synagogue preaching as having been carried on primarily in Greek, whereas the teaching in the rabbinic academy was carried on primarily in Hebrew. David Halperin has made a case for the existence of a 'Greek midrash' on Ezekiel, the logical setting of which would be synagogue preaching; see his The Faces of the Chariot: Early Jewish Responses to Ezekiel's Vision (Tübingen: J.C.B. Mohr [Paul Siebeck], 1988), Chapter 8, 'The Shabu'ot Cycle', section 5, 'The Greek midrash of Caesarea', pp. 346-52. Kimelman suggests ('R. Yochanan', pp. 578-81) that at least one section of R. Yochanan's midrash on the Song of Songs depends on a reading of the text which matches the LXX and differs from the Hebrew (he suggests that this knowledge comes via Origen).

Although not much is known about the Christian community prior to the third century,[16] it was strongly associated with the Greek-Jewish evangelist Philip and the apostle Peter as founding authorities.[17] These associations have been taken to imply that early Caesarean Christianity had a strong 'Jewish-Christian' element;[18] certainly in Origen's own time Caesarean Christians were greatly attracted both to Jewish observances and to Sabbath attendance in the synagogue.[19] It seems likely that with the increase in Caesarea's political prominence (particularly under the Severans), the importance of the Caesarean church as a player in ecclesiastical politics increased as well; by the early third century, although the Jerusalem church retained a special place of honor as the founding Christian community, the Caesarean church and its bishops had begun to take the more prominent position of church leadership.[20] Origen's own presence in Caesarea and the

16. The earliest reference apart from those in the New Testament is Eusebius's description of a synod held there in 190 CE (*Hist. Eccl.* 5.23-25).

17. Acts 8.40 names Philip as the first Jesus-believer to reach Caesarea from the Jerusalem community, but gives no details of his activity there; a reference to Philip and his prophesying daughters in Acts 21.8-9 indicates that he resided there for some years. Acts 10 describes Peter as the founder of the Caesarean Church. The Pseudo-Clementine literature, which took shape in its various forms between the mid-third and mid-fourth centuries, locates Peter in Caesarea as the leader of the Christian community and champion of an anti-Pauline Christianity very sympathetic to Jewish practices. For background, see Georg Strecker, 'Die Pseudoklementinen, Einleitung', in Wilhelm Schneemelcher (ed.), *Neutestamentliche Apokryphen in deutscher Übersetzung*. II. *Apostolisches, Apokalypsen und Verwandtes* (Tübingen: J.C.B. Mohr [Paul Siebeck], 5th edn, 1989), pp. 439-47.

18. E.g. Levine, *Caesarea*, pp. 24-26 and notes. 'Jewish-Christian' should here be taken to indicate a Jesus-believing community which drew the predominance of its members, mores and practices from Judaism. In this time and place, it should not be understood as a term which indicates a form of Christianity either necessarily 'deviant' or practiced by a minority.

19. Cf., for example, *Comm. Ser. in Matt.* 79 where Origen inveighs against the 'Ebionite' practice of celebrating Passover along with the Jews; in *Lev. Hom.* 5.8, Origen scolds his congregation for going to synagogue on the Sabbath.

20. Levine, *Caesarea*, pp. 114-15. The indications in Eusebius are ambiguous; in discussing the two churches together, he sometimes names the Jerusalem bishop first and sometimes the Caesarean. Levine cites the seventh canon of the Council of Nicaea (325 CE) as regularizing the situation which had been evolving during the previous century; the canon says that special honor should go to the bishop of Jerusalem, but that this should not prejudice the rights and privileges of the 'metropolitan' (i.e. the bishop of Caesarea).

school which he founded there brought the city to prominence as well as an intellectual center, a prominence which it enjoyed through the following century.[21]

Thus, in third-century Caesarea we are presented with vigorously growing and politically active Jewish and Christian communities. Within the Jewish community, the rabbis' recent arrival on the scene in institutional numbers might be seen as an element of uncertainty; although the rabbis had some political and economic power, their position of religious leadership was by no means secure. Within the Christian community, the arrival of the rabbis might also have provoked institutional insecurity, since they represented a cadre of authoritative biblical interpreters, to whom Christians might easily turn. It is possible that bishops Theoctistus of Caesarea and Alexander of Jerusalem encouraged Origen to resettle in Caesarea so as to enlist his erudition in combatting this presumed new institutional threat.

Origen is one of our best non-Jewish witnesses to Caesarean Judaism of this period.[22] He frequently draws on Jewish interpretive

21. See Levine, *Caesarea*, pp. 119-27. There is no concrete evidence prior to Origen as to the shape of Christian teaching in Caesarea. In Alexandria in the second century, teaching seems to have been carried on in small groups centered around individual teachers; only when Bishop Demetrius tapped the young Origen was the move made toward consolidating the Church's teaching in a single catechetical school (for a recent sketch of the 'school' situation in Alexandria, see David Dawson, *Allegorical Readers and Cultural Revision in Ancient Alexandria* [Berkeley, Los Angeles and Oxford: University of California, 1992], pp. 219-22). A similar situation may have existed in Caesarea. It is at least possible that Theoctistus and Alexander saw a school on the 'new' Alexandrian model, with Alexandria's star teacher at its head, as just the thing to combat the lure of rabbinic teaching, as well as a means of attracting students from other places and so enhancing Caesarea's prestige (cf. Eusebius, *Hist. Eccl.* 6.30, on Origen's distinguished 'foreign' students).

22. The case has been most recently and thoroughly made by N.R.M. De Lange, *Origen and the Jews: Studies in Jewish–Christian Relations in Third Century Palestine* (Cambridge: Cambridge University Press, 1976). Although De Lange's study suffers some flaws it remains an invaluable collection of materials for the student of this period. De Lange's critics have in the main faulted his tendency to underestimate the significance of Origen's theological anti-Jewish polemic and stereotyping portrayals of Jewish exegesis. See the articles in response to De Lange by, e.g., Roger Brooks, 'Straw Dogs and Scholarly Ecumenism: The Appropriate Jewish Background for the Study of Origen', in Charles Kannengieser and William L. Petersen (eds.), *Origen of Alexandria: His World and His Legacy* (Notre Dame: University of Notre Dame, 1988), pp. 63-95; Paul Blowers, 'Origen, the Rabbis, and the Bible: Toward a Picture of Judaism and Christianity in Third Century Caesarea', in

traditions to lend depth or authority to his own exegesis.[23] He mentions interactions with Jewish scholars (probably to be construed as rabbis): he speaks of seeking them out to clear up textual obscurities, or of 'having heard a Jew expound' on various biblical passages.[24] And he several times refers to public disputes with 'those among the Jews called sages'.[25]

I have identified as direct references to such disputes, instances in which Origen speaks of disputing (διαλέγομαι),[26] meeting

Kannengieser and Petersen (eds.), *Origen of Alexandria*, pp. 96-115; John McGuckin, 'Origen on the Jews', in Diana Wood (ed.), *Christianity and Judaism* (Studies in Church History, 29; Oxford: Basil Blackwell, 1992), pp. 1-13.

23. Often Origen identifies such traditions by such formulas as 'from the ancients' (e.g. *Exod. Hom.* 5.5, 11.4, *Num. Hom.* 13.5), lending the weight of venerability to his citation. In *Peri Pascha* 16.15-30 he cites the practice of 'the Hebrews' to describe the process of 'taking the lamb' on the tenth of Nisan (Exod. 12.4); the practice he describes, naming persons who will partake of each individual paschal sacrifice, is not biblical, but its existence is assumed in the Mishnah (e.g. *Pes.* 6.6; 8.3-4). The practice is invoked in *Peri Pascha* as an authoritative exposition of the literal sense of the verse. On the other hand, an integral part of Origen's theological hermeneutic is a devaluation of Jewish 'literalist' interpretation, set in opposition to 'true' Christian 'spiritual' interpretation; this shows itself as early as his systematic statement on scriptural interpretation, *Peri Archon*, and appears in later (Caesarean) writings as a tendency to style caricatured literal readings of biblical texts as 'Jewish'. See *Peri Archon* 4.3.2; for an example of the caricaturing technique in Origen's sermons, see *Gen. Hom.* 3.4-6. When using Origen's writings as a source for contemporary Jewish and Christian interaction, one must draw distinctions between passages which present data and those which present theological polemic (with no attempt at 'historical' accuracy); cf. the previous note.

24. See, e.g., *Letter to Julius Africanus* 6, *Ez. Hom.* 4.8.

25. *Contra Celsum* 1.55: πρὸς τοὺς λεγομένους παρὰ Ἰουδαίοις σοφούς; *Contra Celsum* 1.45, 56 and 2.31 have slightly different phrasing. The appelation, 'sages', seems most readily to fit the rabbis, known (among themselves at least) by the Hebrew title, חכמים, sages. *b. 'Abod. Zar.* 4a appears to allude to such a dispute; R. Abbahu contrasts the sages in Babylonia with those in Palestine by saying that the former do not need to know their Bible as well as the latter, who 'are always found with you' ('you' being *minim* such as are involved in this dispute). It is perhaps worth noting that none of Origen's explicit references to debates with sages portray them as originating in exegetical disputes, but dispute about the meaning of scriptural passages looms large as part of the subject matter (e.g. *Letter to Africanus* 2 and 5; *Contra Celsum* 1.45).

26. *Contra Celsum* 1.45; *Letter to Africanus* 5 (in fact, that which spurred Africanus's letter in the first place was a public discussion or dispute [the verb is διαλέγομαι] about the book of Daniel with 'our friend Bassus' [*Letter to Africanus*,

(συμβάλλω),[27] or engaging in philosophical inquiry (ζήτησις)[28] with Jews. All three of these terms carry connotations of philosophic debate or dispute; the methods of argument Origen describes come from the arena of dialectic. The primary sources for descriptions of these disputations are the *Letter to Julius Africanus* (c. 248–250 CE), and the *Contra Celsum* (c. 249 CE); [29] *Peri Pascha* also contains an allusion to such a dispute.[30] These works contain perhaps six such explicit references;[31] their dating suggests that these exchanges

p. 2]). In *Contra Celsum*, Origen (probably following Celsus) also portrays Celsus's hypothetical Jew as 'disputing' (διαλέγομαι) with Jesus (*Contra Celsum* 1.28; cf. 1.37); in book 2, Origen takes up the hypothetical Jew's hypothetical dispute (again the verb is διαλέγομαι, cf. 2.52) with hypothetical Jewish Christians.

27. *Contra Celsum* 2.31, *Peri Pascha* 1.34; cf. *Philocalia* 23.22.8, where this verb is used to denote an exchange with a μαθηματικός.

28. *Contra Celsum* 1.55, *Letter to Africanus* 5; in the Pseudo-Clementine literature this term is typically used to designate the encounter in Caesarea between Peter and Simon Magus.

29. It has been demonstrated that Origen's homilies and commentary on the Song of Songs (c. 244–45) contain interpretations which may best be explained as reactions to contemporary rabbinic interpretations of the same text, but the commentary and homilies themselves do not allude to a formal debate as the context in which these ideas would have been exchanged (*pace* Kimelman, 'Rabbi Yochanan', above, n. 13, who uses the term 'dispute', to situate the interchange between Origen and R. Yochanan).

30. The passages in the *Letter* and *Contra Celsum* are anecdotal; that is, they present Origen's allusions to his own past experience. *Peri Pascha* differs from these in that it speaks of the debate as hypothetical: 'But if one of us, meeting with Hebrews, should say recklessly that the *Pascha* is thus named on account of the Passion of the Savior, he would be ridiculed by them as being utterly ignorant of what is meant by the name...' (Καὶ εἴ τις προπετέστερον τῶν ἡμετέρων Ἑβραίοις συμβαλὼν λέγοι τὸ πάσχα διὰ τὸ πάθος τοῦ σωτῆρος οὕτως ὠνομάσθαι, καταγέλαστος ὑπ' αὐτῶν ἔσται ὡς ὅλως οὐκ ἐπιστάμενος τί τὸ σημαινόμενον ἐκ τῆς ὀνομασίας; *Peri Pascha* 1.32–2.2). Because the passage shares vocabulary with some of the other more fully descriptive passages I understand it as a reflection on past experience, rather than as a prediction of hypothetical possibility. De Lange also understands this as evidence that Origen was sometimes compelled to 'revise his ideas' because of his debates with Jewish sages. See *Origen and the Jews*, pp. 94-95.

31. *Contra Celsum* 1.45, 1.55-56, 2.31; *Letter to Africanus* 5, *Peri Pascha* 1.32–2.4. *Contra Celsum* 1.55-56 probably alludes to one single such debate, but it is possible that two distinct occasions are in view. De Lange devotes an entire chapter to 'Debates and Discussions'. However, much of the material he has collected here as evidence of Origen's participation in the 'debate between Church and Synagogue' merely illustrates Origen's use of traditional Christian polemical anti-Jewish

occurred primarily during the last five to seven years of Origen's teaching career.

By 245 CE, when the debates appear to have begun, Origen had been resident in Caesarea some ten to twelve years; the rabbinical academy had flourished for only slightly longer. According to the chronology developed by Pierre Nautin, Origen had by 244 CE preached his way through most of the three-year Caesarean lectionary cycle.[32] We know from the sermon references that during this time Origen had an established practice of seeking out rabbinic biblical interpretations; Kimelman's work on the Song of Songs indicates that at the same time some rabbinic figures came to know Origen's exegesis.[33]

Thus, by 245 CE, Origen and rabbinic sages knew each other as authoritative interpreters of biblical texts. I suggest that these public encounters mark not only Origen's emergence as a champion for the Church, but more basically the emergence of Jewish–Christian public disputation as an institutional strategy of the Caesarean Christian and rabbinic Jewish communities. This strategy was enabled by the coincidence of Origen's arrival in Caesarea with the growing political and economic influence of the nascent rabbinic faction. And I suggest that the disputes served important internal functions, as well as the ostensible external function of demonstrating each group's truth claims to outsiders. Among Caesarean Christians, the debates established the Church's teaching authority, with Origen as its representative, as the legitimate conduit for 'true doctrine' which could defeat Jewish claims;[34] among Caesarean Jews, the debates helped to consolidate the

---

arguments and prooftexts, and provides no further indication that Origen debated these materials on concrete occasions.

32. Nautin argues persuasively that internal evidence in Origen's writings and sermons makes it possible to reconstruct the order of the sermons, that vis-à-vis other writings they must have been preached during a three-year period, covering (but not completing) one turn of the lectionary cycle, and that this stretch of preaching probably took place from c. 239–242 CE. This dating contradicts Eusebius's account, which would place the written sermons after 245 CE, but fits better with other aspects of the Origen chronology than Eusebius' assertion; Nautin, *Origène*, pp. 403-409.

33. See references above, nn. 23, 24; on R. Kimelman's study see nn. 13 and 15 above.

34. This institutional strategy would also have helped consolidate Origen's personal authority as a teacher in the church. The conflict with Demetrius which caused Origen to leave Alexandria seems to have had its roots in some kind of struggle over

authority of the rabbis as spokesmen for the larger Jewish community in the realm of religion as well as those of politics and economics.

It was in this cultural setting of struggle with Jews to establish Christian hegemony in the matter of biblical interpretation, and struggle with Christians to establish the authority of his own method of teaching and its results, that Origen composed *Peri Pascha*. The allusion in *Peri Pascha*'s Prologue to debate 'with the Hebrews' about the meaning of the Passover should not surprise us; as a formative story of central importance for both Judaism and Christianity, the Passover narrative was perhaps an inevitable battleground in the struggle to claim the voice of authoritative teaching.

Peri Pascha: *An Overview*

The only extant manuscript of *Peri Pascha*, discovered in 1941,[35] is a 50-page papyrus codex.[36] The document consists of two parts, unequal

Origen's teaching, either his methods or his authority. It also seems that, by the end of his public preaching life, Origen had run into difficulties with the bishop of Caesarea, again seemingly triggered by Origen's preaching. See G. Bardy, 'Aux origines de l'école d'Alexandrie', *RSR* 27 (1937), pp. 65-90.

35. *Peri Pascha* was discovered by British army workers, in an ancient limestone quarry at Tura, south of Cairo. While clearing the quarry for use as an ammunition depot, the workers discovered a small cache of writings by Didymus the Blind and Origen. It seems probable that the manuscripts originally came from the monastery of St Arsenius, located not far from the quarry. Since the codices were placed in the cave without their covers (suggesting that these may have been removed for reuse) the editors theorize that they were put there not for safe-keeping, but rather as part of a purge of the monastery's library in the wake of the anathemata pronounced on the works of Origen and his followers in 543 and again in 553 CE (Guéraud and Nautin (eds.), *Sur la Pâque*, pp. 21-22).

36. The covers of the original codex had been removed; the four quires of *Peri Pascha* had been rolled up together with the *Dialogue of Origen with Heraclides and his Fellow Bishops on the Father, the Son, and the Soul*. The *Dialogue* was at the core of this roll; quire 2 of *Peri Pascha* (codex pp. 17-32) was on the outside. Quires 1, 3 and 4 of *Peri Pascha* were found to be in relatively good condition, with some pages completely intact. However, quire 2, since it was in the most exposed position, suffered extensive insect damage: The top half of every page is missing from codex pp. 17-30, which encompass the exegesis for most of Exod. 12.3-9, and pp. 31-32 are completely gone (Guéraud and Nautin (eds.), *Sur la Pâque*, pp. 22-23). Nautin was able to restore some of the missing text from passages preserved in Procopius of Gaza and some of the Greek exegetical catenae (Guéraud and Nautin (eds.), *Sur la Pâque*, pp. 52-77).

in length. Part A runs to 39.6;[37] it consists of a Prologue to the work as a whole (1.1–3.31) and a verse-by-verse exegesis of Exod. 12.1-11a, the laws for the sacrifice and eating of the Passover lamb. Part B purports to expound the 'spiritual sense' of the Passover (39.9–41.12). A short allegorical exegesis of Exod. 12.5 (41.13–43.6) is followed by a longer allegorical discourse on the meaning of 'Egypt' (43.6–47.27); Part B then concludes by returning to and expounding Exod. 12.11b: 'Eat it in haste; it is the Passover of the Lord'.

Origen treats Exod. 12.5 exegetically in three distinct locations within *Peri Pascha*:

(1) In the second half of the Prologue, Origen offers a summary of the highlights of Exodus 12–15, citing a few verses explicitly; Exod. 12.5 appears as the first cited verse.

(2) In Part A, Origen comments on the verse as a lemma, in standard fashion (*Peri Pascha* 22.8–23.3).

(3) In Part B, Origen juxtaposes Exod. 12.5 and Isa. 53.7, interpreting the one in the light of the other (*Peri Pascha* 41.36–42.13).

In the Prologue and Part B, Origen makes use of interpretive traditions which are also present in Palestinian Jewish sources; in Part B, in point of fact, he mounts an exegetical polemic against a Jewish delineation of the figure of the Servant in Isaiah 53. In the ensuing discussion, therefore, we will focus on these treatments of Exod. 12.5 in *Peri Pascha*'s Prologue and in Part B.[38]

A. *Exodus 12.5 in* Peri Pascha*'s Prologue*

Origen begins the Prologue with a definition of the term Πάσχα, proffering a meaning 'according to the Hebrews'[39] in opposition to a

37. References to the text are cited by page and line number, following Guéraud and Nautin's edition. Line numbers from the badly damaged pages of quire 2 are given as negative numbers, and are counted from the *bottom* of the page (e.g. 22.-8 signifies the eighth line up from the bottom of p. 22).

38. In fact, the structure of the exegesis of Exod. 12.5 in Part A depends on Philo's interpretation of Exod. 12.5 in *Quaest. in Exod.* 1.7-8. Since the focus of this paper is Origen's knowledge of the interpretations of his Caesarean contemporaries, a fuller exploration of this connection with Philo falls outside the scope of the present study.

39. Actually, Origen's definition, διάβασις, 'crossing over', comes from Philo, who holds that the feast of the Passover (which he most often calls a διαβατήρια, or

commonplace Christian definition, which related the name of the festival to the Greek verb πασχείν, to suffer.[40] The second half of the Prologue opens with a summary of the highlights of Exodus 12–15, and a brief statement of the typological significance of the biblical events for the spiritual life of the Christian. It is the biblical summary which concerns us here:

> ... ἕκαστοι πρόβατον ἄρσεν τέλειον ἄμωμον λαβόντες θύσωσιν καὶ πρὸς ἑσπέραν φάγωσιν ὀπτὸν πυρὶ οὔτε ὠμὸν οὔτε ἡψήμενον ἐν ὕδατι ἵν' οὕτως ὁ ὀλεθρεύων τὰ πρωτότοκα τῶν Αἰγυπτίων μὴ θίγῃ αὐτῶν τὰς φλιὰς τῶν θυρῶν αὐτῶν ὁρῶν τῷ αἵματι κεχρισμένας.

> ... they should each take a *lamb*, *male*, *perfect*, *without blemish*, sacrifice it and towards evening eat it, roasted with fire, neither raw nor boiled in water, so that in this fashion, the Destroyer of the first-born of the Egyptians might not touch them, when he sees the lintels of their doors sprinkled with blood. (*Peri Pascha* 2.23-33)

The Septuagint version of Exod. 12.5a reads: πρόβατον τέλειον ἄρσεν ἐνιαύσιον ἔσται ὑμῖν ('You shall have a lamb, perfect, male, one year old'). Origen's allusion to the verse, πρόβατον ἄρσεν τέλειον ἄμωμον, alters the word order of the LXX and adds the

---

'crossing-feast') took its name from the *people*'s crossing of the Red Sea, coming out of Egypt; see n. 2 above. Palestinian Jewish sources, both in Greek and in Hebrew, use terms which refer the name to *God*'s activity in either skipping over or protecting the houses of the Israelites during the tenth plague (Josephus, *Ant.* 2.311-13: ὑπερβασία; Aquila on Exod. 12.11: ὑπέρβασις). The *Mekilta deRabbi Ishmael*, Tractate Piska 7 debates the notions of God's protecting [חוס] or skipping over [פסע] the Israelites). The interpretive tradition that relates the name to God's protection is quite venerable; the Septuagint on Exod. 12.13 and 27 uses the verb σκεπάζω to translate the Hebrew פסח.

40. The definition can be seen at its most full blown in Melito's *Peri Pascha* 46 (see also Pseudo-Hippolytus, *In Sanctum Pascha* 49; critical edition. For this reason, some have construed that this etymology was a Quartodeciman (or at best deviant) invention, constructed to support a specifically Quartodeciman practice of a Paschal celebration which commemorated Jesus' passion and death (see n. 3 above). However, the explicit or implicit connection of Πάσχα with Jesus's suffering is widespread among second-century Christian writers (e.g. Justin, *Dialogue with Trypho* 40; Irenaeus, *Against Heresies* 4.10.1; Clement of Alexandria *Peri Pascha* [fragment preserved in the *Chronicon Paschale* 1.14-15; *PG* 92.81]); the Valentinian commentator Heracleon apparently also made this association in his commentary on Jn 2.13 (Origen cites and rejects Heracleon's interpretation in *CJn* 10.117-118). It may be noted that Philo himself 'invents' an etymological connection between πάσχα and πάσχειν to suit his own allegorical purposes (*Rer. Div. Her.* 192-93).

seemingly redundant ἄμωμον, 'without blemish'. When Origen explains this verse in Part A, he reverts to the terminology and word order of the LXX; in Part B, he treats the terms in the order given here in the Prologue, inserting ἐνιαύσιον after τέλειον, and treating ἄμωμον as an independent element of the biblical verse.[41]

The Septuagint's word order is matched by Theodotion, Aquila, Symmachus, the Masoretic text and the Targumim.[42] Pseudo-Hippolytus's *In Sanctum Pascha* is the only source predating Origen which shows irregularity in regard to the term ἄρσεν: it is omitted completely from the text citation, paraphrase, and exegetical treatment of Exod. 12.5.[43] It seems possible to see Origen's 'displacement' of and emphasis on the term ἄρσεν in the Prologue and Part B as a subtle exegetical corrective to Pseudo-Hippolytus.

The occurrence of the term ἄμωμον is in some ways even more intriguing than the altered word order. Nautin suggests that the term comes from Lev. 22.19, which is part of a general discussion of the rules for bringing sacrificial animals.[44] He states that Origen would have known of the application of ἄμωμον to the paschal lamb from either Philo[45] or Melito, each of whom draws upon the term's *non-*

41. That is, he treats the terms of the verse in the sequence, πρόβατον ἄρσεν τέλειον ἐνιαύσιον ἄμωμον; he gives each term an exegetical definition, interpreting ἄμωμον as not synonymous with τέλειον.

42. The textual apparatus to this verse shows a lot of variation in later versions of the text, both in the word order generally and by the addition of ἄμωμον. The addition of ἄμωμον is especially prominent in the Byzantine text group (see John W. Wevers, *Notes on the Greek Text of Exodus* [Septuagint and Cognate Studies, 30; Atlanta: Scholars Press, 1990], p. 170); a significant number of variations noted in the Göttingen Septuagint's apparatus are from quotations in paschal tractates and similar documents which may reflect other signs of influence by Origen's *Peri Pascha*.

43. *In Sanctum Pascha* 5, 6, 19.

44. Guéraud and Nautin (eds.), *Sur la Pâque*, p. 116; Sgherri prefers Num. 6.14, which gives the requirement for the sacrifice of the Nazir (*Sulla Pasqua*, p. 66 n. 6); but the language is too dissimilar in other respects to make this verse a likely exegetical source. I agree with Nautin's suggestion, albeit for different reasons, as will become clear.

45. Philo's brief allusion to the Passover lamb in *Congr.* 106 locates this lamb in the context of his more general allegorical interpretation of the sacrificial system. In a discourse on the spiritual significance of biblical tens and tenths, he speaks of taking the Passover lamb on the tenth and keeping it safe, so as to be able to offer 'as innocent and spotless (ἀσίνεις καὶ ἀμώμους) victims its advances on the road to progress'. This phrasing echoes Philo's allegorical connection of the sheep with moral

cultic meaning of moral or spiritual blamelessness.[46] The question, however, is not only where Origen might have seen the term, but what led him to the exegetical choices to employ it first to amplify the meaning of τέλειον as he does in the Prologue, and then as an independent part of the lemma, as he does in Part B.

This question does not have a self-evident answer, because the Septuagint's use of τέλειον in Exod. 12.5 is itself an anomalous feature. When the Hebrew Pentateuch describes sacrificial animals (in our verse and elsewhere), it uses the term תמים, perfect; Lev. 22.21b defines this term in relation to sacrificial animals generally as meaning 'without a blemish'.[47] In a few instances, human beings are also

progress elsewhere in his corpus via an etymological connection of πρόβατον with προβαίνω (e.g. *Sacr.* 112); 'innocence' and 'spotlessness' are here understood as moral or spiritual qualities. The phrase ἀσίνεις καὶ ἀμώμους echoes Philo's own discussion of Lev. 22.19-25, as found in *Spec. Leg.* 1.166: πάντα δ᾽ ὁλόκληρα, περὶ μηδὲν μέρος κηραίνοντα τοῦ σώματος, ὅλα δι᾽ ὅλων ἀσινῆ, μώμων ἀμέτοχα ('All [the sacrificial animals] are to be complete, with no sort of affliction of any part of the body, spotless throughout and free from blemish'). *Spec. Leg.* 1.166-67, which goes on to describe the process of meticulously checking for blemishes, leads into a description of the sacrifices for the various holy days, drawn from Num. 28–29. Thus Philo's use of ἀμώμους in *Congr.* 106 seems not to be an explicit exegetical gloss on the τέλειον of Exod. 12, but rather to be a link with his more general (levitical) conceptualization of the sacrifices and their spiritual meaning. Origen invokes neither the phrasing nor the concepts of these passages in *Peri Pascha*. In *Contra Celsum* 8.22, Origen speaks of the Passover of the soul in language which more closely invokes *Congr.* 106. However, this thumbnail sketch of the διάβασις of the Christian soul makes no reference to 'innocent and spotless victims'.

46. Melito uses ἄμωμον in his paraphrase of Exod. 12.1-13 at the beginning of his own *Peri Pascha* (para. 12). He replaces the entire text of Exod. 12.5 with the phrase, ἄσπιλον ἀμνὸν καὶ ἄμωμον ('a lamb, spotless and unblemished'). The phrase comes altered from 1 Pet. 1.19 (τιμίῳ αἵματι ὡς ἀμνοῦ ἀμώμου καὶ ἀσπίλου Χριστοῦ), where it seems to carry a complex load of Passover associations and bears a sense of Christ's spiritual blamelessness as well. For Melito, this phrase functions literarily to make an initial identification between the paschal lamb (πρόβατον) and the lamb (ἀμνός) referred to in Isa. 53, Jn 1.29 and 1 Peter. Since Origen does not use other language evocative of Melito (or 1 Peter) on this verse, it is difficult to see his use of this term as stemming from the influence of these texts.

47. תמים יהיה לרצון כל מום לא יהיה בו ('it shall be perfect, to be accepted; no blemish shall be in it'). Since the LXX has already chosen ἄμωμος as the translation value for תמים, its translation of this verse is somewhat circular: ἄμωμον ἔσται εἰς δεκτόν, πᾶς μῶμος οὐκ ἔσται ἐν αὐτῷ ('it shall be unblemished, to be accepted; no blemish shall be in it').

described as תם or תמים, usually translated as 'blameless' or 'perfect' in a moral sense.[48] The Septuagint assumes a distinction between the meanings of this term, as applied to animals and to humans; in all cases except that of Exod. 12.5, the LXX uses ἄμωμος to refer to animals and τέλειος or other morally positive terms to refer to human beings.[49] Only in Exod. 12.5 does τέλειος describe an animal; perhaps more significant, the same word was apparently kept in the text versions of Aquila, Symmachus, and Theodotion.[50] Thus, in the Greek translation tradition the Passover lamb differs from all other sacrifices in respect of the translation of תמים.[51] This means that for interpreters of the Septuagint, there was no explicit terminological link between Exod. 12.5 and Lev. 22.19-21 or other passages which describe this characteristic of 'perfection' of sacrificial animals.

The closest literary parallel to Origen's treatment of τέλειον in *Peri Pascha* 2.24 is actually to be found in the Palestinian targumic tradition, which translates תמים as שלם מן מום, 'complete without a blemish'.[52] In fact *Targum Neofiti* consistently translates all

48. E.g. Abraham (תמים, Gen. 17.1), Noah (תמים, Gen. 6.9), Jacob (תם, Gen. 25.27), Job (תם, Job 1.1). Early rabbinic tradition occasionally interpreted תמים/תם, when applied to a person, to mean that that person had been born circumcised; see, e.g., '*Abot deRabbi Nathan A*, ch. 2.

49. Abraham = ἄμεμπτος (τέλειος in the versions); Noah = τέλειος; Jacob = ἄπλαστος; Job = ἄμεμπτος.

50. There are no variants noted among the versions for this term in Field (*Origenis Hexaplorum quae supersunt* [ed. F. Field; Oxonii, 1875]) or in the Göttingen edition's apparatus; see on Exod. 12.5 in *Septuaginta, vol. II,1: Exodus* (ed. J.W. Wevers; Göttingen: Vandenhoeck & Ruprecht, 1991).

51. It is tempting to speculate that the translation itself may have roots in an older midrashic tradition. G. Vermes ('Redemption and Genesis XXII: The Binding of Isaac and the Sacrifice of Jesus', in his *Scripture and Tradition in Judaism: Haggadic Studies* (Leiden: E.J. Brill, 2nd rev. edn, 1973), pp. 193-227), shows that a midrashic tradition linking Isaac's sacrifice with the salvation in Egypt through the blood of the Passover lamb dates to pre-Christian times, at least as early as the book of *Jubilees*. The odd use of τέλειος in the LXX at Exod. 12.5 could be a reminiscence of a midrashic identification of Isaac with the Passover lamb. Certainly, Christian writers like Pseudo-Hippolytus exploited this unusual adjective to link the Passover lamb with Jesus.

52. See *Targum Neofiti* on Exod. 12.5: *Neophyti 1: Targum Palestinense, MS de la Biblioteca Vaticana, II: Exodo* (ed. A. Díez Macho; Madrid/Barcelona: Consejo Superior de Investigaciones Científicas, 1970). A manuscript from the Cairo Genizah contains the same text as Neofiti on this verse (Cambridge University Library MS Or. 1080, B 18.1f. 4v; see Michael L. Klein, *Genizah Manuscripts of Palestinian*

occurrences of תמים, as applied to sacrifices, with this phrase. This interpretive translation is a straightforward adaptation of Lev. 22.21b, bringing together the two halves of the phrase into one technical translation term.[53] The same exegetical limitation to the meaning of תמים occurs in rabbinic literature of the tannaitic period.[54] The *Mekilta deRabbi Ishmael*[55] applies this meaning in its exegesis of Exod.

Targum to the Pentateuch (2 vols; Cincinnati: Hebrew Union College Press, 1986), I, p. 208. The written Palestinian targumim as we have them probably took shape in the third through fifth centuries. However the *practice* of verse-by-verse translation of the Bible in the context of liturgical reading is already known in the Mishnah (e.g. *m. Meg.* 4.4, 6, 10), and the targumim themselves appear to contain earlier traditions. Thus, although I do not wish to seem to indicate that Origen has taken this reading of the text from a literary source in Aramaic, I think it is possible that Origen could have learned orally circulating targumic interpretive traditions, especially since, in this bilingual culture, such traditions might easily have circulated in Greek, albeit coming from a Hebrew–Aramaic interpretive context. De Lange (*Origen and the Jews*, pp. 129 and 206 nn. 66 and 72) notes two instances in the interpretation of the Joseph story where Origen's interpretation of names has a particularly close parallel to the Palestinian targumic tradition.

53. See n. 47 above. That this is an exegetically derived definition and not motivated entirely by linguistic necessity is suggested by *Targum Onqelos* and *Targum Pseudo-Jonathan*, which translate תמים with the more economical שלים, 'complete, whole'. In fact Lev. 22.21 is the only place in *Targum Neofiti* where, presumably to avoid redundance, תמים is translated by the single word שלם.

54. Some tannaitic expositions of Lev. 22.19-21 evince a more complicated legal process at work. *Sifra Parshat Emor* 6 (on Lev. 22.19-21) pits Lev. 22.20-21 against verse 23, which says that a blemished offering will not be accepted; v. 21 then is taken to imply the additional information that one is not even to *dedicate* such an animal (see also *t. Tem.* 1.6). The same passage interprets the two halves of Lev. 22.21b as giving a negative commandment and a positive commandment: (1) to offer one's unblemished animals; and (2) not to place a blemish on an unblemished animal (thereby rendering it unfit for sacrifice). It may be significant that these more complex interpretations are found in the tannaitic texts directly concerned with the Leviticus passage, wherein the details of the logic of the sacrificial system are being worked out. The extant biblical and related texts from Qumran do not have traces of any such explanatory definitions of תמים.

55. The tannaitic commentary on sections of the book of Exodus; references in this paper are given according to the edition of Jacob Lauterbach (*Mekilta de-Rabbi Ishmael* [3 vols.; Philadelphia: Jewish Publication Society, 1933; repr. 1976]). The commentary as a whole begins with Exod. 12.1; later rabbinic tradition sees this verse as the beginning of the heart of the Torah, since it outlines the first commandments that God gives to the people of Israel as a whole. Opinions on the dating of this work have varied widely. B.Z. Wacholder held that it was created in its entirety

12.5; תמים functions להוציא בעל מום, 'to exclude an animal with a blemish', from qualifying as a Passover offering.[56] Thus, this Palestinian exegetical tradition, arising from a Hebrew text in which the same term, תמים, describes all sacrifices including the Passover offering, derives (via Lev 22.21) a halakhic, cultic, definition as the application for the term in Exod. 12.5.[57]

I suggest that it is this cultic application which Origen is appropriating in *Peri Pascha* 2.24. In this passage, he is presenting the historical meaning of the Exodus narrative, the story of what was done by the Hebrews in Egypt. The phrase τέλειον ἄμωμον establishes the literal sense of the Septuagint's unusual term, τέλειου, firmly locating it within the symbolic universe of cultic language. Thus, Origen is using ἄμωμον here, not to connote spiritual blamelessness, but in its technical legal-cultic sense as suggested by Lev. 22.19-21, and assumed by rabbinic exegetes, to describe the lamb of the Passover of Egypt as free from physical blemish. In the context of the Prologue, then, ἄμωμον functions in an anti-typological way: that is, it limits the application of τέλειον to the physical description of the sacrificial animal prescribed for those who sacrifice the Passover, and steers the

in the aftermath of the Arab conquest of Palestine (i.e. subsequent to 637 CE; 'The date of the Mekilta De-Rabbi Ishmael', *HUCA* 39 [1968], pp. 117-44); Jacob Neusner has suggested the fifth century as time of compilation, and maintains that it is in essence a post-tannaitic compilation (*Mekhilta According to Rabbi Ishmael: An Introduction to Judaism's First Scriptural Encyclopedia* [BJS, 152; Atlanta: Scholars Press, 1988]). Menachem Kahana has recently taken on Wacholder's thesis and argued persuasively that the document took its essential shape in the third century, although as with all of the tannaitic midrashim, it may have undergone a final redaction at a later period; Kahana argues for the general reliability of the *Mekilta* as representing tannaitic exegesis and concerns; see Kahana, 'The Critical Edition of *Mekilta deRabbi Ishmael* in the Light of the Geniza Fragments' [Hebrew], *Tarbiz* 55 (1986), pp. 489-524, esp. pp. 515-20.

56. Tractate *Pischa* 4 (J.Z. Lauterbach, *Mekilta de-Rabbi Ishmael* [3. vols.; Philadelphia: Jewish Publication Society of America, 1933], I, p. 28 [l. 3]). *Sifra* on Num. 6.14 (*Parshat Naso* 33) has identical wording. The *Mekilta*'s exposition considers each term of Exod. 12.5 to have an independent halakhic significance.

57. Interestingly, in what may illustrate a case of Christian influence on Jewish interpretation, the much later Palestinian midrashic composition, *Exodus Rabbah*, includes one midrash on Exod. 12.5 which interprets the description of the lamb non-halakhically, that is, not related to the mechanics of the sacrifice. In this midrash, תמים is referred to God by way of Deut. 32.4: הצור תמים פעלו ('The Rock, his works are perfect'); see *Exod. R.* 15.12.

reader away from applying this unusual Septuagint term typologically to Christ.[58]

B. Peri Pascha *41.36–42.13: The Passover Lamb and the Suffering Servant.*

The alliance of Exod. 12.5 and 1 Cor. 5.7 with Isa. 53.7 was an exegetical commonplace among second-century Christian biblical interpreters,[59] usually in conjunction with interpretation of the name *Pascha* as related to πάσχειν.[60] At the end of the introductory section of *Peri Pascha* B, Origen apparently prepares to make the same association. He says that salvation has been accomplished for 'Christ's brethren' (41.9-10) 'by the blood of Christ himself, like a lamb without blemish' (ὡς ἀμνοῦ ἀμώμου).[61] This phrase functions as the caption of a composite quote using Isa. 53.7-9 and 4-5. Origen habitually links v. 7 to Jesus' passion, v. 9 to explanations of his sinlessness, and vv. 4-5 to his saving task of taking on 'our' sins, either in the historical moment of his death on the cross or in the contemporary present.[62]

However, in the following section of text, Origen proceeds to wrench apart Isa. 53.7 from its customary juxtaposition with Exod. 12.5:

58. In fact in *Peri Pascha* A, the term τέλειος is used most frequently to designate the baptized Christian, who is continually striving towards an even higher perfection by *offering* the Passover sacrifice. The exception to this is 22.-8 to -4, which presents the actual interpretation of Exod. 12.5, and where all of the adjectives are referred to Christ.

59. E.g. Justin, *Dialogue* 111; Melito of Sardis, in whose own *Peri Pascha* this is a major literary theme (paras. 4-9 interweave images from Exodus and Isaiah; throughout the rest of the sermon, Exodus language highlights the original redemption from Egypt and the language of Isaiah, the redemption wrought for Christians, but both designate the activity of Christ—see especially paras. 12-17, 30-33, 66-69); Pseudo-Hippolytus, *In Sanctum Pascha* 18, uses Isa. 53.7 and Jn 1.29 to demonstrate that Jesus is the paschal lamb of Exod. 12.5. The connection has already been made by the author of the Gospel of John, who portrays Jesus as the paschal lamb and the ἀμνὸς τοῦ θεοῦ 'who takes away the sin of the world' (Jn 1.29; cf Isa. 53.6, 10, 12).

60. See n. 40 above.

61. This phrase may allude to 1 Pet. 1.19, ὡς ἀμνοῦ ἀμώμου καὶ ἀσπίλου. Both ἄμνος and πρόβατον appear in Isa. 53.7, although ἄμωμος does not appear at all in Isa. 52.13–53.12.

62. See, e.g., *CJn* 28.157-78, and cf. 290; *Exod. Hom* 5.1; *Lev. Hom.* 5.3, 12.2-4; *Contra Celsum* 1. 54-56 (on which see further below).

For just as they[63] were prefigured (προετυπώθησαν) in a male lamb (ἐν ἀρσενικῷ προβάτῳ), so were we in the man (ἐν ἀνθρώπῳ) who is like a lamb (ὡς ἀμνῷ; Isa. 53.7); just [as they were prefigured] in a perfect [lamb] (ἐν τελείῳ), so were we in the fullness[64] of him who has completed (τελειώσαντος) his Father's will; just as [they were prefigured] in a one-year-old [lamb], so are we at the end of the ages (τέλει αἰώνων; cf. 1 Cor. 10.11), for just as the year is the fullfillment of months, so is he the fullfillment of the law and the prophets; just as they [were prefigured] in a [lamb] without blemish (ἐν ἀμώμῳ), so were we in a man without sin (ἐν ἀναμαρτήτῳ; cf Isa. 53.5).[65]

This interpretation is structured by rather straightforwardly opposing fragments of Exod. 12.5 with phrases from Isaiah 53 or the New Testament. The lamb of Exod. 12.5 is said to 'prefigure' 'them' and the 'man like a lamb' to prefigure 'us'. The use of the verb προτυπόω is odd here. The passive can mean: to be previously formed, be set forth as a type, be foreshadowed, be prefigured.[66] It seems contrary to the expectations both of standard Christian typological thinking, and

63. Nautin and Daly understand this 'they' to be the 'Hebrews'. However, both from the ensuing use of the verb προτυπόω (see n. 69), and from the discussion further along (44.5-7) on the failures of those who were supposed to be subject to the law, it would seem that 'they' are Origen's Jewish contemporaries. This understanding makes more sense of the pointed contrasts between 'them' and 'us' developed in this passage.

64. ἐν πληρώματι; cf. Jn 1.16. Note that this passage works by juxtaposing similar but not identical biblical snippets (πρόβατον versus ἄμνος; τέλειος versus πλήρωμα).

65. Ὡς γὰρ ἐκεῖνοι προετυπώθησαν ἐν ἀρσενικῷ προβάτῳ, οὕτως ἡμεῖς ἐν ἀνθρώπῳ τῷ ὡς ἀμνῷ· ὡς ἐν τελείῳ, οὕτως ἡμεῖς ἐν πληρώματι αὐτοῦ τελειώσαντος τὸ πατρικὸν βούλημα· ὡς ἐν ἐνιαυσίῳ, οὕτως ἐν τέλει αἰώνων—ὡς γὰρ ὁ ἐνιαυτὸς συμπληρωτικός ἐστιν μηνῶν, οὕτως καὶ αὐτὸς συμπληρωτικός ἐστιν νόμου τε καὶ προφητῶν—ὡς ἐν ἀμώμῳ, οὕτως ἐν ἀναμαρτήτῳ· (*Peri Pascha* 41.36–42.13).

66. Melito of Sardis appears to play on several senses of this verb in his own *Peri Pascha*, where the verb is introduced in context of explaining the function of a preliminary sketch or model for an artistic work or building (*Peri Pascha* 35-36); it is later used in conjunction with the noun τύπος, which bears a double sense of 'type' and '(builder's) model' (*Peri Pascha* 58; cf. 40). Interestingly, in view of the passage under discussion, Melito makes the statement at one point that 'The salvation and truth of the Lord was prefigured *in the people*' (para. 39); the ensuing paragraphs establish the connection between 'the people' and 'the church' (paras. 39-43; this is more the typological connection we might have expected in Origen's Part B, on the basis of the exegesis in Part A).

those established by Origen's own line of thinking in *Peri Pascha* A,[67] to say that the lamb prefigures 'them' (the Hebrews or the Jews) rather than Jesus, and equally strange to say that the Servant prefigures 'us' (the Christians) rather than Christ.[68] In fact, as Origen proceeds to interpret other verses of Exodus 12 in this passage, he drops the 'them/us' dichotomy and reverts to a more straightforward typological reading which sees elements of Exodus as foreshadowings of 'our' new spiritual reality.[69]

I suggest that this odd opposition between Exod. 12.5 and Isa. 53.7 is made more intelligible if we consider it in the light of Origen's debate with a Jewish sage on the meaning of Isaiah 53 (*Contra Celsum* 1.54-56).[70] In the immediate context of *Contra Celsum*, Origen cites Isa. 52.13–53.8 as the third in a series of three prophecies which refer 'clearly' to the life and times of Jesus. Origen's aim is both to refute as unrealistic Celsus's portrayal of his Jewish interlocutor, and to demonstrate to 'Celsus and his Jew' (1.46) how the events of Jesus' life

67. Especially in view of the pains which Origen takes in Part A to make it clear that the paschal lamb is a figure of Christ himself (*Peri Pascha* 13.15ff.). In fact, as we saw, the introduction to the passage now under discussion makes it clear that Christ is the one 'like a lamb without blemish' whose blood has brought salvation.

68. Presumably in an attempt to get around this difficulty, Nautin translates the verb as *représenter*, explaining that the sacrificial victim (the lamb in the first instance, Jesus in the second) 'represents' those who offer it, being offered in their place (Guéraud and Nautin (eds.), *Sur la Pâque*, p. 138 n. 97). This presents a plausible reading of the passage, but as Sgherri observes, rejecting the explanation, it does not seem that the verb itself can bear this sort of interpretation. Then too, *Peri Pascha* B is characterized as an attempt to explain the 'spiritual' meaning of the Pascha—that is to say, its non-literary-historical sense; it would seem, then, that προτυπόω ought to bear something like its usual meaning, pointing toward a figurative explanation for the literary sense. Beyond this, the verb is unusual for Origen; according to Sgherri, this is its only occurrence in the extant Origen corpus (*Sulla Pasqua*, p. 117 n. 1).

69. The passage continues to *Peri Pascha* 43.6. Origen juxtaposes Exod. 12.2 with allusions to Col. 1.15-16 and Rev. 3.14, Exod. 12.3 with a statement that may draw on Col. 2.9. At Exod. 12.3, the 'they/we' opposition begins to disappear, and the interpretations become straightforward allegory which appears to draw on Philo (compare *Congr.* 103-106 with Origen's treatments of Exod. 12.3, 6; see also *Quaest. in Exod.* 1.21 on Exod. 12.17 and 1.22 on Exod. 12.22).

70. The direction of my argument assumes that the debate, which Origen 'remembers' in *Contra Celsum*, took place prior to the writing of *Peri Pascha* as well. It is suggestive that *Contra Celsum* 8.22 is the only passage outside of *Peri Pascha* in which Origen emphasizes the explanation of Passover as διάβασις.

happened in accordance with the prophecies. Origen invokes this Servant Song as the quintessential prophecy and justification for Jesus' passion.

After citing the text, Origen says (*Contra Celsum* 1.55) that he remembers using these prophecies 'in a discussion with some said to be sages among the Jews'.[71] The Jewish sage responds to his citation of Isaiah by saying that this text refers to the whole people of Israel as one individual, and to their being scattered among the nations so that many may become proselytes.[72] Thus, says Origen, the Jew sought to explain vv. 52.14, 15 and 53.3, all verses which focus exclusively on the Servant.[73] Origen's refutation procedes in three steps. First, he 'produced many arguments' to prove that it was 'not well-reasoned' (οὐκ εὐλόγως) to refer the prophecies about one person to the people as a whole. Then, he brings Isa. 53.4, 5 as counterproofs: if the Servant stands for all the people, then how do we understand these verses, where the text distinguishes between the Servant and 'us', that is, the people of God; who is this 'he' by whose 'stripe we are healed'? In other words, Origen asserts that the grammatical construction of the text raises difficulties for the identification of the Servant with Israel as the people of God.

71. Μέμνημαι δέ ποτε ἔν τινι πρὸς τοὺς λεγομένους παρὰ Ἰουδαίοις σοφοὺς ζητήσει ταῖς προφητείαις ταύταις χρησάμενος.

72. Continuing traces of this understanding of the Servant are found in medieval rabbinic commentaries (see, e.g., *Num. R.* 13.2, as well as the commentaries of Rashi and Radaq on these verses, in *Miqraot Gedolot: The Latter Prophets* [Hebrew] [Tel Aviv: Schocken, 1959]). A reading of the Servant as the whole people of Israel might be considered patently the 'plain meaning' of the text, given the explicit references to Israel as God's servant in the surrounding context of Isa. 40–55 (e.g. Isa. 41.8-10). It should be noted, however, that a messianic strain of interpretation persists as well; the Isaiah Targum dramatically rewrites the song to describes the Messiah's victory over and expulsion of the Gentiles, *Ruth R.* 5.6 uses Isa. 53.5 to prove that the Messiah will suffer before being restored, *b. Sanh.* 98b similarly uses 53.4. *b. Soṭ.* 14b applies Isa. 53.12 to Moses, the servant of God.

73. Isa. 53.3 in Hebrew introduces 'us' as a character in opposition to the Servant: 'we esteemed him not' (ולא חשבנהו). The LXX renders the same phrase in the passive voice, 'he was not considered' (οὐκ ἐλογίσθη), and so avoids introducing the second character. Insofar as Origen reproduces the argument accurately, the sage's initial proof seems to depend on the fact that the text speaks only about the Servant and not about 'us', since Origen represents those verses which speak of both as causing problems for the Sage's interpretation. This might then imply that the sage in question was also employing the LXX as his primary text.

Origen says (step three) that he caused the 'greatest difficulty' for his opponent by bringing up the end of Isa. 53.8 (LXX), 'because of the iniquities of *my people* he was led to death' (ἀπὸ τῶν ἀνομιῶν τοῦ λαοῦ μου ἤχθη εἰς θάνατον).[74] The difficulty Origen raises through this verse is that now 'the people of God' (Origen's phrase) are explicitly mentioned as distinct from the Servant; if that is the case, then how can the Servant stand for Israel, the people of God? According to Origen, then, the Sage's exegesis is grammatically and logically indefensible; on the contrary, these statements can only fit the saving activity of Jesus Christ.

Two things should be noted about the substance of this argument, as Origen reports it. First, the debate is not between a putative 'literal' rabbinic interpretation and a 'spiritual' Christian one, but rather between two competing 'spiritual' or allegorical readings of the contemporary meaning of the Servant.[75] Second, Origen proceeds against his opponent by showing the logical and grammatical difficulties with the opponent's allegorical interpretation. Origen assumes that he has demonstrated 'clearly' (σαφῶς) that the grammatical relationship between the Servant and 'us' supports his own assertion that those who can speak thus about the Servant are those who have been 'healed of their sins by the suffering of the savior'.

In *Peri Pascha* B, Origen disregards the 'grammatical' objections to identifying the Servant with the people of God. He pits Exod. 12.5 and Isa. 53.7 against each other as the prefigurings of the *former* people

74. The Hebrew on this verse is a bit obscure, probably to be understood to mean, 'because of the transgression of my people he was stricken (the stroke was his)' (מפשע עמי נגע למו). The last word is often understood as 'to them' by rabbinic commentators, and understood to mean that the righteous among Israel suffer for the sins of the rest, or that Israel suffers for the sins of all people (cf. the commentaries of Rashi and Radaq on this verse, via the reference in n. 72). The Isaiah Targum reads the verse as saying that 'my people's' sins will be cast upon the Gentiles (see Bruce Chilton's rendition of the entire song, with critical notes, in Bruce D. Chilton, *The Isaiah Targum: Introduction, Translation, Apparatus and Notes* [The Aramaic Bible, 11; Wilmington: Michael Glazier, 1987]). The LXX translators read the last word as למות, 'to death'; it is interesting, considering the importance of this phrase as a passion proof, that Origen makes no reference to the difference of readings in his report of the debate.

75. This is particularly interesting given the hermeneutical opposition posed between Jewish 'literal' and Christian 'spiritual' interpretation throughout Origen's writings (see n. 23 above).

of God (the Jews) and the *new* people of God (the Christians). In the logical context of the passage, these new associations are even more problematic than the Sage's exegesis in *Contra Celsum*. However, within the rhetorical flow of *Peri Pascha*, they play an important exegetical–polemical function. Origen asserts in the introduction to *Peri Pascha* B that he will here try to expound the 'spiritual' meaning of the Passover (*Peri Pascha* 40.31-33). In the passage we have discussed, which opens this exposition, Origen links two biblical 'passion proofs' with unexpected historical antitypes and sets the biblical passages in opposition to each other. By associating the Christians with the figure of the Servant, Origen undermines Jewish (rabbinic) vindication, via spiritual–allegorical exegesis of Isaiah 53, of the Jews' contemporary suffering; by associating the Jews with the lamb of Exod. 12.5, he undermines the Christian application of the Passover to Jesus' death. Further, he has bound inextricably together the Passover celebrated by the 'sons of Israel' in Egypt (*Peri Pascha* 39.9-18) and that celebrated by the Jews of the present day,[76] at the same time marking this Passover of the Jews as 'other' than that which fulfills the type of the biblical feast (cf. *Peri Pascha* 39.24-27, 44.4-21).

Finally, the equation of the Christians with the figure of the suffering Servant/Jesus becomes crucial for the argument in the remainder of Part B. Part A of *Peri Pascha* established the idea that the Christian's celebration of the Passover was to sacrifice, prepare and consume the Logos of God, that is, Christ, via study of the Scriptures. In a number of other writings, Origen develops the idea that the process of scriptural study is one of simultaneously understanding at deeper and deeper levels the message conveyed by the Logos, and of conforming the soul ever more closely to the likeness of the Logos.[77] Part

---

76. Cf. κατ᾽ ἐκείνους in 39.21, referring to the children of Israel in Egypt, and ἐκεῖνοι in 41.36–42.1, referring this time to those 'prefigured' in the lamb. In both instances 'they' is opposed in the text to 'us'; the opposition is picked up again at 44.4ff in a passage contrasting those subject to the law who were unable even to attain to its 'natural' salvation, and those who in the 'haste' (cf. Exod. 12.11) of faith are able to fulfill the Passover truly in accord with the law.

77. See the discussion in Karen Jo Torjesen, *Hermeneutical Procedure and Theological Method in Origen's Exegesis* (Patristische Texte und Studien, 28; Berlin and New York: De Gruyter, 1986]), pp. 77-85. Torjesen demonstrates that each step of Origen's exegetical procedure is motivated by the notion that scriptural study is the means by which the Logos brings about the transformation of the soul (see pp. 87-107).

B of *Peri Pascha* focuses on the 'Passover of the Lord' (Exod. 12.11b), that is, Christ's death on the cross and passage 'beyond the limits fixed by God', into the presence of the Father.[78] By participating in the sacrifice of the Logos in this age (and, the implication is, conforming themselves ever more closely to the likeness of the Logos/Christ), the Christians will be able to participate with Christ in the 'actual realization of the name of the Passover', crossing over the boundaries of death into the presence of God, when this takes place in the 'firmly established age of the Father'.[79]

Conclusions

The interpretations of Exod. 12.5 in *Peri Pascha* show us two facets of Origen's usage of Palestinian Jewish exegetical materials. On the one hand, Origen is capable of employing Jewish materials to lend authority to a particular literal–historical reading of the biblical text. He begins *Peri Pascha* with an explicit appeal to the meaning of 'the Hebrew' to ground his uncharacteristic Christian exegesis.[80] I have suggested that he has implicitly invoked the authority of Jewish interpretation by using the exegetical equivalence τέλειος ἄμωμος in his first statement of Exod. 12.5. The rhetorical effect of the phrase is to 'relocate' the Passover sacrifice within the wider sacrificial system; Origen uses this relocation to focus his Christian readers' attention on the *procedure* of the Passover sacrifice, and on the identity of these *readers* as 'those who sacrifice Christ'.[81] Thus, Origen's recasting of Exod. 12.5 reinforces his redefinition of *Pascha* in the Prologue as a term which describes the liberation of the people of God, and incidentally undermines the historicizing exegesis of Quartodecimans (and others) whose identification of Passover as the anniversary of the

78. *Peri Pascha* 46.24–47.7; 47.34-35.

79. *Peri Pascha* 45.7-13: Περατικοῦ γὰρ ἀντιπερατουμένου κόσμου εἰς τὸν καθεστηκότα πατρικὸν αἰῶνα, γίνεται ἡ τῶν τέκνων ἐπιστροφὴ τῇ τοῦ πάσχα ὀνομασίᾳ ἐνεργῶς τελουμένη. Cf. 47.34–48.10, which speaks of Christ's ascent and entrance into heaven enabling that of those who follow him.

80. See nn. 39 and 40 above.

81. οἱ Χριστὸν θύοντες; *Peri Pascha* 3.20. This is in opposition to the standard Christian reading of the Passover as a type of Jesus' crucifixion, in which 'those who sacrifice Christ' might be understood as those historical figures who performed the crucifixion (Origen argues for his own conception of 'those who sacrifice Christ' in *Peri Pascha* 12.25–13.22).

passion of Jesus might be used to justify a continuing affinity to the Jewish celebration.[82]

On the other hand, as the pre-eminent Christian teacher of Bible in the Caesarea of his day, Origen was well aware of the sophistication of rabbinic biblical teaching and of its attraction for his constituents and would-be constituents. He confronted that attraction on numerous occasions, by scolding his flock, by scathing caricature in his sermons, by careful reasoning in public debates. In *Peri Pascha* B, he confronted what might have been an appealing Jewish counterattack to Christian claims about Jesus.[83] He accepts the exegetical identification of the Servant with the People of God, but substitutes the Christian people of God for the Jewish people of God as the proper subjects of that identification.

This exegetical substitution provides a key to the rhetorical movement of *Peri Pascha* as a whole. In *Peri Pascha* A, Origen substitutes the 'spiritual' Passover sacrifice celebrated by the Christian for the 'literal' Passover celebrated by his Jewish contemporaries. He does this by conflating the historical sense of the biblical sacrifice with contemporary observance, and then setting both aside in favor of the 'true' Passover—the Christian's consumption of the Logos through scriptural study. In Part B, Origen moves beyond the spiritual sacrifice by the Christian to the spiritual sacrifice celebrated by Jesus;

---

82. The reader should remember that Quartodecimans were not the only Christians to hold this understanding of Jesus' death. I note that the Christians against whom Origen rails for celebrating Passover with the Jews (*Comm. Ser. in Matt.* 79) were not strictly speaking 'quartodeciman'; they very likely celebrated Easter along with the rest of the Caesarean church, and in addition ate the Passover on the 15th of Nisan, because this is 'what Jesus did'.

83. Allusions to Isa. 53 in earliest rabbinic literature are rare (cf. nn. 72 and 74 above which mention mostly later interpretations, although the Isaiah Targum may reflect a tannaitic and messianic perception of the Servant); a few isolated allusions appear in the earlier tannaitic literature, with no references at all appearing in Lauterbach's index to the *Mekilta*). It is impossible to conclude from this 'silence' whether the passage was merely of little importance or whether Christian appropriation of this figure resulted in rabbinic self-censorship at this period. On the face of it, I should say that the earliest (Jewish) Christians would have needed very little in the way of prior tradition to find prophecies in this text for some of the more ignominious aspects of the trial of Jesus. Possibly both the Sage's identification of the Servant as the (Jewish) people, and Jewish messianic readings of the text were attempts to counter Christian claims.

he opens this exposition by substituting a Christian spiritual understanding of the Servant for a Jewish spiritual understanding of that
figure. *Peri Pascha* seeks to demonstrate through its exegesis the
inevitability of the supersession of 'the Passover of the Jews'[84] by the
Passover of the Christians via the (in Origen's view) *true* 'Passover of
the Lord'.

I suggest that it is this rhetorical movement of supersession which
accounts for the relative absence in *Peri Pascha* of the explicit appeals
to authority of Jewish interpretation, even in a situation where Origen
found it helpful to draw on Jewish interpretive traditions to revolu-
tionize the way some Christians would understand the Passover.
Sophisticated exegesis was the most effective weapon for both Origen
and his rabbinic contemporaries in the struggle to influence minds and
souls in third-century Caesarea. *Peri Pascha*, like *Contra Celsum*,
demonstrates both Origen's skill at wielding this weapon and his
appreciation for the skills of his adversaries.

84. Cf. Jn 2.13. Prior to *Peri Pascha*, Origen's most extensive commentary on
Passover was his comment on this verse in *CJn* 10. There he went to great lengths to
show that the Passover of the Jews was not the same as (and in fact inimical to) the
'Passover of the Lord' of Exod. 12.11. This opposition is not mentioned explicitly in
Peri Pascha, but it provides the underlying premise for the entire exegetical
demonstration.

PAUL AND THE PERSIAN SAGE: SOME OBSERVATIONS ON APHRAHAT'S USE OF THE PAULINE CORPUS

Stephen S. Taylor

Introduction: The Pauline Legacy Debate

As soon as we begin to talk about the use of the Pauline corpus in later Christian tradition we are plunged, willy-nilly, into the intricate and ongoing debate over the legacies of Paul. It is far too involved to recount here, but in a nutshell the debate began in German Protestant circles about 150 years ago around this question: 'If Paul was such a key figure within the earliest, formative period of Christianity, why did Christianity in the subsequent periods turn out, to put it baldly, so "unPauline"?'[1]

Most of the earlier answers advanced posited some widespread opposition to Pauline thought or at least a period of neglect, perhaps before Paul's letters were collected and published, which allowed Paul to be eclipsed—eclipsed, that is, until some marginalized Christian, usually but not always Marcion, rescued Paul from the shadowy penumbra of competing varieties of Christianity. Indeed, it became essential to appeal to someone like Marcion, since the survival of the Pauline epistles themselves could be explained in no other way.[2] Not

---

1. Much of Walter Bauer's celebrated *Orthodoxy and Heresy in Earliest Christianity* (trans. and ed. Robert A. Kraft and Gerhard Krodel *et al.* [Philadelphia: Fortress Press, 1971; tr. of 1964 German edn], esp. pp. 213-39) was devoted to elucidating this very point. But Bauer was only refining a thesis articulated first by his homonymic predecessor, F.C. Baur. Though there were major differences between Baur and his disciples in the Tübingen School and the Ritschlians, and ultimately W. Bauer's own reconstruction, the long debate was fueled by the vexing problem of the rise of early Catholicism.

2. Marcion became the focal point of what Robert Murray has called 'the idealization of early "heretics"' as foils to the 'orthodox' who so misconstrued or ignored Paul (Robert Murray, *Symbols of Church and Kingdom* [London and New York:

to be outdone, more mainstream elements of Christianity fought to reclaim Paul, but the reclamation proved to be only partial and rather shallow. Thus the Paul that emerged from the century-long tunnel period was but a shadow of his former self. The result was, as Harnack quipped, that the second- and third-century Fathers completely misunderstood Paul, except Marcion—who also misunderstood him.[3]

More recent research has called into question the thesis that Paul was ever eclipsed whether through opposition or neglect. In his 1967 overview of late-second-, third-, and fourth-century Fathers who used Paul, Maurice Wiles concluded:

> There is no single commentator of whom we may assert that he catches and reflects the fullness of Paul's thought... On the other hand, there is no commentator whose work has come down to us in any quantity in whose writings there are not found comments of real and lasting value. For all their real shortcomings, at least the theory that the thought of Paul was totally lost... until the shining of the great Augustinian light is one deserving to be dismissed to the very limbo of outworn ideas in which it would itself seek to place the early patristic commentaries on the writings of the divine apostle.[4]

The works of Andreas Lindemann and Ernst Dassmann reached similar conclusions with primarily second-century materials.[5] In a direct challenge to the reigning consensus, David Rensberger argued that earlier reconstructions of an eclipsed Paul failed to take into

Cambridge University Press, 1975], pp. 5-6 n. 3). Marcion, or his disciples, were credited with virtually every worthwhile development in the second century—from the preservation and collection of the Pauline corpus to the evangelization of the Syriac-speaking lands. The idealization of Marcion continues today, witness R. Joseph Hoffmann, *Marcion: On the Restitution of Christianity—An Essay on the Development of Radical Paulinist Theology in the Second Century* (Chico, CA: Scholars Press, 1984). Hoffmann pushes Marcion's activity into the early part of the second century in order to overcome problems in Harnack's and Knox's theories.

3. Adolf von Harnack, *History of Dogma* (London: Williams and Norgate, 1894), I, p. 89.

4. Maurice F. Wiles, *The Divine Apostle: The Interpretation of St Paul's Epistles in the Early Church* (Cambridge: Cambridge University Press, 1967), p. 139.

5. Andreas Lindemann, *Paulus in Ältesten Christentum: Das Bild des Apostels und die Rezeption der paulinischen Theologie in der frühchristlichen Literatur bis Marcion* (BHT, 58; Tübingen: J.C.B. Mohr, 1979); and Ernst Dassmann, *Der Stachel im Fleisch: Paulus in der frühchristlichen Literatur bis Irenaeus* (Münster: Aschendorff, 1979).

account the genres and purposes of many second- and third-century sources. Once these kinds of allowances are made, the near-universal recognition of Pauline authority emerges full grown out of the second century.[6] Partly inspired by these efforts, a conference held on the campus of Southern Methodist University in 1987 was devoted to the issue of 'Paul and the Legacies of Paul'.[7] The common theme running through most of the papers was that it is incorrect to speak of an 'eclipse' of Paul in the second and third centuries; rather what we have is near-universal appropriation with necessary and natural adaptations.

At a more analytical level, Eugene Lovering's 1988 dissertation examined the various theories concerning the collection and publication of the *Corpus Paulinum* and concluded that a 'tunnel period' is virtually excluded by the evidence that Paul's letters were appreciated and circulated, singly and in a variety of unofficial corpora, from the very beginning.[8] Just a year later John J. Clabeaux built on Nils Dahl's work on the early Pauline prologues,[9] and argued that the Marcionite Pauline citations preserved in Tertullian's *Adversus Marcionem*, the *Dialogue of Adamantius*, and Epiphanius's *Panarion* bear witness not to a precedent-setting Marcionite canon but to an early-second-century, pre-Marcion corpus which underlies the 'Western' text, the Old Latin version of the 'I' type, and the Old Syriac version as

6.   David K. Rensberger, 'As the Apostle Teaches: The Development of the Use of Paul's Letters in Second-century Christianity' (PhD dissertation, Yale University, 1981).

7.   All except two of the major papers and some of the responses read at the conference have been published in William S. Babcock (ed.), *Paul and the Legacies of Paul* (Dallas: Southern Methodist University Press, 1990). The omitted papers have been published elsewhere: Elaine Pagels, 'Exegesis and Exposition of the Genesis Creation Accounts in Selected Texts from Nag Hammadi', in Charles W. Hendrick and Roger Hodgson, Jr (eds.), *Nag Hammadi, Gnosticism, and Early Christianity* (Peabody, MA: Hendrickson, 1986), pp. 257-85; and Albrecht Dihle, 'Philosophische Lehren von Schicksal und Freiheit in der frühchristlichen Theologie', *JAC* 30 (1987), pp. 14-28.

8.   Eugene Harrison Lovering, Jr, 'The Collection, Redaction, and Early Circulation of the Corpus Paulinum' (PhD dissertation, Southern Methodist University, 1988). Lovering still allows a major role for Marcion in the formation of the *Corpus Paulinum*, but this is because he has not availed himself of Clabeaux's work, even though he lists Clabeaux's dissertation in his bibliography.

9.   Nils Alstrup Dahl, 'The Origin of the Earliest Prologues to the Pauline Letters', *Semeia* 12 (1978), pp. 233-77.

attested by Ephrem. Clabeaux theorized that the provenance of this corpus was in the East, perhaps Syrian Antioch.[10]

The evidence for an uninterrupted, broadly attested use of Paul has, in a fundamental way, redefined the question. The basic question now is: 'How do we account for the transformation of Paul in the face of his enthusiastic and virtually uninterrupted appropriation?' In comparison to the old, this is a much more interesting way of framing the problem. It demands that we deal not only with the discontinuities between Paul and his early interpreters, but also, and at the same time, with the continuities. The emphasis has now shifted from the struggle between heroic Paulinists and dull 'early Catholics', to the interplay between text and context and the results of shifting hermeneutical horizons.

In the remaining pages I hope to give a brief overview of the uses and the inevitable abuses of Paul within the *Demonstrations* commonly attributed to Aphrahat, the early-fourth-century Persian Sage.[11] Aphrahat's 23 *Demonstrations*, composed from 337 to 345 CE, constitute some of the earliest surviving witnesses to an ecclesiastically oriented Christianity within Syriac-speaking lands.[12] Frankly, it surprises

10. John J. Clabeaux, *A Lost Edition of the Letters of Paul: A Reassessment of the Text of the Pauline Corpus Attested by Marcion* (Washington, DC: Catholic Biblical Association of America, 1989). This is a revision of his dissertation: 'The Pauline Corpus which Marcion Used: The Text of the Letters of Paul in the Early Second Century' (PhD dissertation, Harvard University, 1983).

11. I admit that 'Aphrahat', unlike 'Paul', is little more than a cipher. The author of the *Demonstrations* never identifies himself. Indeed, any kind of biographical information that might have been passed on by his contemporary coreligionists seems to have been lost or garbled by the middle of the fifth century (see T. Baarda, *The Gospel Quotations of Aphrahat the Persian Sage. I. Aphrahat's Text of the Fourth Gospel* [2 vols.; Amsterdam: Vrije Universiteit, 1975], I, pp. 2-5). Nevertheless, for simplicity's sake, I will continue to call the author 'Aphrahat'.

12. The *Liber Graduum* is probably older, and it was widely used by later ecclesiastics. But, as Murray points out, it does not give 'very clear indications of community self-awareness' (Murray, *Symbols*, p. 3). As for modern translations of the *Demonstrations*, the reader should consult: *Aphrahat: Unterweisungen* (ed. and trans. Peter Bruns; 2 vols.; Freiburg: Herder, 1991); *Aphraate le Sage Persan: Les Exposés* (ed. and trans. Marie-Joseph Pierre; 2 vols.; Paris: Les Cerf, 1988–89). Robert Owens is working on a critical and complete English translation. Until its completion, English readers will have to rely on a hodgepodge of translations of uneven reliability. For *Demonstrations* 1, 5, 6, 8, 10, 17, 21, 22, see Albert Edward Johnson (trans.), 'Select Demonstrations of Aphrahat', in *The Nicene and Post-*

me that the Demonstrations and other early Syriac Christian sources
have been ignored by the principals in the legacies of Paul debate. One
must remember that, except for the Gospels (*Diatessaron*) and Acts,
the Pauline corpus was the Syriac Christian New Testament canon.
Moreover, the Syriac Christian tradition with its own unique trajectory offers a new angle of vision on the old problem of Paul's legacy.

Aphrahat and Paul's Letters

Aphrahat's characterization of himself as 'a student of the holy scriptures' (1.1049.3-4) is certainly devoid of any self-delusion.[13] Anyone
who reads Aphrahat has to be struck by his great propensity to quote
or allude to Scripture. Whether he is teaching, admonishing, polemi-
cizing or merely waxing doxological he is always moving from one
biblical text to another. In his *editio princeps* of the *Demonstrations*
William Wright indexed 794 quotations from the Old Testament
and 446 from the New. Parisot counted 987 quotations of, or close

Nicene Fathers (second series; ed. Philip Schaff and Henry Wace; Grand Rapids:
Eerdmans, 1956), XIII, pt. 2, pp. 345-423; for *Demonstration* 4, see the excellent
translation in Sebastian P. Brock (trans. and intro.), *The Syriac Fathers on Prayer
and the Spiritual Life* (CSS, 101; Kalamazoo, MI: Cistercian Publications, 1987),
pp. 1-28; for *Demonstrations* 11, 12, 13, 15, 16, 17, 18, 19, 21, and parts of 23,
see the generally reliable translations in Jacob Neusner, *Aphrahat and Judaism: The
Christian-Jewish Argument in Fourth-Century Iran* (Leiden: E.J. Brill, 1971), pp.
19-119; and for *Demonstrations* 3 and 9 see the problematic translations by Frank
Hudson Hallock: '*De Caritate*', *JSOR* 14 (January 1930), pp. 18-31, and 'Aphraates
On Penitents', *JSOR* 16 (Jan./Apr. 1932), pp. 43-56, respectively. *Demonstrations*
3, 9, 14, 20, and most of 23 remain untranslated into English. The translations in
this essay are mine unless otherwise noted.

13. References to the *Demonstrations* will be given in the form that has become
conventional in Aphrahat studies. The first number gives the *Demonstration* number
and the second, the section number as determined by William Wright (who first
edited the manuscripts) and adapted by Parisot (William Wright, *The Homilies of
Aphrahat, the Persian Sage Edited from Syriac Manuscripts of the Fifth and Sixth
Centuries in the British Museum with an English Translation*. I. *The Syriac Text*
[London: Williams & Norgate, 1869]). The numbers within the parentheses give the
more precise location according to the volume, column, and line numbers in Parisot's
edition (Ioannes Parisot [ed.], *Aphraatis sapientis persae, Demonstrationes* [2 vols.;
Paris: Fermin-Didot, 1894–1907]). Where the precise location is not an issue, for
example, when a long passage is being referenced, information within parentheses
may be omitted.

allusions to, the Old Testament and 753 to the New Testament. If we rely on Robert Owens's computations, this averages out to about four per column of Syriac text[14] or about one every sixth line. Thus it is not surprising that Aphrahat quotes or alludes to Paul at least 250 times and possibly over 300 times.[15]

Actually in Aphrahat's case, the distinction between quotation and allusion, however crucial it is to the text critic,[16] may be of little significance—not only because of Syriac's heavy dependence on that most slippery relative particle, ܕ, to indicate both direct and indirect speech, or even because of the early Syriac Fathers' almost studied disregard for things like intellectual and literary property rights, but because Aphrahat normally seems to cite Paul from memory. We can see this not only in the interesting conflation of similar Pauline passages,[17] but also in the alterations that appear in often-cited passages. One example will have to do: Aphrahat is fond of Eph. 6.14-17 where Paul describes 'the full armor of God' and admonishes the Christian to don it. In *Demonstration* 6.1 (1.244 and 1.249) he gets it almost right: with the exception of 'faith' which seems to be paired with 'the preparation of the Gospel of peace', each virtue is matched with the correct

14. See Robert J. Owens, Jr., *The Genesis and Exodus Citations of Aphrahat the Persian Sage* (Leiden: E.J. Brill, 1983), pp. 17-18, who conveniently summarizes the data from Wright and Parisot.

15. I will ignore the 'possible' references in this essay. Nevertheless, they are interesting in their own right. A large group of them, for example, are citations of the Old Testament that Aphrahat and Paul share. They raise the interesting issue of Aphrahat's reliance on Paul for his use of the Old Testament. For more on this see my dissertation ('Paul and the Persian Sage: The Legacy of Paul in Aphrahat's Demonstrations' [University of Pennsylvania, forthcoming]).

16. There is a sizable body of literature on the problems that patristic citations pose to text-critical reconstruction of biblical texts. See, for example, M.J. Suggs, 'The Use of Patristic Evidence in the Search for the Primary New Testament Text', *NTS* 4 (1957/58), pp. 139-47; Gordon D. Fee, 'The Text of John in The Jerusalem Bible: A Critique of the Use of Patristic Evidence in New Testament Textual Criticism', *JBL* 90 (1971), pp. 163-73; Bruce M. Metzger, 'Patristic Evidence and the Textual Criticism of the New Testament', *NTS* 18 (1972), pp. 379-400. For discussions of the use of specifically Syriac patristic citations, see Josef Kerschensteiner, *Der altsyrische Paulustext* (CSCO, 37; Louvain: Secrétariat du CorpusSCO, 1970), pp. 112-14, and Owens, *Genesis and Exodus Citations*, pp. 26-29.

17. See 12.10 (1.529.6-8) which seems to conflate Rom. 6.3-4 and Col. 2.12; and 2.6 (1.57.10-12) which amounts to a conflation of Eph. 2.14-15, Heb. 9.17-18, and Gal. 3.15-17. Note also the interesting use of Heb. 1.1 in 11.11 (1.500.22-24).

piece of armor. In 12.9 (1.525.24–1.528.1) however, the loins are girded with faith rather than truth and the shield of faith is left out of the equation. But then in his *Demonstration On Fasting* 3.1 (1.97.2-4) it is fasting, not faith, that is called 'a shield against the Adversaries' darts'. One gets the picture of a man composing at his desk freely without any compulsion to check his Bible.

This is not to say that Aphrahat treats the Pauline text irreverently. Rather he has drunk so deeply of it (or parts of it) that Pauline images and phrases well up spontaneously and naturally.[18] And there is no mistaking it, Aphrahat treats the Pauline corpus as Scripture. He can introduce quotations from it with the formula, 'it is written' (14.42 [1.693.15]; 22.26 [1.1049.13-18], and one of his favorite rhetorical moves is to wrap up a point by quoting first from Jesus and then from Paul. For example, in 22.13 (1.1016.21) he writes: 'And concerning that which I said—that over there they do not take wives, and male and female are not distinguished—it is our Lord (ܡܪܢ) and his Apostle (ܫܠܝܚܗ) who taught us [this]'; and there follows, in quick succession, a quote from Lk. 20.35-36 and one from Gal. 3.28. In these and many other passages like them, one is struck by just how completely Paul has been integrated into 'Scripture'. Moses, Ezekiel, Jesus, and Paul are saying the same thing. The Pauline texts don't seem to have a Pauline context.

3. *Distribution of Citations*

What are those Pauline texts? From what books does Aphrahat make his selections? Aphrahat and his Syriac Christian contemporaries seem to have operated with a 14-book Pauline corpus which included Hebrews and *3 Corinthians*, but excluded Philemon.[19] A glance at the

---

18. Sections 14.31 and 14.37 are good examples of this. Aphrahat can even mistake what Paul has written (1 Tim. 1.9) for his own point—2.7 (1.64.1). Owens, (*Genesis and Exodus Citations*, pp. 20-21) reached similar conclusions in his text-critical examinations of Aphrahat's Genesis or Exodus citations: that they are from memory.

19. We know he regarded Hebrews and *3 Corinthians* as Pauline because he introduces quotations from these books with the same formulae he uses when quoting from other more generally accepted Pauline books. For example in *Dem.* 2.14 (1.77.16-19) Aphrahat prefaces a quote from Heb. 9.11 with the phrase: 'And the Apostle also said...'. By the same token, a clear quotation of *3 Corinthians* 10 in *Dem.* 6.12 (1.285.23-25) is introduced by, 'The blessed Apostle also said...'. See

chart on the following page shows that Aphrahat did not operate on the basis of a 'canon within a canon'. With the exception of 2 Thessalonians,[20] his references are distributed among all the Pauline letters as he knew them.

This is not to say they are distributed evenly, however. Clearly 1 Corinthians stands out: it is used more than twice as often as any other letter and accounts for more than a third of all the probable and certain references. Romans, Hebrews, and 2 Corinthians follow in terms of sheer numbers, but if one considers frequency of citation as a function of letter size, then Ephesians and Galatians would have to receive second and third place.

Nevertheless, 1 Corinthians' predominating representation cannot be accounted for on the basis of its size alone; its nearest competitor, Romans, is even larger. Moreover, a closer look at the data reveals a rather startling imbalance in the numbers for 1 Corinthians. Aphrahat quotes from the letter almost twice as often as he alludes to it (57/30). This is not what one would expect. If someone is well acquainted and profoundly affected by a book, one would expect that explicit quotation of it would be outnumbered by unconscious or conscious allusions

also 13.12 (1.568.13-16) where he quotes Heb. 4.8 and 23.20 (2.64.22), which appears to be a quotation of *3 Corinthians* 5. This is consistent with what we know from other early Syriac authors. Ephrem and the *Liber Graduum* both cite Hebrews frequently as Pauline, while Ephrem (alone among other early Syriac witnesses) cites *3 Corinthians* 5 in his commentary on the *Diatessaron* (26.1). There he introduces the quote with the words: 'And again the Apostle said this...'. For the text of the commentary see the edition by L. Leloir, *Saint Ephrem Commentaire de l'Evangile Concordant, Texte Syriaque (Manuscrit Chester Beatty 709)* (Dublin: Hodges Figgis & Co. Ltd, 1963). Leloir had previously edited the Armenian version in *Saint Ephrem Commentaire de l'Evangile Concordant, Version Arménienne* (CSCO 137, Louvain: Secrétariat du CorpusSCO, 1953). On the extent of the Pauline corpus in the early Syriac canon see the succinct discussion in Harry Y. Gamble, *The New Testament Canon: Its Making and Meaning* (Philadelphia: Fortress Press, 1985), pp. 35-46.

20. It is difficult to judge the significance of Aphrahat's failure to quote from or allude to 2 Thessalonians. The *Liber Graduum* cites it at least seven times, but references elsewhere in early Syriac literature are exceedingly rare. Nevertheless it is treated in the Armenian version of Ephrem's commentary on Paul's letter. Kerschensteiner, *Der altsyrische Paulustext*, p. 172. As Kerschensteiner reports, the commentary reflects the following arrangement of Paul's letters: Romans, 1–2 Corinthians and *3 Corinthians*, Galatians, Ephesians, Philippians, Colossians, 1–2 Thessalonians, Hebrews, 1 and 2 Timothy, and Titus. This is not the place to get into the thorny issue of the order of the letters within the early Syriac canon.

to it. This is precisely the case with most of the other letters. The only other letters to show a preponderance of quotations over allusions are 2 Corinthians (13/9) and 1 Timothy (5/1).[21] 1 Timothy's numbers become less significant when one realizes that three of the five quotations are from the same passage, 1 Tim. 1.8-9.

Distribution of Pauline Citations Within the Demonstrations

Pauline Book	Certain or Probable quotations	Certain or Probable allusions	Total certain/ probable	Possible quotations/ allusions	Total References
Romans	17	18	35	16	51
1 Corinthians	57	30	87	9	96
2 Corinthians	13	9	22	11	33
Galatians	7	13	20	3	23
Ephesians	6	15	21	5	26
Philippians	3	10	13	3	16
Colossians	1	6	7	2	9
1 Thessalonians	3	7	10	1	11
2 Thessalonians	0	0	0	0	0
1 Timothy	5	2	6	0	6
2 Timothy	1	1	2	0	2
Titus	1	1	2	0	2
Philemon	0	0	0	0	0
Hebrews	7	17	24	6	30
3 Corinthians	2	2	4	0	4

So how does one account for the situation with 1 Corinthians? Perhaps Aphrahat had an especially deep knowledge of the letter, or 1 Corinthians was the one book he had at his desk.[22] Part of the answer, it seems to me, must be based on one of the most interesting features of the *Demonstrations* as a whole: except for the sustained skirmish against the Jews,[23] they are remarkably free of polemics.

21. Note, as well, that *3 Corinthians* is balanced (2/2) as is Romans (17/18).

22. This raises the interesting question, which we cannot pursue here, of how and in what physical format the Pauline letters would have been circulated in pre-Peshitta days.

23. Neusner (*Aphrahat and Judaism: The Christian–Jewish Argument in Fourth-Century Iran* [Leiden: E.J. Brill, 1971]) must be credited with pointing out to modern readers the importance of the Jewish–Christian debate to Aphrahat's community, though his skepticism about living contact between Aphrahat and rabbinic-type Jews is probably excessive (see Naomi Koltun, 'Jewish–Christian Polemics in Fourth-

Now polemics tend to multiply scriptural quotations as warring parties seek to prove their positions relative to shared Scriptures. It is quite clear that Paul would have no probative value in the Jewish–Christian debate, and as Naomi Koltun-Fromm has noted,[24] Aphrahat is very careful to stick to the Hebrew Scriptures in these contexts. But there is one instance of an intra-Christian debate within the *Demonstrations*, and that has to do with the resurrection body. And in fact it is in the course of conducting this debate in *Demonstration* 8 that many of the quotations from 1 Corinthians—specifically ch. 15—are made.[25]

Aphrahat's predilection for 1 Corinthians should not be allowed to overshadow the fact, however, that his knowledge of Paul—especially of the Church epistles—was broad and deep. If we include all of the possible references, he draws from 15 of the 16 chapters of Romans, 13 of the 16 chapters of 1 Corinthians, 9 of the 13 chapters of 2 Corinthians, 4 of the 6 chapters of Galatians, 5 of the 6 chapters of Ephesians, 3 of the 4 chapters in Philippians, 3 of the 4 chapters of Colossians, 3 of the 5 chapters of 1 Thessalonians, 10 of the 13 in Hebrews, and by default, all of the chapters of 3 Corinthians! Overall, and using the rather arbitrary chapter divisions as our unit of measurement, that works out to a usage rate of about 76 per cent.

Aphrahat's Attitude toward Paul Himself

With all this use of the Pauline corpus one would expect to find a very high view of Paul, the person, within the *Demonstrations*. This is

Century Persian Mesopotamia: A Reconstructed Conversation' [PhD dissertation, Stanford University, 1994]). What both Neusner and Koltun (now Koltun-Fromm!) miss, however, is that Aphrahat's concern about the Jews is not limited to the demonstrations written explicitly against them. The Jews and their arguments about the Scriptures and the nature of the people of God are never far from Aphrahat's mind (see *Dem.* 1.5-6; 1.10-11 [1.21-28]; 8.21 [1.401.1-2], cf. Lk. 20.9-18; 14.45 [1.709-712]).

24. Koltun, 'Jewish–Christian Polemics', p. 97.

25. It is remarkable, especially in view of the reigning theories on the heterodox origins of Syriac Christianity, how muted and distant Aphrahat's criticisms of competing varieties of Christianity are. Marcion, Valentinus, and Mani are rarely mentioned or alluded to (see *Dem.* 3.9 [1.116.1-18]; 17.7 [1.797]: possibly 13.11 [1.568]). On this, see Pierre, *Les Exposés*, vol. 1, p. 278 n. 21 who regards the 3.9 passage as the only allusion to Christian heresies.

indeed the case. Aphrahat's favorite title for Paul is simply ܫܠܝܚܐ, 'the Apostle'. At times he elaborates on this with 'the blessed Apostle' (e.g. 1.3 [1.9.7]; 1.5 [1.13.11]; 1.8 [1.20.19]) or 'the glorious Apostle' (e.g. 13.12 [1.568.13]; 15.2 [1.732.8]). Once, immediately following a reference to the Lord Jesus, Paul is called 'his [the Lord's] Apostle' (ܫܠܝܚܗ, 1.22.13 [1.1016.21]). Only once, in the citational formulae, does Aphrahat feel the need to further identify the Apostle by adding his name (23.44 [2.85.5] 'Just as the Apostle Paul testified'). This is significant when one realizes that for Aphrahat ܫܠܝܚܐ is still a title which others shared. Aphrahat knows about the 'other apostles' and refers to stories about Peter and the others recorded in the Gospels and the canonical Acts. Jesus himself is called 'the Apostle of the Most High' (14.39 [1.684.11]). But it is only Paul who is called 'the Apostle', absolutely.[26] Students of Syriac Christianity have yet to integrate this fact with other traditions that assign the central place within Syriac Christian history to 'Judas Thomas'.[27]

For Aphrahat, then, Paul is preeminently the Apostle, the Doctor of the Gentiles, one of God's mouthpieces. Nevertheless, it is still remarkable how little interest Aphrahat evinces in the biographical details of Paul's life. Once Paul appears in a list of early Christian martyrs (along with Jesus (!), Stephen, Peter, and others—21.23 [1.988.17]).[28] But in the only other two references to events in his

26. A new title for Paul appears in *Demonstration* 23: 'The Doctor of the Peoples (Gentiles)'—23.2 (2.4.21-22); 23.9 (2.25.13-14); 23.62 (2.128.24).

27. I have yet to find one reference to Thomas in the *Demonstrations*. He is not listed in Parisot's index. For more on the role of the 'Judas Thomas' tradition in early Syriac, and more specifically Edessene, Christianity, see Helmut Koester, 'Gnomai Diaphoroi: The Origin and Nature of Diversification in the History of Early Christianity', in James M. Robinson and Helmut Koester (eds.), *Trajectories through Early Christianity* (Philadelphia: Fortress Press, 1971), pp. 114-57; L.W. Barnard, 'The Origin and Emergence of the Church in Edessa during the First Two Centuries A.D.', *VC* 22 (1968), pp. 161-75; and more broadly, F. Forrester Church and Gedaliahu G. Stroumsa, 'Mani's Disciple Thomas and the Psalms of Thomas', *VC* 34 (1980), pp. 47-55.

28. 21.23 (1.988.12-17): 'Great and excellent is the testimony [=martyrdom, ܣܗܕܘܬܐ] of Jesus. He outdid in affliction and confession all of those who came before and afterward. After him was the faithful witness, Stephen, whom the Jews stoned. Also Simon and Paul were complete witnesses. Jacob [James] and Yohannan [John] walked in the path of their master, the Messiah. Also some of his apostles in various places confessed and went forth true witnesses' (according to Neusner, *Aphrahat and Judaism*, p. 111, with some changes).

life, Paul is always paired with Jesus as the object of Jewish persecution:

> Our savior they laid hold of, treated shamefully, condemned unjustly, suspended on a tree. And [as for] Paul, sometimes they bound him, sometimes they stoned him, and sometimes they let him down the city wall in a basket (14.45 [1.713.23]).

Aphrahat confuses here the actions of Paul's Jewish enemies with those of his Jewish-Christian friends (2 Cor. 11:32-33; Acts 9.24).[29] In any case, the basic point is clear enough: Paul is Jesus' faithful and intimate apostle; his experience recapitulates the Master's. These three references establish the fact that Aphrahat knew the stories relating Paul's biography and could view Paul as an *exemplum ad imitatum*. At the same time, however, they are the exceptions that prove the rule that, for Aphrahat, Paul's abiding greatness could no longer be imitated for it lay in his membership in that exclusive club of 'inscripturated' authors.

Aphrahat's Faithfulness to Paul on Law and Grace

Now, of course, the use of Scripture in later traditions is not only a matter of explicit references and citations. It is also about fidelity to basic and distinctive concepts in Scripture. In this particular case we would have to ask: Was Aphrahat faithful to Paul? Did he use Paul's terminology? Did he employ that terminology in the same way, with the same valence? The answer must be a resounding yes and no! A complete case would require an examination of Aphrahat's use of all the key terms and concepts in Pauline thought. Clearly that is beyond the scope of a single paper. I will limit myself to one complex of ideas in Paul: the contrast between law and grace.

---

29. See also 14.45 (1.713.5-13). 'And again God said concerning all the prophets: "I have cut off my prophets and I have killed them by the speech of my mouth, but the sons of Israel have not turned from their sins." And as for our Savior, the sons of his people even called him a Samaritan, and they named him Beelzebub, as if he were demon-possessed. And Paul, when he was teaching they called him a speaker of foolish things.' Note that here, as well, Aphrahat misconstrues a detail of Paul's life: he seems to think that Paul's taunters in Athens were Jews (possibly interpolating Acts 17.17 into 17.18). The strange reading of Hos. 6.5 reoccurs in 19.3 (1.853.7-11), this time conflated with Mal. 3.6-7.

Paul on Law and Grace

One of the distinctive themes in Paul is the distinction between law, or the works of the law, and grace.[30] With admonitions such as Rom. 6.14—'Do not let sin rule over you, for you are not under law but under grace'—we are brought face to face with the great conceptual divide in Paul's thought. For Paul the watershed event in history, indeed the event that marks the end of history, was the redemptive death and resurrection of the Messiah. The word 'grace' (χάρις) is Paul's most comprehensive rubric for this event.[31] At least two-thirds of the incidences of this term in Paul refer to the unmerited favor of God in Christ. So strong is the bond between χάρις and salvation in Christ, that Paul will only rarely use it as a static quality of the godhead (2 Cor. 1.11 possibly). He normally uses it of the eschatological, saving activity of both God and Christ (Rom. 1.7; 2 Cor. 9.14; Gal. 1.6; 2.21; Phil. 1.2; 2 Thess. 1.12), or of God through/in Christ (Rom. 3.24; 5.15; 1 Cor. 1.4), or even (and quite frequently) of Christ alone (Rom. 1.5; 1 Cor. 16.23; 2 Cor. 8.9; 12.9-10; 13.14; Phil. 4.23; 1 Thess. 5.28). For Paul, moreover, this grace in Christ was no afterthought, but was already God's overarching intent 'before the foundation of the world' (2 Tim. 1.9) and was, in fact, the motive force in God's covenantal dealings with Israel, as far back as the covenant with Abraham (Gal. 3.6-29). Paul does not develop a theology of 'common (providential) grace', but had he done so, he most likely would have rooted that also in 'God's grace in Christ'. For even the financial help (χάρις) he hopes the Corinthians will give to believers in Jerusalem is founded on the χάρις of Christ (2 Cor. 8.9). Thus,

30. I am fully aware of the vast complexities in every aspect of Pauline research, particularly since the publication of E.P. Sanders's *Paul and Palestinian Judaism: A Comparison of Patterns of Religion* (Minneapolis: Fortress Press, 1977). The bibliography alone is staggering. Yet one cannot be paralyzed by it. For those who are interested in the use and transformation of Scripture and tradition there are no firm footholds in either the parent or daughter traditions, though perhaps those who work in the Pauline tradition feel the shifting sands more keenly. The thumbnail sketch of Paul's understanding of the law and grace provided below is both provisional and cursory. Yet I believe it faithfully reflects the general consensus on these issues and is adequate for the task at hand.

31. Of the 155 occurrences of the word 'grace' (χάρις) in the New Testament 100 are found in the books that comprised the *Corpus Paulinum* of the Syriac Church. If we assume, with Hennecke, that the benediction of *3 Corinthians* was indeed tripartite, then we can add one occurrence to the two numbers above.

for Paul, grace was an eschatological blessing secured at the end of salvation history by the work of the Messiah.

It is clear within this scheme of things that, soteriologically speaking,[32] there is little room for any other agent or means of rightstanding with God—this applied to the law as well. Through the lens of the eschatological Christ-event, the law was seen to have a subservient and relatively negative (though essential) role in the positive scheme of salvation history. It was a custodian or a schoolmaster until the Christ should come (Gal. 3.24). It was added not so much because of transgression, but for transgression's advantage, to increase it, pile it up, and concentrate it,[33] so that the Messiah could, 'in the fullness of time', 'be born of a woman, under the law' (Gal. 4.4) and so take its curse. Thus for Paul, the flip-side of Christ, the quintessential expression of God's grace, was Christ, the end or goal (τέλος) of the law (Rom. 10.4).

Aphrahat's Understanding of Law and Grace
How does Aphrahat do? Is he faithful to Paul on this issue of law and grace? Well, the issue is complex and Aphrahat may not be entirely consistent.[34] Nevertheless, there are certainly many continuities. The issue of the law is a major theme in the *Demonstrations*. Aphrahat's favorite word for the law, ܢܡܘܣܐ, occurs more than 175 times. Other terms, such as ܐܘܪܝܬܐ (= Torah), are less frequent but certainly add to the impression that for Aphrahat the status of the Old Testament law was a living issue.

---

32. 'Soteriologically speaking' is an important qualification, for Paul never questions the validity of the law as a declaration of God's character and will and therefore of God's judgment against sin. One must assume that for Paul those not 'in Christ' were very much 'under law'. One would not be too far off the track to see behind Paul's various statements about the law a sustained polemic, along the same lines as the polemic of Jesus as presented in the Gospel tradition (Mt. 5.17-48), against the 'taming' of the law within a 'covenantal-nomistic' framework. For Paul the law (=scripture=God, compare Gal. 3.22 with Rom. 11.32) has shut everybody except Jesus the Messiah out of the covenant (and even he is caught up in its curse [Gal. 3.13]!).

33. Gal. 3.19—taking the preposition χάριν to have a purpose rather than a causal force, as the presence of τῶν παραβάσεων and 3.22 seem to demand; see Rom. 5.20; cf. Rom. 3.11-19; 11.32.

34. And, of course, the issue of Paul's consistency is a hotly debated topic. See Heikki Räisänen, *Paul and the Law* (WUNT, 29; Tübingen: J.C.B. Mohr, 1983).

And well it should have been. A careful reading of the *Demonstrations* reveals that Aphrahat's community felt keenly the force of Jewish polemics.[35] Aphrahat's thinking about the law, like Paul's, was shaped by the necessity of delineating the purposes of God over against a Jewish understanding of those purposes. It is no surprise, then, that Aphrahat is thoroughly acquainted with Paul's arguments regarding the law:

(1) The law was added on account of (ܡܛܠ) transgression (2.3 [1.52.10] echoing Gal. 3.19, cf. Rom. 5.20; 2.4 [1.56.9] echoing Gal. 3.17).[36]

(2) As an addition, the law cannot abrogate the prior promise given to Abraham (2.4 [1.56.5-13] following the argument in Gal. 3.17-19).

(3) The law was a 'keeper' or 'nurse' until 'the seed' should come in whom the Gentiles would be blessed (2.3 [1.52.15] reading Gal. 3.25 in conjunction with Gal. 3.16).

(4) Circumcision without faith is of no use and profits nothing (11.2 drawing on Gal. 5.6; Rom. 4.11 (11.3 [1.476.2-5] drawing on Rom. 4.10).

(5) 'By the works of the law, no one is justified', for no one can keep the works of the law (15.8 [1.757.1] quoting Gal. 3.11).

Many more examples could be given, but these are enough to make the point: most of the Pauline pieces are there. Nevertheless, one must hasten to add that for Aphrahat the puzzle seems to be a different one.

This comes out clearly in Aphrahat's two most programmatic statements about the law in the demonstration *On Love* (*Dem.* 2) and the demonstration *On Jewish Food Laws* (*Dem.* 15). In the former he argues that all the law (or all that is valid in the law) is fulfilled in the law of love, already explicit in the law but brought to supreme prominence in the teaching of Jesus. Aphrahat establishes this point by appealing to Eph. 2.14.

> And (then) the Testator of the Testament died and he confirmed the two covenants, and he made the two one and he abolished the law of commandments by his commandments.[37]

---

35. See n. 23 above.

36. See the slightly different reason given in 2.7 (1.64.3) where he quotes 1 Tim. 1.9: 'And you remember, my beloved, what I wrote to you before, that "the law was not imposed for the righteous". For whoever guards righteousness is above the commandments, even the law and the prophets'.

37. ܒܪܡ ܕܟܕ ܡܝܬ ܡܩܝܡܢܗ ܕܕܝܬܩܐ ܘܫܪܪ ܬܪܬܝܢ ܕܝܬܩܣ ܘܥܒܕ ܠܬܪܬܝܗܝܢ ܚܕܐ ܘܒܛܠ ܠܢܡܘܣܐ

The conflation of Eph. 2.14-15 with Heb. 9.17-18 and Gal. 3.15-17 cannot detain us here. What interests us at this point is the way in which Aphrahat empties the Ephesians passage of its obvious personal referents. In context τὰ ἀμφότερα clearly refers to the two divisions of humanity (see vv. 13, 15b-c), but Aphrahat construes it as a reference to the Mosaic and the New Covenants. Likewise (and much more significantly), Aphrahat passes over the all important phrases in 14d and in 15b, ἐν τῇ σαρκὶ αὐτοῦ and ἐν αὐτῷ, respectively, and rests the full agency or means of the 'abrogating' on the phrase ἐν δόγμασιν. Thus whatever his understanding of 'making the two one' or 'abrogating of the law' was, it was not accomplished in the person of Christ himself but in what Christ taught (his dogma), namely the two love commandments. It is no accident, then, that Aphrahat's positive statements on the law would be concentrated in a discussion of love. In this way, we are tipped off that for Aphrahat the fundamental categories are not law and grace (or faith) but the law codified in the Old Testament and the law of love as taught by Jesus.

It only follows from this that when Aphrahat eventually gets around to spelling out what is wrong with the law, as he does in *Dem.* 15.7-8, his critique does not plumb the depths of its soteriological inadequacy. Rather Aphrahat is at pains to make distinctions within the law itself. Drawing on Ezekiel's claim in 20.25-26 that God gave Israel commandments which were not excellent, by which they could not live, he makes an explicit distinction between the Decalogue (and I assume this would include the laws of love) and the rest of the law.[38] It is by the latter set of (largely) ritual laws—the laws that define and confer Jewish privilege—that 'no one can be justified'. Moreover, says Aphrahat, it is these laws that no one can keep. Though Aphrahat clearly has Paul's arguments in mind throughout his discussion, his distance from Paul is palpably evident. Paul consistently maintained the unity of the

---

ܠܟ ,ܡܢܝܗܘܢܟܒ ܟܐܢܐܝ ܟܡܚܒܘ (2.6 [1.57.10-12]). See also 2.5 (1.56.16): 'And that word was in safe-keeping 1364 years from after the imposition of the law. That word preceded the law 430 years. And when it arrived, it abolished the observances of the law. The law itself and the prophets were concluded upon these two commandments concerning which our Lord spoke.'

38. Note, however, that in 13.8 [1.557] even part of the Decalogue is relativized by the normative experience of Abraham. Aphrahat points out that Abraham (and other pre-Mosaic saints) was not justified by Sabbath-keeping.

law (Gal. 3.10; 5.3), and indeed, when he wanted to make the point that the law was unobservable, he bypassed ritual laws and went straight to the Decalogue's tenth commandment (see Romans 7).

Aphrahat's distance from Paul on this point accounts for the strange inversion of Paul's Romans 4 argument about the justification of Abraham before the giving of the law. As noted above, Aphrahat was clearly aware of Paul's argument and indeed was greatly indebted to it.[39] He was fond of quoting Gen. 15.6 ('Abraham believed the Lord, and He reckoned it to him as righteousness') in the light of Rom. 4.3 (2.4 [1.53.19]; 11.3 [1.476.11-13]; 11.12 [1.504.20-21]; 13.8 [1.557.15-18]). He even went to great lengths to establish for his readers the chronological priority of the promises to Abraham over the promulgation of the law at Sinai.[40] Nevertheless, for Aphrahat, one of the implications of the chronological sequence so carefully worked out was that 'Abraham kept the righteousness which is in the law while the law was not yet laid down' precisely in that 'he brought the captives of Sodom back in the strength of his God and did not stretch out his hand for the spoil' (2.2 [1.49.11-13]). The extension of the argument to cover the patriarchs and Moses makes Aphrahat's essential point unmistakable: Abraham was morally and ethically righteous vis-à-vis the law before the law's promulgation. It is a point that Paul's opponents (as reflected in Romans 4) would have gratefully grasped with both hands!

Thus Aphrahat does not offer a fundamental critique of the law as a soteriological category. Why he does not do so—given his knowledge and appreciation of Paul—cannot be argued in this essay. Suffice it to say that Aphrahat is not so much taken with the centrality of Christ in salvation history as he is with the inclusion of the Gentiles. Aphrahat's overarching aim in all the passages cited above is to safeguard the calling of the Gentiles over against Jewish claims. The Mosaic legislation must be shown to be secondary and therefore abrogated, but only insofar as it confers and safeguards Jewish privilege. We certainly cannot dismiss Aphrahat's exegesis here; he anticipates by 1500 years one of the central conclusions of the so-called 'New Perspective' on Paul advanced (with much greater care) by James Dunn and others![41]

---

39. Note how closely Aphrahat sticks to Paul's point in 11.3 (1.476.2-13).

40. Read the extended chronological discussion in 2.3-5.

41. James D.G. Dunn, 'The New Perspective on Paul', *BJRL* 65 (1983), pp. 95-122.

When we turn to Aphrahat's understanding of grace (ܛܝܒܘܬܐ), we find the same mix of discontinuity within continuity. It too is an important theme within the *Demonstrations*.[42] Aphrahat certainly knew himself to be a recipient of grace. He prefaced his *Demonstrations* with an assurance to an inquirer that he would gladly share what he knows about the faith, 'For (echoing Mt. 10.8) whoever by grace receives, should by grace give' (1.1 [1.5.8]). In the same vein he reminded his fellow pastors and church leaders that:

> Although we are sinners and imperfect, nevertheless my beloved ones, upon this foundation we build and from (its) leaven we have received, and upon our earth the Lord's seed has fallen and from the coming merchant we accept money. And upon all flesh his spirit is poured out and his grace from men is not withheld (14.47 [1.716.20-25]).

Like Paul, Aphrahat could speak with great feeling on the theme of God's grace towards humankind:

> And you are as good as you are long-suffering toward the sons of men. Before your judgment [day] you have not judged us, you have not accused us, and you have not condemned us; and you have not withheld your grace from the wicked (14.15 [1.608.7-10]).

> You, our King, are accustomed to demonstrate your compassion; we are accustomed at all times to entreat your compassion. We beseech you upon the confidence of your kindness, [knowing that] your grace is not withheld even from the wicked, [since] you cause your sun to shine on upon the good and upon the wicked (23.56 [2.113.26-116.4]).

> Far be it from you that you should withhold your compassion in your wrath; for at no time is your grace conquerable by our wickedness, nor is your mercy restrained because of our iniquity. Indeed, your nature is not corrupted because of us. Your name is 'Good': Demonstrate your grace. Your grace is for us since, also, your justice is against us (ܩܒܠܢ ܐܢܬ ܥܠܝܢ ܟܐܢܘܬܟ). Both are found with you, and they are in your hands (23.57 [2.117.4-10]).

But it is clear here as well that, relative to Pauline usage, there has been a conceptual shift. As the last quotation indicates, Aphrahat defined 'grace' almost exclusively over against God's justice or judgment. As he explained in 7.27 (1.360.7-15):

---

42. The term 'grace' (ܛܝܒܘܬܐ) occurs some 61 times in the *Demonstrations*. A full appreciation of the concept of God's unmerited favor would have to take into account Aphrahat's use of related terms such as 'mercy'.

> It is [in] this age/world that grace exists and, until its end, repentance. The
> time draws near when grace will be spent, and justice will reign. There
> will be no repentance in that time. Justice will dwell in peace, because, in
> its strength, it will have subdued grace.[43] And whenever the time of jus-
> tice draws near, grace will not seek to accept the penitents, because the
> limit determined for [grace] is death (lit. 'the departure'), after which there
> is no repentance.

The antithetical coupling of grace with justice (rather than with the
salvation-historical concept of 'the law'), while perfectly correct relative to Paul's theology, subtly alters Paul's redemptive-historical,
eschatological understanding of χάρις. The term is, in fact, emptied of
much of its eschatological force, and becomes descriptive of God's
dealings in human history as a whole. As the passages cited above
indicate, by 'grace' Aphrahat usually has in view God's providential
grace shown throughout history on the just and the unjust, or specific
acts of divine kindness, such as when God took Ezekiel's wife away in
a plague in order to safeguard Ezekiel's virginity (18.7 [1.833.24]) or
allowed Moses to survey the promised land from Mount Nebo (8.9
[1.377.16]). Thus, for Aphrahat, 'grace' is very rarely God's unmerited favor specifically in the salvation provided in the Messiah. Indeed
it is startling that of the 60-plus uses of 'grace' in the *Demonstrations*,
only four times is it predicated of Christ (2.20 [1.92.8], [1.92.20]; 6.1
[1.241.16]; 14.47 ([1.716.25]) and only one of these is likely to be a
reference to Christ's grace expressed in his death and resurrection
(2.20 [1.92.20]).

Conclusion

In the case of Paul and the Persian Sage this pattern repeats itself over
and over again: eager and constant appropriation beside baffling trans-
formations, use hand in hand with abuse. So how do we account for
the transformation of Paul in the face of Aphrahat's enthusiastic
appropriation of him? The historical factors that account for this are

---

43. Or 'because grace has (will have) increased in its strength', or with Hallock
'because grace, in its strength, has prevailed.' The passage is ambiguous since there
is no direct object marker. But Aphrahat's point is not that grace will win out in the
end, but that justice will. This is a point he makes repeatedly: see especially 8.20
(1.400.4-5), where he speaks of the coming 'world where grace is consumed in justice'. See also 22.13.

likely to be many, even if we must rule out eclipses, tunnel periods, and mere benign neglect. There is, frankly, a lot of work to be done on the 'why?' of all this. Nevertheless, it is interesting that, again and again, the 'what' that drops out of Paul for Aphrahat seems to be the systemic and pervasive centrality of Christ or what Sanders and others have called Paul's 'participationist eschatology'.

Can we fault Aphrahat for this? Can we accuse him of infidelity? Or even dismiss him with amused condescension? Not at all. The Pauline horizon was defined by the great tensions between the Old and the New occasioned by his experience, as a first-century Jew, of the resurrected Messiah: the tension between the Old understanding of God and the New, the Old understanding of Scripture and the New, the Old understanding of the people of God and the New, and the Old understanding of the End and the New. For Paul these theological, hermeneutical, sociological, and eschatological tensions were all held together, even if not fully dissipated, quite literally 'in Christ'. Reading Paul in a different horizon—300 years later and hundreds of miles east of the Roman Empire—Aphrahat looked to Paul for the resolution of different tensions. So perhaps it is not a case of 'use and abuse' but of 'use and therefore abuse'. What we have here is a classic example of what happens ineluctably when a scripture's historical context is not transmitted with its text.

INDEXES

INDEX OF REFERENCES

OLD TESTAMENT

OTHER ANCIENT REFERENCES